MW01618235

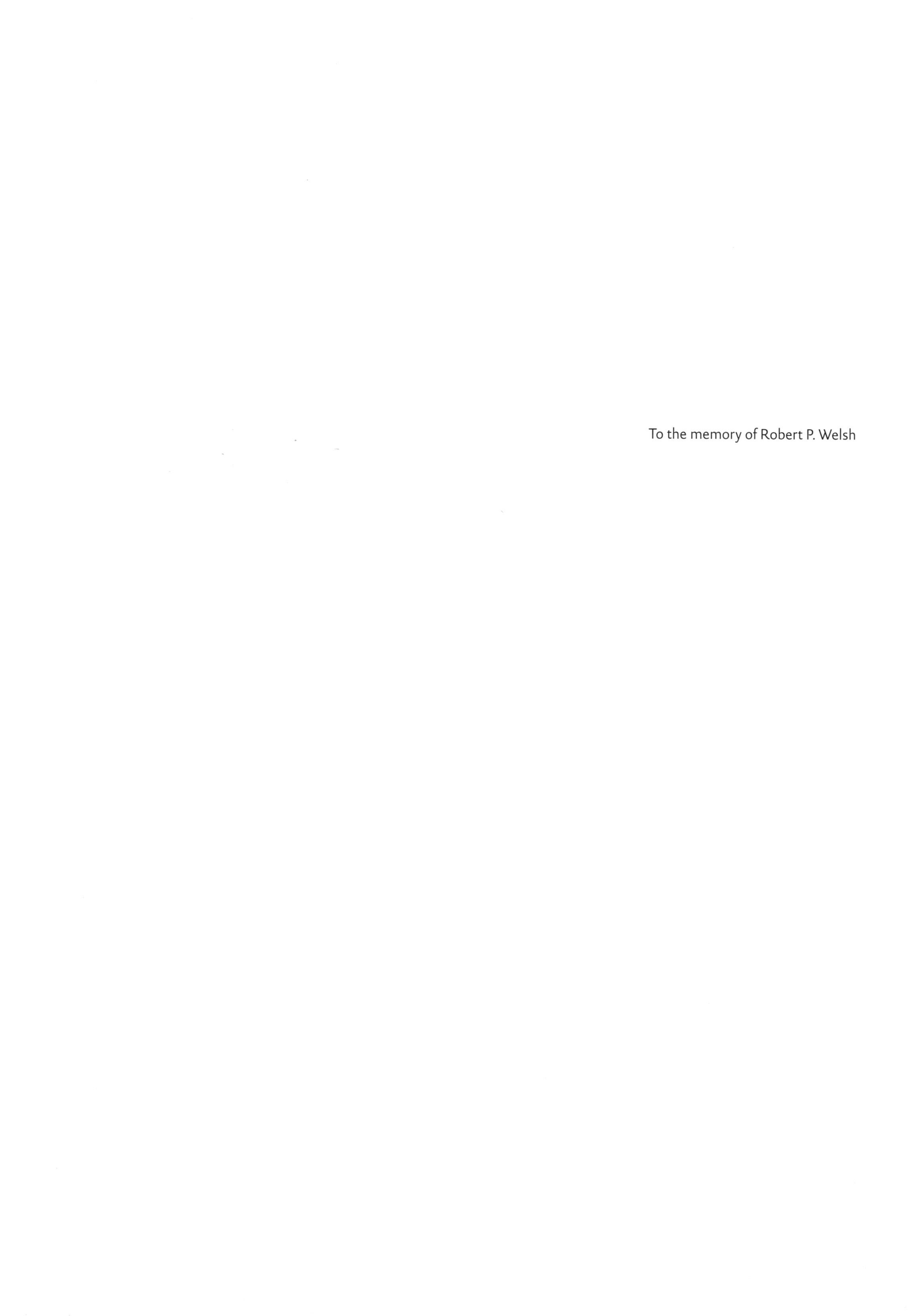

To the memory of Robert P. Welsh

voor Mont Juni 1906.
portret van
Piet Mondriaan &
het Gein, al schilderend

Mondrian 1892–1914
The Path to Abstraction

mondrian 1892–1914
The Path to Abstraction

Catalogue by
Hans Janssen and
Joop M. Joosten

Musée d'Orsay, Paris
March 25–July 14, 2002

Kimbell Art Museum, Fort Worth
August 18–December 8, 2002

Waanders Publishers, Zwolle
Kimbell Art Museum, Fort Worth
Réunion des Musées Nationaux, Paris

This exhibition was organized by the Réunion des Musées Nationaux, the Musée d'Orsay (March 25 - July 14, 2002), and the Kimbell Art Museum of Fort Worth (August 18 - December 8, 2002) and was made possible thanks to an exceptional loan from the collection of the Gemeentemuseum, The Hague.

Cover front:
Molen (Mill), 1910

Oil on canvas
The Hague, Gemeentemuseum,
Bequest of Salomon B. Slijper, 1971 (cat. 90)

Cover back:
Large landscape, 1907-1908

Oil on canvas
The Hague, Gemeentemuseum,
Bequest of Salomon B. Slijper, 1971 (cat. 63)

Library of Congress Control Number:
2002/07008
ISBN 90 400 8695 8 (paperback)
ISBN 90 400 8708 3 (hardback)
NUR 642

Organizing Committee

Hans Janssen
Chief Curator of the Gemeentemuseum, The Hague

Joop M. Joosten
Co-author of the catalogue raisonné of Piet Mondrian

In Paris
Serge Lemoine
Director of the Musée d'Orsay

In Fort Worth
Timothy Potts
Director of the Kimbell Art Museum

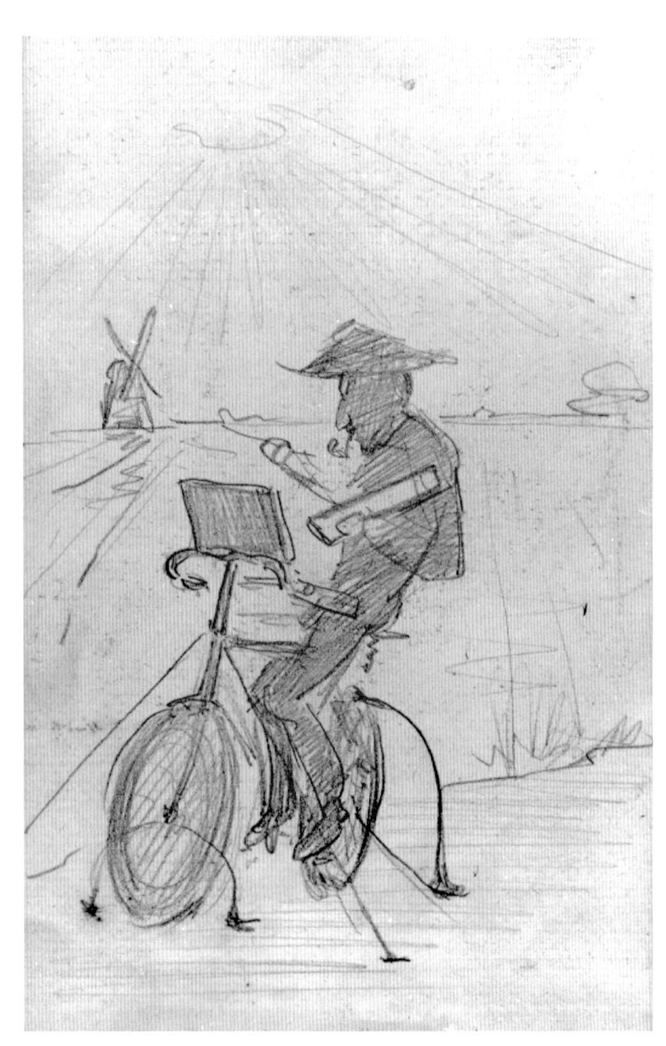

Lenders to the Exhibition

Gemeentemuseum, The Hague
Beyeler Foundation, Riehen/Basel
The Carnegie Museum of Art, Pittsburgh
Dallas Museum of Art
Gemeentearchief, Amsterdam
Solomon R. Guggenheim Museum, New York
Frans Halsmuseum, Haarlem
Kimbell Art Museum, Fort Worth
Kröller-Müller Museum, Otterlo
Musée d'Orsay, Paris
The Museum of Modern Art, New York
Stedelijk Museum, Amsterdam
Tate Gallery, London
Ver. Het Museum, Winterswijk
Zeeuws Museum, Middelburg

Director's Foreword

Piet Mondrian is one of the most recognizable artists of the twentieth century. His grid paintings, beginning in 1920 (when he was nearly fifty) and continuing up to his death in 1944, are perhaps the most iconic statement of the modernist aesthetic, their impact having penetrated far beyond the art world itself into the collective visual vocabulary of the twentieth century. This "classic" Mondrian, however, is less than half of the whole. Preceding what he called his "Neo-Plastic" paintings stands a career of nearly thirty years during which Mondrian evolves from a painter of atmospheric landscapes in the tradition of the Hague school, through immersions in various forms of post-Impressionism, Symbolism, Fauvism, Expressionism, and Cubism, until he finally strikes out on a novel and distinctive path towards abstraction that comes to its first consummation in 1914–15.

This exhibition is the first to focus exclusively on this process of Mondrian finding his abstract style, analyzing in depth the disparate influences upon him–aesthetic, historical, intellectual, and spiritual–in the years up to 1914. Its point of departure is the landmark retrospective of Mondrian's work in The Hague, Washington, and New York in 1994–96, to which the curators of this exhibition, Joop Joosten and Hans Janssen, also contributed. Much of the commentary on that exhibition related to the reappraisal of Mondrian's emergence as an abstract painter by Yve-Alain Bois and, in particular, the claim that this process should be understood primarily in terms of formalist analysis internal to the paintings as aesthetic objects, eschewing traditional appeals to Mondrian's European roots in the Dutch landscape tradition, his commitment to Theosophy, and other "extraneous" factors. While not ignoring Mondrian's Dutch origins, the retrospective directed the focus of critical insight and understanding elsewhere: the closer Mondrian gets to his fundamentalist repertoire of flat primary colors within a black-and-white grid, the more each step forward is determined by the aesthetic code of Neo-Plasticism itself, and the less it owes to any vestige of representational subject or style.

While many were persuaded that this approach goes a long way towards accounting for the evolution of Mondrian's work within Neo-Plasticism, it was less clear that it provides the key to understanding his earlier work. One reviewer cited "the radical telescoping of the first half of the artist's career. Represented by only a handful of paintings, Mondrian's long involvement with Theosophy and Symbolism is all but banished from the record." Another drew out the implications of this imbalance: "This 'contemporary' Mondrian for the end of the twentieth century is distinctly different. . . . There are three important gaps: the early work (pre-1907), the most obviously Symbolist/Theosophist work of 1908–11. . . . The first two omissions represent a pair of complementary critical judgements which have profound implications for any understanding of Mondrian's painting as a whole. In the first case, the belief that the early 'naturalist' painting anticipates the late work is rejected, and Mondrian the 'naturalist' is set aside as a 'mediocre' and peripheral figure in turn-of-the-century Dutch painting. In the second, the long accepted identification of *Devotie*

(*Devotion*) [cat. 68], the *Evolution triptych* [cat. 91] and the other most transparently Theosophist paintings as the foundation of Mondrian's mature art is overturned, on the grounds that Mondrian himself comprehensively rejected the use of symbol. . . . The selectors' anathema against Mondrian's Symbolism is, however, too total. . . . The need remains as strong as ever for analyses of his achievement within the context of inter-war 'Constructivism' in Western Europe, that place his internationalism, his Idealism, and even his passion for jazz in context." Yet another concluded simply: "But to see more of his early work, we must wait for a different show."[1]

It was this widespread feeling that the early Mondrian required further consideration, and that this in turn necessitated a more extensive presentation of his work, that gave rise to the present exhibition. It is curated by two of the leading Mondrian scholars, who bring to it an intimate knowledge of his pre-Neo-Plastic works, especially those in the unrivaled holdings of the Gemeentemuseum, The Hague, which form the backbone of the exhibition. Bringing together a larger selection of Mondrian's early works than has before been made, the exhibition undertakes a fundamental reexamination of his emergence as an abstract artist. It is unapologetically didactic, addressing a topical debate in which a range of approaches is actively in play and not flinching from taking alternative points of view. Its success will be measured not only by the response of our visitors but also by its contribution to this debate, which we hope to advance by bringing paintings and scholars together in a symposium at the Kimbell on September 28, 2002.

The attractions of a formalist interpretation of Mondrian's work are not difficult to see. Indeed, of few other artists could it be said that their choice of pictorial elements, the disposition of these elements on the canvas, and the technique of building up the painted surface are based on principles as purely formal and "abstract" as Mondrian's, in the sense that they refer to nothing outside the process of painting itself. But the fundamentalist monism of Mondrian's visual means in his Neo-Plastic maturity may in this respect disguise the historical, aesthetic, and psychological complexity of the process that brought him to this point. Mondrian was born deep in the nineteenth century and his immersion in the Dutch landscape tradition through the 1890s and into the 1900s was almost total; there is as yet no real hint of the radical artist to come. The explosive eclecticism of his work in 1908–10 comes as a thunderbolt, as if Mondrian had suddenly and simultaneously happened upon the whole spectrum of progressive art from van Gogh, Seurat, and the Symbolists to Munch and Matisse. In fact it was Mondrian's readiness to engage with these aspects of progressive art that had advanced. At this point he often seems more a sponge than an active agent of change; and so it remained until his second great transformative encounter, that with Cubism in 1911. The effect this time was to be different, inspiring him not just to imitative flourishes, but setting Mondrian on a trajectory that would lead to an altogether new mode of painting. Even here, however, at the point of his most radical break with the

1. Holland Cotter, "Abstraction and the True Believer," *Art in America* 83 (Nov. 1995), 70; Christopher Green, *The Burlington Magazine* 137 (March 1995), 199–200; Jo Ann Lewis, "Between and Beyond the Lines," *The Washington Post* (June 11, 1995), sec. G, p. 4.

past, it is possible to glean shadows of his representational past. For Mondrian, abstract art did not mean non-Realist art, which is the point of Joosten and Janssen's seemingly category-defying characterization of his mature style as "realist-abstractionist."

The Kimbell's painting *Tableau No. 1*, 1914 (cat. 105) is a case in point: despite the now formally abstract character of the grid (punctuated by the occasional arc) Mondrian still floats this "figure" on a colored ground whose transition from cool slate blue at the bottom to warm pink/ocher at the top mirrors the chromatic and tonal shift of his riverine landscapes, from dark water, riverbank, and trees to luminous dusk sky. The grid itself fades into and out of this misty colored field, as atmospheric and moody as its landscape forebears. Despite its formally abstract credentials, this work, and others like it, still hovers on the brink of an ambivalent representationalism, one in which the familiar world of trees, rivers, and all such things has been replaced by abstract geometrical objects, whose corporeal status, despite their abstract character, is powerfully affirmed by the still very "real" space and light within which they subsist. It was only in his Neo-Plastic paintings that Mondrian succeeded fully in suppressing any figure-ground reading of his images–that his paintings truly become, in visual as well as material terms, "a flat surface covered with colors arranged in a certain order," as Maurice Denis famously remarked.

While this exhibition reaffirms the critical path of Mondrian's abstraction as running through Cubism, it also allows us to see more clearly in some earlier work his predilection in this direction–although he might not yet have recognized it as such, and had not yet developed the pictorial means to articulate it. Two works in particular stand out: *The Red Cloud* (cat. 60) and *Geinrust Farm in the Haze* (cat. 51). In *The Red Cloud*, it is only the horizon line–a visual imperative bequeathed by centuries of landscape painting–that forces us to read this image as a landscape. Otherwise, the flat areas of scumbled blue and the floating patch of orange provide no three-dimensional triggers, no unambiguous declaration of subject. Similarly, in *Geinrust Farm*, the silhouette of farmhouse and trees along the riverbank is recognizable only by reference to the other works in this series. All solid form has dissolved in a wet slurry of expressive brushstrokes that unhinges any reading of three-dimensional space or figure/ground distinction. The only space is that of the picture surface itself and the paint its only "subject." Mondrian here is on the brink of full abstraction via the *dissolution* of form and space. But this was a consequence that clearly did not suit him; he was not prepared to let go of form and thus continued no further down this path. Cubism, on the other hand, provided a path to abstraction not through the dissolution of form and space but through its structured dissection and rearticulation within a new space defined by the picture plane itself. This matched Mondrian's reductionist-essentialist-realist instincts much better–as we see him working through in this exhibition–and indeed it was to remain the underlying principle of his art throughout the rest of his career.

In 1909–10, Mondrian painted the floor and wainscoting of his studio black and the walls and furniture white, as if prefiguring the spare, Calvinist aesthetic that would soon emerge in his painting. Later in his career he covered the walls of his studios with sheets of monochromatic cardboard, extending the principles of Neo-Plasticism overtly to the three-dimensional world. The philosophical basis of this curious habit lay both in Mondrian's utopian fantasy of a completely aestheticized environment, one in which the spiritual power of art would pervade all of society; and in an idealistic otherworldliness (by turns Platonic, Hegelian, and Theosophical) that allowed him to believe, while he was distilling art to its most primal elements, that he was still painting the ultimately most *real* world of all—that, as he said in 1942, he had always been a realist. Indeed, a critical aspect of Mondrian's entire career is his coming to terms with an evolving conception of the real, and it is against this background that we should understand his statement that: "Nature (or what I see) inspires me, gives me, as it gives all painters, the emotion which brings forth creative élan, but I am seeking to approach truth as closely as possible, and to abstract everything from it until I reach the foundations (always visible foundations!) of things. That is for me a truth. . . ."

Mondrian is one of the few artists whose impact has been equally great on both sides of the Atlantic, which makes it doubly gratifying that the many lenders to this exhibition, both public and private, have generously agreed to allow their works to travel to the United States. At its core lie the paintings from the unparalleled holding of Mondrian's early works in the Gemeentemuseum, The Hague, founded on the collection of Salomon B. Slijper, which have very generously been lent to the Kimbell Art Museum for this exclusive United States showing of the exhibition. To the Gemeentemuseum and the many other lenders, both public and private, who have made this exhibition possible, we extend our sincere thanks and appreciation. It comes to Fort Worth after its debut at the Musée d'Orsay, Paris, where the exhibition was initiated. Our thanks for this very fruitful collaboration go to Dr. Wim van Krimpen, director, and Dr. Hans Janssen, chief curator of the Gemeentemuseum, The Hague; Dr. Henri Loyrette and Dr. Serge Lemoine, former and present directors of the Musée d'Orsay; and Dr. Philippe Durey, administrateur général of the Reunion des musées nationaux, France, and the staff at the RMN, especially Anne Fréling and Bénédicte Boissonas in the department of exhibitions, and Anne Latournerie, Dagmar Rolf, and Béatrice Foulon in the publications department. Here at the Kimbell, the exhibition has been coordinated and installed by Malcolm Warner, senior curator, assisted by Julie Herrick. The English translation of the catalogue was coordinated by Wendy Gottlieb, manager of publications and public access, assisted by Anna Lazarus. Together with the rest of the Kimbell staff, their efforts have contributed greatly to the success of the project.

Timothy Potts
Director
Kimbell Art Museum

Note to the Reader

After March 1912, following the Salon des Indépendants, and while Mondrian found himself removed from his traditional Dutch surroundings, he completely abandoned the practice of signing his name "Pieter Mondriaan" in favor of "Piet Mondrian." For the sake of coherence, we have maintained this later spelling. For the signatures of works in the catalogue, we have chosen a means of exact transcription, respecting the typographic inadequacies of this method.

The technical notes on the works will permit the reader to distinguish the original titles (that is to say, those given by Mondrian himself) from those given to the works and modified over time (original titles followed, if necessary, by the translation).

Numbers preceded by A, B, or U refer to the catalogue raisonné of Mondrian's works (see Joosten and Welsh, 1998). A-numbers refer to the first volume, the work up to 1911, by the late Robert P. Welsh; B-numbers refer to the second volume, the work from 1911 to 1944, written by Joop M. Joosten; and U-numbers refer to works that are "unidentified," for which references exist but no clues as to which actual work is meant.

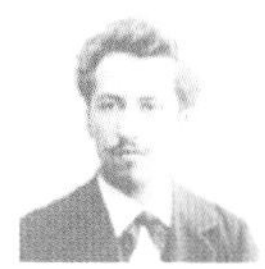

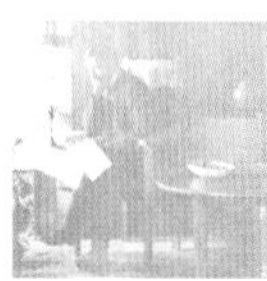

Contents

"I was always a realist."

Piet Mondrian

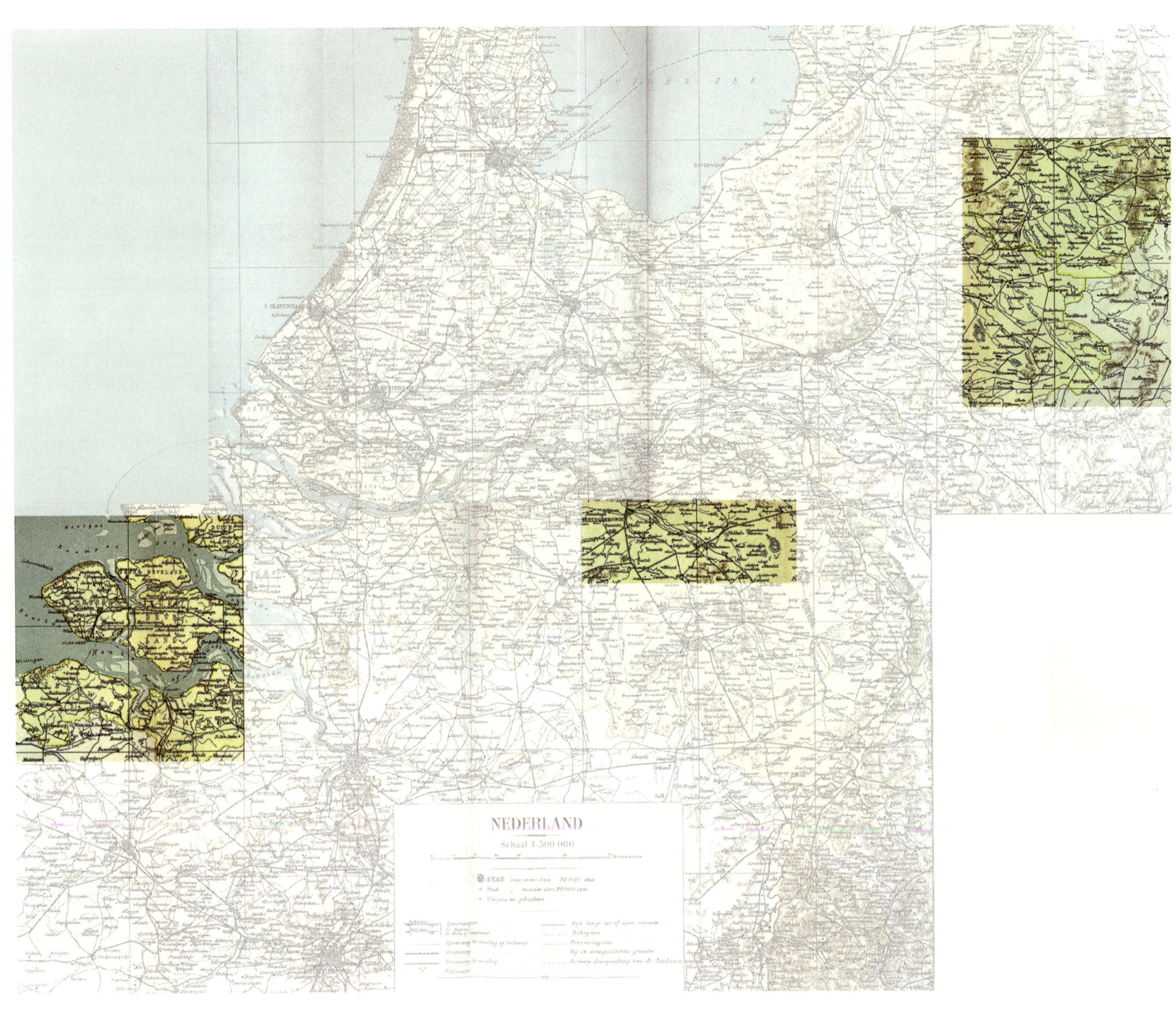

Map of Holland, c. 1910
Van Oosthoek Encyclopedia, 1924

Introduction

Hans Janssen and Joop M. Joosten

The Mondrian retrospective organized in 1994 by the National Gallery of Art in Washington, the Gemeentemuseum in The Hague, and The Museum of Modern Art in New York inspired the desire for a meticulous reexamination of the painter's early work.

The treasury of knowledge amassed over a period of thirty years by the late Robert Welsh, an endeavor that resulted in the catalogue raisonné of 1998, broke the ground for a radically new approach to this period of Mondrian's oeuvre. Although many questions remain, it is now possible to trace convincingly the beginnings of the painter's career. The paintings and drawings of this early period reveal not only a pictorial tradition tied to the nineteenth century, but also, without question, a much earlier tradition deeply ingrained in the history of Dutch art.

Mondrian has always been considered an innovator; indeed, he was one of the first to abandon copying from nature as the standard means of representation. The consequences of this step, the results he achieved, and his constant search toward developing the theories he defined in an original way can make us forget all that tied him to the past.

We have chosen instead to limit ourselves as closely as possible to the historical facts. Moreover, we have selected only the creative work in which Mondrian made a contribution to the evolution of the plastic arts as a whole. We have, therefore, excluded copies of other masters (old and new), commissions, and portraits. Only when a painting or a work on paper constitutes a step forward in one aspect or another has it been included. We do not want to disqualify the commissioned work: it gave Mondrian the means to do what he really wanted to do, to make a contribution to the development of the pictorial arts. From the beginning of his career, Mondrian resigned himself to the idea of having to accept commissions, make saleable works, and paint portraits to support himself.

My environment conditioned me to paint the objects of ordinary vision; even at times to make portraits with likeness. For this reason, much of this early work has no permanent value. At the time, I was earning my living by teaching and commercial drawing. [2]

Until now Mondrian has been considered the creator of two separate oeuvres, an artist who underwent two distinct forms of artistic development. On the one hand, there is the naturalistic work in which landscape plays a dominant role. On the other, there is the adventure of Neo-Plasticism, originally coined by Mondrian in 1917 as "Nieuwe Beelding".

The word "Beelding" is highly unusual in Dutch, being the virtually non-existent present participle of the Dutch verb "beelden", which in the Dutch dictionary of 1881 was still described as 'to form something material, in order to give it a certain shape', but it was also indicated that the word had fallen into "disuse" at that time.

Usual in Dutch is the noun "afbeelding" or "voorstelling", literally meaning "representation", as used in the figurative arts. "Beelding", as used by Mondrian, refers back to the older, pre-1881 wording. In this sense the word "beelding", as used by Mondrian, is a sort of regressive archaism. In coining the term, Mondrian takes out the referential and stresses the expressive potential, but leaves enough room for the old figurative functions to be included too. Thus, "Beelding" is a new category, encompassing both figurative and non-figurative art. The first was described by Mondrian as natural-realism; the other as abstract-realism.

The addition of the adjective "Nieuwe" (meaning "New") made Mondrian's intentions even more clear: that he was aiming for a new, non-representational form of art, in which the function of form was solely to stress the sheer visualization of content. "Beelding" focuses on this immediate, decisive function of visualization. The problem with the term is that it is untranslatable. In 1920, Mondrian translated 'Nieuwe Beelding' into French as "Néo-Plasticisme". This designation was later generally utilized and promoted by Mondrian to describe his new art. Used as an adjective, it becomes "Neo-Plastic" or, more generally, "plastic". We choose to use the same terminology, although we are conscious of its limitations.

This exhibition aims to demonstrate that there is no question of a break in Mondrian's development, a point of view that was clearly the artist's own, as captured by Charmion von Wiegand, in

1942, in her journal. After she had looked with Mondrian at his earliest works, he said: "For me there is no difference between these early ones and the last ones–they are all part of the same thing. I do not feel the difference between the old and the new in art as really different, but as a continuity."[3] He had already revealed similar thoughts on his own evolution in 1922:

Here you have an album of photographs representing my pictures extending from the earliest period to those of today. I began as a naturalistic painter. Very quickly I felt the urgent need for a more concise form of expression and an economy of means. I never stopped progressing toward abstraction. One period flows logically from the one before. I embraced the results of this interior progression. In the last eighteen months a period of calm set in. I am convinced that this progression has not yet reached its culmination. It will continue in the same direction and it will not retreat. [4]

We also want to emphasize the extent to which Mondrian was apprehensive about influences from other artists on his own artistic vision. He believed only in the evolution inherent in his own work. Herman Hana noted as early as 1924:

I do not mean by this that he distinguished himself straightaway through this great force of character or by the audacity that would develop only later, but that from the beginning, he knew how to avoid copying one or another great master. What he does imitate is nature, and what touches us in these reproductions is his sincere and loyal spirit. [5]

Nearly all those who associated with Mondrian arrived at the same conclusion. That constitutes the point of departure for our description of the evolution of his work. When Mondrian arrived in Amsterdam in 1892, he was confronted with an artistic environment that could be characterized as very conservative. Contrary to what was going on in other Dutch cities—especially The Hague and Rotterdam—in Amsterdam, at the dawn of the twentieth century, nineteenth-century realism was still flourishing. Thanks to critics like Théophile Thoré and Eugène Fromentin, realism was considered to be the distinctive mark of Dutch art as a whole. It was to the glory of this tradition that the Rijksmuseum, at that time the largest museum in the world, had been inaugurated in 1885, only a few years before Mondrian's arrival.

At this time the artists heralded as the most modern school of French art and exhibited frequently at the Rijksmuseum and the Stedelijk Museum, as well as in other halls and in commercial art galleries, were not the French Impressionists but masters of the Barbizon school and other realists.

The reactions of Dutch artists, faced with the trends emerging abroad, were quite significant and represented the sentiments of the Dutch public at large. They believed that art belonged to one's country, city, or cultural tradition and should not be under the authority of some other, unknown foreign country. The idea was particularly anchored in Amsterdam, among the artists, the public, and especially the collectors. It is in this context that one must understand the paradox of Mondrian, for whom a life consecrated to art "signifies the decline of old-fashioned life and its advantages of intimacy, of homeland and family; the charm of traditional friendship and love–all this is no real loss since it leads to a superior life."[6]

In the 1950s, Albert van den Briel remarked subtly that if there was anything Dutch in Mondrian's character it was the gradual progression of his development. Yet in another sense Mondrian was, and remained throughout his whole career, a Dutch artist. "I never painted these things romantically; but from the very beginning, I was always a realist," Mondrian wrote in spring 1941 at the start of his well-known retrospective essay, *Toward the True Vision of Reality*. For those who are acquainted with the artistic climate in Holland at the end of the nineteenth century and the beginning of the twentieth, what Mondrian wrote in this passage confirms the idea that his early work should be seen in relation to that belated Amsterdam realism. However, there is a fundamental difference. Mondrian's later writings continue to remind us precisely what makes a work of art a work of art: determined relationships. It was Maurice Denis (1870–1930), Mondrian's elder by eighteen months, who in August 1890, in the flower of his youth, pronounced this revolutionary statement: "Remember that a painting—before being a warhorse, a naked woman, or some trite anecdote—is essentially a flat surface covered with colors arranged in a certain order."[7]

"A flat surface covered with colors arranged in a certain order": isn't that what characterizes each of the Neo-Plastic works of Mondrian? We are convinced that Mondrian aspired to just such a "certain order," at the moment he chose, in 1893, to embark on a career as an artist. Simply stated, art was still ruled by colors, lines, and forms borrowed from life, *representing* cows, trees, houses, sky, clouds, and the like. Deeply rooted in the Dutch tradition, Mondrian believed that "to paint" was synonymous with "to represent reality"; not to illustrate thoughts, ideas, and scenes idealistically, but to render them purely and simply in terms of what the artist sees. For this reason we reject the approach that views Mondrian's work as the simple vehicle of spiritual content.[8] Mondrian was a realist, realist-naturalist in his earliest works and realist-abstractionist in his later works, as he himself stated repeatedly. It must be added that, as much in his first as in his later periods, Mondrian approached his subjects from many angles, not in order to create series or to penetrate the essence of the object, but to define the "certain order" that he perceived as clearly and explicitly as possible.

In 1893, when Mondrian made his debut into Amsterdam's artistic milieu, he must have harbored great hopes for his artistic work. Until 1904, nowhere do we see him make explicit use of horizontals and verticals, or flat-painted surfaces of color or form. What always fascinated him, and increasingly as he acquired greater technical skills, was the way his subjects could be translated into a clear, plastic composition.

Two landscapes dating from 1893 (cat. 2 and 3), permit us to understand the impetus behind Mondrian's first attempts to liberate himself from the pictorial practices illustrated by the earlier still lifes that he made (cat. 1).

In 1897, a year after finishing his training, we see him participate in exhibitions organized by different art societies, something he never did during his studies. He took part for the first time in two exhibitions in Amsterdam. We also find him in Utrecht in an exhibit of the Kunstliefde (Love of Art) Society, to which he had not contributed since 1893. These facts clearly reflect a determined will to make himself known as a professional painter.

Until 1901, Mondrian's work is characterized by a great diversity of rural and urban motifs, often complex, and by a no less great diversity of procedures in his technique. Everything seems to indicate that he aimed to search for diametrically opposed ways of rendering, so as to acquire mastery over the means of plastic expression. His range of techniques extends from painting in its pure state to drawing in its most exacting sense, from the synthetic approach of the ensemble to the strong affirmation of details, from a heavy use of contrasts to a light.

A more in-depth examination reveals a break between 1900 and 1901. Certain events in the artist's life, more or less linked to one another, clearly influenced his working methods. First there is his introduction to Simon Maris, a year younger than Mondrian and son of one of the leaders of the Hague school, Willem Maris, the youngest of the three famous Maris brothers. They probably met in the milieu of the Saint Lucas artist's society, after Simon Maris had returned from Antwerp, probably during the second half of 1899. This meeting and the close friendship that developed permitted Mondrian to be introduced into a new network of friends and to meet Simon's father. In the year 1900, the senior Maris contributed three works, from a private collection, to the annual exhibition of the Saint Lucas society. At the same time, the Amsterdam art gallery F. Buffa & Son showed the paintings of Willem Maris chosen for the Dutch contribution to the Universal Exhibition in Paris. Curiously, before that date, Willem Maris had been only rarely shown in Amsterdam. Until this time he had remained in the shadow of his two older and more famous brothers, Jacob and Matthijs.

In 1901, Mondrian shifted his working terrain to the pastures in the polders south of Amsterdam, along the little river Gein, known for its wooded banks. The works born in that countryside strongly recall those of Willem Maris. The acquaintanceship with Simon Maris and Willem Maris, and the sudden choice of the Gein region are strongly linked.

This first Gein period came to an abrupt end with Mondrian's departure for Brabant in 1904. During his stay in this region, Mondrian learned to give his motifs more solid form. The characteristics of the countryside and its rural landscapes must have played an important role in the process. Mondrian was able to maintain the new solidity of form after his stay in Brabant, working again in the marshy area of the Gein. His acquaintance with the solid landscape of Twente in 1906 may also have helped him to maintain a preference for solid form.

His evening landscapes, which can be dated to 1907 and 1908, characterized by the strange discoloration of the setting sun, immediately followed by the dark blue night landscapes, can be considered Mondrian's first reaction to modernist trends—Neo-Impressionism, Fauvism, Expressionism—which were gaining in importance in Holland.

The moment he accepted these international developments, he immediately positioned himself preeminently in the modern art movement that was now taking hold in the Netherlands. Going back and forth between foggy Amsterdam and the summer light of Domburg, he produced a series of extraordinary masterpieces, in which violently contrasting or subtly balanced colors reveal an iconoclasm that was the first sign of a radical new approach. Mondrian decided that the colors of nature cannot be reproduced on canvas and that he had to find a new way to express the beauty of nature. The breakthrough came when he encountered the work of Cézanne and Picasso, which put him on the right track.

This exhibition was first planned for the Musée d'Orsay, Paris. The suggestion of Timothy Potts, director of the Kimbell Art Museum, that the exhibition also be shown in the United States, provided a welcome opportunity to present this new perspective on Mondrian in the country where he ended his life and where his impact has been so great. The cooperation took on the amplitude of a major and authentic step toward a new and accurate survey of Mondrian's beginnings, toward a true vision of reality.

Hans Janssen
Joop M. Joosten

1. Joosten and Welsh 1998.
2. *Toward the True Vision of Reality* (1941), in Holtzman and James 1986, 338.
3. Charmion von Wiegand, unpublished journal, September 16 and 17, 1942.
4. [H. van Loon], "Bij Piet Mondriaan" ("With Piet Mondrian"), *Nieuwe Rotterdamsche Courant*, March 23, 1922, Evening edition.
5. Herman Hana, "Mondrian de pionier" [Mondrian the Pioneer"], *Wil en Weg (The Will and the Way)* 2 (1924), 603–4).
6. Piet Mondrian, "L'art nouveau, la vie nouvelle, la culture des rapports purs," 1931 (unpublished manuscript), translated in Holtzman and James, 1986, 258.
7. Maurice Denis, "Définition du néo-traditionisme," *Art et Critique*, August 1890.
8. This approach is summarized in the words of Robert Rosenblum, "It was precisely the material surface of things that Mondrian, too, [following C. D. Friedrich] thought of only as an outer layer that veiled hidden, intangible forces in Nature." In: Robert Rosenblum, "Notes on Mondrian and Romanticism," in *Piet Mondrian, 1872–1944*, exh. cat. (Toronto, Philadelphia, The Hague), 1966, 18.

Chapter One

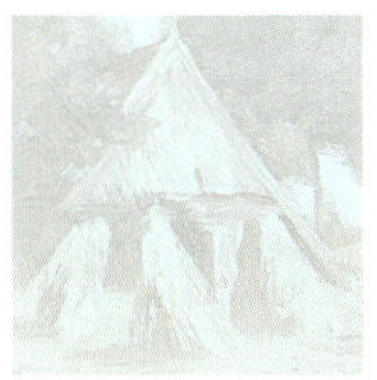

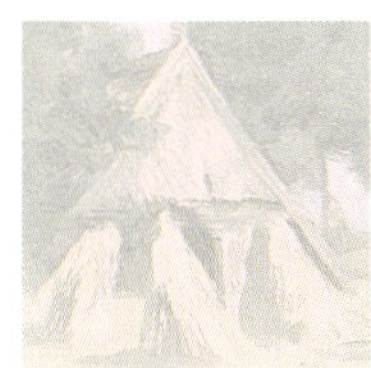

1893

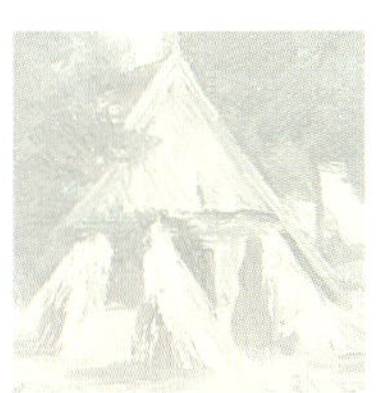

"My father was always drawing, though it was only a hobby with him, and I began like anybody else." [1]

Hans Janssen

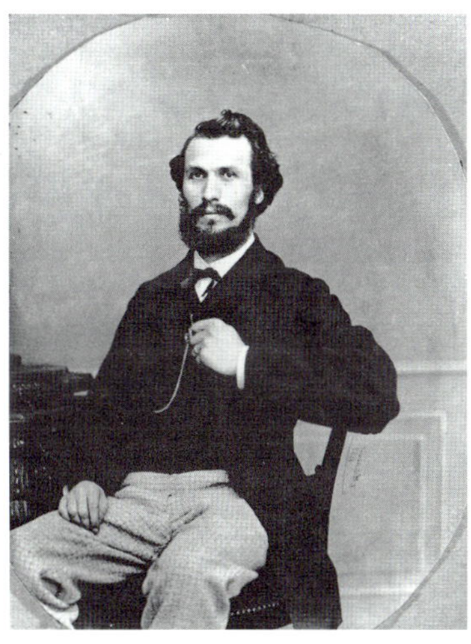

Fig. 1
Mondrian's father, P. C. Mondrian (1839–1921), 1867
Gemeentemuseum, The Hague

In November 1892, at the age of twenty, Piet Mondrian entered the National Academy of Fine Arts in Amsterdam. He came from a conventional, church-going family, a milieu not especially known for encouraging an artistic calling. However, his father, Pieter Cornelis Mondriaan (1839–1921), the director of a Christian (national) primary school in Winterswijk, was a passionate draftsman (fig.1). He inspired the developing curiosity of the child and encouraged him as much as possible. As the older son, Mondrian had attended his father's elementary school for six years, then received two more years of advanced schooling that culminated in foreign language studies.

When Mondrian told his father of his intention to

1. Bradley 1944, 17.

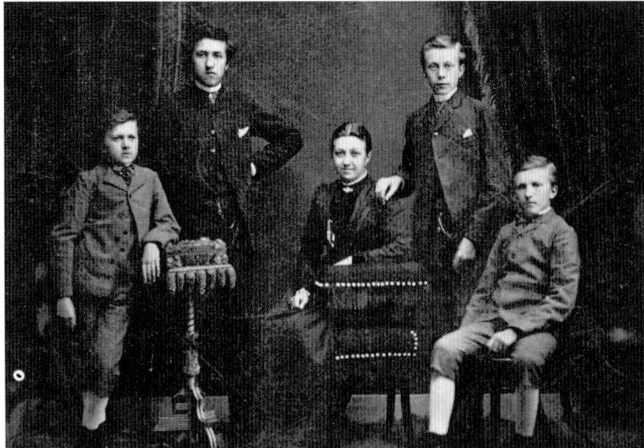

Fig. 2
The Mondrian children, c. 1890
Left to right: Carel (1880–1956), Pieter Cornelis (Piet), Johanna Christina (1870–1939), Willem Frederik (1874–1945), and Louis (1877–1943)
Gemeentemuseum, The Hague

become an artist he met with opposition, a reaction that could be explained less from radical Calvinism's hostility to art than by the scarcity of family resources. The possibility of sending one of the children to study in faraway Amsterdam certainly could not be taken for granted (fig. 2). Piet had learned oil painting from his uncle Frits (1853–1932), who, around 1886, often came to Winterswijk to paint in the open air with his nephew. The innovation of painting *en plein air* had recently arrived from France and would soon become popular in artistic circles. In the eyes of the public, however, it was more or less synonymous with infidelity to art. [2]

Mondrian's father required that his son first obtain the certificates necessary to become a drawing teacher. He would then be able to teach, a proposition that was not especially attractive to the future artist.[3] However, the fact that these certificates might provide access to one of the national schools of fine arts led Mondrian, from 1888 to 1892, to undertake conscientious and intensive preparations for the exams while he lived at home in Winterswijk, where he had transformed the former playroom into a studio. He studied anatomical and botanical works, taught himself mathematics and perspective, and dragged huge plaster casts of Michelangelo's *Moses* and the ancient Greek *Laocoön* around Winterswijk so he could draw them. On September 10, 1892, he was awarded the last of his certificates and was thus permitted, without further exams, to enroll directly in the National Academy of Fine Arts.

Upon arriving in Amsterdam, he found himself in an artistic milieu of considerable diversity, in which it was not easy for a young artist of his generation to make his mark. The year 1893 therefore proved decisive, marking a starting point for the young artist. Not much is known about this period in Mondrian's career. The great attention he paid to describing and documenting his evolution after 1908 is in direct contrast to his seemingly deliberate concealment of everything that took place before. "I began like everybody else," was the brief résumé of this period that he offered at the end of his life![4] It was not until long after his death that it was possible to form a precise idea of the maturing of the artist. His first autobiography, albeit quite succinct, dates from 1907:

2. Welsh 1977, 181, note 51. Welsh mentions, without citing any sources, that Mondrian painted out-of-doors around Winterswijk. Dutch journals from the years 1880–90 are filled with pejorative references in any discussion of painting *en plein air*.
3. Letters from Carel Mondriaan (1880–1956), brother of Piet, to Salomon Slijper, November 29, 1945, and January 20, 1946, Slijper Archives.
4. Bradley 1944, 16–17.

Piet Mondrian at first practiced drawing under the guidance of his father, who often drew. Then, at the age of fourteen, he began painting under the guidance of his uncle Frits, who came from The Hague to Winterswijk to paint out of doors.[5]

This information gives a bit of breadth to his laconic, "I began like everybody else." It was therefore his close family environment that fostered his enthusiasm for painting.

The National Academy trained artists in genre painting or portraiture–hardly the free practice of art of which Mondrian was dreaming. His father described the situation clearly in a request to the Queen Mother Emma (1858–1934), regent for the young Queen Wilhelmina (1880–1963), from whom he requested financial aid. "For *four years* without a break, he [Piet] has pushed himself, taught *himself*. But he is only too conscious of the fact that he will not be able to persevere on his artistic path without extreme difficulties, even if he is permitted to practice his talents more fully than in the fashion authorized by those about him."[6] In the fall of 1892, Mondrian registered as a "Drawing Master" in urban Amsterdam.[7] Even though he augmented his stipend for a long time by giving drawing lessons, and even applied, in 1898, for a position as professor of drawing in Enschede, these were the limits of his teaching aspirations.

Before his son's enrollment in the National Academy, the senior Mondriaan had to pay a visit to the director, August Allebé (1838–1927). He himself also settled the fees for room and board in a Protestant pension on Kalverstraat and even asked that the administration of the Academy provide him with "the rules and regulations or something similar," so that he and his son could get their bearings and review the various disciplines and schedule of course hours before Piet enrolled on November 1.[8] All these actions lead us to believe that his father actively supported Mondrian in his ambitions. On the other hand, it was no doubt difficult for the novice student to leave the family home.

The relationship between father and son was complex, but a strong link must have existed between them.[9] This bond is apparent from the regular visits Mondrian continued to make to his family in Winterswijk and, after 1900, in Arnhem. All the holidays and many summer vacations drew him back to the fold, and this habit lasted until his final departure for Paris in 1919.

August Allebé's style of directing the Academy determined to a great extent the ambiance that reigned within (fig. 3). Under his authority, the relatively conservative bastion of art training experienced one of its more productive periods. The director emphasized practical exercises, consisting essentially of drawing after the model (in plaster); but he also inspired students to reflect on the more theoretical aspects of the work. "He ceaselessly pushed us toward simplicity and truth, which, in the most modest way, he called 'exactitude,' persuaded that there could be no beauty except that founded in truth."[10] During the first year, Mondrian enrolled in all the classes, but it was the "little painting class" of Nicolaas van der Waay (1855–1936) that he attended most diligently. There one practiced painting still lifes, and painted and drew from plaster casts or copies of the old masters. The free style that the painters of the Hague school used to render variations of weather in their landscapes were taboo, and French Impressionism–called "Luminism"–was not recognized at all. Jan Sluijters (1881–1957) consequently earned a reprimand when he dared to discuss van Gogh (1853–1890) within the walls of the Academy.[11]

According to several sources, not only had Mondrian wanted to be a painter since the age of fourteen, but, what is more, he was firmly

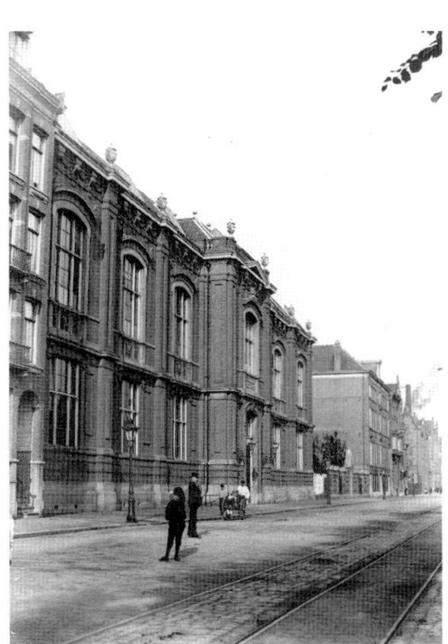

Fig. 3
Jacob Olie, *The Stadhouderskade, Amsterdam, with the façade of the Royal Academy of Fine Arts (Rijksacademie)*, July 14, 1897
Municipal Archives, Amsterdam

5. Lurasco 1907, n.p.
6. Letter from Piet Mondrian (very probably written by his father), of February 27, 1892, to Her Majesty, the Regent, quoted by Van Adrichem-Ammerlaan 1933, n.p.
7. Bakker, Bax, and Welsh 1944, 43.
8. Letter from Mondriaan's father to August Allebé, October 21, 1892, in Mali, Booij, and Scholtz 1994, 105.
9. Albert van den Briel's is the most detailed description of the relationship between father and son. See "Mondriaans persoonlijkheid" ("Mondrian's Personality") in Henkels 1988, 53.
10. Roland Holst 1928, 220.
11. Loosjes-Terpstra 1959, 40.

convinced that he was going to reveal the very essence of painting.[12] In 1915, he wrote that he was on the one hand raised "in the craft of painting, on the other hand compelled by the ardent desire to discover [his] own interior self." "It's of the same order," he insisted, "as spiritual revelation—religious even."[13] Nothing was more serious than his quest for truth in painting.[14] From the beginning, Mondrian aspired to painting as art, to a painting more or less closely related to the Dutch landscape tradition. But landscape painting was forbidden at the National Academy. Indeed, many artists believed that the Academy had largely sacrificed the awakening of observation through contact with nature.

The first paintings in which Mondrian asserted his independence—these were not, of course, those he prepared for his exams—were not landscapes. *Stilleven* (*Still Life*), dating from January 1893 (cat. 1), is a good example. Mondrian sent it to the spring exhibition of the Kunstliefde (Love of Art) Society in Utrecht, which he had joined in 1892. It is a painting of surprising freedom. One's attention is concentrated on light, which, falling on the glazed bowl, the fish scales, and the little lemon, ties the compositional elements together. But the artist also covers the canvas with a light green, a harsh yellow, and a dull gray, varied according to their placement, without much attention to their color contrasts or luminosity.[15]

It was not only his use of colors, but also his choice of subjects that enabled Mondrian to escape from the grip of academicism. Until 1908 he continued making this kind of still life for a market comfortably ensconced within the limits of the Dutch tradition of *vanitas* paintings, so characteristic of "Dutch realism." In Mondrian's time, the two major attributes of this style were fidelity of reproduction and attention to the specific features of each object. These two principles had been restated in 1856 in a treatise by the very influential Dutch art historian and art critic Tobias van Westrheene. This study, dedicated to Jan Steen, had an extraordinary impact. In Holland of the 1880s, it contributed greatly to the artistic climate that favored a freer brushstroke combined with a realist vision.[16] It was not until 1908 that Mondrian became involved in the path of modernism by breaking with this entrenched tradition.

Van Westrheene distinguished "the principle of individuality" and "the faithful and naïve study of nature" as the two principal, essential elements of Dutch art.[17] Dutch painters searched for the particular characteristics of an object, unlike idealist French and Italian painters, who strived for the representation of universal and timeless models. "Dutch artists never thought of wrapping an abstract idea in forms that only suggested nature, neither did they seek to express great ideas through the use of the conventional language of painting."[18] According to Van Westrheene, Dutch artists were averse to tradition and relied purely and simply on observation. In imitating a fragment of the real, Dutch artists believed in the simplicity of their subjective approach, the promise that poetry and truth would be found in whatever they represented. This conviction was as valid for seventeenth-century artists as for most of Van Westrheene's contemporaries. During the 1880s, even though young artists and critics opposed their predecessors and became propagators of a new style, the new generation still adhered to these principles. So it was that in 1892 a young painter again assured one critic, "One must have courage to be a man, face to face with nature, entirely free, ingenuous, liberated from all conventions, motivated by the sole and unique intention of producing the art that nature has revealed to him."[19] One of the most eminent critics for the *Beweging van Tachtig* (the Literary

12. Letter from Albert van den Briel to J. M. Harthoorn, December 3, 1965, in Henkels 1988, 107.
13. De Meester-Obreen 1915, 399.
14. Joosten and Welsh 1998, vol. 1, 159.
15. "Er is meer idee in zijn licht en bruin en de eenheid is juist veel grooter geworden juist daadoor" ("There is more thought in his light and his brown, and that is exactly what gives it a greater unity"), in B.A.R. [sic], "De Schilderijen-tentoonstelling" ("The Painting Exhibition"), *Utrechtse Courant*, April 29, 1893.
16. Streng 1995, 336.
17. Van Westrheene 1856, 18–19.
18. Ibid.
19 Letter from Jan Voerman to Filippo Tassaro, November 23, 1892, quoted in Wagner 1977, 38.

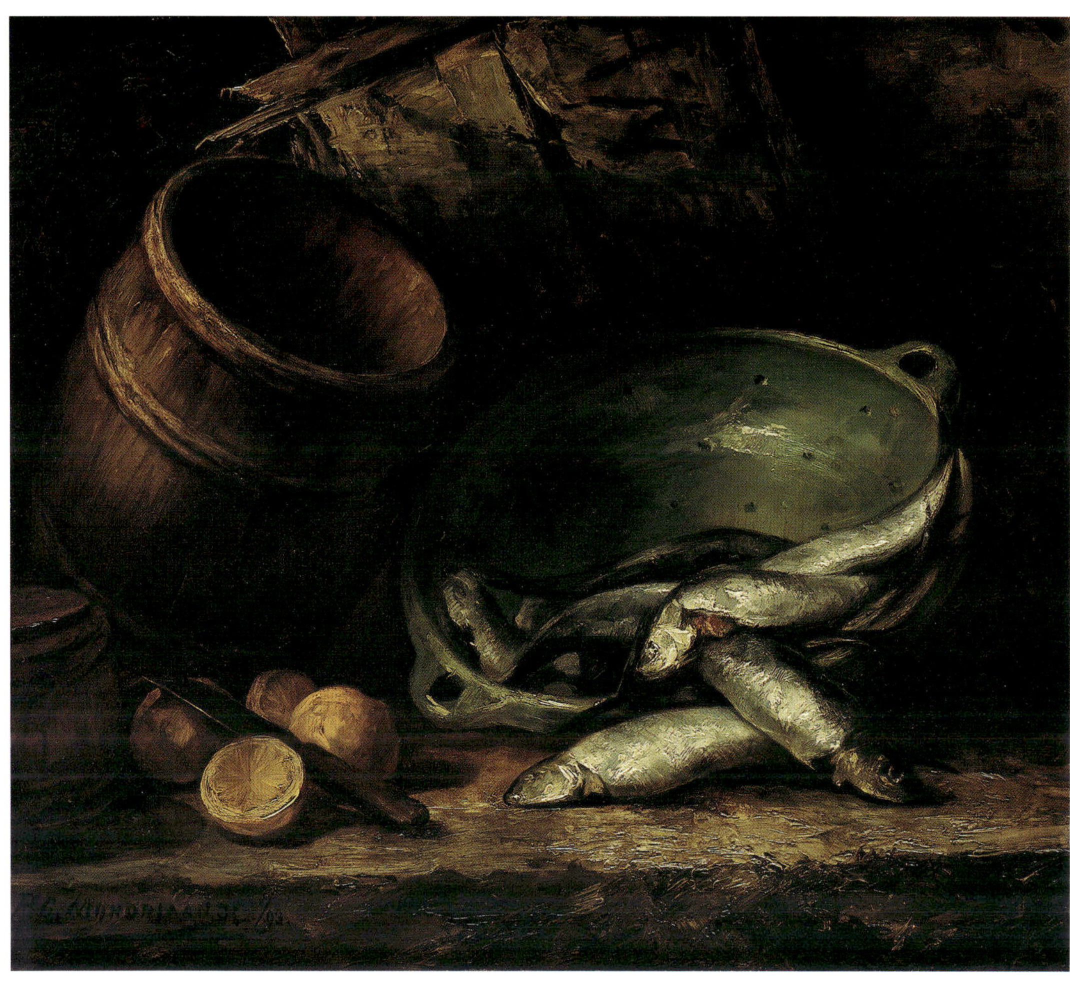

1

Movement of the 1880s), Maurits van der Valk (1857–1935), pronounced in 1898, in an article on Rembrandt, words that every artist should adopt as his motto, "The more we understand simple things, the more we understand God."[20] For the Protestant community, the reproduction of everyday reality guaranteed the revelation of "supreme truths" and participated, in an exalted form, in the fundamental conception of the work of art, as derived from seventeenth-century aesthetics.

At the end of the nineteenth century, this idea of realism remained unchallenged. From the most authoritative art critic to the most naïve art journalist, "image-representation" was credited with the unsurpassed fame that the tradition of seventeenth-century Dutch art had enjoyed. Twenty-five years later, in his theoretical text entitled *De Nieuwe Beelding in de schilderkunst (The New Plastic in Painting)*, Mondrian relied heavily on this principle of individualization, and even mentioned Jan Steen as a model of "clarity" in both form and content in seventeenth-century painting, in contrast to the "vagueness" of Matthijs Maris.[21] When, at the end of his life, in his *Toward the True Vision of Reality* (published in 1942), Mondrian emphasized that he had been a realist from the beginning and not a romantic,

Cat. 1 *Stilleven (Still Life)*, 1893
Oil on canvas
26.2 x 30.5 in. (66.5 x 77.5 cm)
Signed and dated lower left: *P.C. Mondriaan Jr. 1/93.*
Stedelijk Museum, Amsterdam, inv. A 8756 (A 23)

20. Maurits van der Valk, "Bij de Rembrandt-tentoonstelling" ("At the Rembrandt Exhibition"), *De Kroniek* 4 (October 1898), 341.
21. Piet Mondriaan, "Het Bepaalde en het Onbepaalde" in *De Nieuwe Beelding in de schilderkunst* ("The Determined and the Undetermined") 2, 1918–19, 15, as translated in Holtzmann and James 1986, 71.

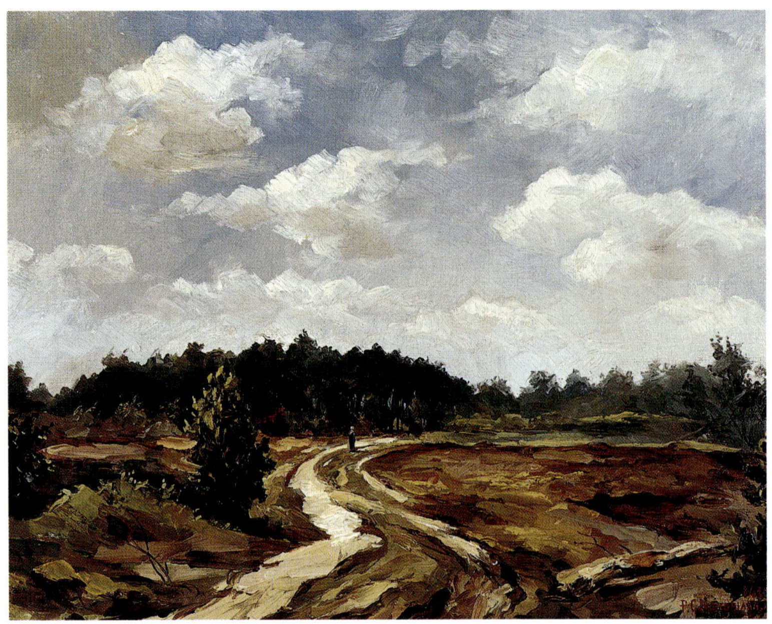
2

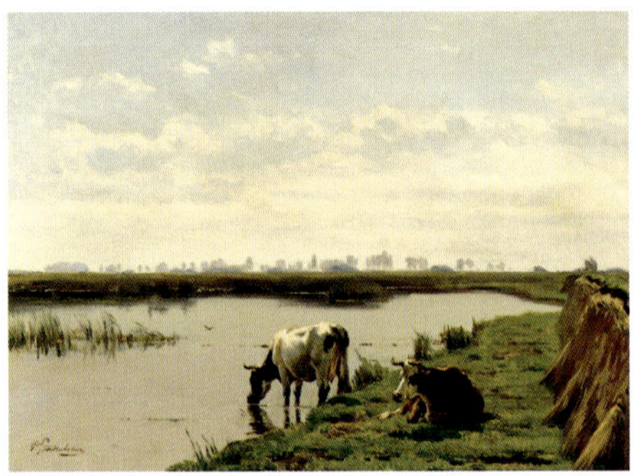

Fig. 4
Pieter Stortebeker (1828–1898), *Cows beside the Water*
Oil on canvas
Private collection

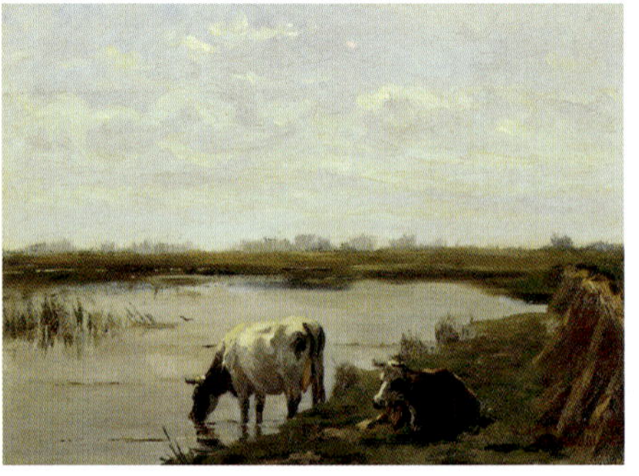

Fig. 5
Piet Mondrian, *Copy after Stortebeker*
Oil on canvas
Private collection (A -)

this remark must be interpreted according to the perspective outlined here. The very idea of "true vision" derives from a personal and obsessive search for truth, such as it had been defined and universally accepted in Dutch art since the seventeenth century. The complete liberty and freedom towards past conventions in Mondrian's relationship with nature is magnificently manifested in three paintings, *Country Road, Country Road and Farm,* and *Warmte* (*Warmth*) (cat. 2, 3, and 4), painted in 1893. These works must have been painted during his free hours after classes at the Academy. Until a short time ago, the existence of two of these paintings was unknown (cat. 2 and 3) Sometime around 1898, Mondrian probably gave them to one of his friends, Cornelis van den Berg (1863–1923), with whom Mondrian taught drawing classes from 1895 to 1898. Van den Berg was an instructor of gymnastics and drawing and lived a few steps

Cat. 2 *Country Road,* 1893
Oil on cardboard
16.3 x 20.9 in. (41.5 x 53 cm)
Signed and dated lower right: 8/93 P.C.M;
painted over with: 8/93 P.C. MONDRIAAN Jr.
Private collection (A -)

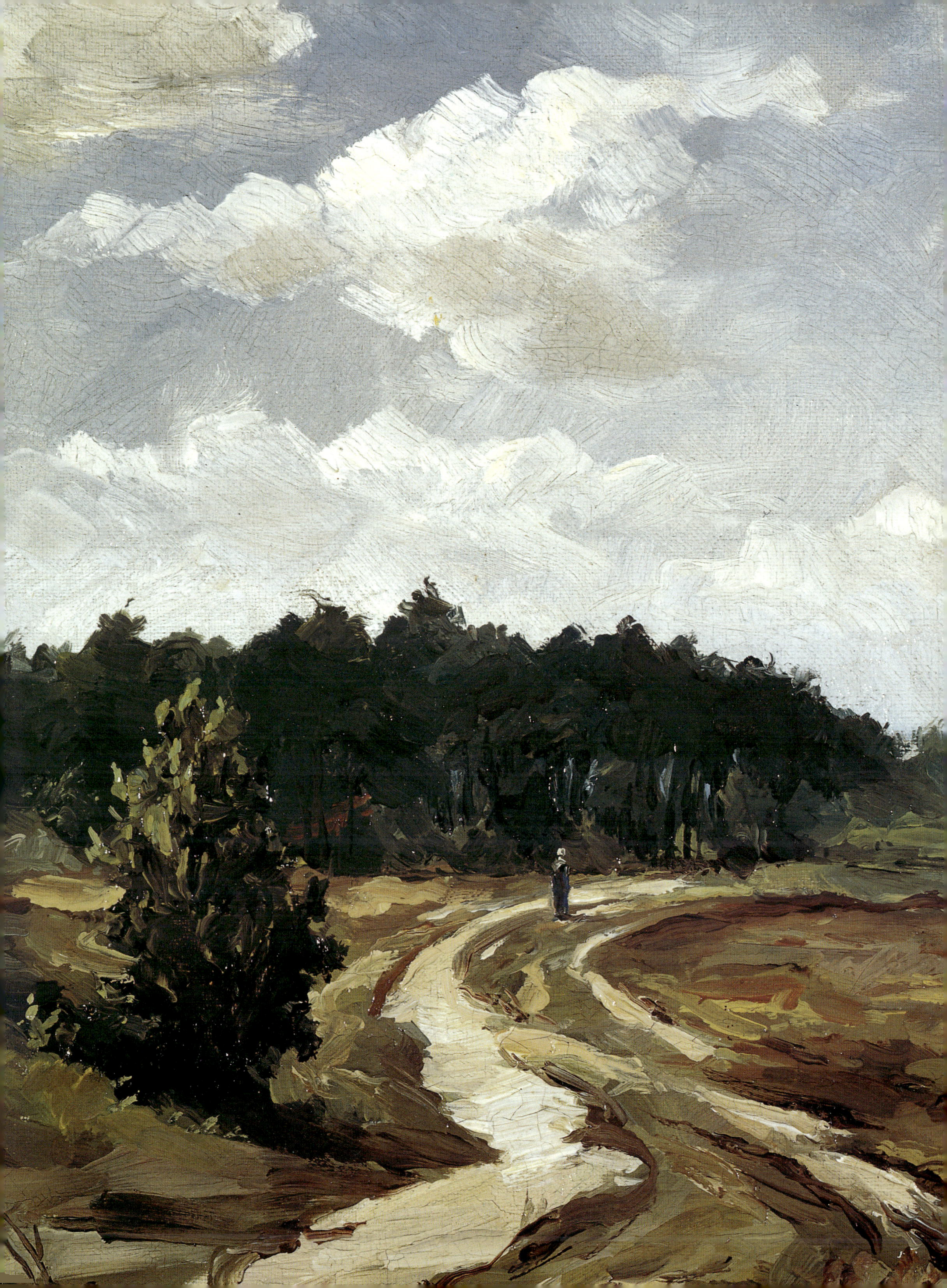

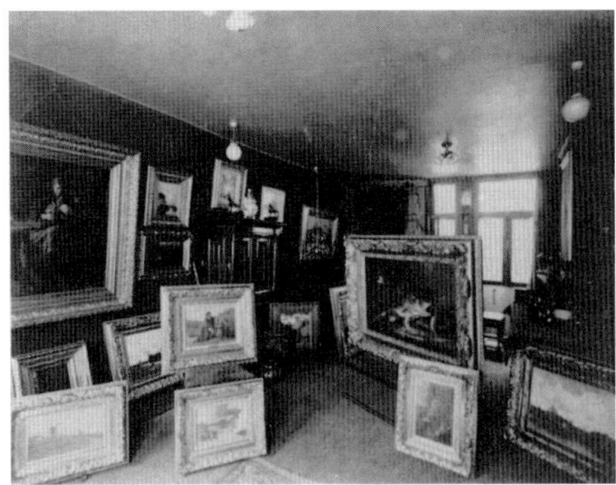

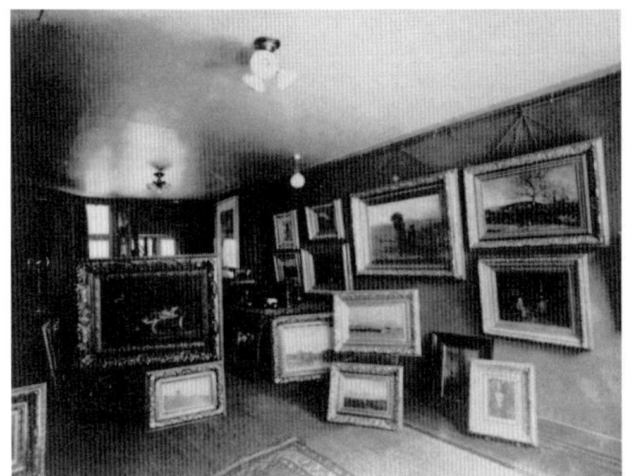

Fig. 6a and b
Gallery Van Wisselingh, located at 194 Kalverstraat, Amsterdam, c. 1893
Private collection

away from the room Mondrian had lived in since August 1895 in the Oosterpark quarter. Married and with a small child, Van den Berg had taken Mondrian into his home during the time when the artist was suffering from a serious illness. One cannot fix the dates precisely, but it must have been somewhere between 1896 and 1899.[22] The third landscape, coming from another source than the preceding two paintings, is a rather striking picture. It was never shown, although there is abundant documentation about it.

During his convalescence, Mondrian copied a painting by Pieter Stortebeker (1828–1893) that today still belongs to the family[23] (fig. 4 and 5). Soon after his recuperation, Mondrian seems to have signed these works in bright red, in the style of the Barbizon school painters, with a clear "P.C. MONDRiAAN Jr."[24] He superimposed this new signature over an earlier one, an elegant monogram combining the letters PCM, in the "old Dutch style," scratched into the painted surface. Mondrian had abandoned this type of monogram after his first year at the Academy, using various signatures in between: Pieter Mondrian and P. Mondriaan. It seemed to him less appropriate than the red capital letters that he had probably seen on Corot's paintings in the Mesdag Collection in The Hague, or when they were shown again at the Stedelijk Museum or by art dealers in Amsterdam (fig. 6a, 6b, and 7). The new signature also resembled somewhat that of George Hendrik Breitner (1857–1923), uncontested master of the moment to all the students at the Academy. The change of signature also raises the possibility that Mondrian reworked some of his paintings before offering them as gifts.[25]

These three canvases reveal a style of painting that was at once free and highly constructed, and employs a thick, creamy paint applied wet-in-wet with great confidence. The rapidity of the brushwork is especially striking. *Country Road* (cat. 2) represents a little lane winding across a kind of moor, sprinkled here and there with bushes and trees. A small, wooded area closes off the horizon. *Country Road and Farm* (cat. 3) depicts a lane running along the back of a farm and some sheaves of wheat. Mondrian reproduces the relief of the foliage by enhancing the color without trying to give the illusion of depth. The ruts in the road are indicated by simple, oblique brushstrokes. The two works are remarkable for their form; one senses no great effort on the artist's part in their creation, but neither are they chance beginnings. The sky in both paintings is treated soberly and sparingly, in contrast with the world below, which, one could say, is constructed on a ground of coarse, irregular dashes of color. The sky was probably painted in later, which would corroborate the view that Mondrian probably corrected his canvases before re-signing them and giving them away.[26] In spite of the rapidity of the brushwork, the painting style

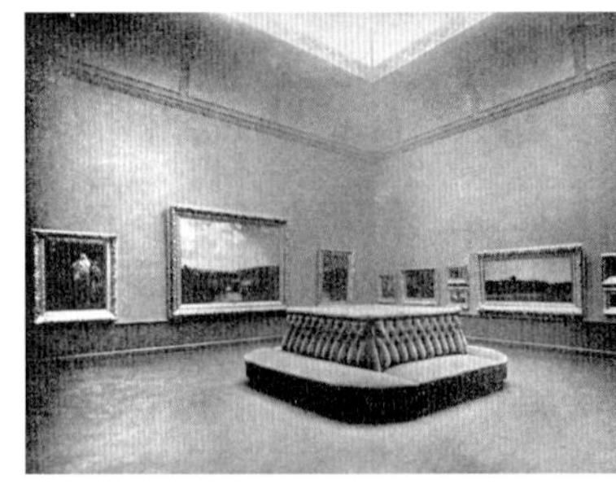

Fig. 7
"Square Gallery" on the first floor of the Stedelijk Museum, Amsterdam, exhibiting a selection of works of French nineteenth-century painters for the benefit of *Vereniging tot de Vorming van een Openbare Verzameling van Hedendaagse Kunst (The Association for Establishing a Public Collection of Contemporary Art)*, c. 1905
Stedelijk Museum, Amsterdam

22. In 1896 Mondrian painted the portrait of van den Berg's son at the age of five. He signed it, "PiET MONDRiAAN/ Jan. 1896." The last appearance of the signature "P. C. MONDRiAAN Jr." dates from 1899, on a ceiling painting done for Doctor Van de Velde, 608 Keizersgracht, Amsterdam (A 133).
23. The "copie after Stortenbeker [sic]/ P. C. MONDRiAAN Jr" is painted on a linen canvas mounted on a small nineteenth-century stretcher with pine fastenings set in a perpendicular manner.
24. Barbizon school exhibitions were quite numerous in Holland between 1893 and 1897. In January 1893, at the Arti et Amicitiae Society, Corot, Daubigny, Diaz, Dupré, Michel, Ribot, and Vollon were exhibited. Vincent van Gogh and Eduard Karsen also signed this way, but without using printed capital letters.
25. Mondrian always signed his works at the time of sale or when he exhibited them, or when, in one way or another, they became public. The best documentation available about this practice concerns the late work. This practice was so systematic with Mondrian that one can be fully confident that he used the same form for his earlier works. See Joosten and Welsh 1998, vol. 2, 189–90, and Cooper 2001, 29.

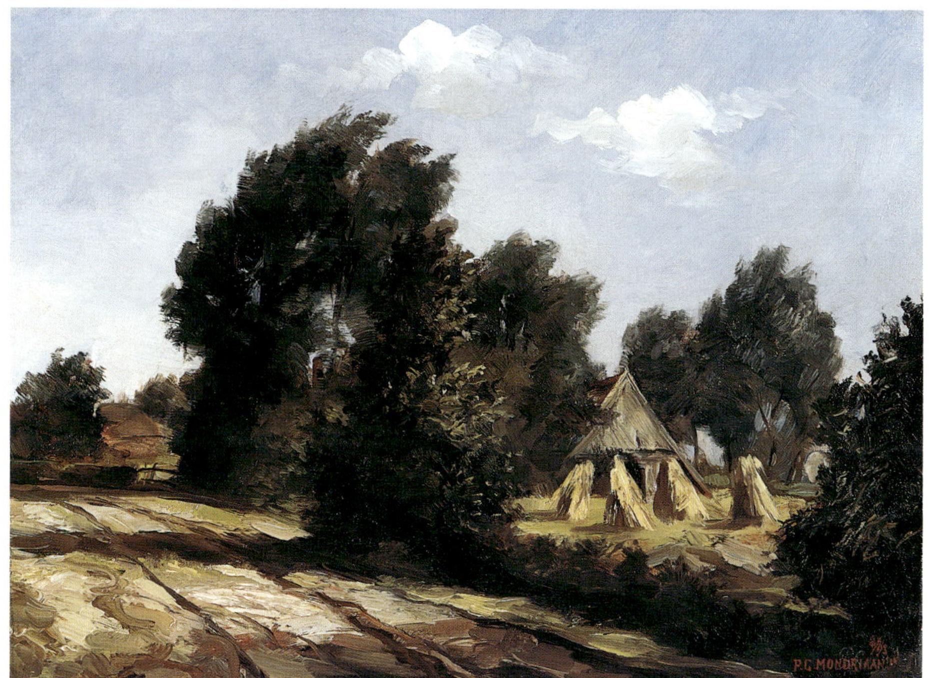

3

conforms to academic rules. It constructs forms by superimposing light layers upon dark ones. To differentiate the foreground from the background, vigorous and broad brushstrokes in the foreground become increasingly slender and delicate toward the background. Mondrian utilizes forms that lead the eye toward the horizon line, which was constructed in stepped stages. But at the same time, he seems deliberately to want to escape all these rules. He creates a rudimentary relief and a limited number of transitions between light and dark that produce an indistinct sense of light. Colors admit gradations reluctantly. Contrasts are stronger, due to the use of a palette dominated by ochers and greens, to which are added dashes of red, yellow, and violet. It is a bit like the "peinture couillarde" ["ballsy" painting] of which Cézanne spoke in 1866 as he shed the conventional rules that bound him. The fluidity of Mondrian's technique also relates to the manner of Vincent van Gogh, whose work Mondrian may have seen during the first months of his stay in Amsterdam. Theo van Gogh's widow, Johanna van Gogh-Bonger, had organized a large exhibition of Vincent's paintings at the Panorama.[27] In the works exhibited, van Gogh, too, was committed to the material aspect of the paint and to the visibility of technique in the final results. The implementation of his technique is not without a sense of organization; his brushwork has something impetuous and cutting edge about it. In this respect, the painting *Warmte* (Warmth) (cat. 4),[28] painted in 1893–94, is completely different, the treatment of the paint standing in total contrast to the "delicate painting" that Mondrian had taught himself in order to pass his exams. The thick, uneven, furrowed layers obscure the perception of the object being represented. With the accent placed on facture, one detects no "sensation," an essential idea in the aesthetics of the Literary Movement of the 1880s, used to designate the immaterial aspect of the artist's temperament, the pictorial effect corresponding to the painter's mood. In *Country Road,* the small silhouette of a woman is the focal element of the painting, an element that creates movement in the picture without, however,

26. The paintings were stretched once they were painted. This practice was very habitual with Mondrian. But the last modifications carried out on the skies were made after the canvas had already been stretched.
27. From December 17, 1892, to February 5, 1893.
28. The signature "Pieter Mondriaan" appears on the works of this period. The shorter version, "Mondrian," on *Warmte* (*Warmth*) (cat. 4), was probably the result of the limited space available for his signature.

Cat. 3 *Country Road and Farm,* 1893
Oil on canvas
17.1 x 23.7 in. (43.4 x 60.2 cm)
Signed and dated lower right:
P.C.M 10/93; painted over with:
8/93 P.C. MONDRIAAN Jr.
Private collection (A -)

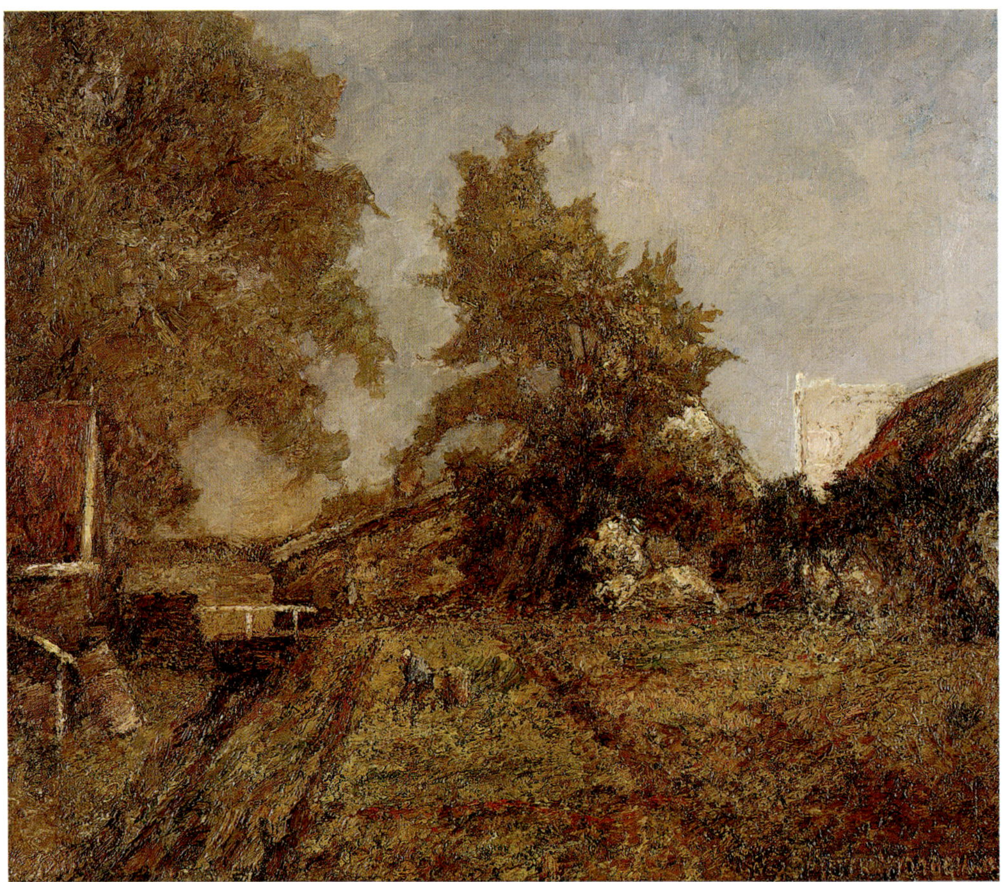

4

having any significance by itself. This woman is seen again in *Warmte*, this time working in the cottage garden; here again, she has no decisive meaning.

It does not appear that these three paintings are the result of direct observation, or that Mondrian might have been able to paint them *en plein air*, even if the current owners of the farm say that they are pictures of the Gooi landscape. On the contrary, what is striking, precisely because of the excessive impasto of the surface, is the extent to which these landscapes fit into the tradition of "mapped landscape," revealing an enclosed and flat world. This was a landscape tradition that relied on the addition of several characteristic elements without a hierarchical structure, in clear opposition to the "rhetorical landscape," essentially derived from French art.[29] Mondrian did not deny his origins, not even in this respect.

29. Alpers 1983, 147 *passim*.

Cat. 4 *Warmte* (*Warmth*), c. 1893–94
Oil on canvas
25 x 29.5 in. (63.5 x 75 cm)
Signed and dated lower right: PIETER MONDRIAN
Private collection (A 20)

Chapter Two

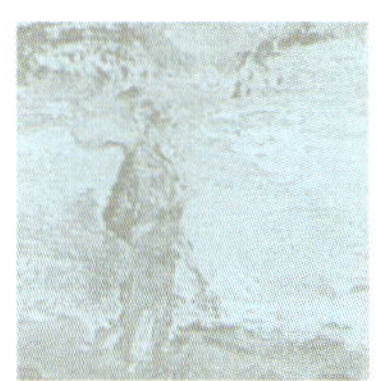

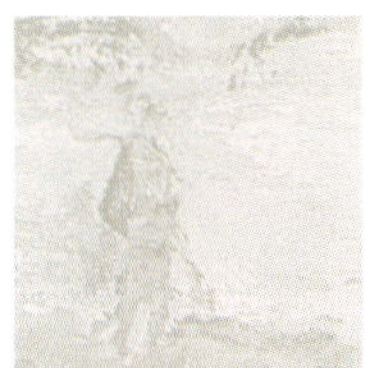

1893–1897

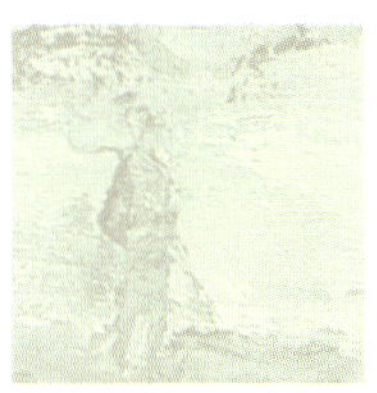

"The artist, born of the past, advances as far as his intuition permits." [30]

Hans Janssen

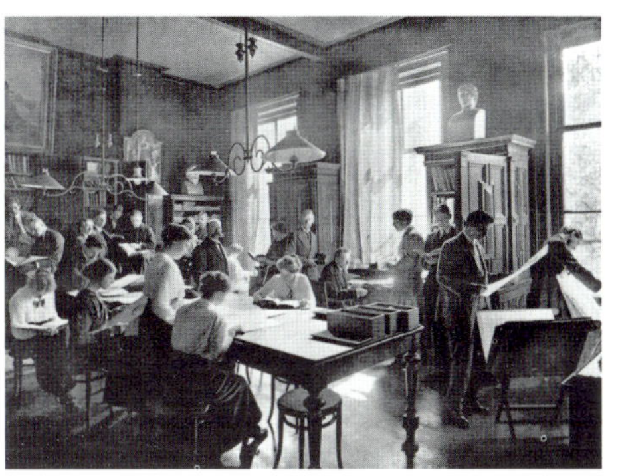

Fig. 8
The class of Professor Jan Six, in the library of the Royal Academy, c. 1910
Gemeentemuseum, The Hague

We may assume that Mondrian, during his two years of study at the National Academy, did not have much time to paint for himself. The program was quite full and was centered on drawing, painting after the model, and aesthetics, the science of beauty. Without being brilliant, Mondrian was "hard-working" and demonstrated "talent," as evaluations show. Notably he exhibited a lively interest in aesthetics, in which, according to these same reviews, he ranked above average. His interest was rewarded in the end, when he received the highest grade, a ten, given by his aesthetics professor, Jan Six (1857–1926) (fig. 8).

In the summer of 1895, Mondrian stopped taking daytime courses. He was no longer receiving

30. Mondrian 1921–22, 308 (translated in Holtzman and James, 1986, 159).

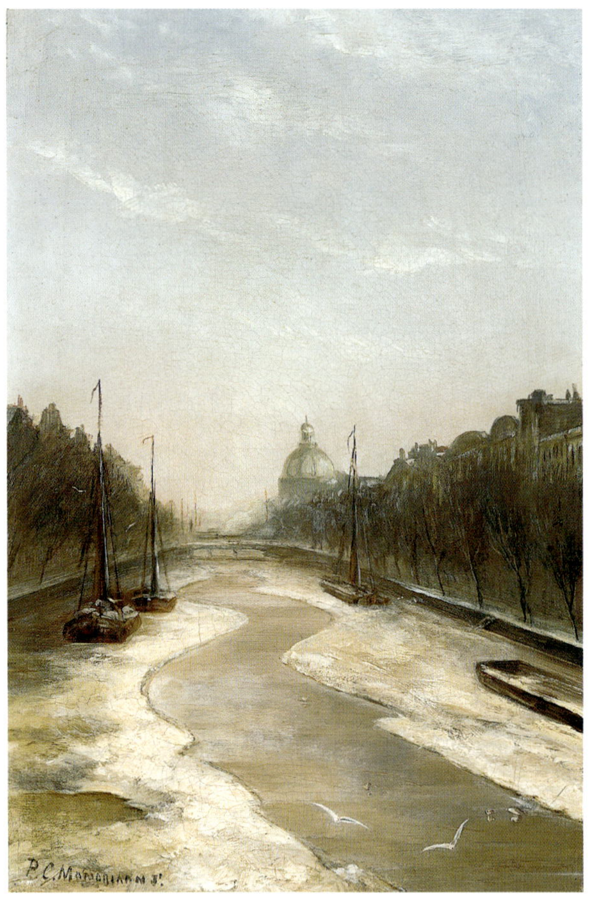

5

financial aid and was now supporting himself.

At 22 began a very difficult time for me. To make a living, I did many kinds of work–bacteriological drawings used for textbooks and in schoolrooms, portraits, copies of pictures in museums, and taught as well, and then I began to sell landscapes. It was a hard struggle but I managed to make a living and was glad to be able to make just enough money to be able to do what I wanted to do.[31]

The fairly large and carefully framed painting entitled *The Singel—Old Amsterdam* (cat. 5) may serve to illustrate the kind of work Mondrian had in mind. It represents a winter view of the Singel Canal in Amsterdam, looking out over the round dome of the Lutheran church building, the quarter known as "Old Amsterdam." It is probable that Mondrian began the painting in 1893, when there was a hard freeze in Amsterdam and the canals were iced over.[32] He painted the canvas while it was tacked in place on a panel. Only after he was finished did he determine its final size, and the paint continues over the border of the stretcher. He tried his hand at the technique of the Hague school, omitting the *ébauche,* or first sketch in diluted paint. But he simply painted the contours, which he then filled in, wet-in-wet. He had the canvas well framed and signed it as he had signed *Country Road* and *Country Road and Farm* (cat. 2 and 3). From all this it can be deduced that this is the painting with the title "Oud-Amsterdam" that Mondrian exhibited in 1898 at the exhibition of the Arti et Amicitiae Society, which he had

31. Bradley 1944, 18.
32. See, for example, the information published in the newspaper *De Telegraaf,* January 17–22, 1893.
33. Welsh, in Joosten and Welsh 1998, vol. 1, 473, identifies U A9 as *Oud-Amsterdam* (referring to A 179.) However, the combination of water-related elements and the disorder that reigns in the foreground, as well as the similarities between this painting and the description given by the *Arnhemse Courant* of September 9, 1898–which discusses "faithful observation" and the much applauded rejection of Breitner's "banal realism"– make it clear that this work corresponds rather to the one with the designation no. 78 in the Arti exhibition of 1898. Its title is *Scheepstimmerwerf* (*Shipyard*). The other painting that Welsh identities as *shipwork* (A 177) is far too much a sketch.

Cat. 5 *The Singel-Old Amsterdam,* c. 1893–97. Oil on canvas
27.2 x 18.1 in. (69 x 46 cm)
Signed lower left: *P.C.* Mondriaan Jr.
Gemeentemuseum, The Hague, bequest of Salomon B. Slijper, 1971, inv. S 98–1971 (A 30)

joined in 1894.[33] The particular reasons he chose to exhibit this stereotypical work are easy to guess. "The Dutch like their painting traditional," he remarked as late as 1944 while describing to a journalist the reaction of the Dutch public when they saw he had abandoned conventional patterns of painting.[34] In 1898, his work consisted for the most part of little experimental sketches, through which he researched and explored, and it seems unlikely that he would have chosen to put these small works at stake at the moment of his "debut" in one of Amsterdam's most prominent art venues.

Mondrian enrolled again for the academic year 1894–95 in the "little evening drawing class" at the National Academy; then again, after a year's interval, in 1896–97. These classes were supervised by Carel L. Dake (1857–1918), who had previously taught Mondrian life drawing. Apparently Mondrian felt the need to perfect his skill in the disciplines of the art of the sketch and drawing after the model: solidity of forms, firmness of composition, and accuracy of execution. That he devoted so much of his attention at this time to the execution of sketches might be explained, as has often been suggested, by his less than stellar talent for drawing the human figure. Even if this is true, one must not forget that in the artistic context of the era, increasing importance was attached to precision of line. Certain conservative critics upheld the idea that, even though Impressionism, coming from France, led to perversion, to excess, and to disaster, one could, nonetheless, defend it in a way. The foundation of art was no longer situated in some "external reality," but was now a question of perception, of sensations aroused in the artist by his environment. The ideas of "impression" and "sensation" played an ever-increasing role in art criticism after 1880.[35] Next to technical virtuosity, the quality that impressed critics was the inner depth with which the artist was endowed.[36] In Holland, as in France, the principle that art is "nature" combined with the sensitivity of the artist was commonly accepted. However, Impressionist casualness and lack of "finish" were more associated in Holland with indecisiveness and fuzziness than with the idea of an active search for power of expression. Even collectors and artists showed scarcely any interest in what was being done in France. The prestige of Dutch realism, linked as it was to the history of Holland, made the acceptance of *"peinture claire"* (light painting) and "the unfinished " difficult. There were some artists who, because of their professionalism, could appreciate a beautifully made sketch. "On the other hand, a collector who trusts his own eyes, will not easily decide to purchase a work in which harmony of colors and movements are well done but in which the drawing is inconsistent or sacrificed to other elements."[37] Thus, in the artistic environment of Holland, Impressionism had a very negative connotation.[38] In 1893, on the occasion of an exhibition of Monet, Pissarro, Sisley, and Renoir at the Haagsche Kunstkring (Art Circle of The Hague), a critic wrote of her reaction in no uncertain terms:

It is true, their aesthetic is different from that of Rousseau, Troyon, Corot–different also from that of the Maris brothers, whose ideal consists of converting what is seen into a perfectly proportioned work of art, opposing tones and hues, having unity, concentrating the light, and thereby inscribing themselves into the tradition of our own seventeenth century [fig. 9]. The "plein air-painters" are different. Their unique concern is to render the moment of the day as objectively as possible, like an instantanée, a snapshot, in which only the essence of each individual color is striking and gets recorded.[39]

34. Bradley 1944, 18.
35. Blotkamp 1991. 75–88.
36. Herwerden 1927, 381–82.
37. *A. C. Loffelt, Het Vaderland,* May 29, 1884.
38. Tempel 1999, 113–29.
39. G. [H. Marius], Haagsche Kunstkring ("Art Circle of The Hague"), *De Nederlandsch Spectator* 16 (October 14, 1893), 327.

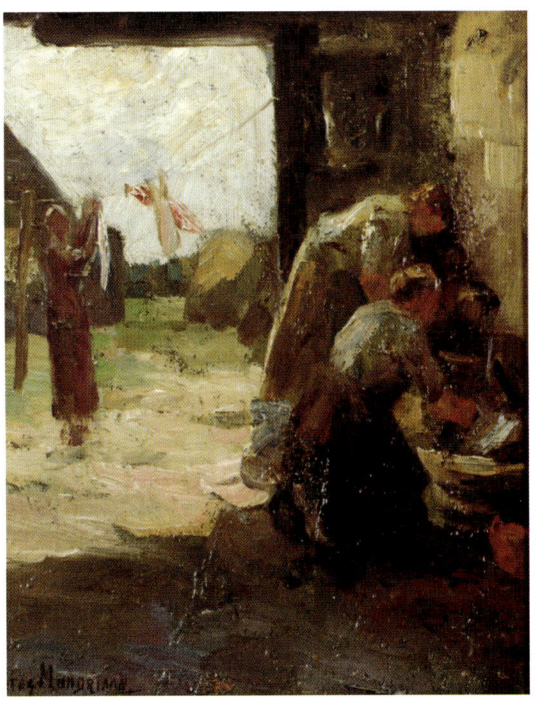

6

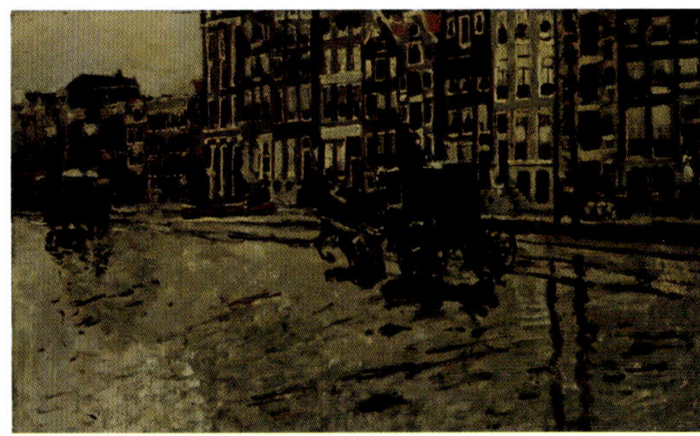

Fig. 10
Georg Hendrik Breitner, *Rokin*, c. 1890
Oil on canvas
Gemeentemuseum, The Hague

The gulf between the *"peinture grise"* (gray painting) of the Hague school, still tied to the Dutch seventeenth century, and the "light painting" of the French nonconformists seemed unbridgeable. In the late period of the Hague school, the work of Breitner and Isaac Israels (1854–1934) shows a preference for the sketch, borrowed from the Barbizon school, a freedom of brushwork, and a minimal attention to detail that led critics to refer to it as "Dutch Impressionism" (fig. 10). But the expression bore no real reference at all to Monet, Renoir, or Sisley, and hardly any more to the Barbizon artists, who were still being promoted by Dutch art dealers. Rembrandt and Frans Hals constituted the only accepted touchstones for assessing the freedom and character of the brushstroke. Mondrian's encounter with the artistic world of Amsterdam took place under this constellation of ideas in 1894. One had to be born extremely fortunate to believe oneself capable of achieving and adapting, as for example Breitner did, that which had been the sole province of Rembrandt. It is therefore quite possible that Mondrian continued to take night courses at the Academy because he wanted more training in spontaneous precision of execution.

In all his early landscapes, Mondrian tried his hand at a great variety of styles and techniques that permitted him to practice spontaneity and precision. One indication that he was engaged in constant experimentation was his use of at least three different types of signature. He painted, at this time, almost exclusively on little pieces of roughly cut canvas or cardboard, on which can be found traces of earlier work, or even on pieces of paper that have ultimately been glued to a canvas. This way of working reveals a painter with little money who could not afford high-quality materials, and at the same time a passionate artist who was not especially patient and sometimes even negligent. All of these characteristics will be continued until 1904, the date after which this type of sketch disappears. Until the end of his career Mondrian was to create most of his paintings on supports whose final size was determined during the working process.

Women Washing (cat. 6) depicts a small group of women busy with their laundry. Light penetrates the interior through the open door and caresses

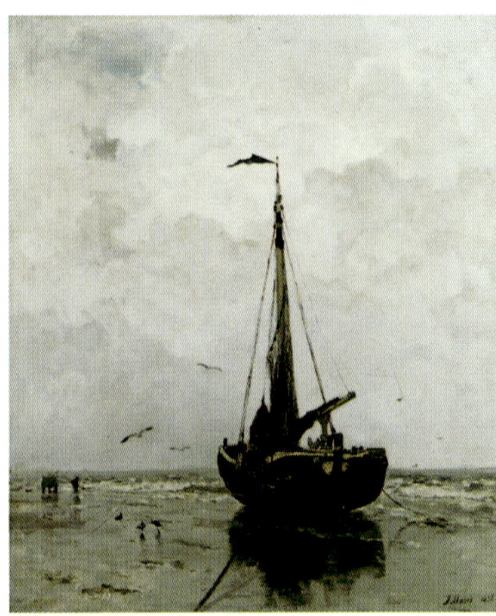

Fig. 9
Jacob Maris, *The Barge*, 1878
Oil on canvas
Gemeentemuseum, The Hague

Cat. 6 *Women Washing*, 1894–95
Oil on canvas
11.3 x 9.4 in. (28.8 x 23.8 cm)
Signed lower left: PIETER MONDRIAAN.
Private collection (A 29)

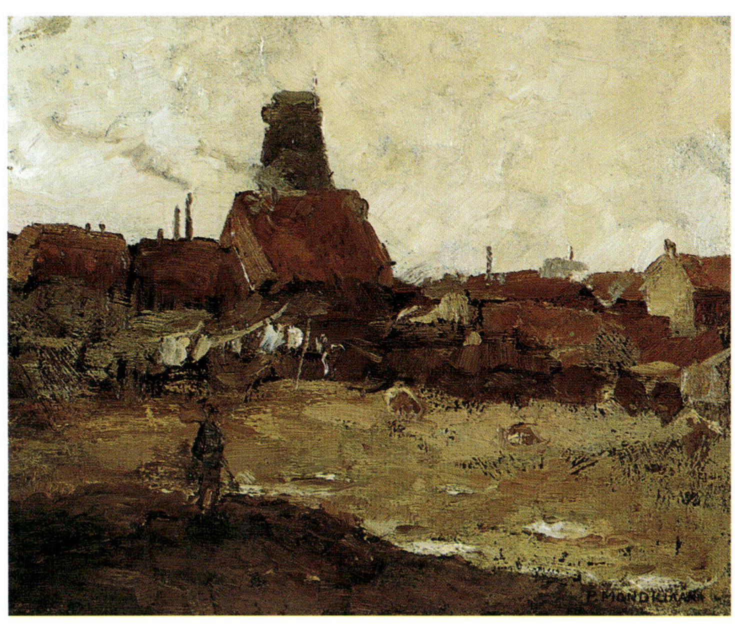

7

their skirts. In the background a woman is busy hanging laundry on a line. This little painting is of sober coloring, favoring browns. Spots of white and pink, and light and dark ocher stand out among the broken brushstrokes. The faces and feet are not painted in detail. As in many scenes of everyday life in which one searches for the poetry of the moment, one senses an awkwardness in the placement of elements, something that had created problems for Mondrian from the beginning. The sense of volume, depth, and verisimilitude is simply replaced by clearly organized strokes. His brushstroke shows that the artist knew how to paint accurately. He succeeded in awakening, with his broad brushwork, the sensation of the fleeting moment, of the instant. Strengthened with this ability, though he placed himself under the banner of the young Dutch Impressionists, he did not necessarily seek to be recognized as such. In any case, even though it appears that he sold this little sketch around the mid-1890s or even before, he did not make this part of his work public.[40]

The paintings *View of Schinkelbuurt* (cat. 7) and *Irrigation Ditch with Bridge* (cat. 8) are also an amassing together of wide brushstrokes. The first is a light-filled view of the Schinkel quarter on the southwest edge of Amsterdam. Mondrian painted it over an earlier painting, which he apparently covered over with a layer of black paint. The composite, complex brushwork keeps the surface as open as possible and enables the black ground to contribute to the optical unification of the final painting. To accentuate the design, he incised lines with the wooden tip of his paintbrush into the still-wet paint.

Although the canvas might appear to have been finished in one session, this does not mean that it was painted *en plein air*. The shadow of a silhouette in the foreground is not at all lifelike, and what is more, the sky–a crazy tangle of whites–and the smoke rising from the chimney were painted in later, as were the white spots in the foreground and the wild, white splashes that represent laundry hanging from the line. What counted above all was creating unity.

Irrigation Ditch with Bridge shows drying cracks that indicate several stages of work. Mondrian used a wide brush and a lively palette, in which red and light green are used to color the painting

Cat. 7 *View of Schinkelbuurt*, c. 1894–95
Oil on canvas
12.2 x 15.2 in. (31 x 38.5 cm)
Signed lower right: P. MONDRIAAN
Gemeentemuseum, The Hague, bequest of Salomon B. Slijper, 1971, inv. S 86–1971 (A 186)

40. We do not know who might have been the first owner of this little painting. One can infer, by comparing the signature with others, that it should be dated before the mid–1890s.

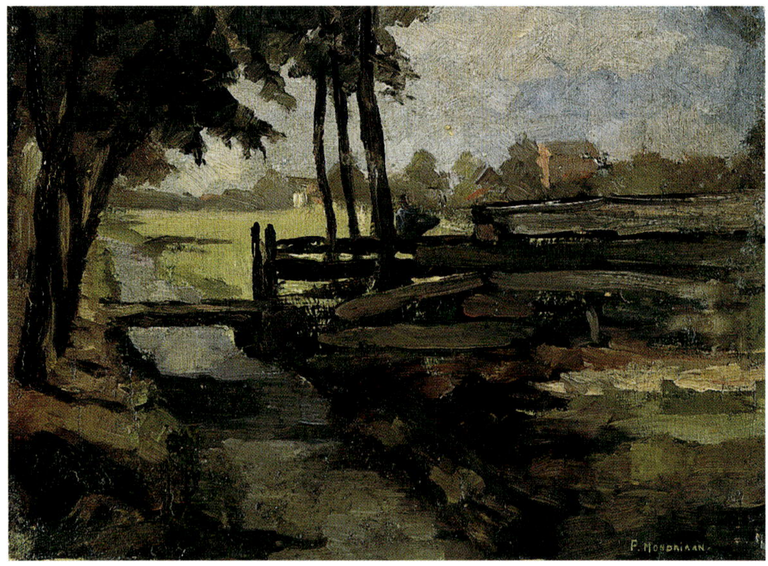
8

and bathe it with light, a process Willem Maris (1844–1910) himself also used frequently at this time (fig. 11). This image, too, was painted over another, earlier painting. The surface irregularities of the earlier painting contribute to the overall effect of the work. This little piece of canvas was glued to cardboard, apparently by Mondrian himself. He followed this studio procedure with other works, pasting a watercolor and an oil-on-paper onto canvas, for instance (fig. 12 and 13).

In *Irrigation Ditch with Bridge* the artist began with the horizon, the light-filled meadows below, and the sky above. He closed in the painting with a dense wooded area on the left painted in three different tones of umber. In the right foreground, an area emerging from the umber and extending upward is built up with horizontal strokes. This mass could represent a woodpile or the combination of a lean-to and a gate, but above all it is a fascinating, organized mass of paint. Everything here is clearly painted from observation; however, one can also see how, guided by enthusiasm, Mondrian lets himself get carried away by his technique. Behind the gate there is a man in a blue smock absorbed in his work. He is only vaguely present, since Mondrian did not find it necessary to provide him with anything more than a torso. The perspective on the horizon and the meadows, accentuated by the bright sunshine, stems from the notion of "simple truth," which, as pointed out earlier, ruled landscape theory. Originating in the seventeenth century, it had been inflected by another, completely specific meaning under eighteenth-century Neoclassicism and nineteenth-century Romanticism: the artist was encouraged to go out into the open air and, face-to-face with his subject, to fix on his canvas the ever-changing aspects of the prosaic Dutch landscape. The goal was fidelity to nature; it was a matter of "seeing through one's own glasses." Even at the close of the nineteenth century, the art of the seventeenth century was thought to teach the painter not to see coldly as a camera, but that he had to add to "simple truth" the sense of his own impression. It was only one step from there to the Barbizon school, and the concept that made "the soul of nature" the subject and spirit of landscape aesthetics.

Aleid Loosjes-Terpstra, one of the first to describe Mondrian's earliest career, arrived in 1956 at this fundamental conclusion:

[The earliest works] are a probing exploration of the elements of nature, in which the motif is not chosen to create a play of tones and colors (as

Cat. 8 *Irrigation Ditch with Bridge*, 1894–95
Oil on canvas mounted on cardboard
10.4 x 14.8 in.(26.5 x 37.5 cm)
Signed lower right: P. MONDRIAAN.
Gemeentemuseum, The Hague, bequest of Salomon B. Slijper, 1971, inv. S 58–1971 (A 37)

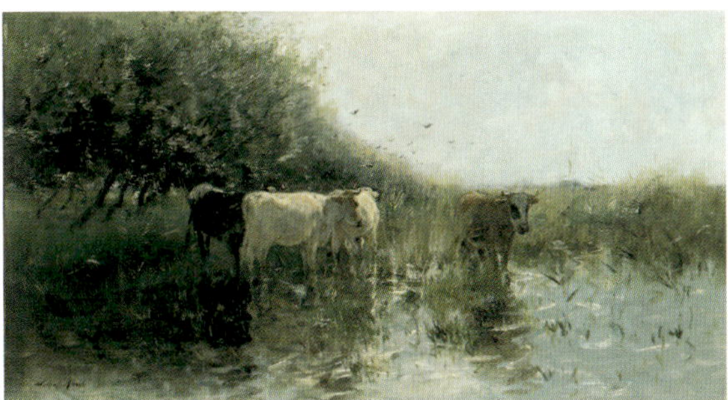

Fig. 11
Willem Maris, *Cows among the Reeds*, c. 1885
Oil on canvas
Gemeentemuseum, The Hague

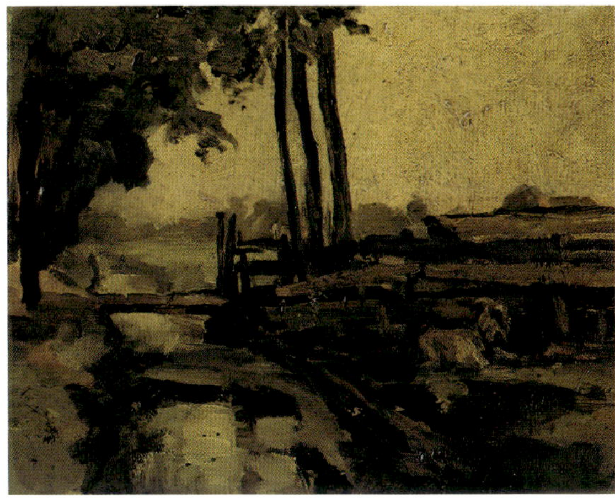

Fig. 12
Piet Mondrian, *Irrigation Ditch with Bridge*, c. 1894–95
Oil on canvas
Private collection (A 38)

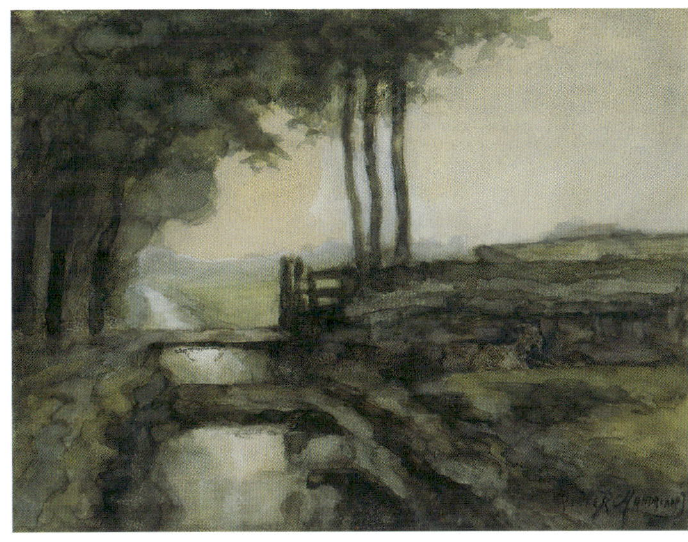

Fig. 13
Piet Mondrian, *Irrigation Ditch with Bridge*, c. 1894–95
Watercolor
Gemeentemuseum, The Hague (A 39)

with the painters of the Hague school), but in which nature maintains all its values and "speaks" for itself to suggest a certain atmosphere.[41]

Exploration is an essential principle of man's identification with nature. The principle might constitute the most obvious point of agreement between Mondrian and the Barbizon school painters. Mondrian himself —and along with him almost all of the painters of his time—had been seduced by the idea of atmosphere, by the notion of an art of impressions, by a "lyrical art." But this seduction is much less evident in Mondrian than has been supposed.

It has been claimed that Mondrian in his early work chose to train himself in the style of the Hague school, that he was seeking a way to capture the "atmosphere" of his subject. But his earliest works absolutely contradict this assumption. Between 1893 and 1904, Mondrian strived always for a scrupulous realism avoiding all exaggeration, blurring, or vagueness. Around 1898, an anonymous critic for the *Arnhemse Courant* defined his position as follows:

Without risking unusual color effects or affectedness in the draughtmanship, there rests over this painting a careful but straightforward

41. Loosjes-Terpstra 1959, 49.

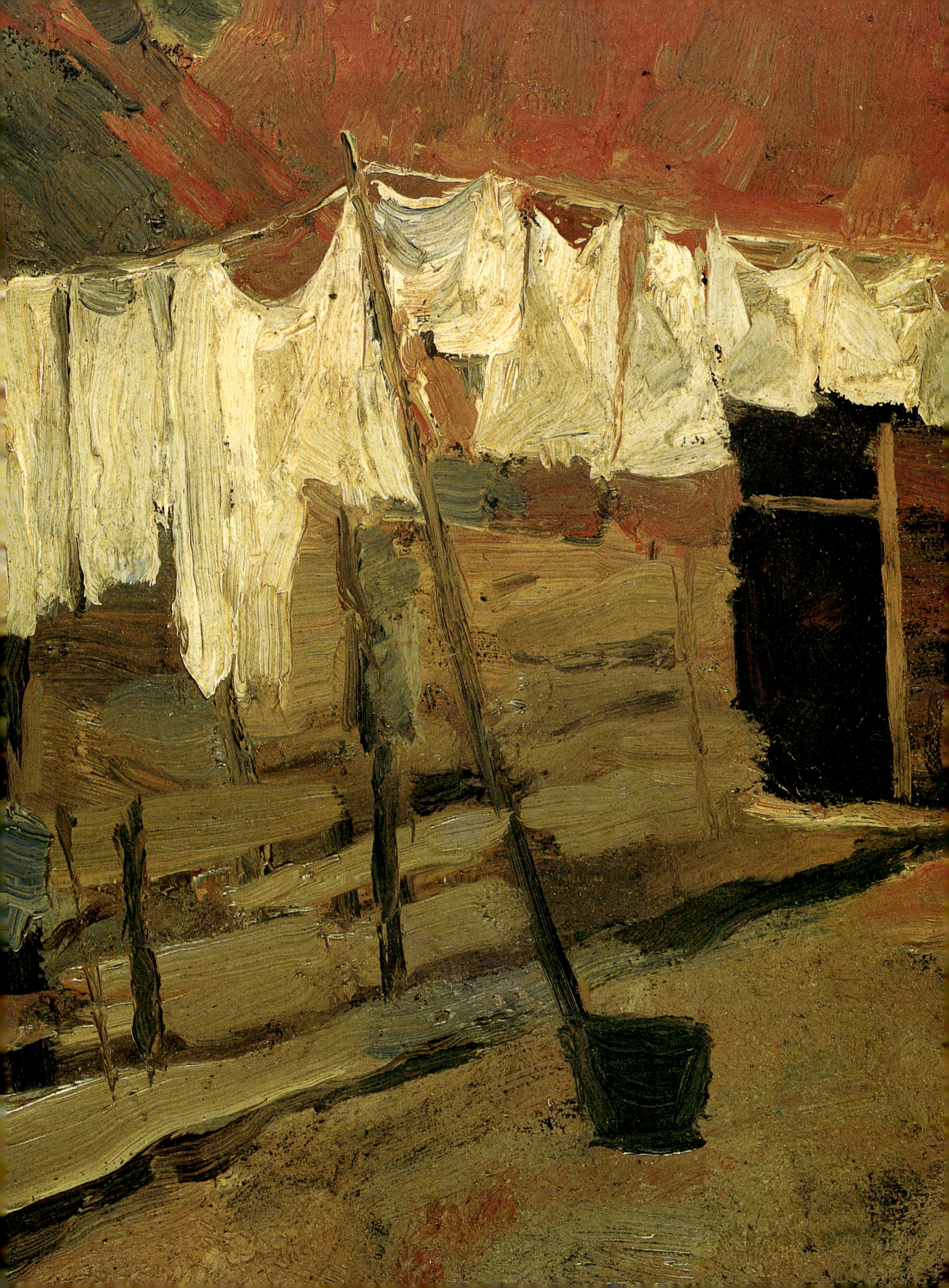

tone that holds him back from a more exuberant realism, as manifested, for example, in Breitner; the Golden Way, which leads so many painters into a morass of banality, has been trodden by Mondrian with success.[42]

During the 1890s, as Carel Blotkamp has correctly observed, Mondrian clearly distanced himself from all avant-garde movements–such as they existed in Holland.[43] However, one must challenge the idea that he refused to engage in any experimentation. He hoped to form his own, unique position without deciding prematurely what form it would take.

Mondrian never abandoned himself to the worship of the artist's personality, so widespread in the Dutch Literary Movement of the 1880s. But in his earliest works as well as his later work, one can detect characteristics that are constants: "a feeling for rhythm, which quickens to the pulse of life and seems somehow to be connected with his positive sense for the new; and the other, a love of order and balance, which is at the root of his search for unity and fullness."[44] One sees the manifestation of these characteristics for the first time in oil sketches painted between 1893 and 1897: *Farmhouse with Clothesline* (cat. 9), in which rhythm plays an essential role; *Farmstead and Ditch* (cat. 10), in which the striving for order and organization dominates; and *Country Road and Row of Houses* (cat. 11), characterized by the balance between rhythm and order.

The canvas of *Farmhouse with Clothesline* displays many tack holes, indicating the existence of several stages of work. Here, too, Mondrian trimmed the canvas on all edges after completing it. In so doing he accentuated the compact and complex structure of the composition. To achieve this–from his very first traces in white chalk forward–he abandoned traditional composition based on foreground and background and opted for a strongly foreshortened perspective that

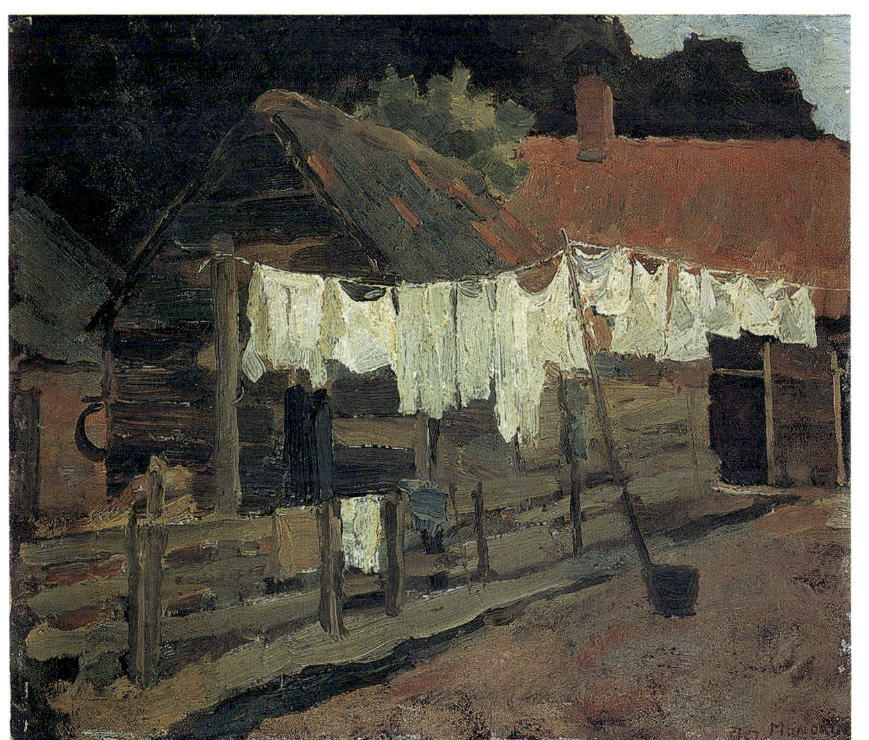

9

Cat. 9 *Farmhouse with Clothesline*, c. 1895
Oil on cardboard
12.4 x 14.8 in. (31.5 x 37.5 cm)
Signed lower right: PIET MONDRIAAN
Gemeentemuseum, The Hague, inv. S 27–1960 (A 171)

42. *Arnhemse Courant*, September 9, 1898, in reference to the exhibition *Arti et Amicitiae*, which was to open in the fall of 1898.

43. Blotkamp 1994, 20.

44. Riley 1997, 9.

imparts surface and volume to the barns at the "back" of the painting. Working with a wide brush, he revealed the black ground, leaving many areas uncovered. A later stage reveals the addition of a violet gray in the courtyard in the foreground and a new layer of color on the sky, probably placed there in order to reestablish balance. The artist engages the eye by creating a play of rhythms and variations in the abrupt contrast between the laundry on the line and the mass of colors that compose the gates, the posts, and the courtyard.

Everything leads us to believe that Mondrian, during several years of practicing this method of painting, mastered a veritable arsenal of techniques that allowed him to compose rather audacious and solid compositions. Among them is *Farmstead and Ditch*, probably painted around 1897. Here again, there is a complex structure: much more than the objects actually represented, the principal motif of the painting is the idea of reflection. Each detail indicates that Mondrian meant to surpass the stage of the sketch and produce a new, finished work of art. The image is condensed, layered, and organized in hierarchical form. Various devices are employed to direct the gaze: the boat in the right foreground that invites the eye to penetrate the shallow space of the painting; the foliage in the upper right that accentuates the composition of the scene; as well as the almost indecipherable tangle that reveals itself partially to our sight on the left. The farm, "plastered up" along the line of the raised horizon, deliberately contrasts with the illusion of reality that radiates from the work. Mondrian temporarily glued this little canvas to a piece of plywood, to be stored in the pictorial archive that was taking shape in his studio at that time. The panache and brio at work in *Country Road and Row of Houses* suggest that it might have been made in one session in the open air. However, a

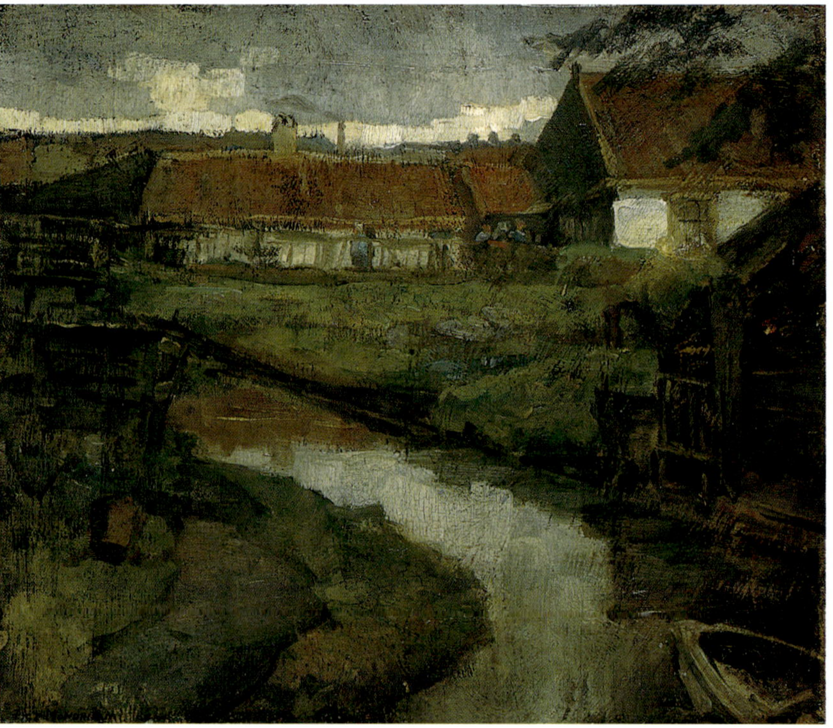

10

Cat. 10 *Farmstead and Ditch*, c. 1897
Oil on canvas mounted on panel
15.6 x 18.5 in. (39.5 x 47 cm)
Signed lower left: PI ET MONDRIAAN
Gemeentemuseum, The Hague, purchase Chr. Veldt, 1956, inv. S 39–1956 (A 154)

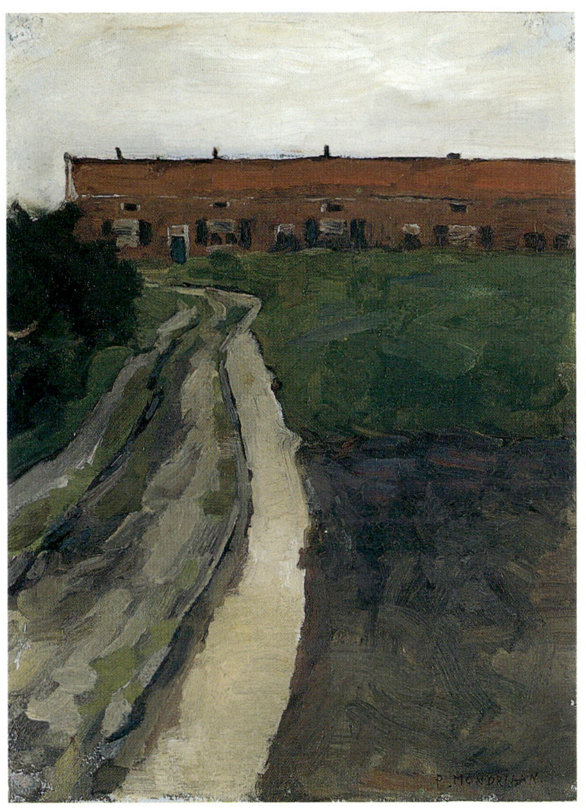

11

closer look reveals at least three distinct stages of work, in the course of which each layer was somewhat dry before the artist picked up the piece of cardboard again. Continuing to paint wet-in-wet, with distinct strokes, Mondrian formed the large shapes and perfected and animated them as he made corrections. Then he worked to make the contours clearer, working them in an open fashion, adding nuances and different colors.

These works are the result of Mondrian's roaming about the countryside around Amsterdam, making studies or sketches, "withdrawn and self-sufficient, with the attitude of one who is awaiting and whose wait, however, is not a cautious approach, but hard labor, even extending into the night. His was a particular kind of wait, filled with certitude and a firm, steadfast confidence."[45]

Cat. 11 *Country Road and Row of Houses*, c. 1897
Oil on paper mounted on panel
15.3 x 11.6 in. (39 x 29.5 cm)
Signed lower right: P. MONDRIAAN.
Gemeentemuseum, The Hague,
bequest of Salomon B. Slijper, 1971, inv. S 57–1971 (A 160)

45. Letter from Albert van den Briel to J. M. Harthoorn, quoted in Henkels 1998, 60.

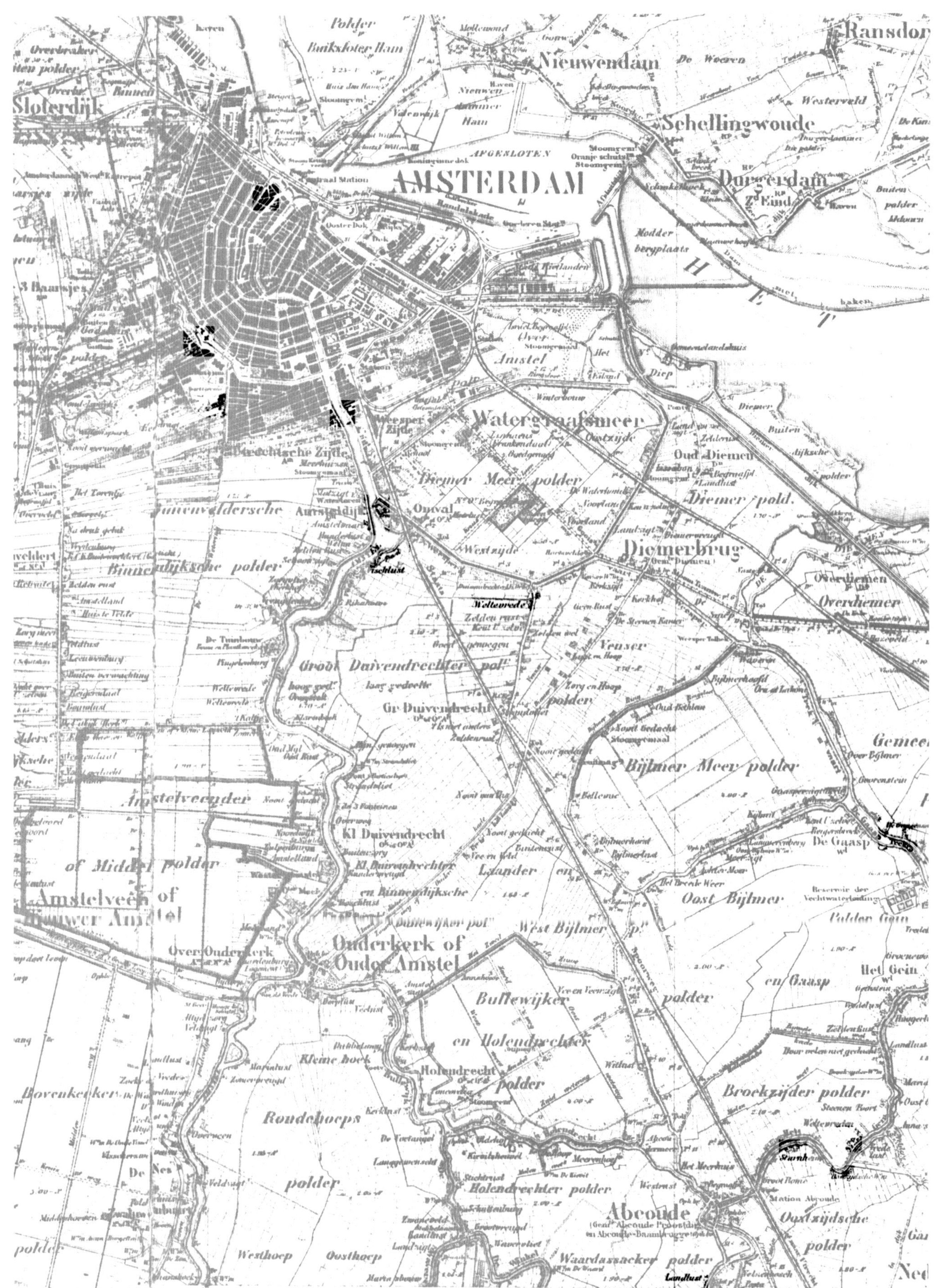

AMSTERDAM
Sloterdijk
Nieuwendam
Schellingwoude
Durgerdam
Watergraafsmeer
Diemer Meer polder
Diemer pold.
Diemerbrug
Oud Diemen
Overdiemen
Venser polder
Groot Duivendrechter pol.
Gr Duivendrecht
Kl Duivendrecht
Bijlmer Meer polder
Oost Bijlmer
West Bijlmer
Amstelveen
Amstelveender of Middel polder
Ouderkerk of Ouder Amstel
Bullewijker en Holendrechter polder
Holendrecht
Holendrechter polder
Roudehoeps polder
Broekzijder polder
Abcoude
Waardassacker polder
Oostzijdsche polder
De Gaasp
Het Gein
Westhoep
Oosthoep
De Nes
Weltevrede
Landlust

Chapter Three

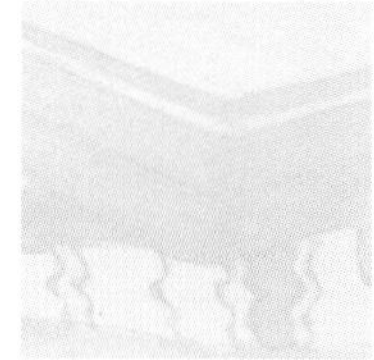

1897–1900

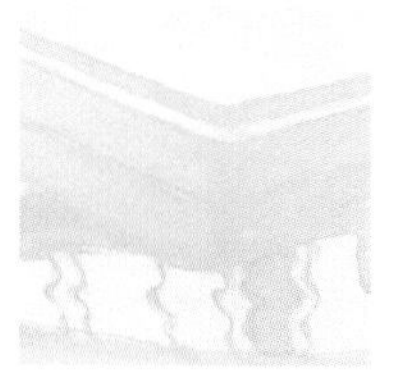

"It is precisely the essential line of any object which I find fundamentally important and, also, the color.[46]

Hans Janssen

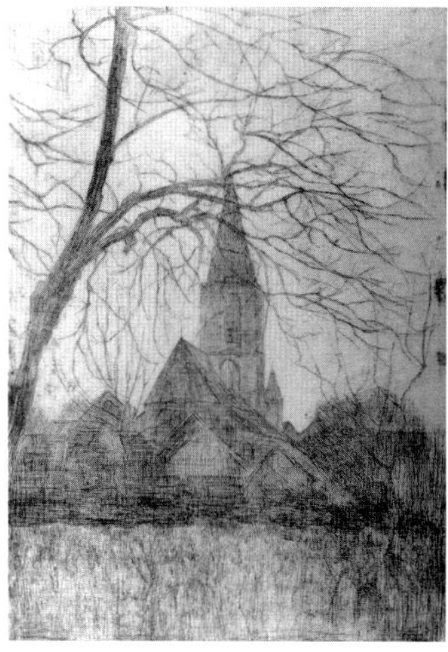

Fig. 14
Piet Mondrian, *Church at Winterswijk*, c. 1898
Engraving
The Museum of Modern Art, New York (A 60)

On June 28, 1897, August Allebé noted in a letter of recommendation for Mondrian that the artist came to the Academy in the academic year 1896–97 "to study the art of printmaking." Allebé then reports that, due to his financial situation, Mondrian was forced increasingly to pursue his training independently, and that studying in foreign schools—and, if possible, a stay in England—would have been extremely beneficial. We have hardly any examples of Mondrian's talents as a printmaker. Aside from his etchings, some bookplates are known. One etching representing the church in Winterswijk exists (fig. 14). The relationship established in the letter between "the art of printmaking" and a stay in England could lead us to believe that

46 Letter from Mondrian to Israel Querido. See Querido 1909–10, 11, as translated in Welsh and Joosten 1969, 10.

Opposite:
Administrative map of Amsterdam and environs, 1896
Municipal Archives, Amsterdam

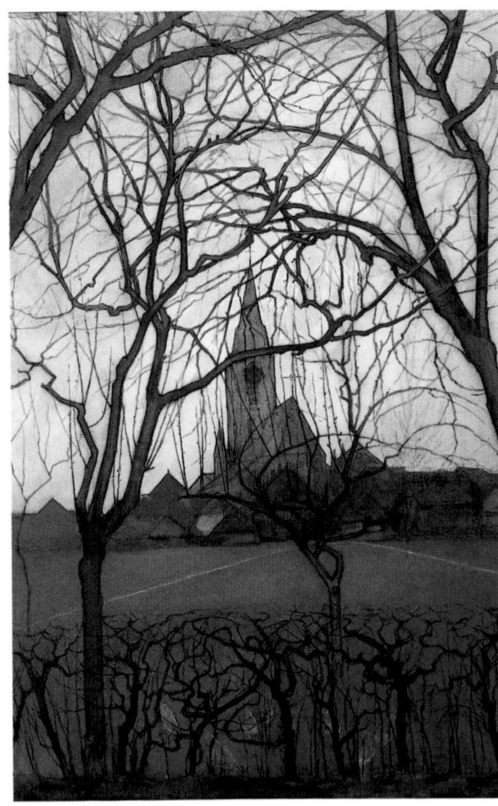

15

Mondrian–following the example of his colleagues Willem Witsen (1868–1923), Willem de Zwart (1862–1932), and Geo Poggenbeek (1853–1903)–hoped to reach an international market, then dominated by the art dealers Van Wisselingh & Co., of London and Amsterdam.[47]

The etching representing the church of Winterswijk belongs to an ensemble of works on paper, conceived by Mondrian as preparatory steps in the creation of a large work that would ultimately be shown at the May 1898 exhibition of Arti et Amicitiae, and then in June 1899 in the exhibition of the Saint Lucas society of artists. The ensemble is interesting in that it so well documents the development of an idea in Mondrian's early work. It looks as if the artist prepared his compositions elaborately, working out groups of drawings. Few such series have survived, and the series relating to *Dorpskerk (Village Church)* (cat. 15) is the most complete. Two of the drawings (cat. 12 and 13) are highly detailed studies that Mondrian later sold as independent works. *Tree Sketch for Dorpskerk* (cat. 12) represents a small, pruned tree, drawn in great detail, with a rapidly executed setting. In *Church, Winterswijk* (cat. 13), the view from the family house toward Jacob's Church occupies the central area of the scene. Behind a hastily sketched hedge appear the roofs of the old village. In the foreground stands a tree, its branches drawn with care and precision. The charcoal sketch *Church, Winterswijk* (cat. 14) is a variation on the same motif, but, in contrast to the other drawings, this one has meaning only within the group.[48]

In the large, final watercolor *Dorpskerk (Village Church)* (cat. 15), Mondrian combines various elements from the studies and sketches. In the center rises the silhouette of the church, amid tightly clustered roofs. Colors range from a soft red to a light bluish gray, with lilac accents passing through a gray green. In front of the church, the

47. Poggenbeek had an extraordinary success in a one-person exhibition at Goupil & Co., dealers in London, announced in the newspaper *De Telegraaf* of June 27, 1899–by coincidence the day before Mondrian asked Allébé to write the letter.

48. This page from a sketchbook was among the documents saved by Mondrian in his studio, probably until he sold most of his works—a large number of his important early works—to Salomon B. Slijper of Blaricum, Holland.

Cat. 15 *Dorpskerk* (*Village Church*), 1897–98
Pencil, watercolor, gouache, crayon, and pastel on paper
29.5 x 19.7 in. (75 x 50 cm)
Signed lower left: PIET MONDRIAAN
Private collection (A 61)

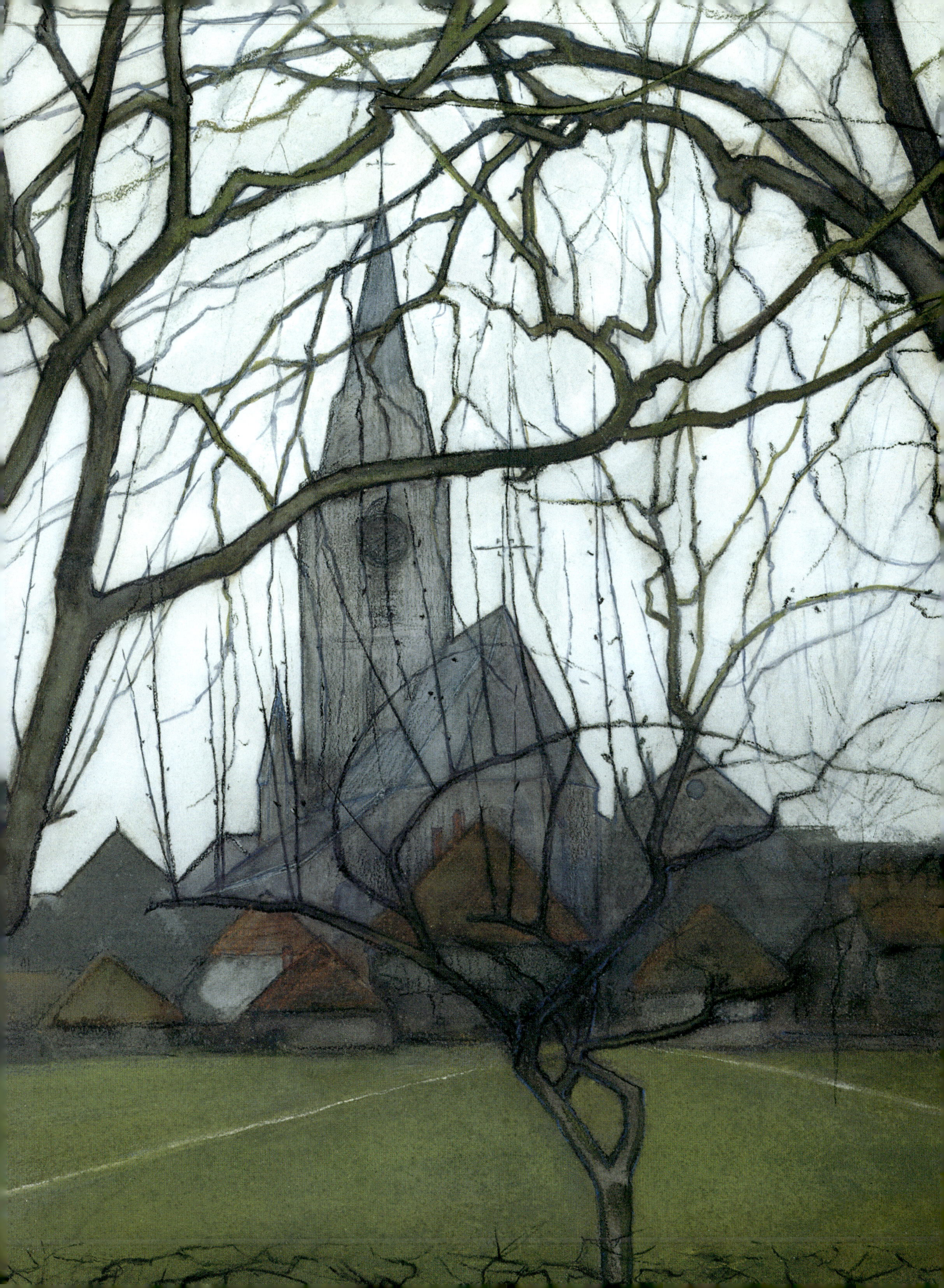

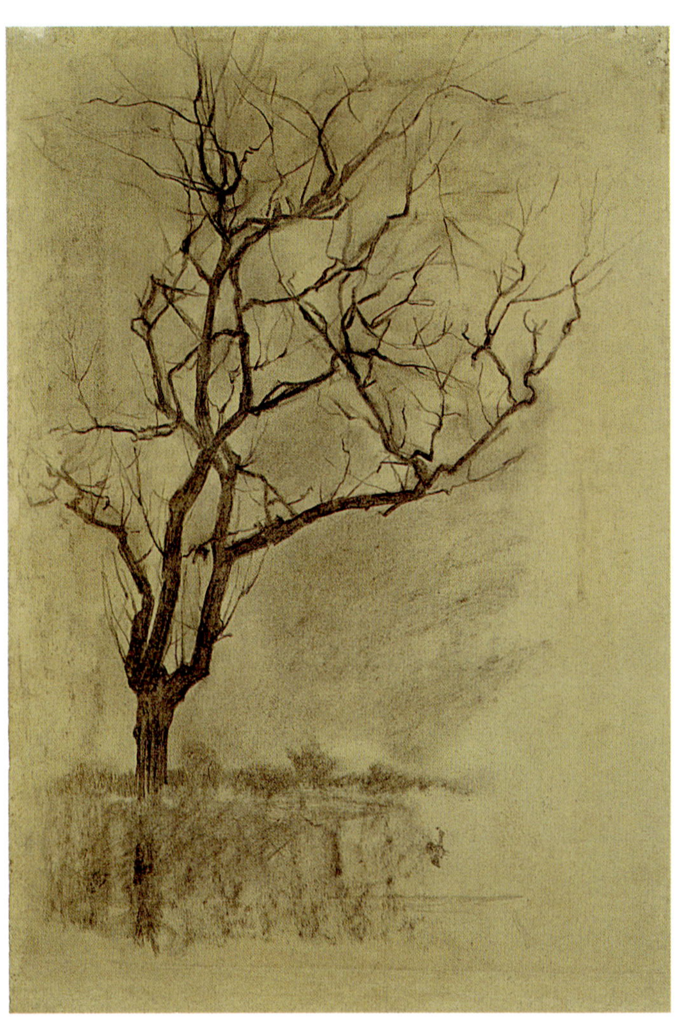

12

Cat. 12 *Tree Sketch for Dorpskerk,* 1896–97
Charcoal and crayon on paper
19.7 x 14.2 in. (50 x 36 cm)
Not signed
Musée d'Orsay, Paris, anonymous life-interest gift accepted by the State, 2000, inv. RF 52 078 (A 57)

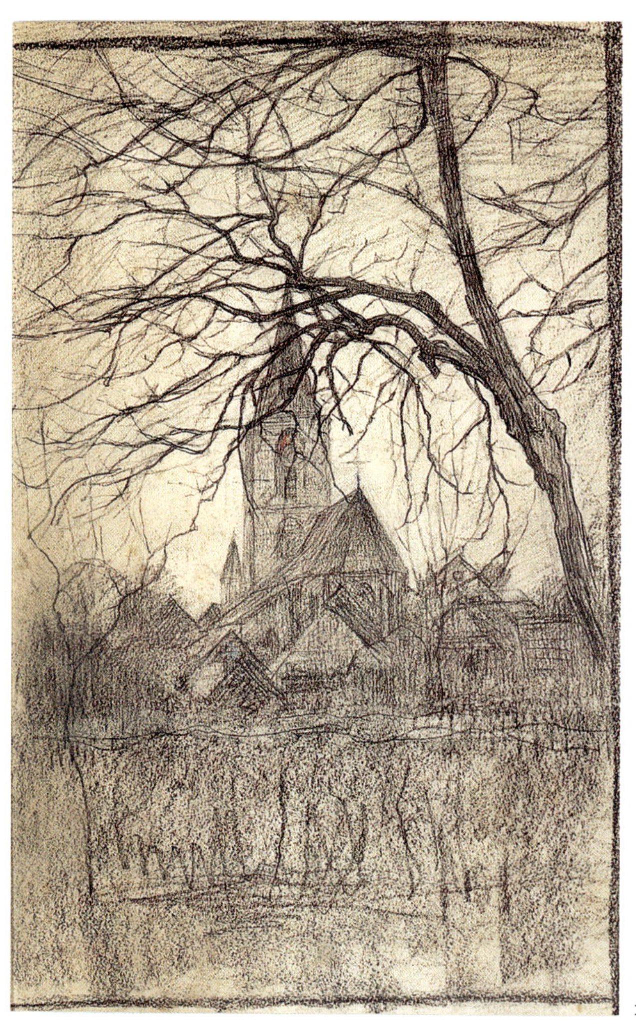

13

Cat. 13 *Church, Winterswijk*, 1897–98
Charcoal and crayon on paper
15.9 x 10 in. (40.5 x 25.5 cm)
Not signed
Winterswijk Museum (A 59)

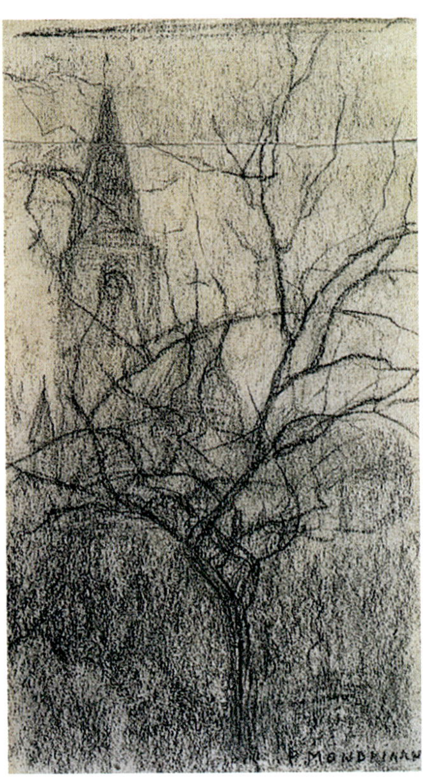

14

effects of yellow, radiating lines on a solid green serve to define the flat expanse. The church tower is set within a fine network of branches, rising toward the pale sky. The low, bare hedge in the foreground is parallel to the picture plane and rooted in a stripe of gray brown earth.

The image has no actual reference to Jacob's Church in Winterswijk itself. Its assembly is harmonious, not only in the interaction of the various elements, but also in their relationship to the margins. There is nothing haphazard in the dense drawing of the branches: in order to obtain the effect, Mondrian had to become visibly involved in juggling and adjusting, ensuring that each element had its place within a balanced whole. The chickens behind the hedge, for example, echo the roofs. The image is also highly constructed on the symbolic level. The church, centrally placed amid cultivated and trimmed nature, is symbolic of community. Even the young shoots of the tree, representing that which is irrepressible and irresistible in all forms of growth, are charged with meaning, placed as they are against the church in the background. The intensely probing stylization accentuates the Symbolism found in a poem, presumably by Mondrian himself, written on the back of the drawing:

And the little branches of the young tree
rejoiced
to join those which, sharing
the peace of the gray sky,
hanging from the mature trees

Cat. 14 *Church, Winterswijk*, 1897–98
Charcoal and crayon on paper
8.3 x 4.7 in. (21 x 12 cm)
Signed lower right: P. MONDRIAAN
Gemeentemuseum, The Hague, bequest of Salomon B. Slijper, 1971, inv. T 77–1971 (A 58)

and below,
the mute green expanse
and the church rising tall, above the village.
M.[49]

This is a lame little poem. The author is trying to associate the vegetal force with the movement of the steeple rising toward the sky amid the peace and silence of nature. A critic meanly opined that Mondrian had not succeeded in representing nature "with these masses of branches resembling a tangle of spider legs and the little, well-polished landscape behind."[50] In the context of the Dutch traditionalism of the period, the work was a fatal step: an artist who did not satisfy the demands of truth obviously had a problem.

Since the beginnings of the 1890s, Jan Toorop (1858–1928) and Johan Thorn Prikker (1868–1932) had shown that line and color, rhythm and measure, could create a universe no longer founded in the perception of observable reality. Opposition to this idea was lively, especially in painters' circles, and was motivated above all by its theoretical content. Dutch artists did not put much stock in theorizing and in words ending in "ism" (usually coming from France), but Symbolism topped everything! Nevertheless, in Amsterdam Rik Roland Holst (1868–1938) and Antoon Derkinderen (1859–1935) devised a watered-down version of Symbolism. Also, around 1895–1900, there was a turn of the tide among younger artists, and Mondrian's *Dorpskerk (Village Church)* could be considered an example of this. It is characterized by a longing for form and for clear, pure line. It is possible that this student, so brilliant in aesthetics, might have read

49. This text is no longer on the back of the work; it disappeared around 1994.
50. Giovanni [J. Kalff], "Schilderijen en teekeningen, 3" ("Paintings and Drawings, 3"), *Algemeen Handelsblad,* June 5, 1898.

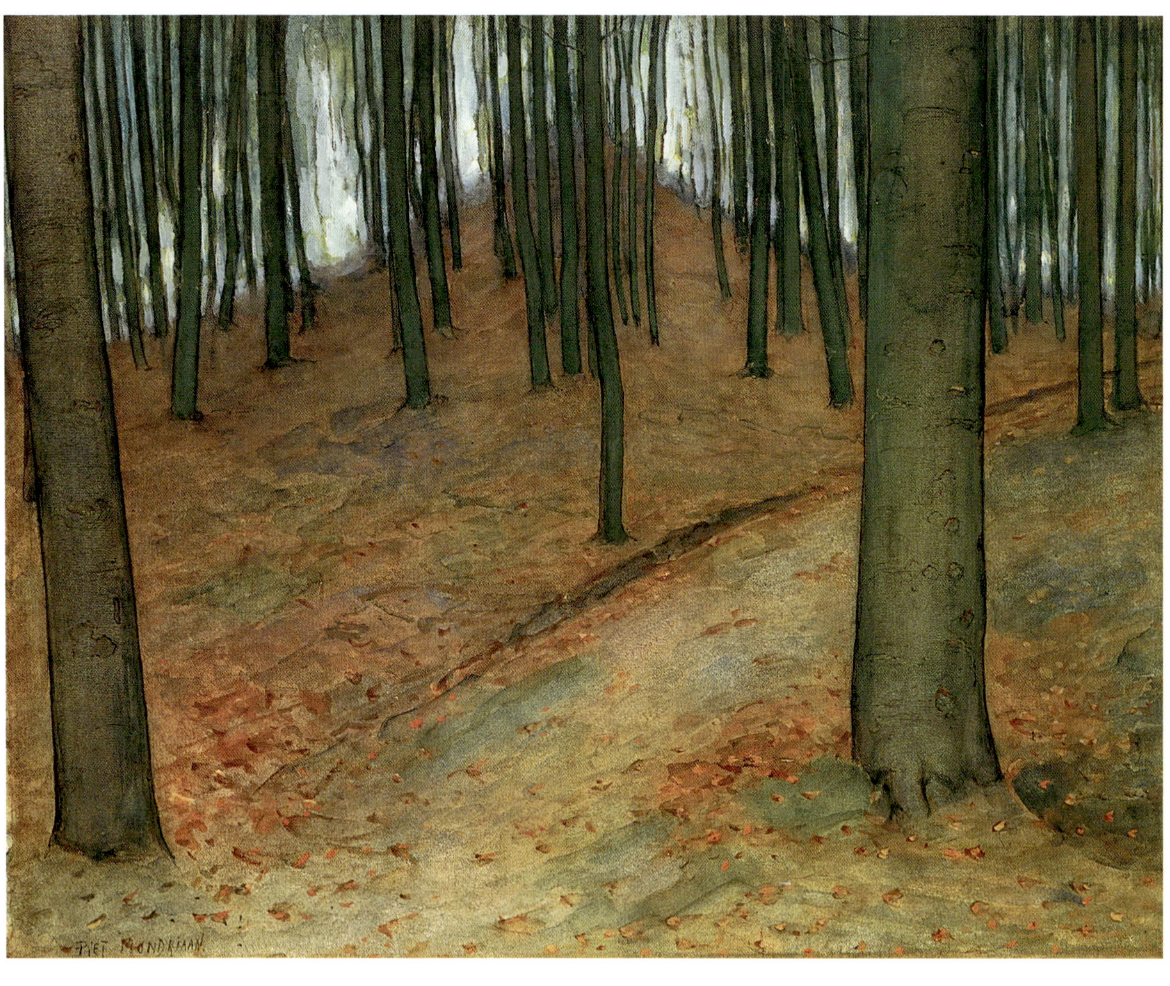

16

Cat. 16 *Forest*, 1899
Watercolor and gouache on paper
17.9 x 22.4 in. (45.5 x 57 cm)
Signed lower left: PIET MONDRIAAN.
Gemeentemuseum, The Hague, bequest of Salomon B. Slijper, 1971, inv. T 58–1971 (A 88)

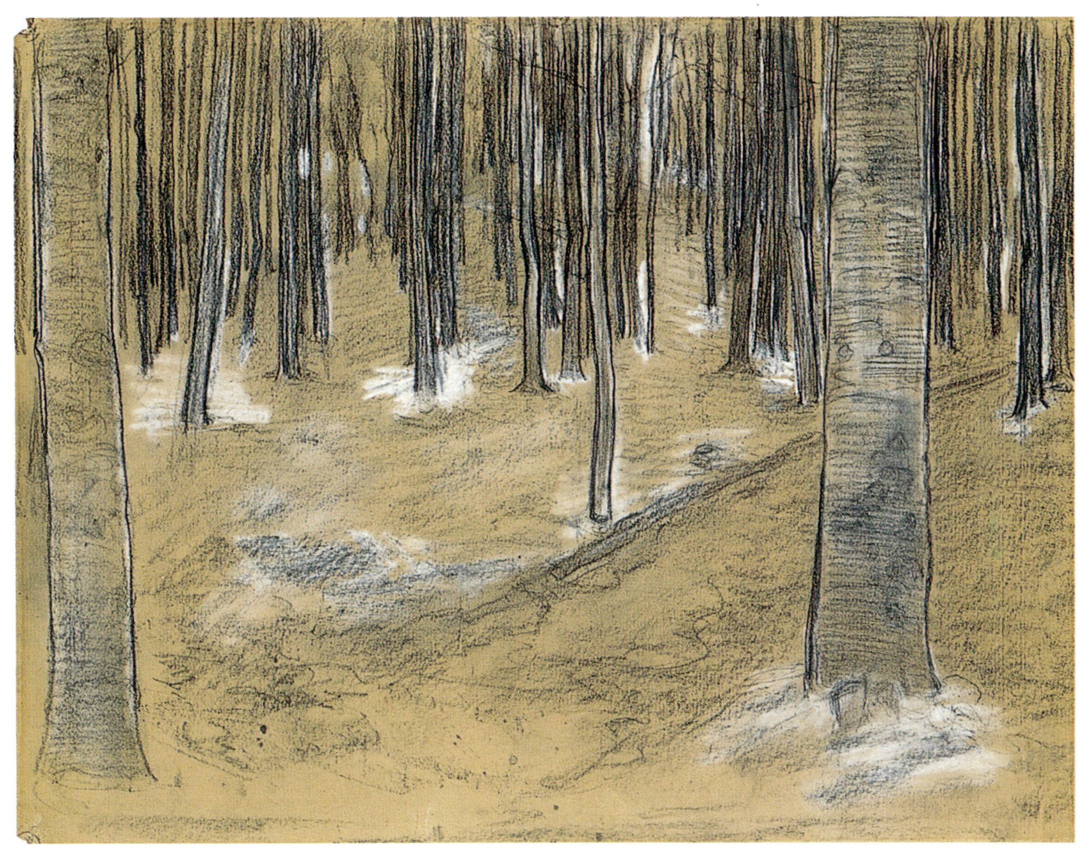
17

Cat. 17 *Forest,* 1899
Lead pencil, colored pencils, and conte crayon on paper
12.1 x 15.9 in. (30.6 x 40.5 cm)
Not signed
Gemeentemuseum, The Hague, inv. T 34–1987 (A 87)

The Elements of Drawing (1857), by John Ruskin, an author highly esteemed in Holland. Ruskin associated moral qualities with the use of line and color. A "good" work of art was the result of a balanced interaction between its various elements: Principality, Repetition, Continuity, Curvature, Radiation, Contrast, Interchange, Consistency, and Harmony. Among these "Nine Laws of Beauty," one particularly stands out: the "Law of Radiation," or the harmonious play of lines radiating from one single point. According to the author, the law of radiation shows how "healthy human actions should spring radiantly (like rays) from some single heart motive; the most beautiful systems of action taking place when this motive lies at the root of the whole life, and the action is clearly seen to proceed from it..."[51] It is not certain that Mondrian knew this text, but it is remarkable to read, years later, in 1918, in his *De Nieuwe Beelding in de schilderkunst (The New Plastic in Painting: From the Natural to the Abstract, From the Indeterminate to the Determinate)* about the rapport between aesthetic perfection and the effect of radiating lines.[52] This principle of composition was to return in other works, figurative as well as abstract, becoming the very foundation of many of them.[53] We are not proposing, however, that Mondrian was, or became, a Symbolist around 1898. To those who knew him, he was before anything else and above all a painter. As the friend of his young adult years, Albert van den Briel (1881–1972) emphasized: "One cannot, in regard to Mondrian, truly speak of 'influences.' He liked to meet; to inquire, gladly walked a little farther with you to get to know you better, but he always remained himself, even in his technique, and his works bear witness to this fact.[54] To make visible the idea was also what Mondrian was likely trying to achieve in the two versions of *Forest* (cat. 16 and 17). In these two works he showed nothing but the bare trunks of beech trees, all standing straight. Greenish, they stand out from the tawny, leaf-colored ground. Space is minimized and without depth; the path running obliquely toward the right collapses

51. Ruskin 1904, 133, 187.
52. Mondrian 1917–18, 41–45, as translated in Holtzmann and James 1986, 48.
53. Locher 1994, *passim.*
54. Henkels 1988, 46.

toward the foreground. Here again, the composition is strong; rhythm and balance are primary. The horizon line rises strangely from the margins of the sheet toward the center, forming a butte whose pointed summit is hidden from view by the trees. Above, white and pale blue reveal the glow of an opening in space.

These last details permit a symbolic interpretation. The art of "the Nordic romantic tradition" toward 1900 produced many wooded landscapes. The interpretation Mondrian gives them, however, is utterly sober and realistic.[55] The true subject is the strange light that results from the moderate contrast between the green of the trunks and the red of the dead leaves.

Welsh mentions *Forest* (cat. 17) as the last study before the watercolor version.[56] It seems reasonable, however, to give this chalk drawing independent status. The yellowing of the paper modifies the effect that the original in white chalk would have produced: the white chalk on the white paper was certainly stronger, and would have enhanced the radiant quality of the still and peaceful composition. It is possible that this drawing is the first appearance in Mondrian's art of a phenomenon that, after 1900, would become a characteristic, the repetition of a single subject by different means of expression, whose distinctive features would operate separately from one another, in a systematic and almost didactic manner. In *Forest* (cat. 16), color plays the primary role. Greens and reds fulfill their roles as complementary colors and form a vivid and active contrast with the yellowish and bluish white light at the edge of the woods. The other version (cat. 17) gives primacy to black and white. This systematic exploitation of the technical possibilities of a motif would play an increasingly important role in Mondrian's future work.

His turning to the use of color of equal value and a heavier line characterizes the first version (cat. 16). Here Mondrian tried to escape from the domination of the mastodons of the Hague school who, due to the art dealers, dictated the aesthetic of the market in Amsterdam around 1900. Jan Voerman (1857–1941), who had

55. The horizon that rises toward the middle of the image, if one refers to the study *Two Women in the Woods* (A91; Saint-Germain-en Laye, departmental Museum Maurice Denis), made around 1898, could be interpreted as a closing of the landscape, in which a tumulus seems to appear in the background.
56. Joosten and Welsh 1998, vol. 1, 190.

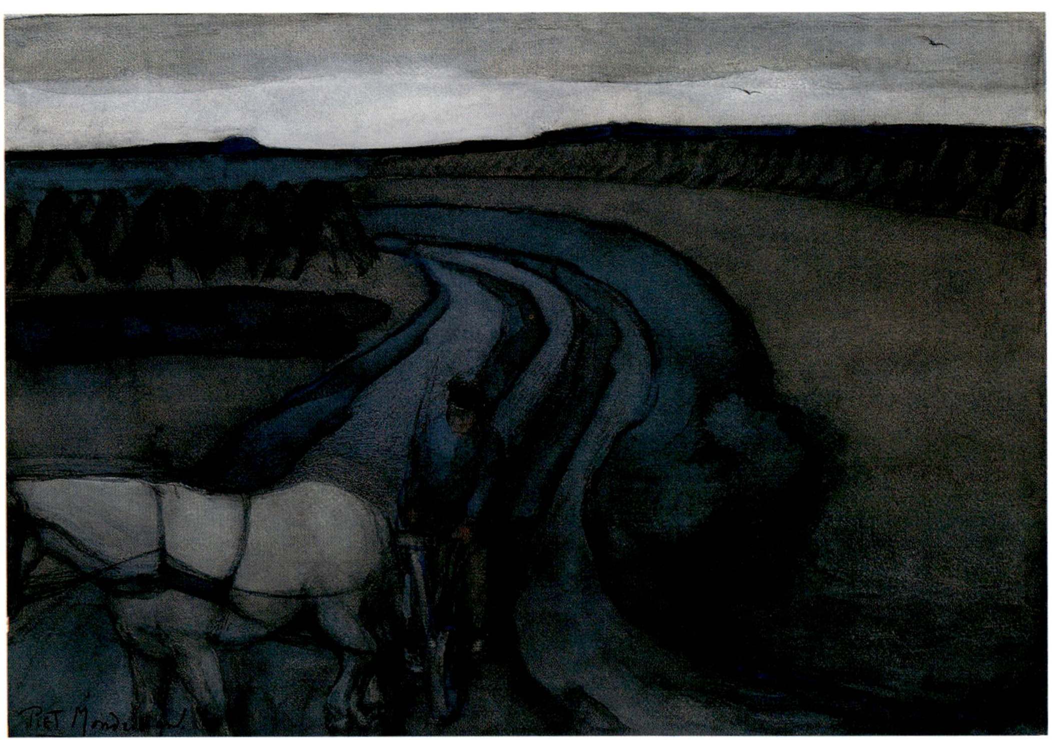
18

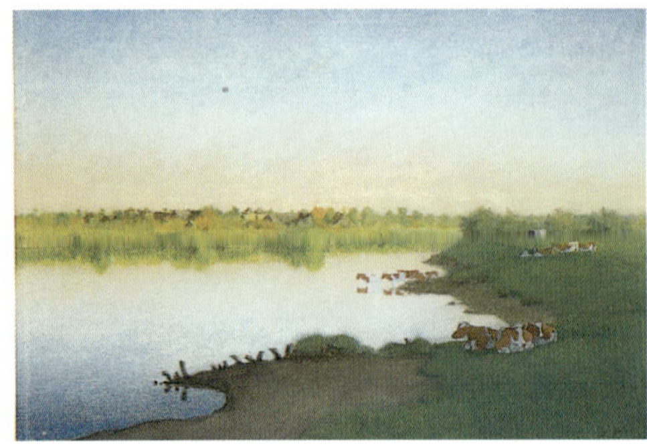

Fig. 15
Jan Voerman, *River landscape with Cows*, c. 1900
Watercolor
Gemeentemuseum, The Hague

Cat. 18 *Aan den arbeid/Op het land* (*At Work/In the Fields*), c. 1898
Watercolor on paper
21.4 x 31 in. (54.4 x 78.7 cm)
Signed lower left: PI ET Mondriaan.
Signature partially painted over in lower right:
PI ET MONDRIAAN
Gemeentemuseum, The Hague, inv. T 66–1986 (A 85)

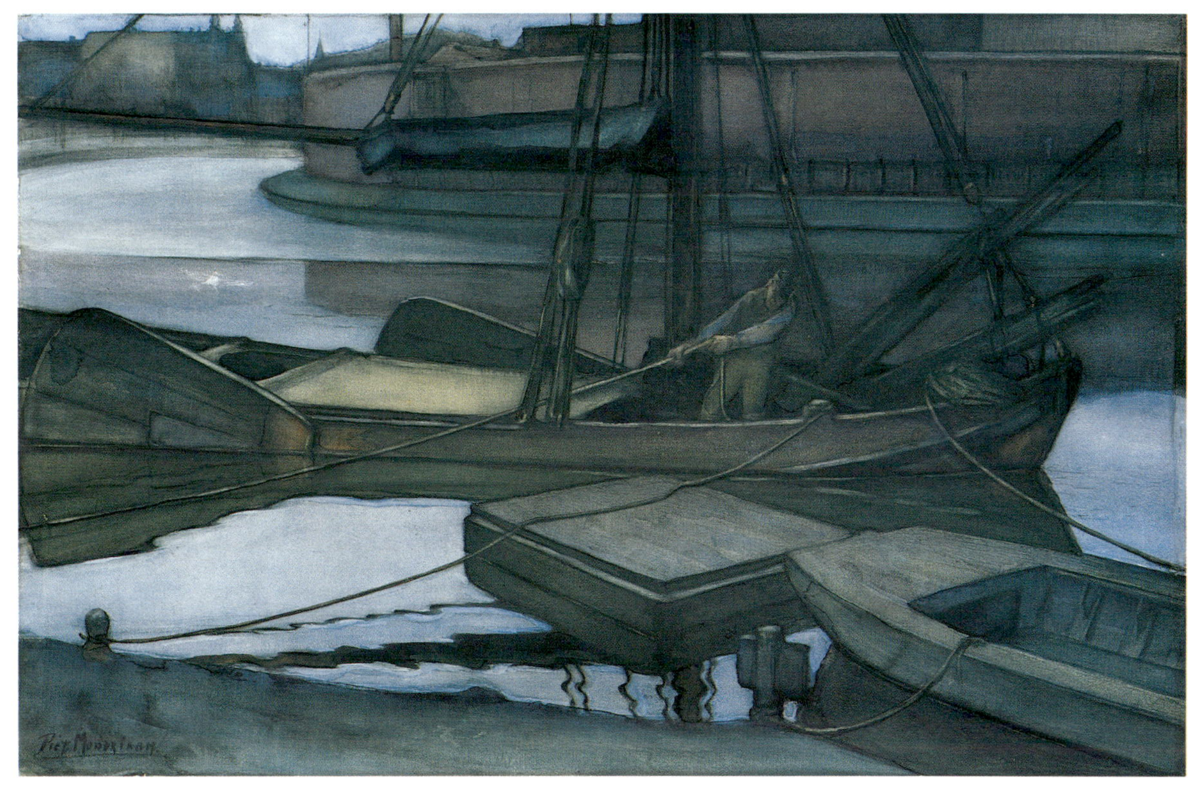
19

Cat. 19 *Aan de Stadhouderskade te Amsterdam* (*At the Stadhouderskade, Amsterdam*), 1898–99
Charcoal, watercolor, and pastel on cardboard
24.4 x 39.3 in. (62 x 100 cm)
Signed lower left: *Piet* MONDRIAAN.
Musée d'Orsay, Paris, inv. RF 41 384 (A 196)

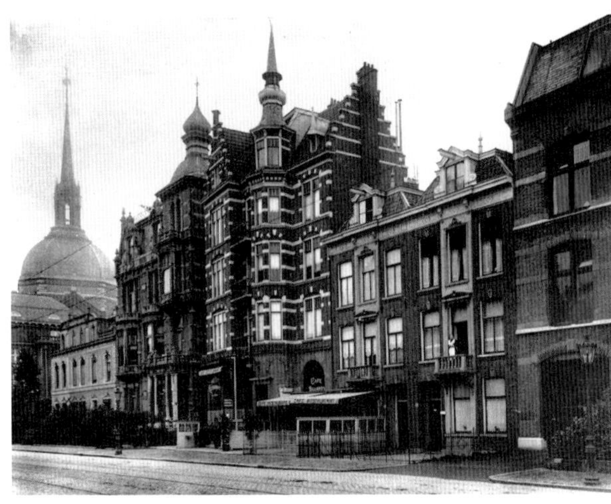

Fig. 16
View of the Stadhouderskade near the Overtoom, before 1910
Between 1897 and 1899, Mondrian lived in this house with large bay windows that formed a small projecting tower.
Municipal Archives, Amsterdam

undertaken to paint with clear and pure colors, to "have done with the dirty sauce,"[57] may have served as an example of this solid style for Mondrian (fig. 15).

Through his large watercolors of this period, Mondrian searched for elements he would select as his own options for doing away with "the dirty sauce." All signs indicate, however, that he was apprehensive about choices that might be too abrupt. He was careful to keep a prudent distance from the established order, which meant the Hague school, as much as from circles more oriented toward Symbolism—perhaps to help assure his chances on the art market. The saturation of the market and the near impossibility for young artists to have access to it constituted a great subject of discussion in 1898.[58] Mondrian's candidacy for the Prix de Rome that year—another means to make his name known—failed. He made a long visit to Winterswijk and applied for a position as drawing instructor in the nearby town of Enschede. In truth this stay reveals more about the increasing financial problems of the young artist, with his peculiar but distinguished taste in clothing, than about his ambitions. During this period, Mondrian established numerous amicable contacts with "the greatest art dealers"–yet another effort to secure a place in the art market.[59]

He did not stop there, however. In October 1898, he participated in an exhibition organized to support a project for a monument to Frans Hals at the municipal museum in Haarlem.[60] Although we cannot identify his contribution precisely, the fact that he participated proves that the art of the seventeenth century still enjoyed an unquestionable prestige in Mondrian's eyes. One senses this attitude also from the first descriptions of his studio. Albert van den Briel, who met Mondrian around 1900, described an

57 A letter, dated July 18, 1903, by Jan Voerman to G.H. Marius, published in Wagner 1977, 58.
58. See the reports in the newspaper *De Telegraaf* of November 9 and 15, 1898, evening editions.
59. Henkels 1988, 147–48. Included in this expression "major art dealers" are presumably P. C. Eilers and K. Groesbeek of the firm Wisselingh & Co., as well as J. Slagmulder of Frans Buffa & Fils.
60. "Kunsten en Wetenschappen: Kunst en letternieuws" ("Arts and Sciences: Artisitic and Literary News"), *De Telegraaf,* Ocober 20, 1989, evening edition.

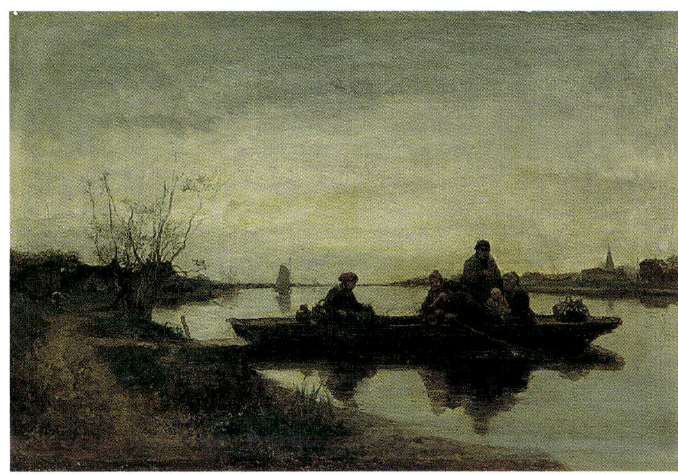

Fig. 17
Jacob Maris, *The Ferry*
Oil on canvas
Gemeentemuseum, The Hague

interior arranged "artistically": a period church chandelier with candles, and antique Dutch furniture in the "Oud Hollandse" style.[61] It was chic to decorate studios this way in the artists' circles in which he now moved.[62] From 1900 he often visited the new meeting room of the Saint Lucas society on the Rokin (he was already a voting member), and this was furnished in the same style:

The room immediately gives the impression of intimacy. The wide and massive armchairs cordially invite you to sit down, as does the fireplace with its antique wrought-iron fire screen, its mantel of an antique design, and its copper chain, as well as its stew, and its blue china.[63]

This was the context in which Mondrian worked. It was strongly turned toward the past and meditating from there on the present. Nothing indicates that Mondrian distinguished himself in this circle by his work.

For the drawings *Aan den arbeid/Op het land (At Work/In the Fields)* (cat. 18) and *Aan de Stadhouderskade te Amsterdam (At the Stadhouderskade, Amsterdam)* (cat. 19), Mondrian employed a palette of dark blues and blue grays. The two drawings are intensely washed, freeing the pigments, giving the paper's texture a granulated look. This method was not accepted as a virtue at the time. However, it allowed Mondrian to regulate in detail the internal harmony of extremely subtle and close contrasts. In this he remained close to the atmospheric techniques of the Hague school, designed to render the smallest variations of weather. At the same time, with his planes of flat colors and serene subjects, related to Japanese prints and characteristic of artists such as Jan

61. Henkels 1988, 44.
62. For example, a number of important period chandeliers and pieces of furniture were sold at the auction of the studio contents of Pieter Stortebeker on November 15, 1898.
63. [Henriette Hendrix], "Saint Lucas," *De Telegraaf*, October 4, 1899, evening edition.

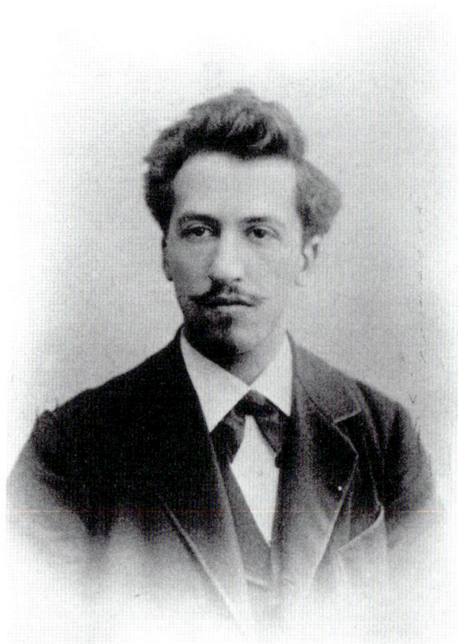

Fig. 18
Piet Mondrian, 1899
Photograph dedicated to his parents (on back)
Gemeentemuseum, The Hague

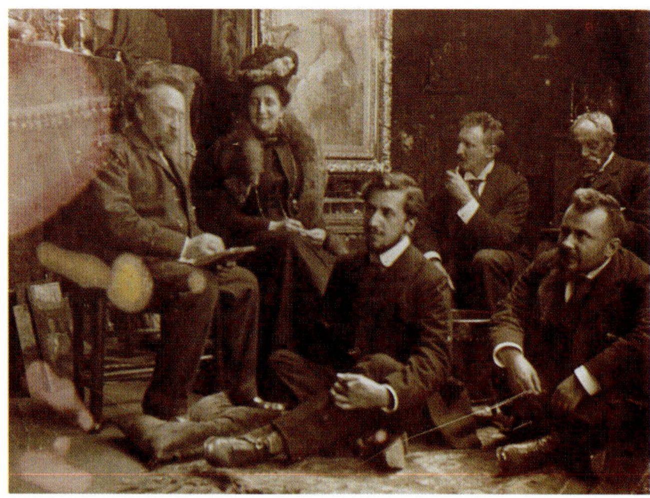

Fig. 19
In Simon Maris's studio, c. 1900
On the left, Willem Maris sketches a portrait of Piet Mondrian, seated at his feet and wearing a beard and mustache. Near Willem Maris sits his second wife, Johanna van Bijlevelt, then Simon Maris, an unidentified older man, and the poet and broker G. H. Kroon, a friend of Simon Maris and of Piet Mondrian.
RKD (Simon Maris Archives), The Hague

Voerman, he took something of a stand against convention.

In *Aan den arbeid/Op het land* (*At Work/In the Fields*), a peasant walks with heavy steps along a country road, his horse harnessed in front of the plow. The almost fluorescent white animal, whose head is cut off at the margin of the paper, resembles a ghostly apparition. The landscape, with its little haystacks, is rapidly rendered in planes according to a certain planned rhythm. The few accents are produced by a vivid lilac blue in front of the plow and a lighter blue on the horizon line.

Aan de Stadhouderskade te Amsterdam (*At the Stadhouderskade, Amsterdam*) is much more elaborate. Mondrian wrote about it with pleasure in 1931: "I thought it good at the time, and it was on show at an Arti exhibition. Although it was painted in broad lines, it is properly finished."[64] The scene is viewed from Mondrian's bedroom in Amsterdam, at 5 Stadhouderskade, no. 2, where he lived from December 19, 1897, until December 22, 1898 (fig. 16). Tones of blue, turquoise and gray blue dominate, and scattered touches of dark ocher take from these colors an appearance approaching a warm red. The sky and the water are almost lilac. The scene represented is somber and private; it is a gray day. It would be easy to see a Symbolist idea in the melancholy that emanates from the painting. The poems of Maurice Maeterlinck (1862–1949) on serenity, falling night, and stages of twilight as expressions of a mood, caused a furor in Holland at the time. But the atmosphere that emanates from *At Work/In the Fields*, as well as from *At the Stadhouderskade, Amsterdam*, more closely recalls Jacob Maris, with his ferries, than artists of the moment and their more modern inspirations (fig. 17).

In 1899, Mondrian made the acquaintance of a painter very much in vogue at the time, Simon Maris (1873–1935), son of Willem Maris and nephew of Jacob Maris (1837–1899), who established himself that year in Amsterdam (fig. 18 and 19). In contact with the jovial Simon,

64. Letter from Mondrian to Salomon Slijper, November 13, 1931. Slijper Archives, RKD, The Hague.

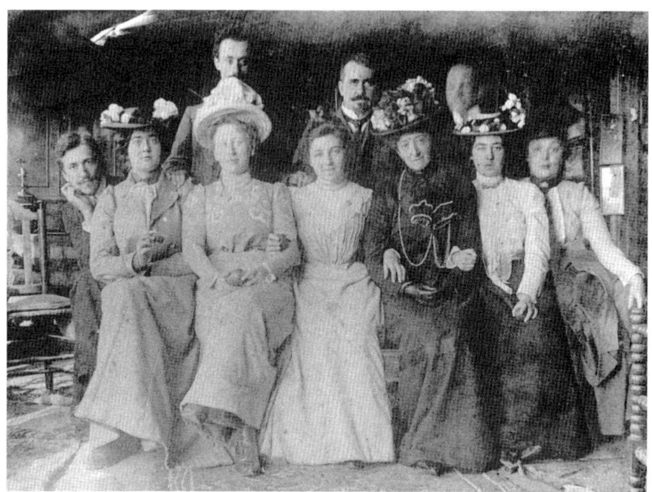

Fig. 20
In Simon Maris's studio, June 8, 1901, after the opening of the Saint Lucas Society exhibition
On the far left, Mondrian, and seated in the center, Henriette Hendrix.
RKD (Simon Maris Archives), The Hague

Mondrian gained a vast circle of friends, among whom was Henriëtte Hendrix (1877–1933), art critic for *De Telegraaf.* The commentaries of this young woman evoked the ideas of the coterie of artists she frequented (fig. 20). On May 29, 1900, mentioning Mondrian's name in a review for the first time, Hendrix judged the watercolor *At the Stadhouderskade, Amsterdam* (cat. 19) "very well done, but grave and somber."[65] Other critics also began to notice Mondrian. Willem Steenhoff (1863–1932), art critic for the review *De Amsterdammer Weekblad* and future director of the Rijksmuseum, wrote in 1901 that Mondrian could be counted among the most remarkable of young artists: "He does not show himself to be a facile dauber of paintings like so many of his colleagues, who know only too well how beauty is to be found in color; and he does not take his calling lightly." Not that Steenhoff entirely spared him from criticism: "Many things must be distilled within this little lad, and he still has many skills to master if his efforts to express himself are to culminate in the birth of a viable child."[66] What skills had to be mastered is evident in *The Royal Wax Candle Factory* (cat. 20). The impenetrable and somber shadow of a factory reflected in the water of a canal was painted with a wide brush in dominant tones of gray and dark ochers. Painters at the turn of the century often treated the urban, industrial landscape as the incarnation of a rich patrimony handed down from a glorious past. This is not the case with Mondrian. He did not value the urban as an expression of his own personality. He sought to translate something of the inalterable beauty of nature through the motifs of a church, a wood, a river, or an urban scene.[67]

It is generally maintained that around 1900 Mondrian became interested in Theosophy, a doctrine that announced the fusion of all spiritualist currents into one universal "supra-religion." If such is truly the case—and solid proof is lacking—we must insist on the fact that he was far from being the only one. Theosophy was

65. H. Hx [Henriette Hendrix], "Saint Lucas," *De Telegraaf,* May 29, 1900. A short time after this article appeared, Hendrix wrote a letter to Simon Maris in which she told of the violent criticism she had endured apropos of her article, especially because of her marked preference for Mondrian. She added, "Please do not compare what I said about Mondrian's work with what I wrote about you; a little child could see the essential difference." She had written in *De Telegraaf* of November 20, 1900, an especially emphatic article praising Simon Maris. Maris was obviously jealous that she had written "delicate and idealistic things created by the painter's imagination" about Mondrian, in a tone used previously for Maris. This statement contradicts the earlier interpretations of this letter, which concludes with a negative vision of Mondrian's work. (See Gorter, van Burkom, and Joosten 1998, no. 2, 25.) The dating of the letter is based on the critique of Simon Maris and the use of the word *waarder* (truer), which Hendrix used in her review of May 29, 1900. Simon Maris Archives, RKD, The Hague.

66. W. Steenhoff, "Saint Lucas Exhibition," *De Amsterdammer Weekblad,* no. 1253, June 30, 1901, 2.

67 Bakker 2000, 126, 131.

highly fashionable, and not only in artistic circles.[68] Mondrian would only become a member of the Theosophy Society in 1909. During this first period, around 1899, Theosophy would have had no more than a vague stimulating effect on his ideas about the occult. It seems proper to rely on Albert van den Briel's observation:

Our friendship dates from 1899, and it was during the winter of 1899–1900 that we discussed Theosophy in depth. He had just gone through a difficult period, as his correspondence, among other things, shows, but details on this point would take me too far from my subject. He was the child of a Calvinist milieu that stressed strict obedience (his father was the friend and partisan of A. Kuijper), and even though he had long before decided on his own path (he lived in Ringdijk Diemermeer with two of his brothers), he was not yet completely free of childhood influences. He believed that he had to liberate himself entirely and develop his personality, and in following this path to deliverance he encountered Theosophy. Mondrian was sensitive to the sublime in this belief, but he had a pronounced antipathy to its exterior manifestations, such as "Theosophy maidens," which took rather frivolous forms, or to joining a club, for example, in Amsterdam. It is possible that he had been a member of the Theosophical Society for several years, but he did not make much of it. In a stricter sense, one cannot say that he was then a theosophist. He was always an artist above all else and always searched for ways to express his sentiments and the moods of his spirit.[69]

68. Annie Besant herself led a campaign in 1898 in the west of Holland. On January 30, she gave a lecture in Haarlem, the following day in Amsterdam, and the next day in The Hague.
69. Letter from Albert van de Briel to Salomon Slijper, November 25, 1945. Slijper Archives, RKD, The Hague.

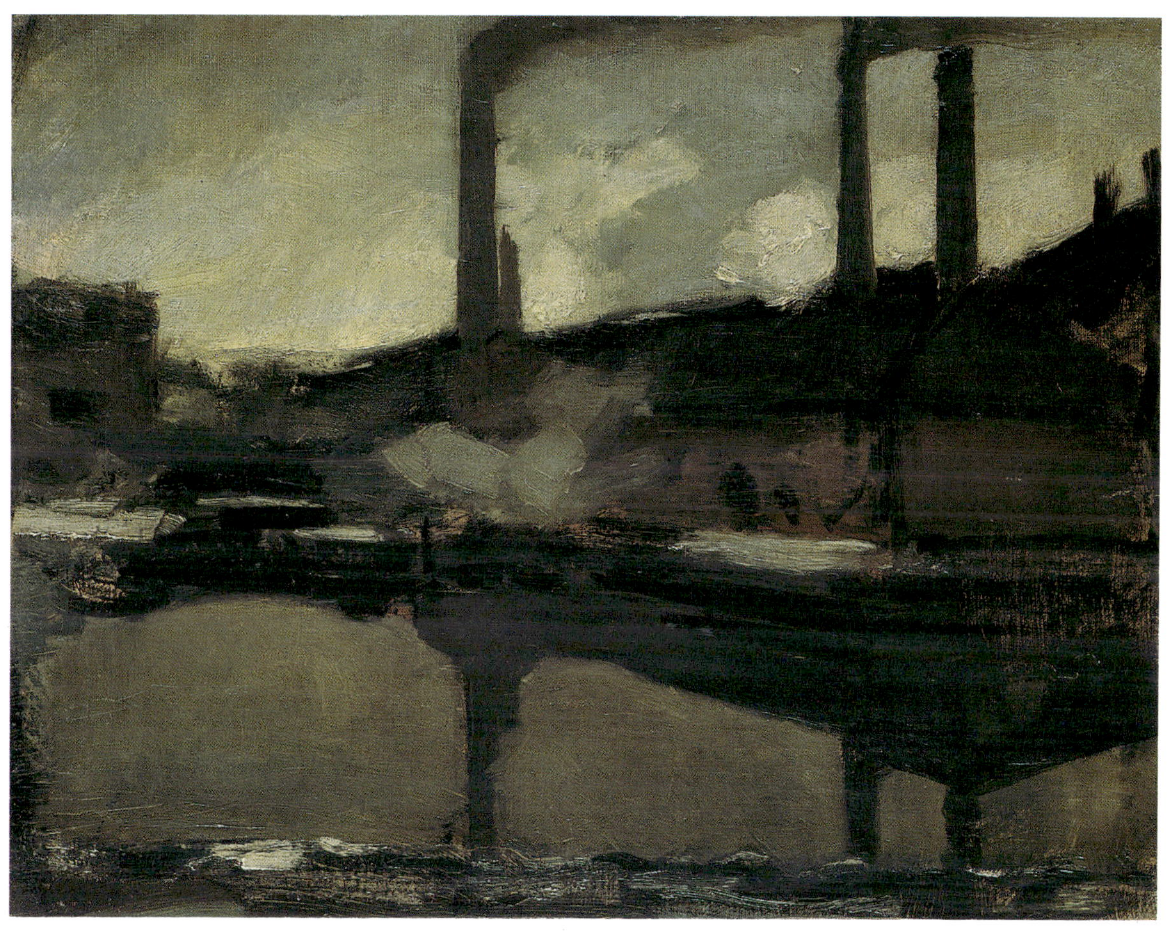

20

Cat. 20 *The Royal Wax Candle Factory*, c. 1899
Oil on canvas mounted on cardboard
13.8 x 18.9 in. (35 x 48 cm)
Not signed
Gemeentemuseum, The Hague, gift of Albert van den Briel, inv. S 7–1965 (A 190)

Chapter Four

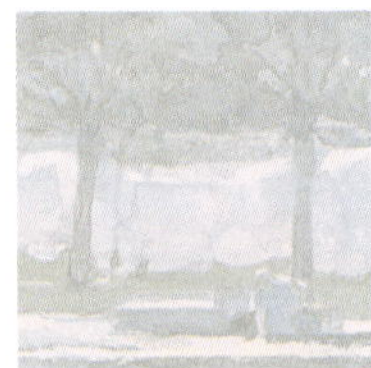

1900–1904

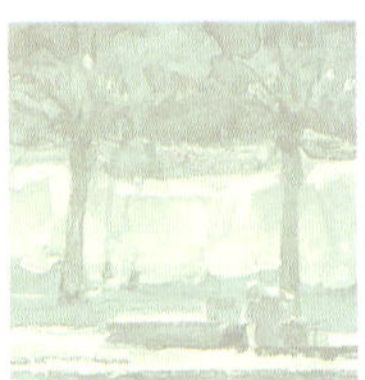

"After several years, my work unconsciously began to deviate more and more from the natural aspects of reality." [70]

Hans Janssen and Joop M. Joosten

In December 1898, Mondrian had moved to 158 Albert Cuypstraat. He was looking for new subjects: along the Amstel, the Weesperzij, the Omval, and further afield on the banks of the river Gein. Traditionally, the area along the banks of the Gein had been a place of relaxation for the inhabitants of Amsterdam, "an enchanting resort that, during much of the year, lures different sorts of people from the area, essentially inhabitants of Amsterdam, Weesp, and Abcoude, to come and spend a few hours of leisure under shady trees (fig. 21)."[71] In these bucolic surroundings, nature provided the most typical Dutch landscape: grassy pastures under high skies in a setting of trees and undergrowth into which nestled farms, little streams, and ditches that one could follow across the countryside as far as the horizon (fig. 22).

Painters of the Hague school had rediscovered this mythical landscape. They aligned themselves with a long and rich Dutch tradition in which painting the landscape meant revealing the immutable and transcendent essence of nature, beyond the accidental dress of the temporal. The enthusiasm manifested by the Hague school for its Dutch landscapes, its vast green expanses, and its high skies indeed bordered on the religious. Seventeenth-century Dutch landscape painting –down to its final reverberations in the nineteenth century–was generally perceived as

70. Mondrian 1942.
71. Van der Aa 1843, 489.

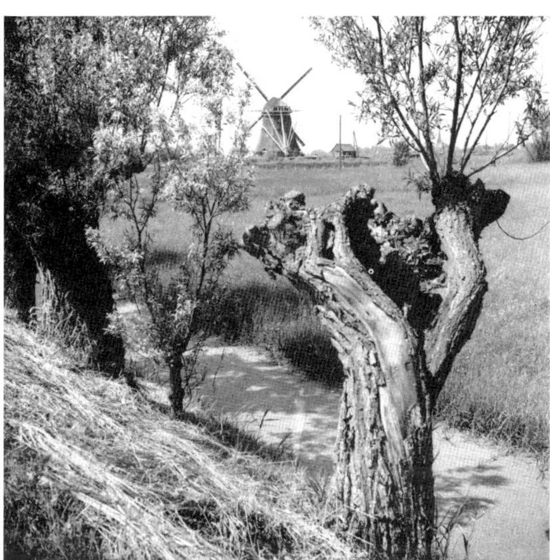

Fig. 21
The Gein near Abcoude, with the Oostzijde Mill
Municipal Archives, Amsterdam

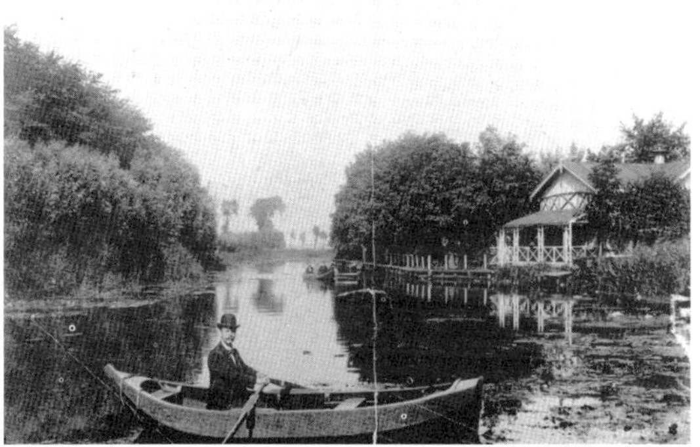

Fig. 22
The Kalfje Tearoom on the Gein
RKD (Simon Maris Archives), The Hague

one of the earliest illustrations of what developed into the doctrine of art for art's sake. The French painter and writer Eugène Fromentin promoted the idea in his book *Maîtres d'autrefois* (*Masters of the Past*), 1876, in which he described the Dutch landscape tradition in terms of art for art's sake. This point of view–and above all, the interpretation of seventeenth-century Dutch landscape painting as the visualization of the relationship with God–became the subject of lively polemics in the art historical literature. The Dutch saw nature as a "second book"–coming immediately after the "first divine book," the Bible–in which there were many lessons to be learned about simplicity, truth, the course of

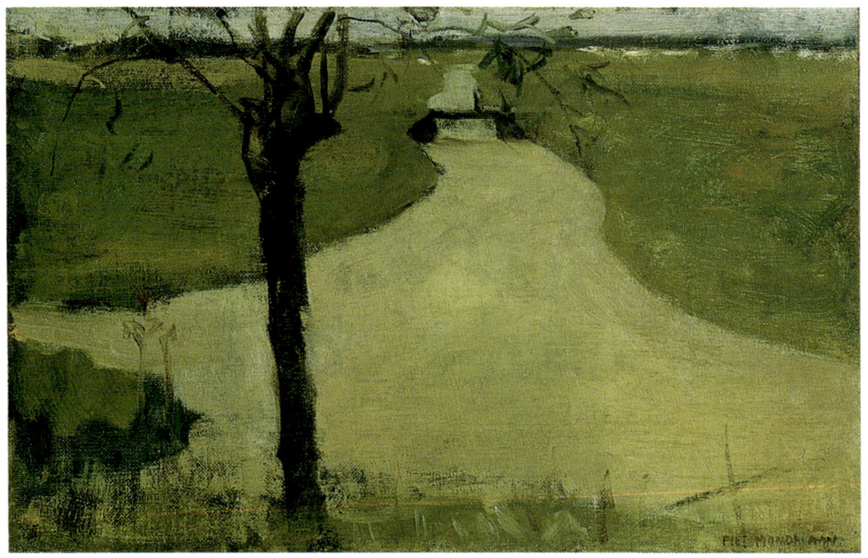

21

events, and Divine Will. An important part of the Dutch landscape tradition, including its hold on the nineteenth century, is understandable only from this point of view. In the beginning of the twentieth century, as Mondrian was discovering the Gein, Dutch landscape painting remained tied to the idea of an emanation of the Divine and eternal that transcended the mundane and particular.[72] This specific form of expression of the universal, which Mondrian searched for all his life and which served as a prologue to his modernist enterprise was, in fact, a typical descendant of the Dutch landscape tradition.

Landzicht farm lay in the heart of the Gein, near Abcoude, and served as a vehicle for Mondrian's ideas in many works. *Ditch near Landzicht Farm* (cat. 21) is characterized by a raised horizon line that closes off the view of the upper part of the landscape, leaving scarcely any space for the canal, and by sallow colors equal in intensity and tone. In the foreground the willow, pruned so that its branches are tufted on top, acts not as a *repoussoir*–rather than offsetting the lack of depth, it reinforces it. However, the most captivating thing about this picture is the somber light created by the play of barely contrasting colors flowing into vigorous shapes.

A little drawing is known, showing Mondrian on his bicycle, firmly held in place by metal hoops, lines, and pickets. He appears nonchalant, pipe in his mouth, cap on his head, and a palette and brushes ready at hand (fig. 23). His box of colors is mounted on the handlebars with a little canvas or piece of cardboard attached to its open lid. According to Albert van den Briel, Mondrian often worked seated on his bicycle. It is possible that he painted *Ditch near Landzicht Farm* in this position and that it is an open-air study. Holes and imprints of thumbtacks confirm this idea.

There are many known variations of the motif. It is tempting to conclude that, here again, we are dealing with a series. The drawing *Ditch near Landzicht Farm* (cat. 22), is a much larger version that at first sight appears to be a sketch, a preparatory step toward a painting, or, as Welsh suggests, toward a watercolor.[73] However, the drawing gives us another aspect of the subject, a detailed representation of the tree in the foreground that contrasts with the spreading landscape of the background. This work reveals the ability of line and shape to suggest space, light, and sky, possibilities Mondrian uses in such

Cat. 21 *Ditch near Landzicht Farm*, c. 1900
Oil on canvas
9.3 x 14.8 in. (23.5 x 37.5 cm)
Signed lower right: PIET MONDRIAAN
Gemeentemuseum, The Hague, gift of Albert van den Briel, 1956, inv. S 25–1956 (A 212)

72. Bakker 1993, 97–115, and Leeflang 1994, 18–32.
73. Joosten and Welsh 1998, vol. 1, 241.

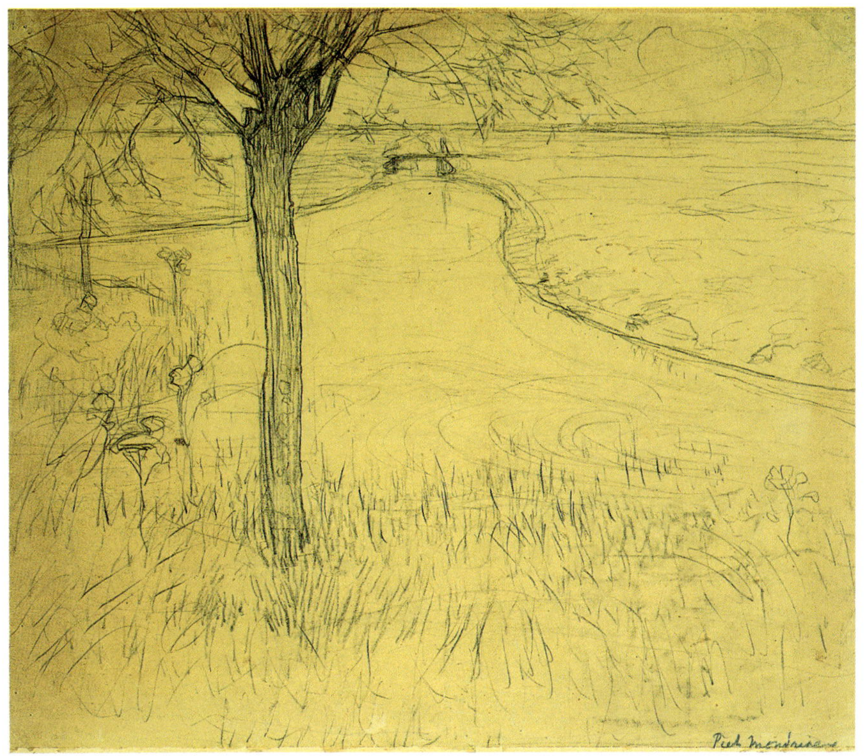

22

Fig. 23
Simon Maris, *Piet Mondrian painting on his bicycle*, c. 1906–7
Pencil drawing taken from a sketchbook
RKD (Simon Maris Archives), The Hague

Cat. 22 *Ditch near Landzicht Farm*, 1900
Conte crayon on paper
15.3 x 24.3 in. (39.2 x 61.6 cm)
Signed lower right: *Piet Mondriaan*
Gemeentearchief, Amsterdam, inv. M 254–2 (A 215)

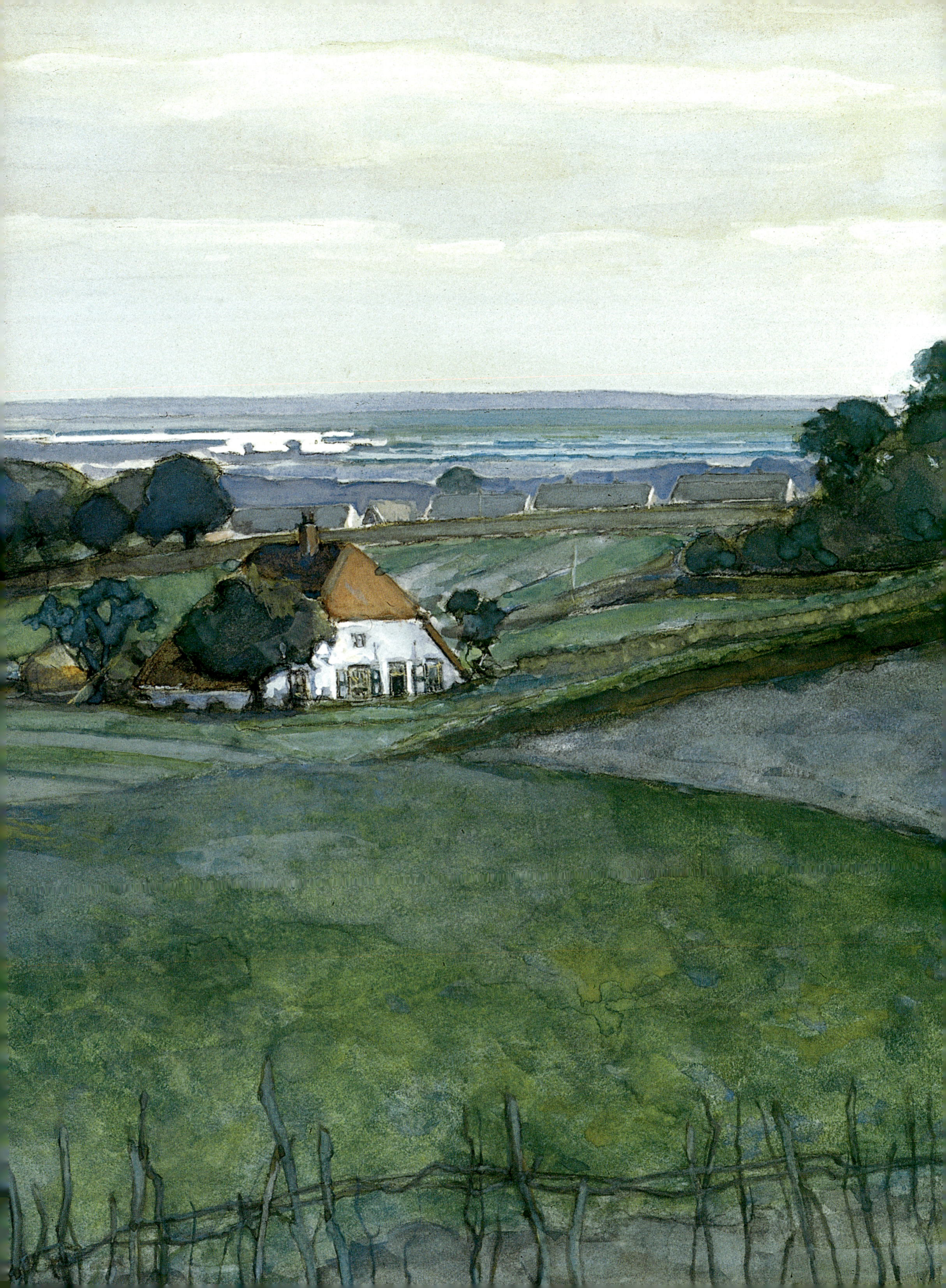

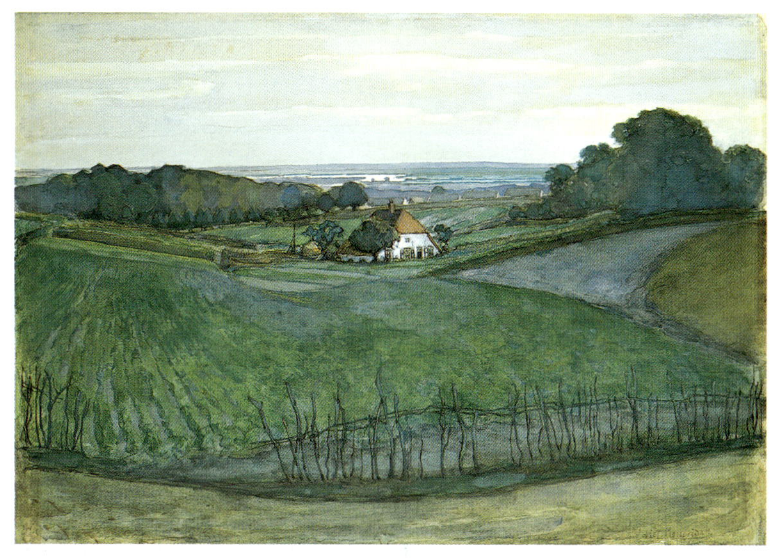
24

a way as to attest to his belief that drawing, painting, and watercolor all have their own intrinsic value.

The watercolor *Bij Arnhem* (*At Arnhem*) (cat. 24) was painted during a visit Mondrian made to his parents, who had moved to Arnhem in 1901. Bright and strong, brushed in with frankly bold colors, it deliberately focuses one's view on the white façade of the farm lying in a depression in the landscape, and on the perspective opening in the background toward the Rhine Valley. The fact that in the spring of 1902 Mondrian proposed a price for this watercolor that doubled the one he had asked six months earlier, suggests that he painted it at a moment when he was able to approach the market with greater confidence. A different tonality, the result of fuller colors and more acute contrasts, appears in *Bleekerij aan het Gein* (*Bleachworks on the Gein*) (cat. 27), which depicts the activities of the residents along the river. The tonality recalls that of Theophile de Bock (1851–1904), a student of Jacob Maris, who was enjoying considerable attention at that moment. The difference is that Mondrian amplified his contrasts, chose less transparent colors, and conceived the composition of the image so that the idea of rendering weather conditions was nearly abandoned. These differences kept him closer to the more mannered style of Symbolism. When Mondrian showed his watercolor in the fall of 1902, the work struck a chord among the Dutch critics. Reactions were numerous. Giovanni (Jan Kalff, 1873–1954) judged it a little "false in its colors" (it

Cat. 24 *Bij Arnhem* (*Near Arnheim*), 1901
Watercolor and gouache on paper
18.3 x 26 in. (46.5 x 66 cm)
Signed lower right: *Piet Mondriaan*
Private collection (A 285)
Courtesy Simonis & Buunk

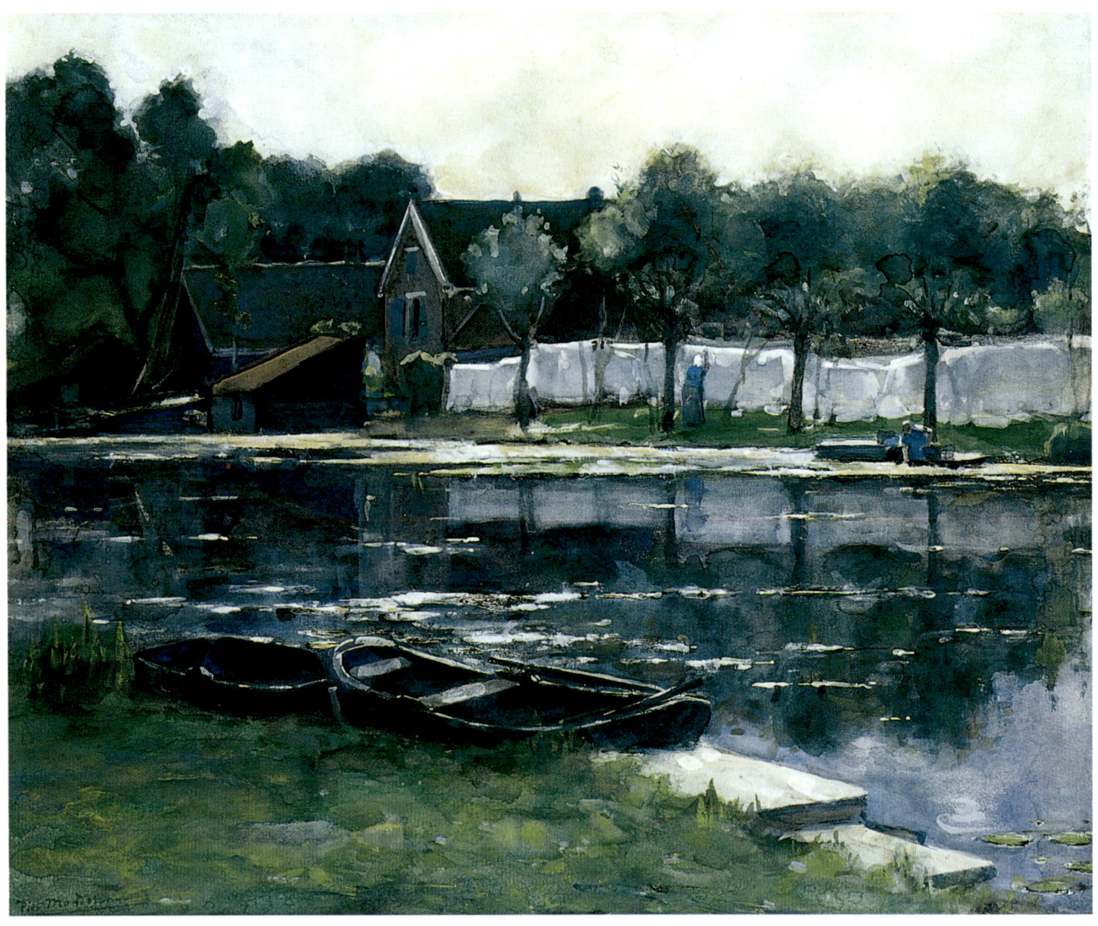

27

distanced itself from De Bock's palette), and Willem Steenhoff spoke of "a powerful object, even though not entirely successful."[74]

It is interesting to connect the watercolor *Bleekerij aan het Gein* (*Bleachworks on the Gein*) (cat. 27) and the bright oil sketch of the same subject (cat. 28). One immediately thinks that Mondrian conceived the oil sketch as a preparatory step for the watercolor. But it might very well be that the sketch was made later. It is not only the absence of tack marks that argues for this conclusion.[75] The tree on the far right of the oil sketch, necessary for balancing the composition, is an addition made as a "touch-up" over still-fresh paint and is unlike the tree in the watercolor. The shapes in the oil sketch are so brief, fleeting, and loose that it is difficult to see it as anything other than a "reflection" of the watercolor (see fig. 24). Above all, the execution is telling. In most cases, an oil sketch allows the artist to test the overall modulation of lighting for a painting or a watercolor. The absence of chiaroscuro in the sketch (in contrast to the watercolor, in which the effects of chiaroscuro actually are exaggerated), and the spatial construction by blocks that results from this absence, as well as its very bright palette, bring this work dangerously close to the Impressionism of Claude Monet, for example. In January and February 1901, Mondrian would have been able to see works of this artist and also of Sisley, Renoir, Pissarro, and others at the Arti exhibition of

Cat. 27 *Bleekerij aan het Gein* (*Bleachworks on the Gein*),
c. 1901–2
Watercolor on paper
18.9 x 23.2 in. (48 x 59 cm)
Signed lower left: *Piet Mondriaan*.
Private Collection (A 282)

74. W. S. [Steenhoff] "Tentoonstelling in Arti, 2," *De Amsterdammer Weekblad*, no. 1325, November 16, 1902, 3.
75. The little piece of canvas was, until its recent restoration, mounted on a piece of cardboard and partially covered with paint along its edges.

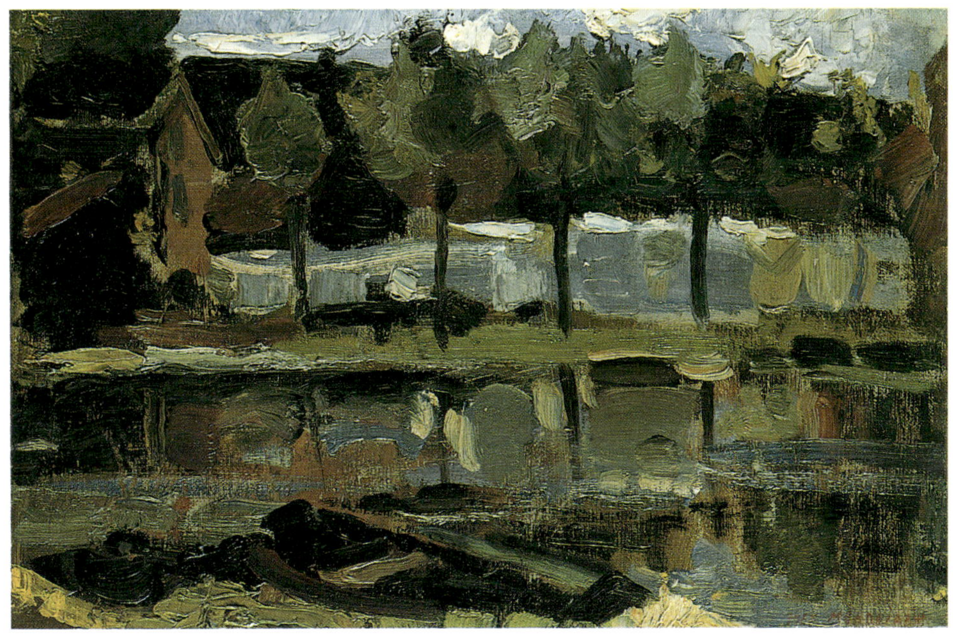
28

Impressionism.[76] The exhibition was organized by the critic and supporter of Medardo Rosso, Etha Fles (1857–1948).[77]

The similarity was dangerous since French Impressionism was not considered an acceptable option in Holland, especially among painters in Amsterdam. No one appreciated such French frivolities. There is no evidence at all that Mondrian cared for Monet, Sisley, Pissarro, or Renoir. Van Gogh was no better received, but the most detested artist was Cézanne. In 1899, his work, rarely shown in Holland, must have struck Mondrian and the circle of Simon Maris as "atrocious." A year later, Cézanne's work was accused of being "crude," "of secondary importance," and "created with extreme harshness of lines and colors."[78] In February 1901, when the Impressionists "liberated" the premises, the Arti society quickly organized–almost as a ritual of purification–an exhibition of the Barbizon school. By her efforts to make French art known in Holland, Fles attracted the anger of the Dutch critical establishment, beginning with Jan Veth (1864–1925).

However, there was a new excitement stirring, also in Holland, the country born in the mist. Within the group of Mondrian's associates–Simon Maris's circle of friends–opinions began to change. The critic Henriëtte Hendrix could not restrain herself from heaving a sign of relief in her commentary on the Van Lynden collection shown in Amsterdam:

Cat. 28 *Bleachworks on the Gein*, 1901
Oil on canvas mounted on cardboard
10 x 15.1 in. (25.5 x 38.5 cm)
Signed lower right: *PIET MONDRIAAN.*
Gemeentemuseum, The Hague, bequest of Salomon B. Slijper, 1971, inv. S 114–1971 (A 296)

76. The exhibition of paintings of the modern French school and sculptures of Medardo Rosso, in the headquarters of the Arti et Amicitiae Society, from January 29 to February 19, 1901.
77. Information appearing in the evening edition of the newspaper *De Telegraaf* on December 22 and 24, 1900, shows that Etha Fles, critic and curator of exhibitions, also succeeded in presenting this exhibition (borrowed from the Durand Ruel collection) in Utrecht (Voor de Kunst Society), and then in The Hague in March.
78. Henriëtte Hendrix, "Haagsche Kunstring" ("Art Circle of the Hague"), *De Telegraaf*, February 23, 1899, and Franz M. Melchers, "Kunst Centenale, Paris 1900" ("A Century of Art in Paris"), *De Telegraaf*, September 12, 1900 (morning edition.)

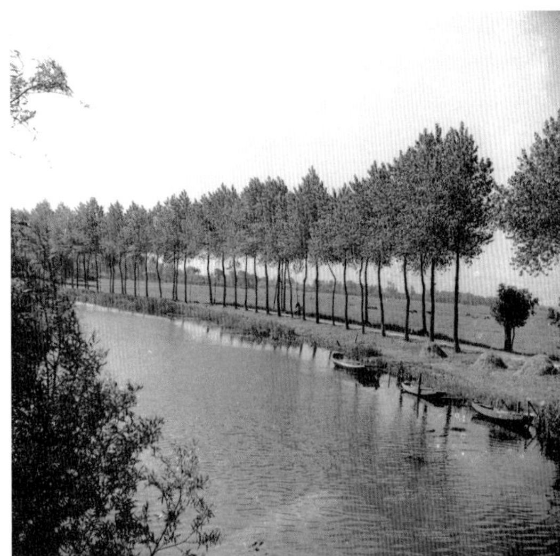

Fig. 24
Trees on the banks of the Gein
Municipal Archives, Amsterdam

. . . Then, as if, coming from the South, we cross the Dutch border, and see the Dutch landscape again spreading out before us, simple, beautiful, and reserved, after that full unfolding of luxurious colors; that is the impression that our Dutch masters stir in us again.[79]

It was also Hendrix, who, now close to Mondrian, demonstrated through sustained attention in various reviews what Fles had to endure. But she began also to write with passion and energy about van Gogh at this time.[80] In April 1901, when all eyes were fixed on this artist in an exhibition organized by the art dealer C. M. Van Gogh-Commerce d'art, she gave an extremely positive report in *De Telegraaf* of April 21:

Those who do not know Vincent will not gain a complete picture of his work through what is shown here. One cannot see him in all his aspects. We do not meet here the man of genius who aspired to the absolute without being able to reach it. This is how I have always felt about him. And so have I seen him, striving to depict Earth in all its majesty.

During the years from 1900 to 1904, we see Mondrian experimenting with what in Amsterdam was understood of van Gogh and Monet.[81] This meant he remained utterly close to the more familiar model of Willem Maris, whose palette was more restrained.[82] This is the case in *Polder Landscape* (cat. 29), as in *House on the*

79. H. Hx [Henriëtte Hendrix], "Schilderkunst in de Stad" ("Painting in the City"), *De Telegraaf*, May 24, 1900.
80. Henriëtte Hendrix, "Jan Toorop and Vincent van Gogh," *De Telegraaf*, January 5, 1899 (evening edition.)
81. Willem Steenhoff, in an article entitled "Important New Acquisition at the Rijksmuseum," *De Amsterdammer Weekblad*, April 29, 1900, wrote that Monet endeavored to relate "being and seeing."
82. At this time Claude Monet's *Corniche de Monaco* (*Monaco Coastal Road*), 1884, was donated to the Rijksmuseum.

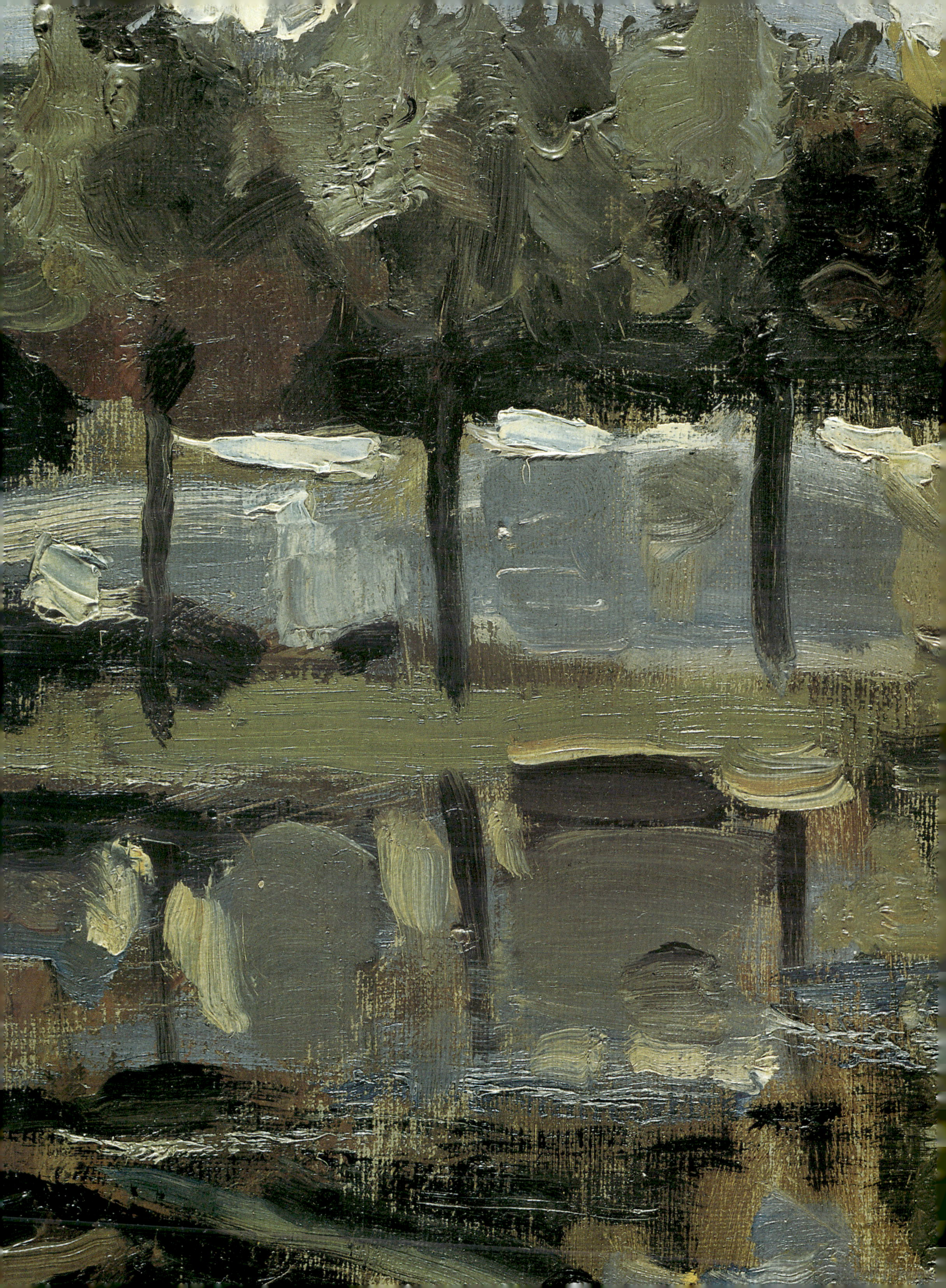

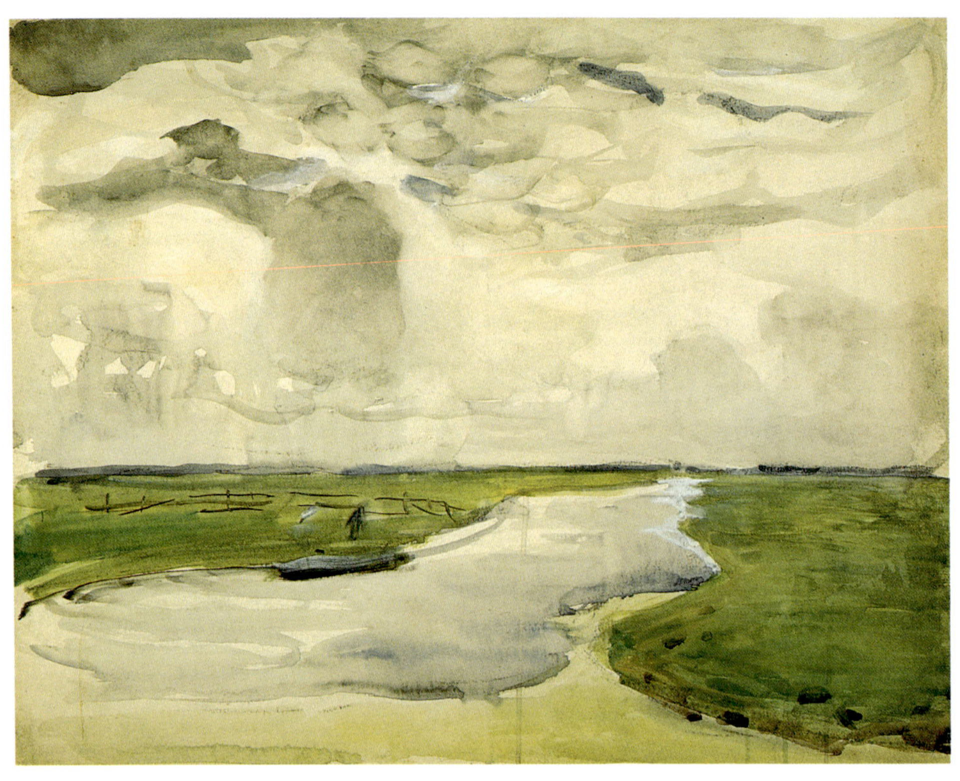

29

Cat. 29 *Polder Landscape*, c. 1900
Watercolor on paper
19.7 x 25.6 in. (50 x 65 cm)
Not signed
Musée d'Orsay, Paris, anonymous life-interest gift accepted by the State, 2000, inv. RF 52 079 (A 510)

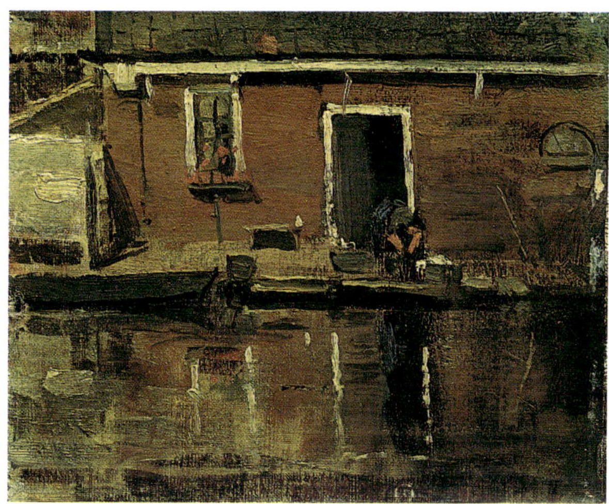
30

Water with Woman (cat. 30), in which Mondrian concentrates, with a heavily charged palette, on sunlight splashing on the gutters and window frames of a peasant house on the banks of a stream. In *Farmyard with Chickens* (cat. 31), made with extraordinary energy, and in *Cows in an Orchard* (cat. 33), Mondrian investigates again the possibilities of the loaded brush. In *Farmyard with Chickens*, he succeeds in creating depth while harmonizing the sunlight behind the farm with the grass of the orchard to create a blinding effect of backlighting. In *Cows in an Orchard*, he uses a thicker impasto and works without the palette knife, the result being a less structured but highly accurate painting.[83] In *Willowgrove on the Gein* (cat. 32) and *Oostzijdse Mill* (cat. 34b), however, he returns once again to the familiar palette and chiaroscuro of earlier days.

Mondrian offers a completely different vision in *Passiebloem* (*Passion Flower)* (cat. 25), a watercolor in the Symbolist tradition, in which an image of a woman is the carrier of allegorical meanings. During the 1890s, artists had considered isolated flower motifs–which had served up to that time only to render the idea of "sensation"–to be alternatives to landscapes. The flowers represented nature as if alive. The woman in *Passion Flower*, deep in ecstatic meditation, wears two heraldic passion flowers attached to her shoulders. In Christian iconography the passion flower embodies the instruments of Christ's Passion; in Theosophy, in a more general way, it becomes the expression of the tragic tied to the search for the spiritual. It remains to be

Cat. 30 *House on the Water with Woman*, c. 1900–1902
Oil on canvas mounted on panel
8.9 x 10.8 in. (22.5 x 27.5 cm)
Not signed
Gemeentemuseum, The Hague, inv. S 29–1960 (A 254)

83. This procedure is the same in *Grazende kalfjes* (*Grazing Calves*) (UA 16), shown in the exhibition *Works of Art by Living Masters* at the Stedelijk Museum in the fall of 1903.

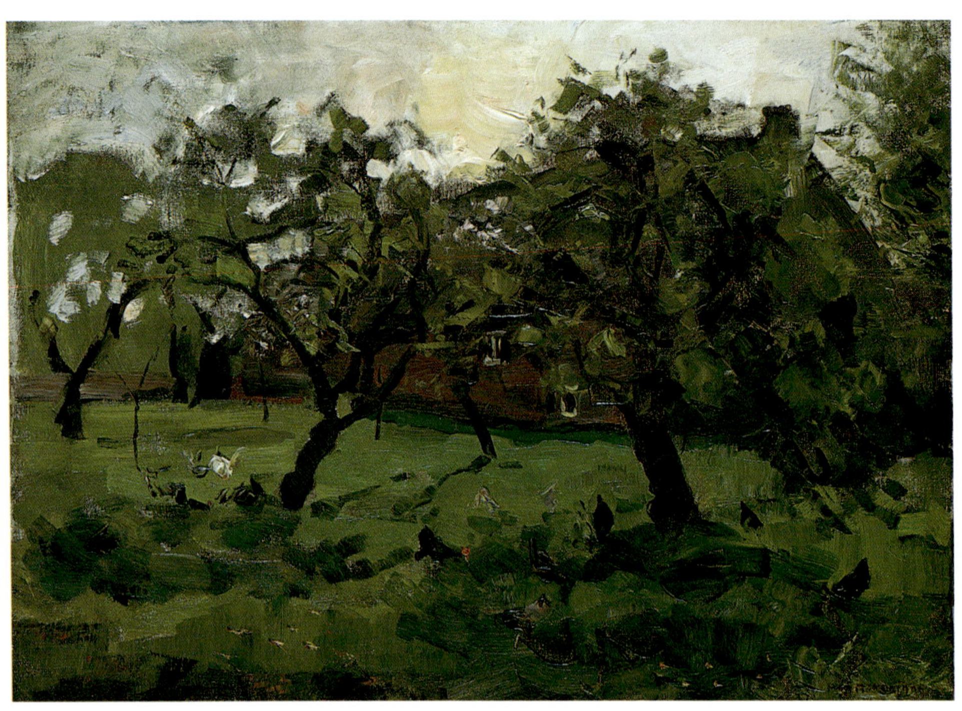
31

Cat. 31 *Farmyard with Chickens,* 1901
Oil on canvas
19.3 x 27 in. (49 x 68.5 cm)
Signed lower right: PIET MONDRIAAN.
Gemeentemuseum, The Hague, bequest of Salomon B. Slijper, 1971, inv. S 66–1971 (A 330)

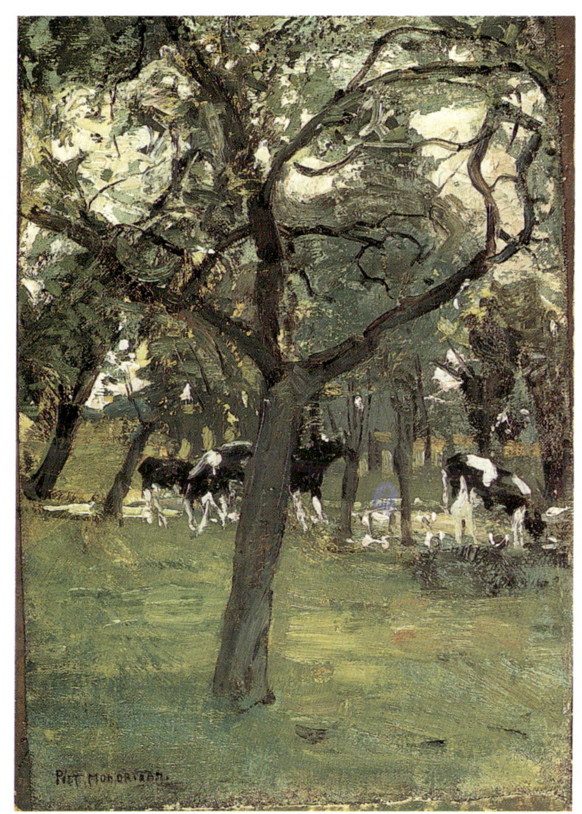

33

Cat. 33 *Cows in an Orchard,* c. 1902–3
Oil on canvas laid down on cardboard
14.7 x 10.7 in. (37.4 x 27.1 cm)
Signed lower left: PI ET MONDRIAAN.
Private collection (A 46)
Courtesy Simonis & Buunk

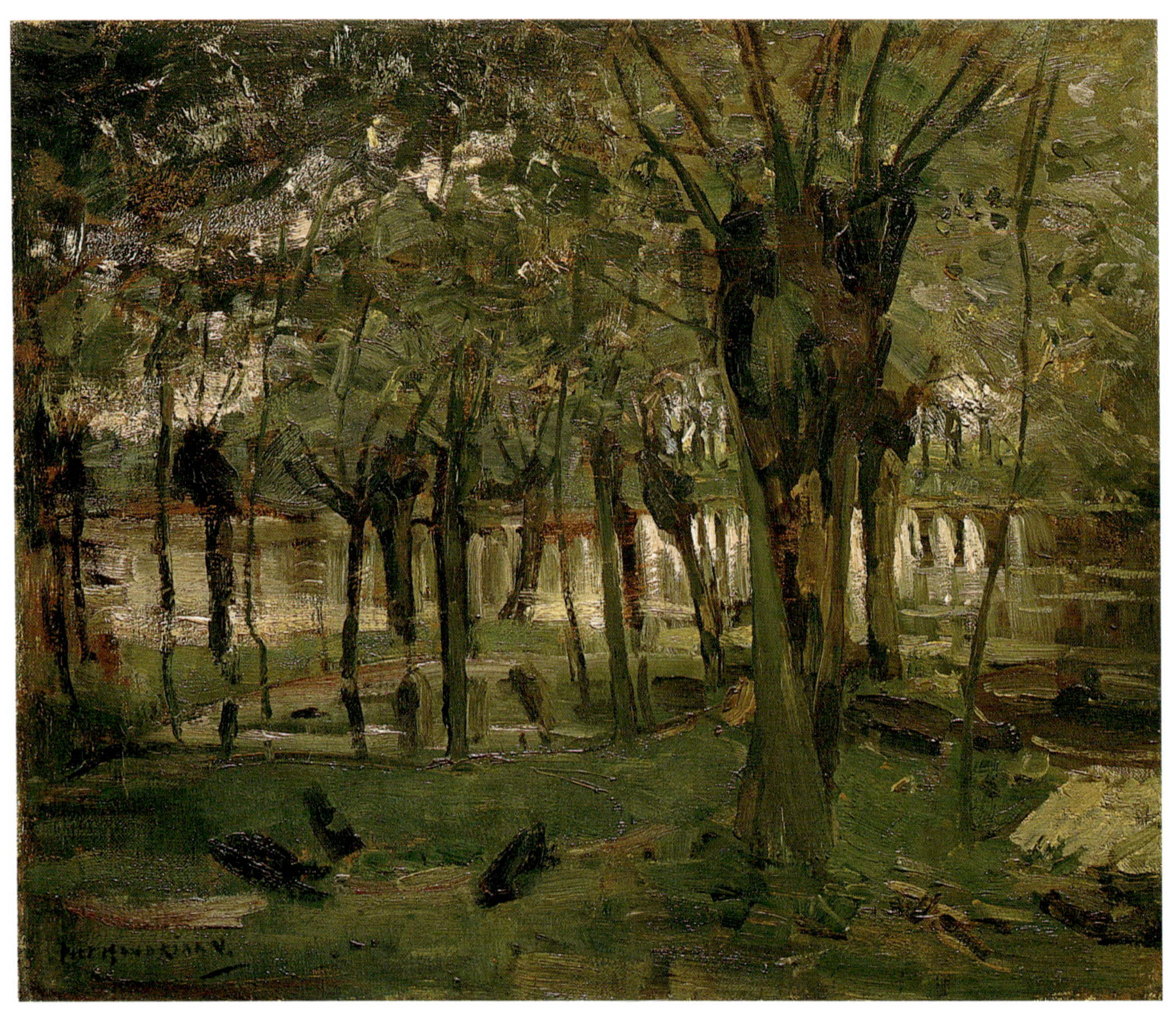

32

Cat. 32 *Willowgrove on the Gein*, c, 1902–3
Oil on canvas
21.3 x 24.8 in. (54 x 63 cm)
Signed lower left: PIET MONDRI AAN.
Gemeentemuseum, The Hague, bequest of Salomon B. Slijper, 1971, inv. S 105–1971 (A 470)

Cat. 25 *Passiebloem* (*Passion Flower*), c. 1901
Watercolor on paper
28.5 x 18.7 in. (72.5 x 47.5 cm)
Vertical inscription lower left: PASSIE BLOEM.
Signed on the vertical lower right:
PIET MONDRIAAN.
Gemeentemuseum, The Hague, gift of Albert van den Briel, inv. T 81–1957 (A 145)

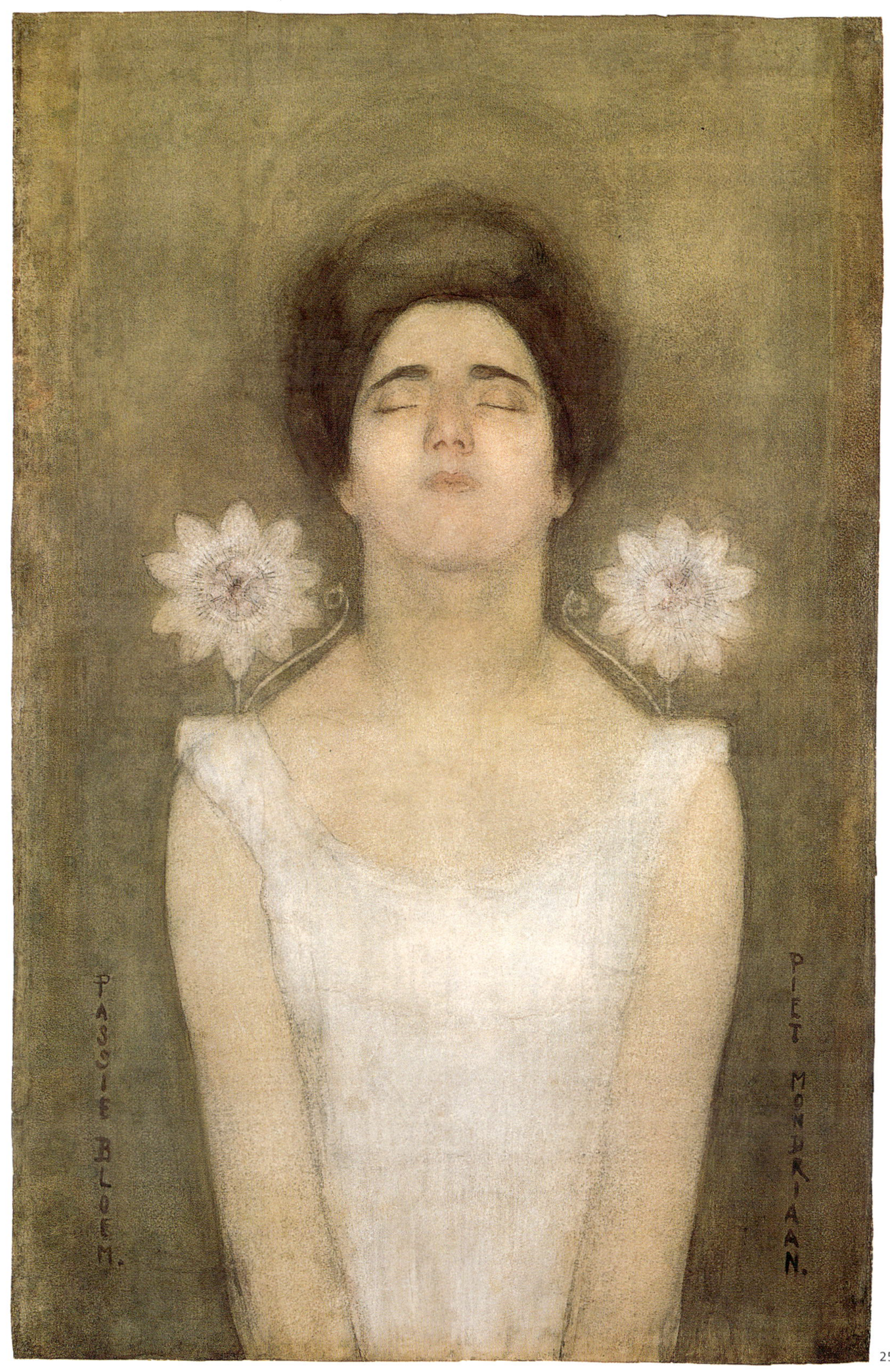

25

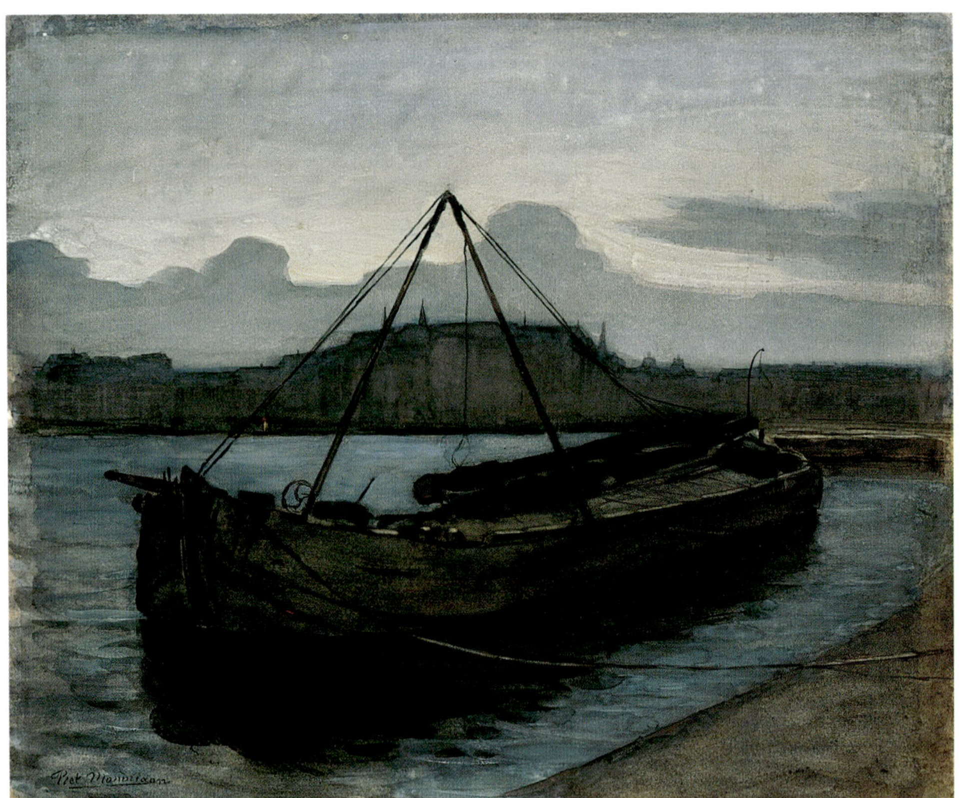
26

determined if Mondrian intended to attribute this latter meaning to the woman as she turns inward into herself in meditation, or if he was trying to show her passions in the light of the Passion of Christ. The symmetry, the position of the flowers, and their conspicuous placement in the foreground, as well as the textual elements, recall the metaphorical representations practiced by artists engaged in Theosophy, such as Mathieu Lauweriks (1864–1932).[84] Whatever his intention might have been–stylistically *Passiebloem* is not motivated at all by Theosophy–in this watercolor Mondrian shows himself not insensitive to the occult.

Avond aan de Weesperzijde (*Evening on the Weesperzijde*) (cat. 26) turns to the occult under the guise of the evening landscape, in which simple realities can take on a deeper meaning on a symbolic level. Mondrian represents a barge with its mast lowered in the peace and calm of an evening landscape; the sun has already set, but objects are still bathed in light, and twilight marks the time before night begins to cover the earth.

Along with these sorties into the realm of Symbolism, Mondrian continued to pursue his studies of landscapes in the environs of Amsterdam. *Op het land* (*In the Country*) (cat. 23) is part of a series of oil sketches (see cat. 11, 21, and 22) in which he tried out finely harmonized colors of delicate intensity, and a very high placement of the horizon. He was so satisfied with this study that he sent it, along with an

Cat. 26 *Avond aan de Weesperzijde* (*Evening on the Weesperzijde*), 1901
Lead pencil, crayon, watercolor, and gouache on paper
21.7 x 26 in. (55 x 66 cm)
Signed lower left: Piet Mondriaan.
Gemeentemuseum, The Hague, bequest of Salomon B. Slijper, 1971, inv. T 50–1971 (A 205)

84. It is interesting to note in this regard that J. M. Lauweriks gave a well-attended lecture at the Saint Lucas society on "Beauty and Philosophy."

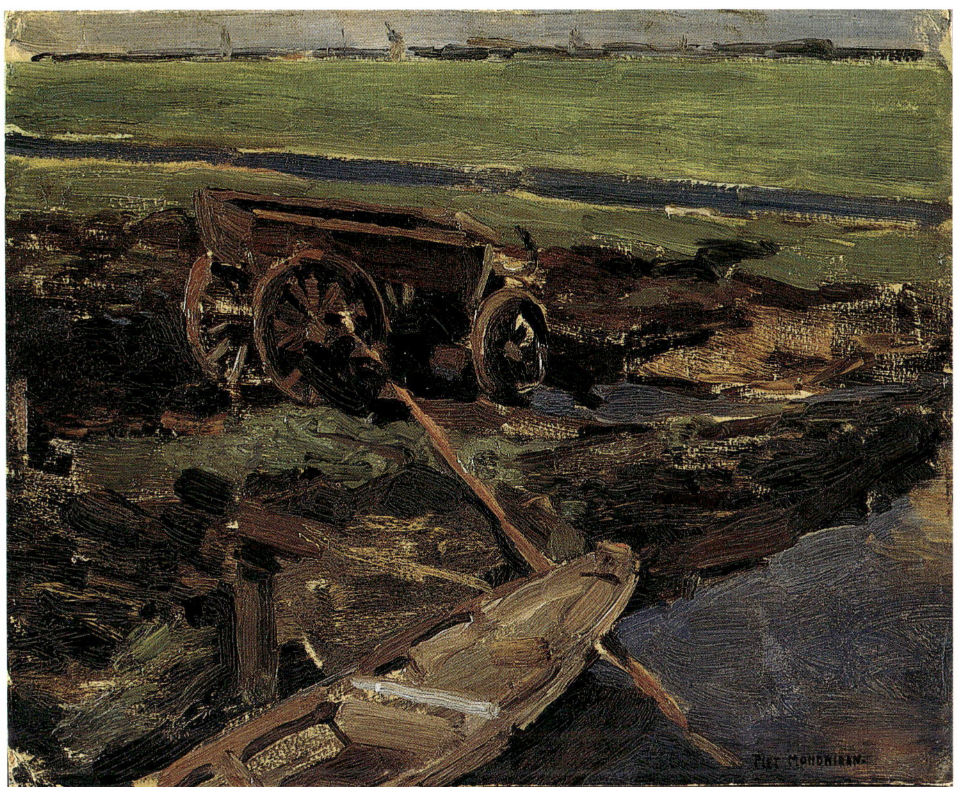

23

unidentified watercolor of a flower and *Evening on the Weesperzijde* (cat. 26), to the spring exhibition of the Saint Lucas society in May 1903. At the time, however, he was indirectly implicated in the violent social agitation that broke out in Amsterdam on the occasion of the general railroad strike, and even had to go into hiding to avoid falling into the hands of the police.[85] Given this situation, one wonders whether he would have been able to give attention to the selection of works for the exhibit. During the summer of 1903, he left for several days to Brabant where he was welcomed by Albert van den Briel, who lived there. In September, he traveled to Spain with Simon Maris and Frits Bodenheim (fig. 25 and 26). His stay in Brabant was extended as Mondrian decided this same year, under circumstances we know little about, to continue working there. Illness? Overwork? Religious crisis? Many hypotheses have been suggested but none substantiated. What is certain is that he had his name removed from the registry in Amsterdam on January 18, 1904, and that he left for Uden, a little town near the area in which Albert van den Briel worked as a professional forester. In Amsterdam as in Arnhem, this decision was received in various ways. Carel, Piet's brother, saw in it a mania for adventure:

[Piet] put on a corduroy suit and wore waterproof boots, had his hair cut in a crew cut, and left to

Cat. 23 *Op het land* (*In the Country*), 1902–3
Oil on cardboard
12.0 x 15 in. (30.5 x 38 cm)
Signed lower right: PI ET MONDRI AAN.
Gemeentemuseum, The Hague, gift of Albert van den Briel, inv. T 26–1956 (A 278)

85. See Baar 1994, 33. Mondrian clandestinely sheltered Louis Gondman, a former classmate, in his studio on Albert Cuypstraat; though required to do so as a soldier, Gondman refused to take part in the repression of the railroad strike (January–April 1903).

paint at Uden with van den Briel. There they stayed together in a little house, eating mutton, as far as I know, or consuming great bowls of milk or buttermilk by the spoonful at a garden table built around the trunk of an enormous tree.[86]

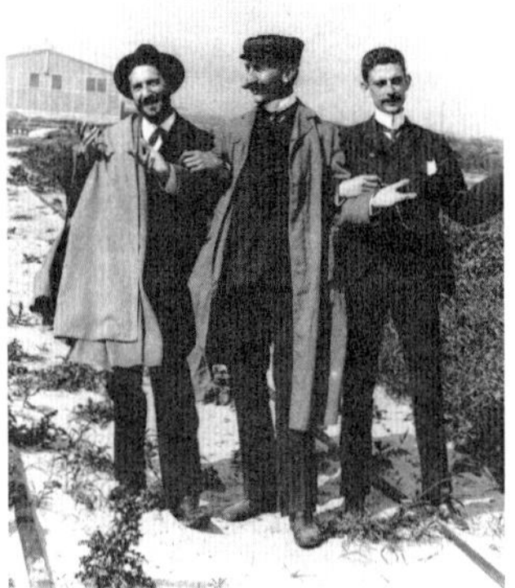

Fig. 25
Piet Mondrian and his friends, 1903
This photograph, taken when Mondrian was leaving Ijmuiden, shows him chatting on the quai of the port with Simon Maris (center) and Ewoud Groeneveld (right), before embarking for Bilbao.
RKD (Simon Maris Archives), The Hague

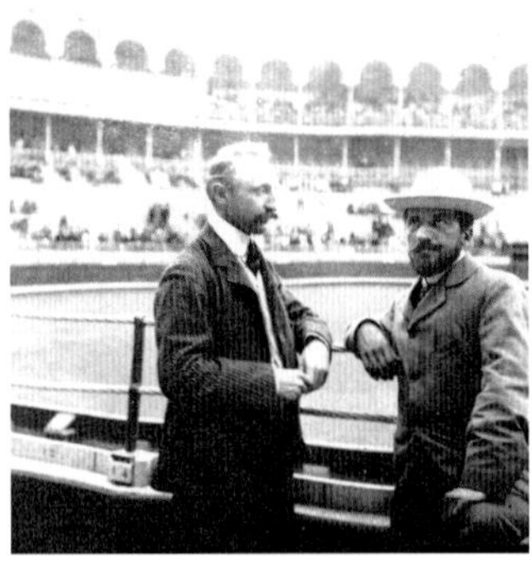

Fig. 26
Piet Mondrian in Spain, 1903
Photograph taken at a bull fight: on the left, Simon Maris; on the right, Mondrian
RKD (Simon Maris Archives), The Hague

In Brabant, his choice of subjects changed abruptly. Landscapes and panoramas gave way to closed motifs, interiors, or closed doors of barns. The most striking fact is that Mondrian now seemed to abandon the tradition from which he came, the tradition of landscape painting that rendered atmospheric conditions and the play of light. He suddenly opted for dense, pure colors, and renounced nuances and the use of gray to create harmony among colors. He reinforced effects of chiaroscuro. In his execution, he sought fluidity and dynamism. He abandoned the short, patchy stroke that he had used so freely in earlier sketches, and used only long, loaded, flat strokes filled with gaudy colors.

One result of this was a greater simplicity of execution. It is as if Mondrian wished to limit himself to pure notation and simple objects painted in a naïve and schematic manner, as in *Barn Interior* (cat. 35) or *Bij de Ossenstal (Near the Oxstall)* (cat. 34a). The perspective of *Oostzijdse Mill* (cat. 34b), which must have been painted just before his departure for Brabant, is complex compared to the arrangement of colors and surfaces in *Barns at Nistelrode* (cat. 37). The strange and powerful colors in *Farmhouse, Brabant* (cat. 36) and *Barns at Nistelrode* stand in dramatic contrast to the softness of *Polder Landscape* (cat. 29) and *Evening on the Weesperzijde* (cat. 26). In these latter two works the colors are still atmospheric and born of a uniform light that extends over the entire surface of the scene. *Farmhouse, Brabant* (cat. 36) reveals an almost primitive need to limit each individual color to its own zone, to build the image from local colors that are related in a new kind of balance. All brightness is stifled so that colors appear somber and heavy, in spite of the variety of the palette. In this sense, Mondrian takes yet another step in the Brabant works to free himself from the Dutch tradition. It is significant that during his stay he must have removed and sold a large piece of brown leather that he had brought from Amsterdam to hang over the window of his studio in order to obtain a warmer, more golden brown light. He was saying goodbye to a palette that he had cherished for a long time.

Later Mondrian mentioned these works as examples of the evolution of Neo-Plasticism – and, therefore, above all, of his own evolution. For him the "plastic of pure relationships" was already in its infancy in these efforts to seek liberation from the indeterminate (the visual appearance of things) and attain "pure plastic of the

86. Letter from Carel Mondrian to Salomon Slijper, November 15, 1945. Slijper Archives, RKD, The Hague.

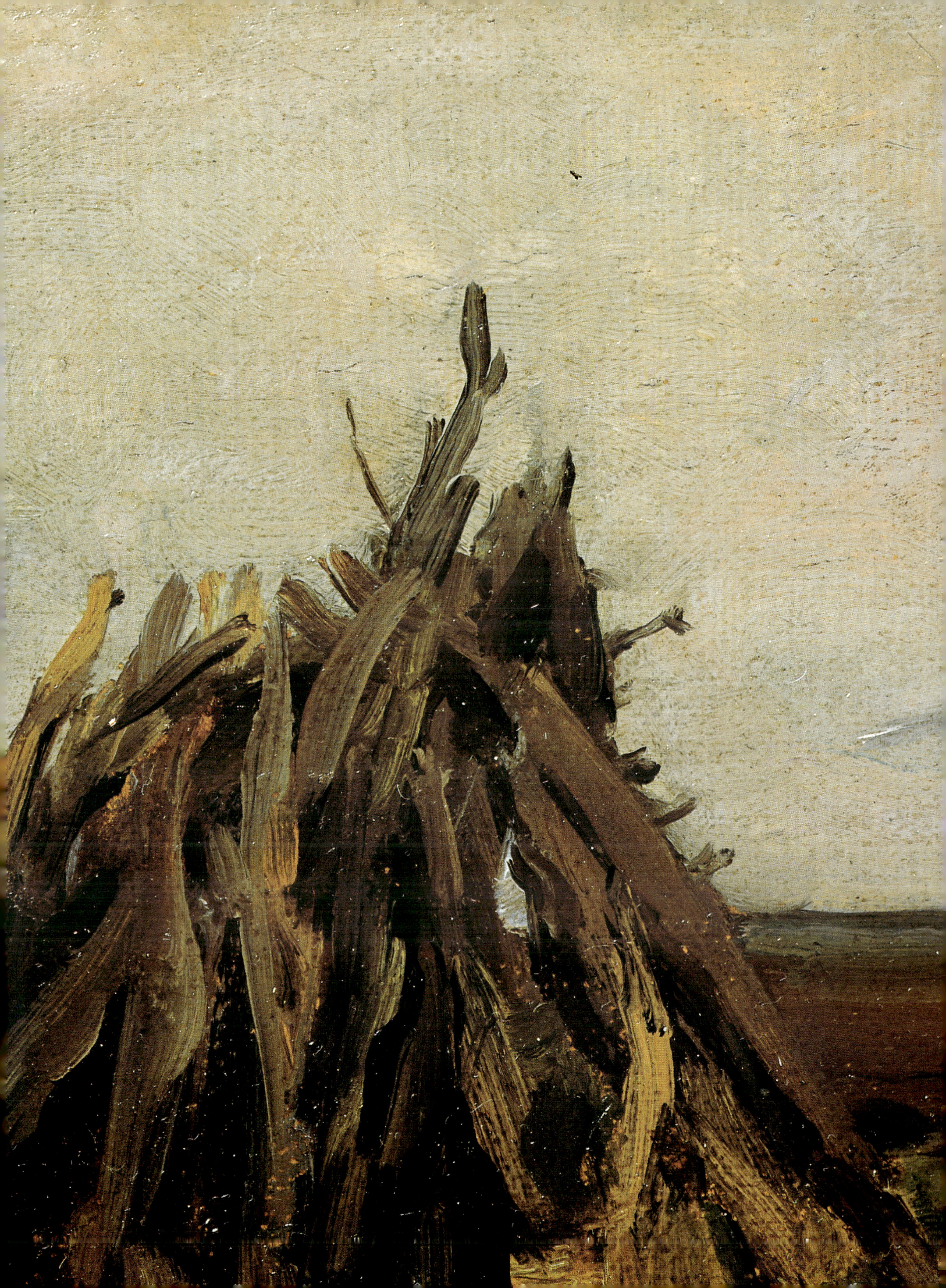

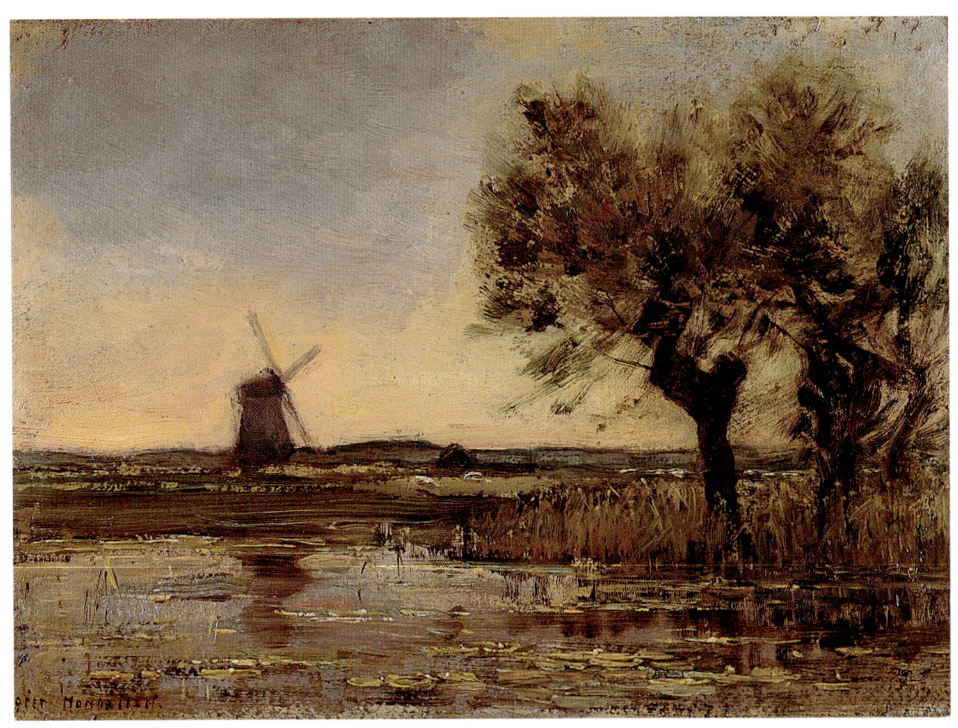
34*bis*

Cat. 34b *Oostzijdse Mill,* c. 1903
Oil on cardboard
11.8 x 16.5 in. (30 x 42 cm)
Signed lower left: PIET MONDRIAAN
Private collection *(Fort Worth only)*

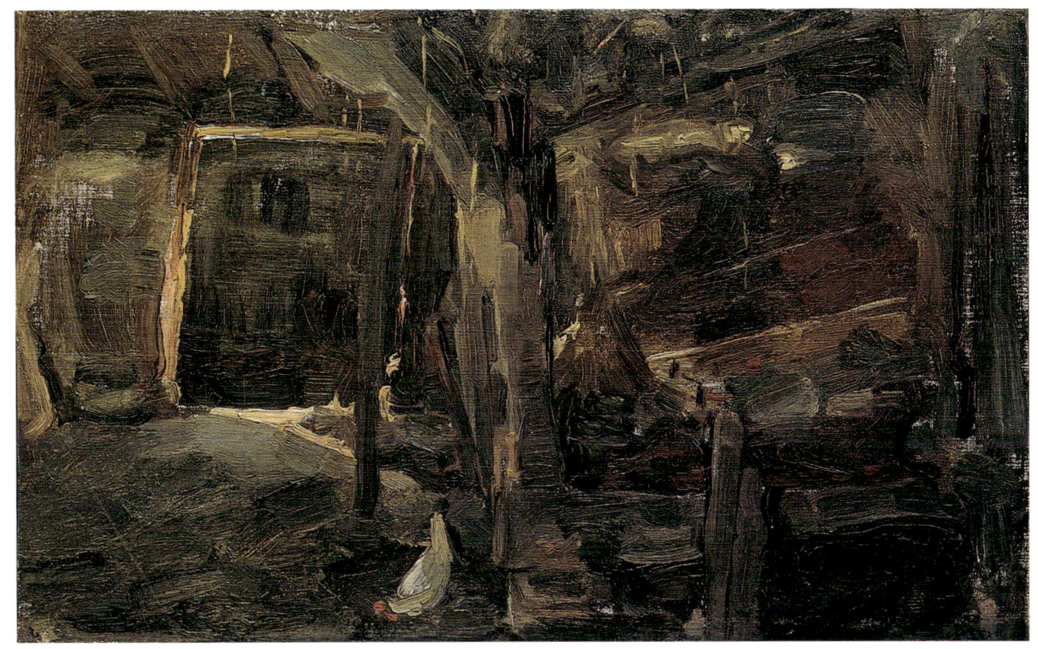

35

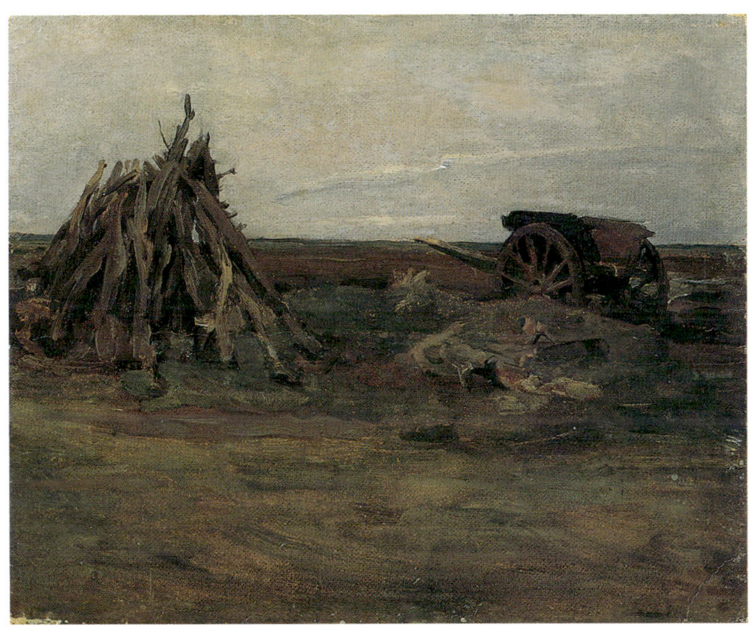

34

Cat. 35 *Barn Interior*, c. 1904
Oil on canvas
12.6 x 19.7 in. (32 x 50 cm)
Not signed
Gemeentemuseum, The Hague, bequest of Salomon B. Slijper, 1971, inv. S 52–1971 (A 357)

Cat. 34a *Bij de Ossenstal* (*Near the Oxstall*), 1904
Oil on cardboard mounted on panel
12 x 15 in. (30.5 x 38 cm)
Not signed
Gemeentemuseum, The Hague, gift of Albert van den Briel, inv. S 27–1956 (A 379)

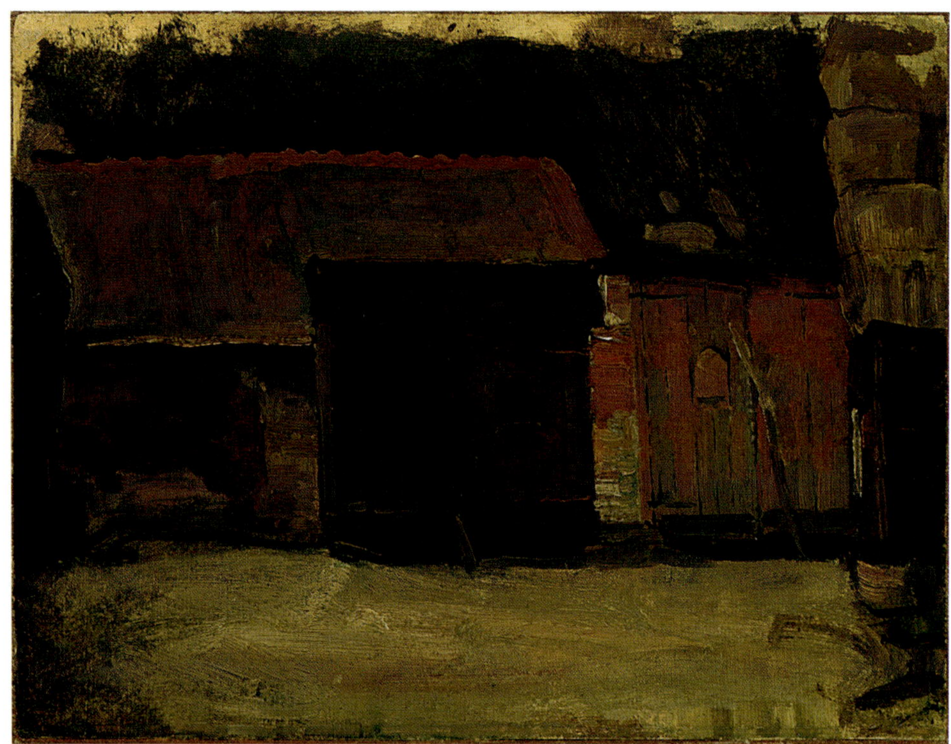

37

determinate." "Was it by chance," Mondrian wondered, "that [the founders of Neo-Plasticism] found such an appropriate subject through which to express their feeling for determinate relationships in an unforeshortened (nonperspectival) view of a farmhouse, with its mathematical articulation of planes (large doors and grouping of windows) and its primary (basic) colors?"[87]

Mondrian was also preoccupied with Theosophy in Uden, and he exchanged ideas about it with Van den Briel. He must have been intensely interested in mathematics and in geometrical proportions. Theosophy may have helped him in organizing his ideas and in helping him to develop a certain manner of reflection on his art. But one cannot state with certainty that the doctrine had a direct influence on the evolution of his expressive resources and of his art. The particular style that Mondrian developed in Brabant was not born from a belief, but from a change in the way he approached his subject matter.

Cat. 37 *Barn at Nistelrode*, 1904
Oil on cardboard mounted on panel
13 x 16.9 in. (33 x 43 cm)
Not signed
Gemeentemuseum, The Hague, gift of Albert van den Briel, inv. S 29–1956 (A 365)

87. Mondrian 1918–19, 17.

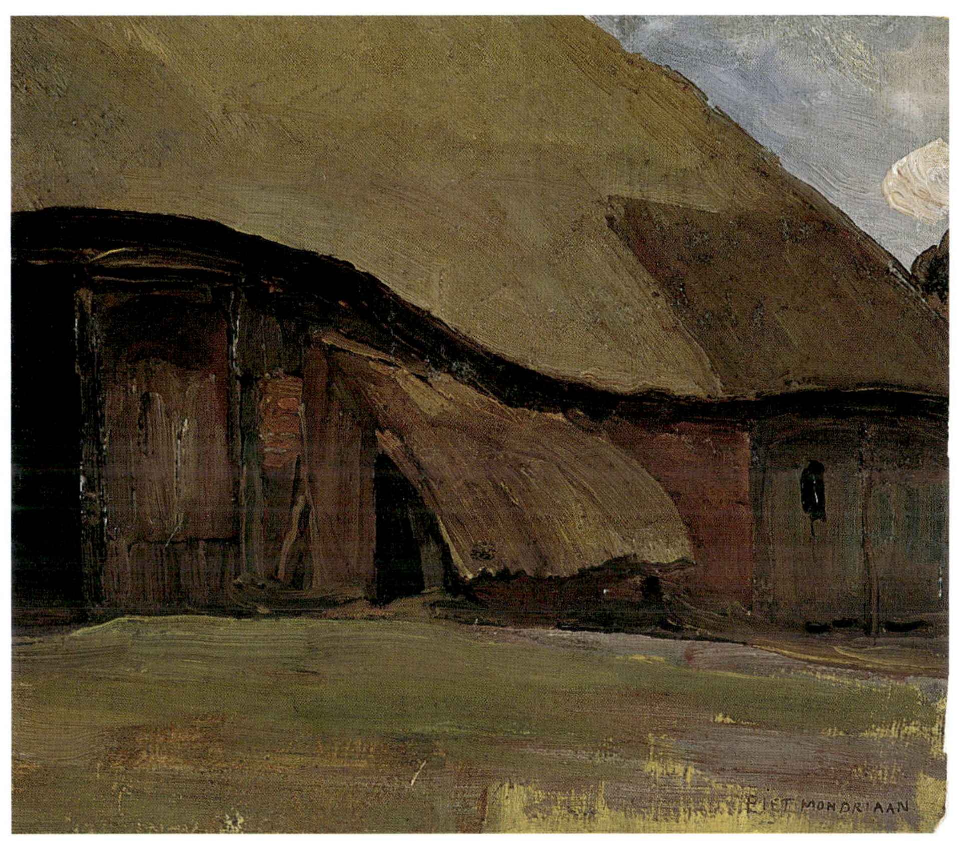

36

Cat. 36 *Farmhouse, Brabant,* 1904
Oil on paper mounted on cardboard
11.2 x 13.4 in. (28.5 x 34 cm)
Signed lower right: PI ET MONDRIAAN.
Gemeentemuseum, The Hague, bequest of Salomon B. Slijper, 1971, inv. S 85–1971 (A 362)

Chapter Five

1904–1908

"Experience was my only teacher." [88]

Hans Janssen and Joop M. Joosten

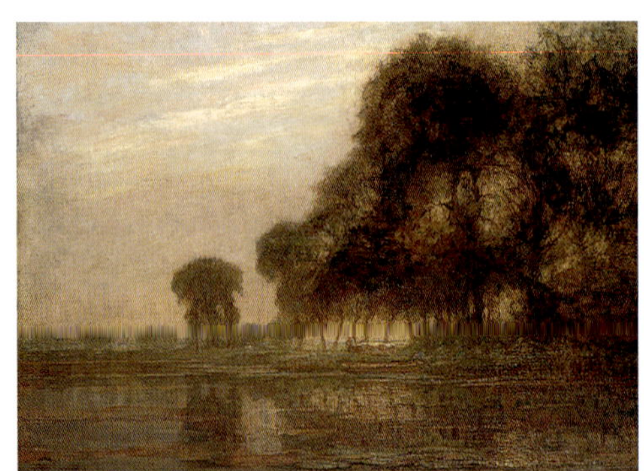

Fig. 27
Piet Mondrian, *Trees beside the Water*, 1907
Oil on canvas
Gemeentemuseum, The Hague (A 482)

Returning from Brabant, Mondrian devoted himself to new research. His characteristic little oil sketches gave way to series: he treated one motif a great many times; more than fifteen variations are known of certain subjects, each employing different means of expression. But the change was, above all, a return to the colors and the style he used before 1904 (fig. 27). The motif of *Farm at Duivendrecht* (cat. 38, 39, 40) seems to have originated in an oil sketch (cat. 38). The sketch was executed in the studio, however, and not *en plein air*, as has often been supposed. Whatever might have been the original design, a great number of increasingly bold variations on it were created around 1905. From large forms

88. Bradley 1944, 18.

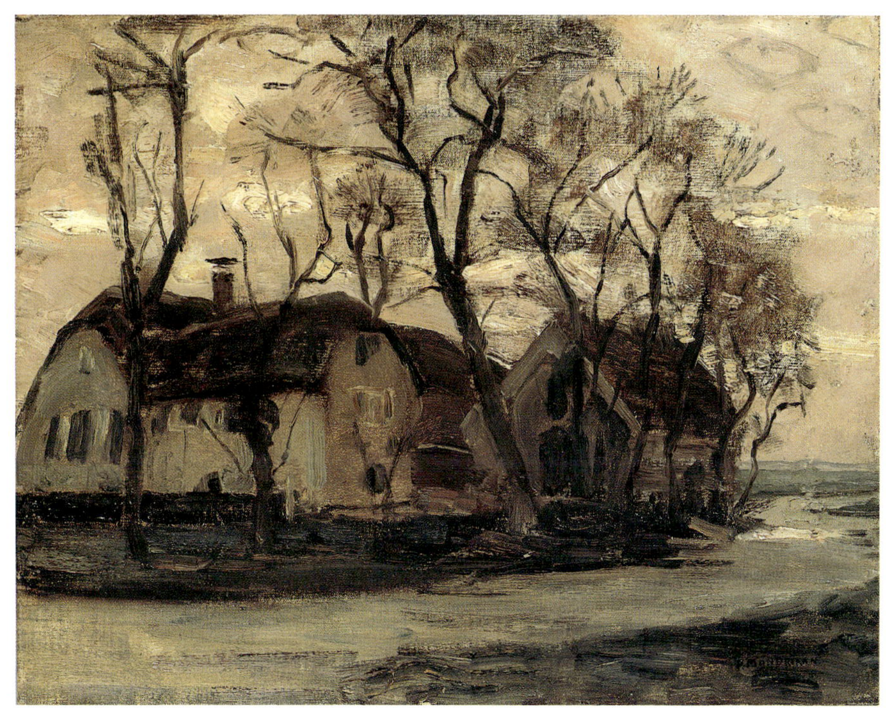

38

Fig. 28
Piet Mondrian and Simon Maris on the banks of the Gein, on the grass and under the willows, "among the city people," summer 1904
On the right, in the foreground, Simon Maris; to his left, Piet Mondrian.
RKD (Simon Maris Archives), The Hague

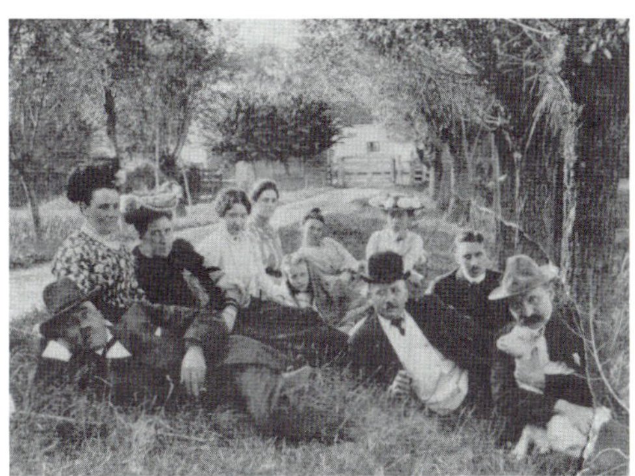

worked in oil to those combining several techniques (cat. 39 and 40), Mondrian continued to advance his research into the possibilities of materials, both in the area of form and in that of content.

As indicated in the introduction, this particular manner of working has engendered many hypotheses on the role of the series in Mondrian's work.[89] We would like to confine ourselves to the observation that Mondrian was not at all the only Dutch painter to work this way. Many of his colleagues repeated motifs, introducing shifts and minimal changes in composition, atmosphere, and weather effects. This practice was also very widespread in Dutch art at the end

Cat. 38 *Farm at Duivendrecht*, c. 1905
Oil on canvas
18.1 x 23.2 in. (46 x 59 cm)
Signed lower right: P. MONDRIAAN.
Gemeentemuseum, The Hague, bequest of Salomon B. Slijper, 1971, inv. S 91–1971 (A 390)

89. See Seitz 1956, 45; and J. Coplans 1968, 38–44; and especially Bois 1994, 313.

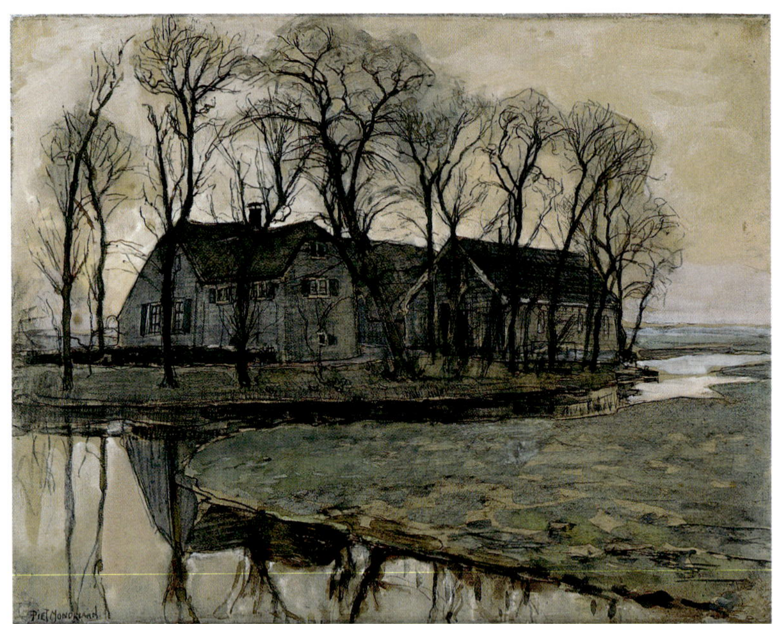

39

of the nineteenth century, and the Maris brothers were especially experienced in the art of the variation (fig. 17). It was a matter, on the one hand, of assuring a regular income thanks to what were called "pot boilers"; on the other hand, however, there was in this practice an authentic search for virtuosity and increasing depth, a desire for precision to the nearest millimeter. At the time of the great Jacob Maris exhibition of 1899, a critic developed this last point, comparing the work of Maris to the work of an actor who, each evening, gives a new presence and brilliance to his role by varying his way of playing the part.[90]

In Mondrian's case, an additional element came into play. By repeating the motif of farms on the banks of the Gein, he was really testing the potential and the limits of his material. He proceeded with his experimentation in *In't Gein* (*In the Gein*) (cat. 41), painted in full, strong colors reminiscent of Jan Voerman, whereas *Landzicht Farm* (cat. 42), dated 1905, presents the veiled tonalities of the work of Willem or even Matthijs Maris. *Geinrust Farm* (cat. 43), with its subtly mottled clump of trees, is almost an intermediate state. While the reflection in the water and the light that falls on the cattle are rich in contrasts, at the same time they create a play of pale colors. *Evening on the Gein* (cat. 44) and *Isolated Tree on the Gein* (cat. 45) approach the motif in a different manner. In the former, the surface of the water in the foreground becomes a calm mirror; the silhouette of the tall tree that

90. "Exposition Jaap Maris," *De Telegraaf*, December 21, 1899 (evening edition). This critical review was probably the work of Henriëtte Hendrix, who frequented the circle of artists surrounding Jacob Maris and who came to know Mondrian at their gatherings around this time. We are given first-hand information here, an unexpected glimpse into the elaboration of Hague school theories of painting.

Cat. 39 *Farm at Duivendrecht*, c. 1905
Chalk, watercolor, and gouache on paper
19.7 x 27.8 in. (50 x 65.5 cm)
Signed lower left: *PI ET MONDRIAAN.*
Frans Halsmuseum, Haarlem, inv. no. 702 (A 393)

dominates the closed horizon and the solitary star in the sky become the focal points of the landscape. *Avond* (*Evening*) (cat. 46), painted in 1906, evokes the same world of calm, closed in upon itself, as do the two versions of *Geinrust Farm* (cat. 47 and 48), another motif that appears in both drawn and painted variants.

These images are a first peak in Mondrian's work. In them is found the expression of a universe as orderly as a poem, in which neither things concrete nor things sensed are sacrificed for the benefit of abstract ideas, but are condensed into a form in which nothing can be changed, added, or subtracted without impairing the whole. This unity of the aesthetic object, originating in the subject represented, constituted a fundamental lesson for Mondrian. "I preferred to paint landscape and houses seen in gray, dark weather or in very strong sunlight," he later wrote, "when the density of the atmosphere obscures the details and accentuates the large outlines of objects."[91] In these works, the artist developed a language of forms that would guide him toward the universe of abstract art. Notions such as "truth" and "fidelity of reproduction" were no longer his guiding principles. The work of art aspired to the ideal of an absolute, total presence. And presence was silence. His thinking was a visual equivalent to Mallarmé's expression that a poem should be "white." The spectator was pure

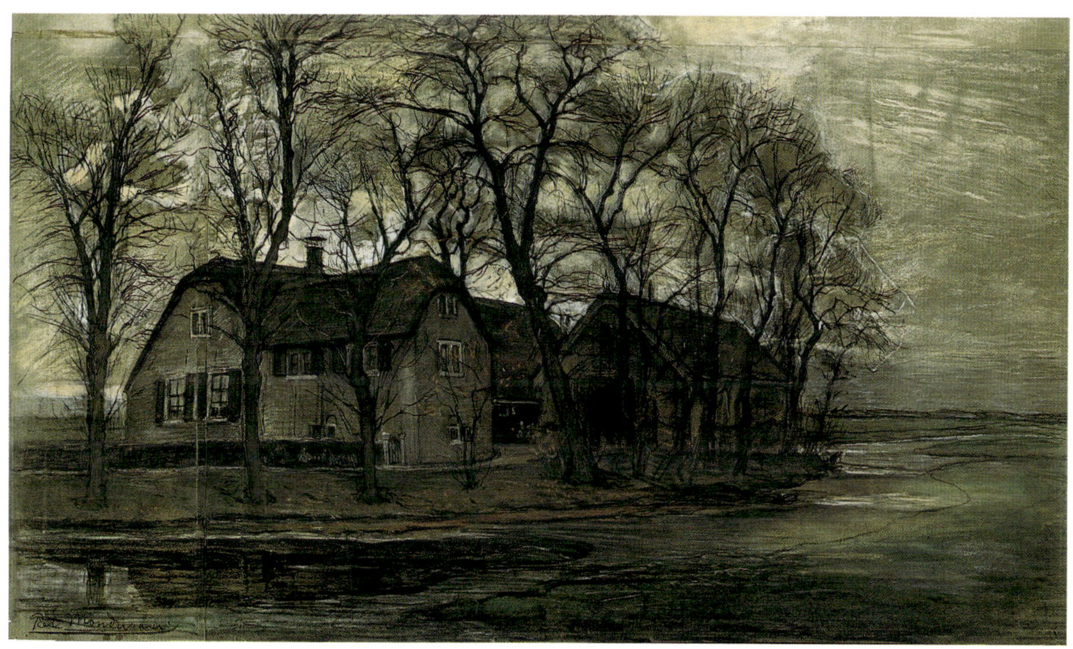

40

Cat. 40 *Farm at Duivendrecht*, c. 1905
Charcoal, crayon, gouache, and pastel on assembled pieces of paper
17.4 x 30.1 in. (44 x 76.5 cm)
Signed lower left: *Piet Mondriaan.*
Gemeentemuseum, The Hague, inv. T 80–1979 (A 395)

91. Mondrian 1942.

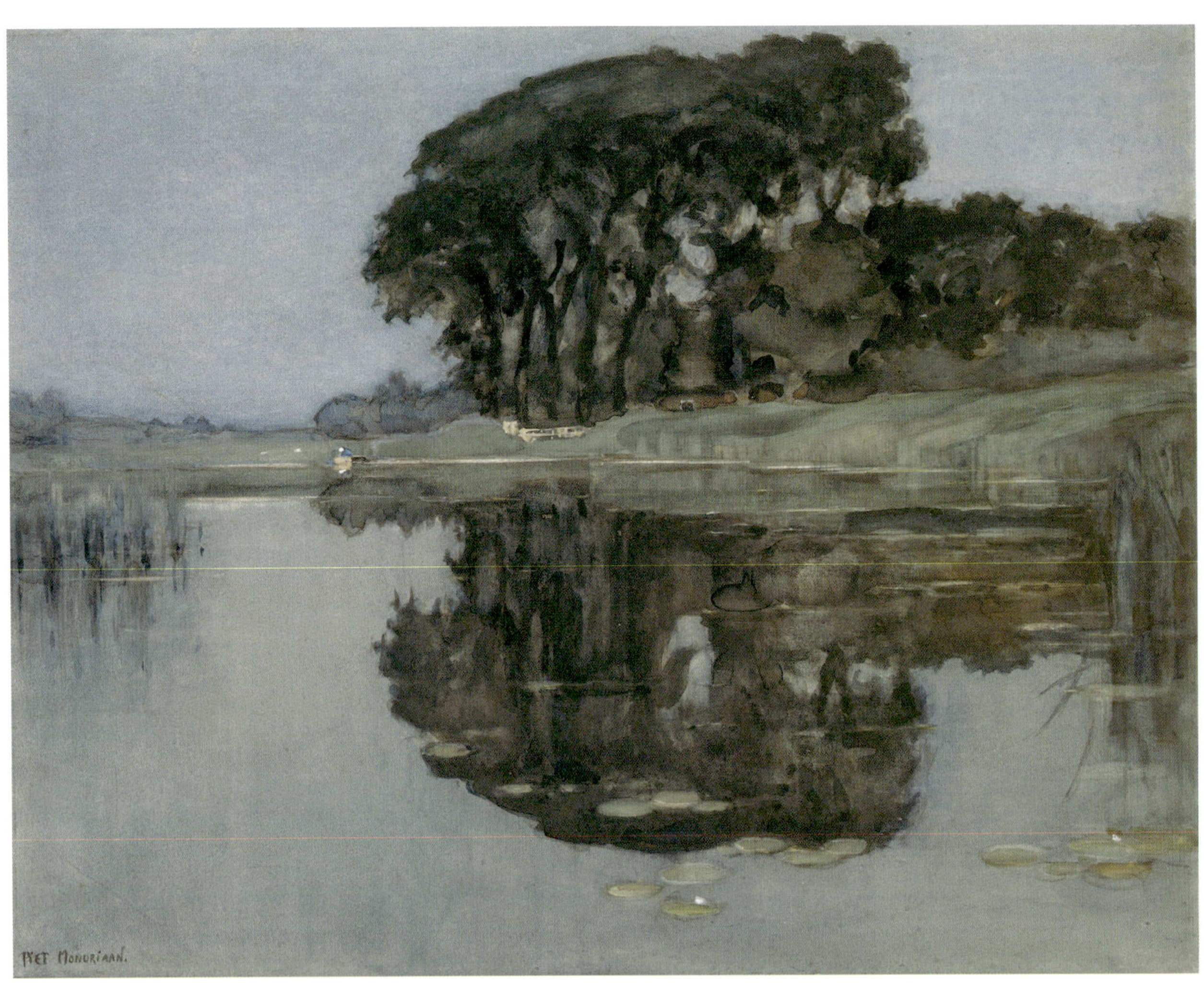

41

Cat. 41 *In't Gein* (*In the Gein*), c. 1905
Watercolor on paper
19.7 x 25 in. (50 x 63.5 cm)
Signed lower left: PI ET MONDRIAAN.
Private collection (A 431)

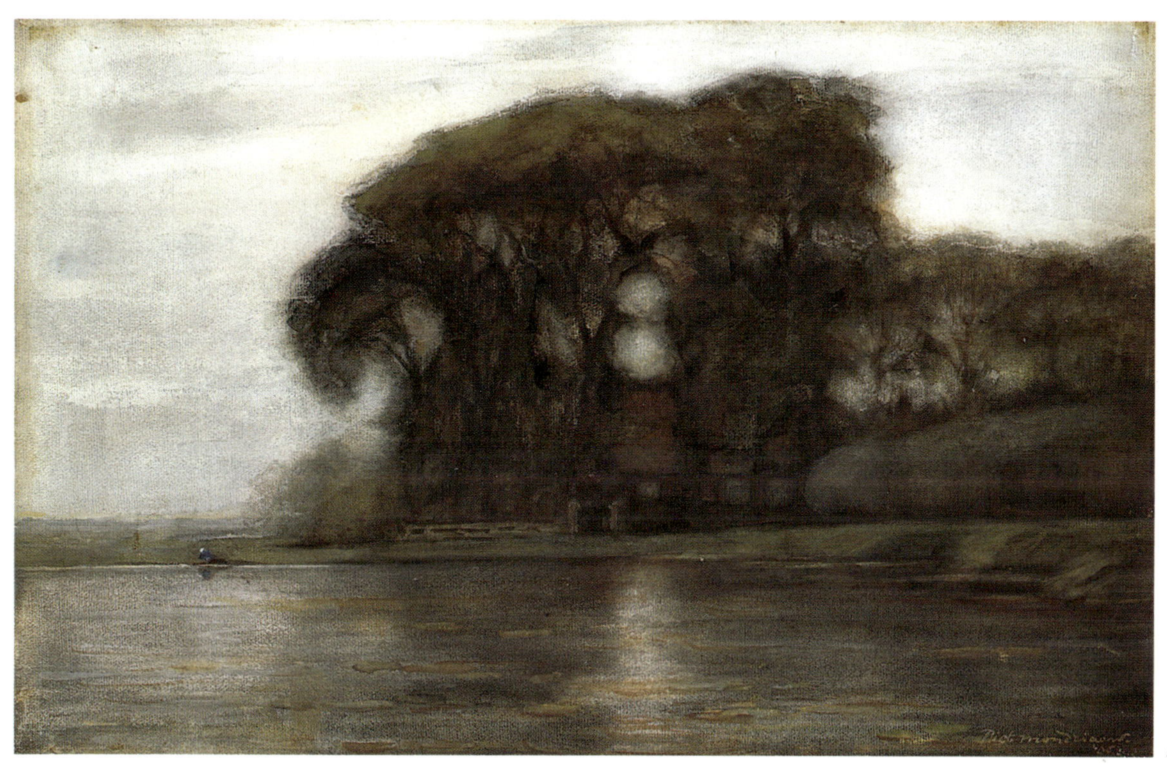

42

Cat. 42 *Landzicht Farm*, 1905
Watercolor on paper
15.2 x 24 in. (38.5 x 61 cm)
Signed and dated lower right: *Piet Mondriaan.'05*
Gemeentemuseum, The Hague, gift of P. A. Scheen, inv. T 46–1960 (A 432)

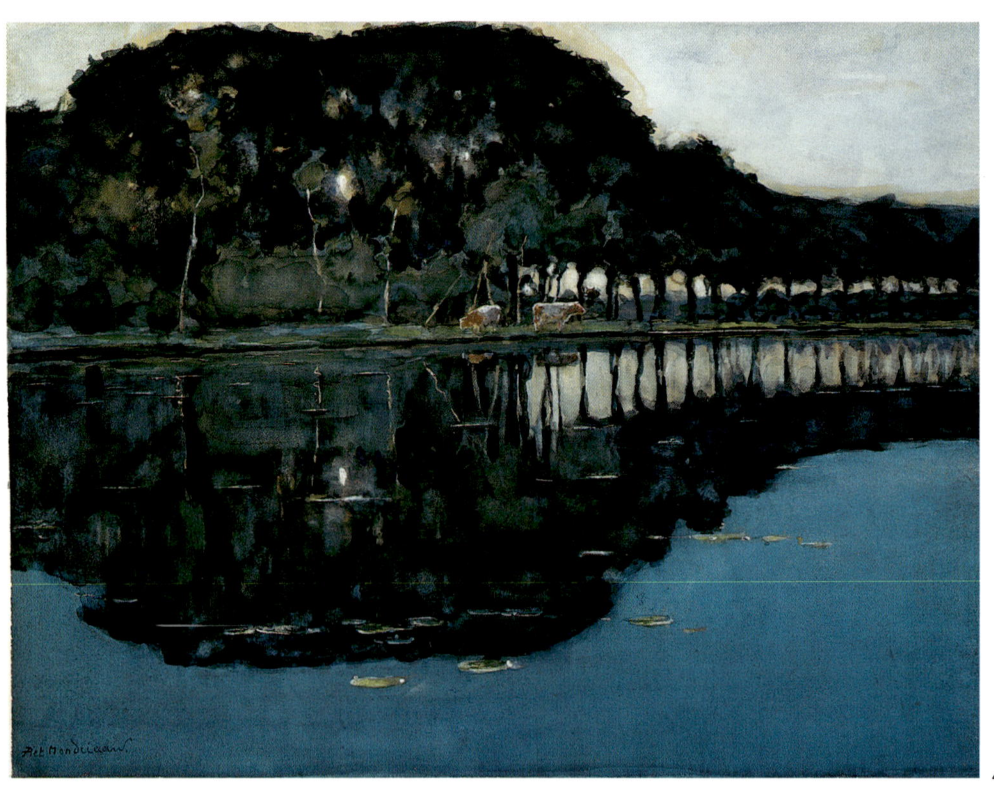

43

Cat. 43 *Geinrust Farm,* 1905–6
Watercolor on paper
19.5 x 26 in. (49.5 x 66 cm)
Signed lower left: *Piet Mondriaan.*
Private collection (A 448)

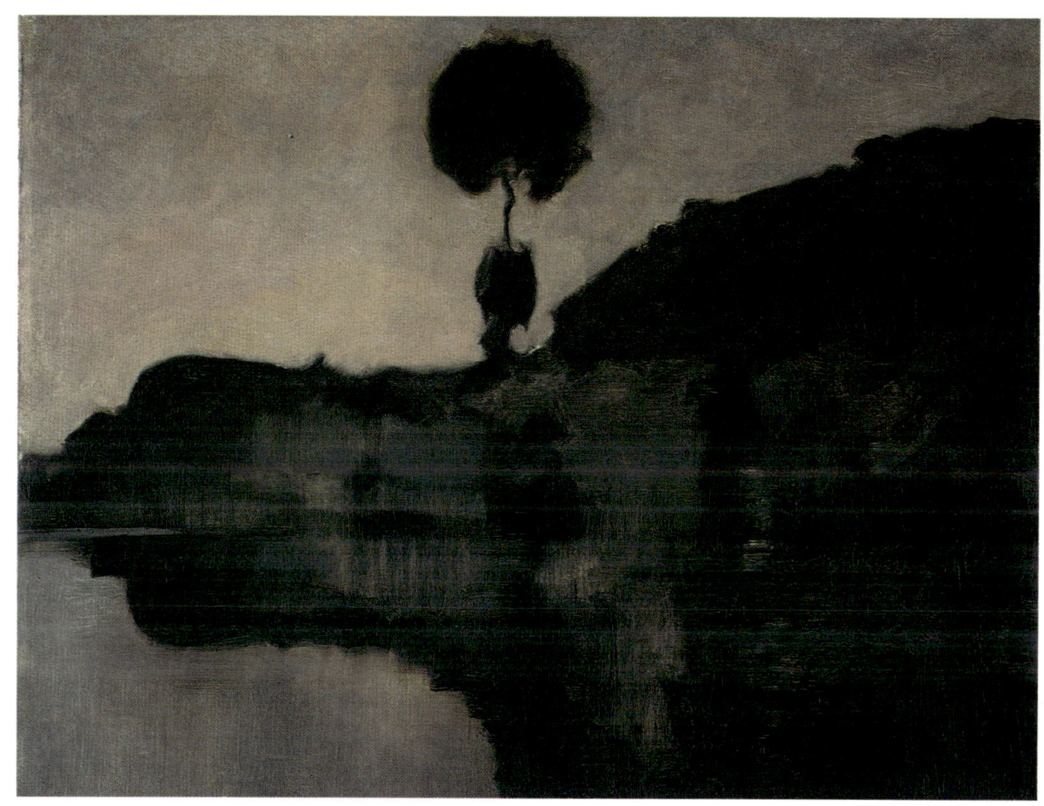

44

Cat. 44 *Evening on the Gein*, 1906
Oil on canvas
25.6 x 33.8 in. (65 x 86 cm)
Not signed
Gemeentemuseum, The Hague, gift of Albert van den Briel, inv. S 28-1956 (A 463)

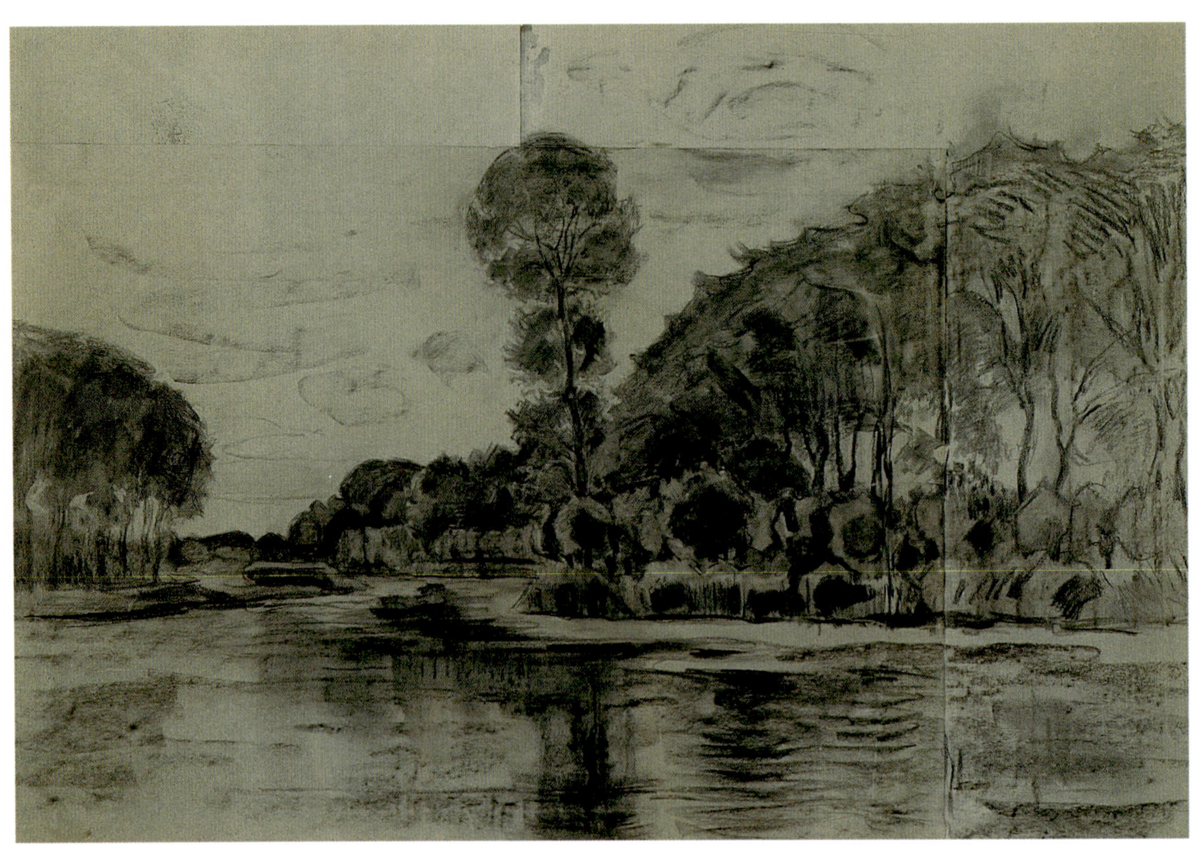
45

Cat. 45 *Isolated Tree on the Gein*, c. 1906
Charcoal and crayon on assembled pieces of paper
22.1 x 32.9 in. (56.2 x 83.5 cm)
Not signed
Musée d'Orsay, Paris, anonymous life-interest gift accepted by the State, 2000, inv. RF 52 077 (A 455)

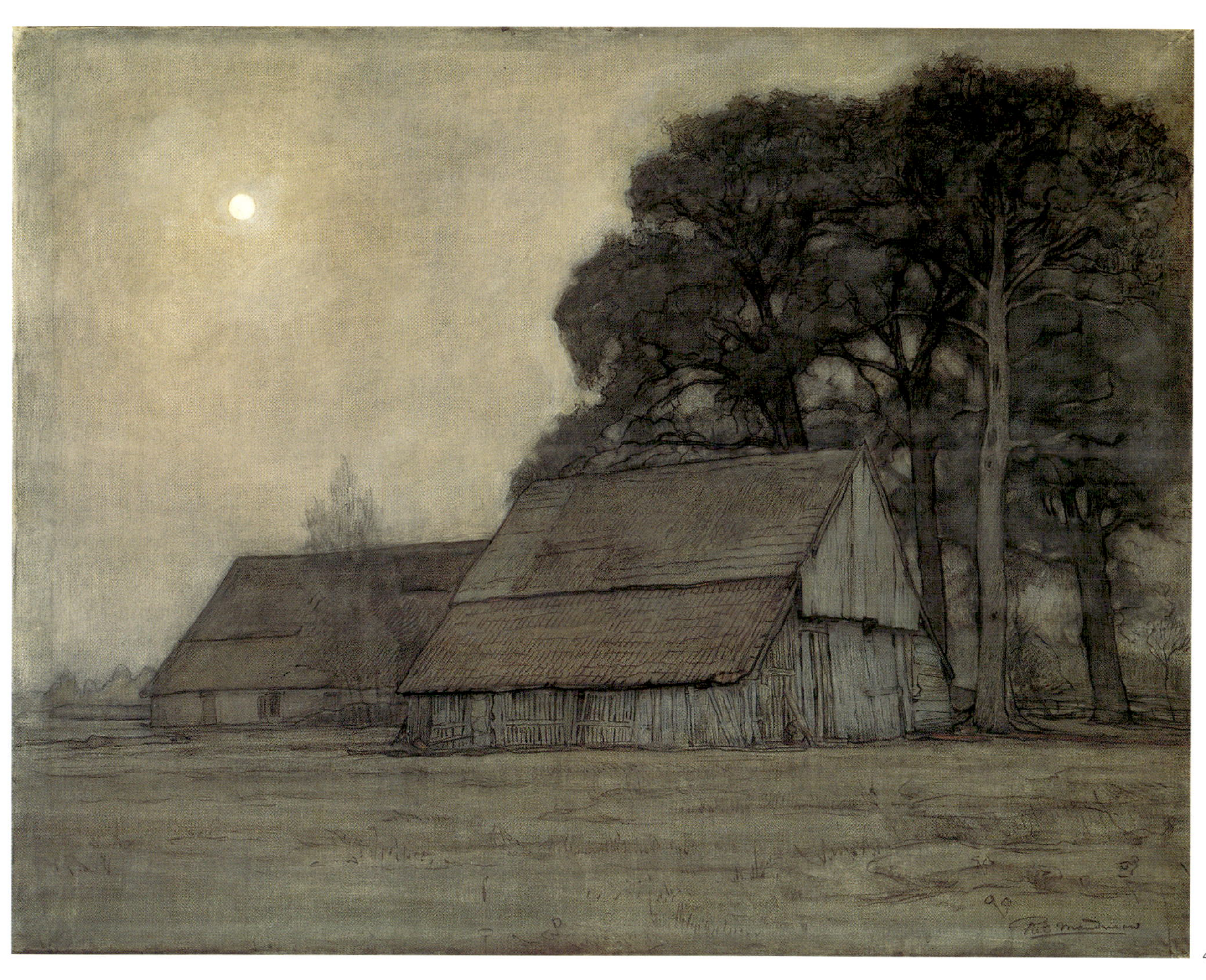

46

Cat. 46 *Avond* (*Evening*), 1906
Charcoal, crayon, and watercolor on paper
29.1 x 38.6 in. (74 x 98 cm)
Signed lower right: *Piet Mondriaan*
Gemeentemuseum, The Hague, bequest of Salomon B. Slijper, 1971, inv. T 51–1971 (A 545)

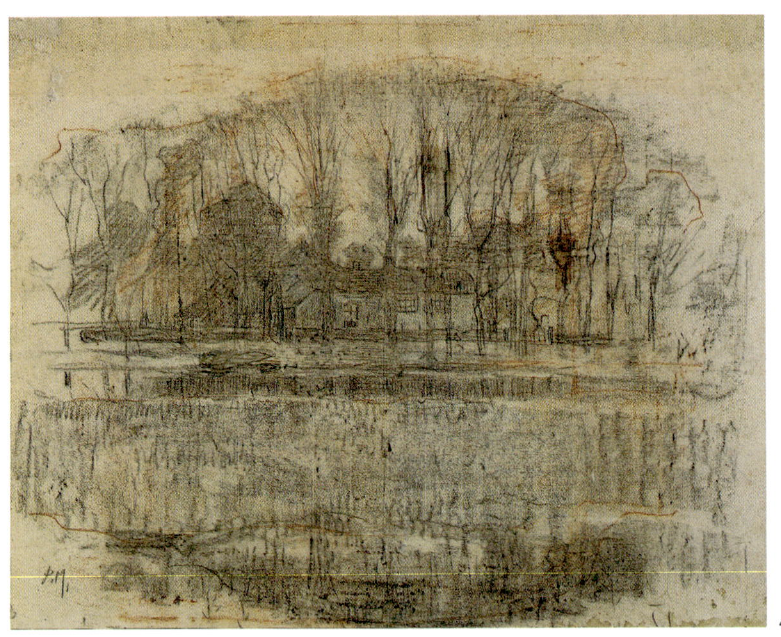

47

Cat. 47 *Geinrust Farm*, c. 1906
Crayon, sanguine, and pastel on paper
18.7 x 25.6 in. (47.5 x 65 cm)
Monogrammed lower left: P.M.
Gemeentemuseum, The Hague, bequest of Salomon B. Slijper, 1971, inv. T 74–1971 (A 440)

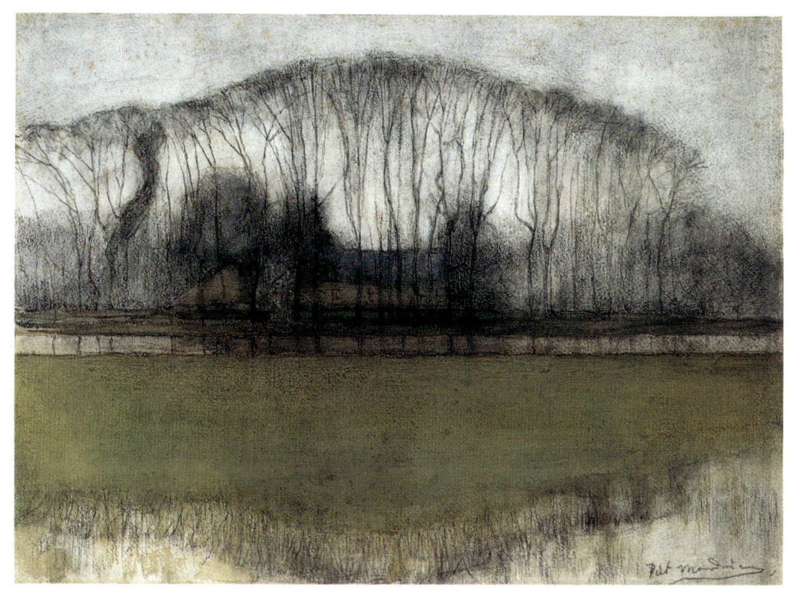

48

Cat. 48 *Geinrust Farm*, c. 1906
Watercolor, crayon, and pastel on paper
19.1 x 26.5 in. (48.5 x 67.2 cm)
Signed lower right: *Piet Mondriaan*
Frans Halsmuseum, Haarlem, inv. no. 455 (A 441)

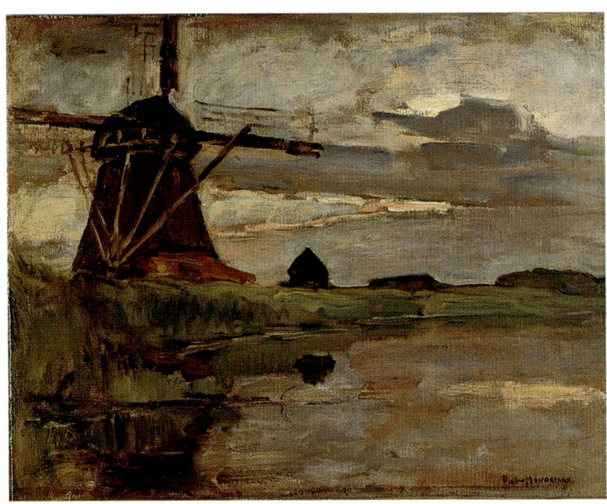

49

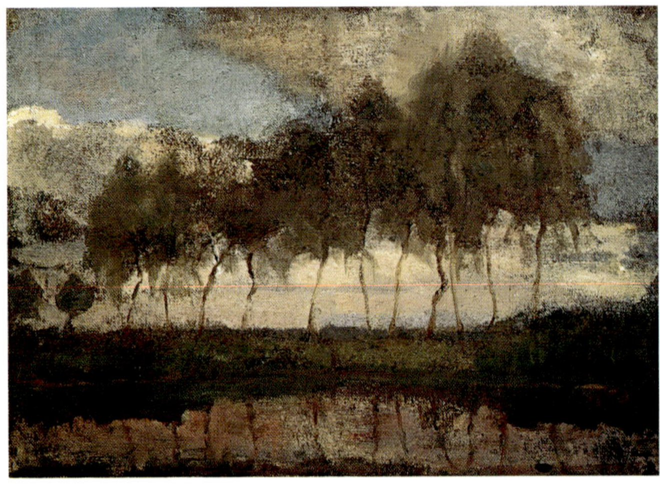

50

Cat. 49 *Oostzijdse Mill on the Gein*, c. 1906–7
Oil on canvas mounted on panel
13.6 x 17.5 in. (34.5 x 44.5 cm)
Signed lower right: Piet MONDRIAAN.
Gemeentemuseum, The Hague, bequest of Salomon B. Slijper, 1971, inv. S 108–1971 (A 405)

Cat. 50 *The Gein: Trees along the Water*, 1906–7
Oil on canvas
17.7 x 26 in. (45 x 66 cm)
Not signed
Gemeentemuseum, The Hague, bequest of Salomon B. Slijper, 1971, inv. S 109–1971 (A 488)

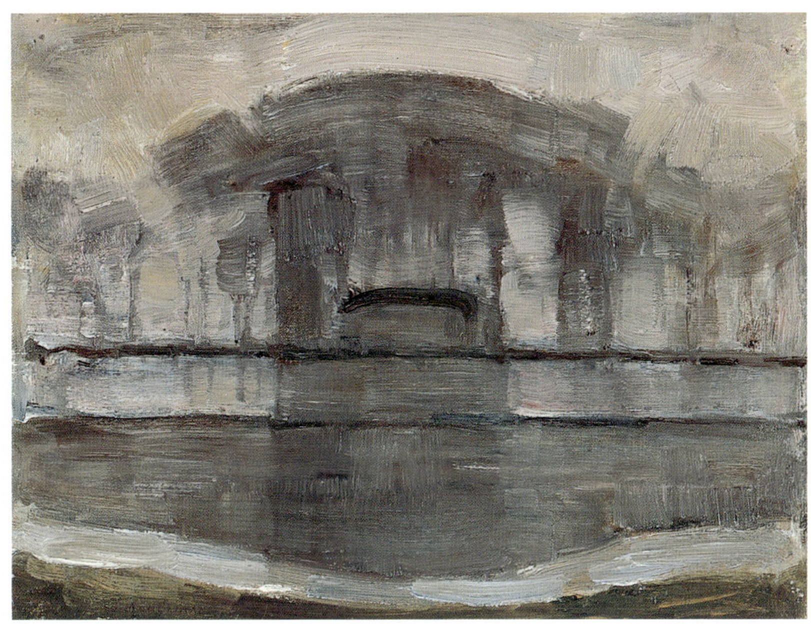

51

Cat. 51 *Geinrust Farm in the Haze*, 1906–7
Oil on canvas
12.8 x 16.7 in. (32.5 x 42.5 cm)
Signed lower left: P. MNDRIAAN *[sic]*
Gemeentemuseum, The Hague, bequest of Salomon B. Slijper, 1971,
inv. S 122–1971 (A 444)

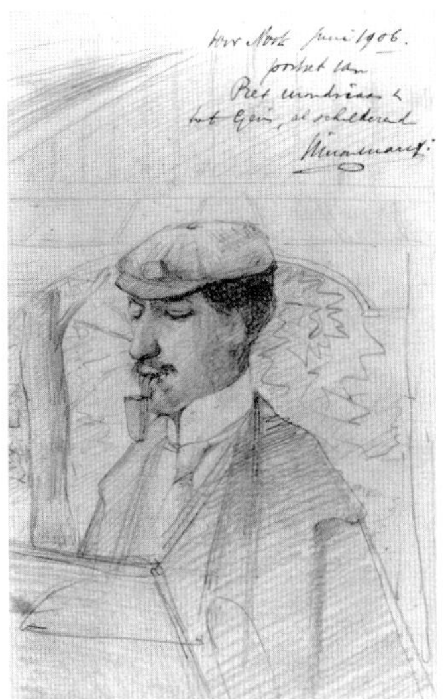

Fig. 30
Simon Maris, *Mondrian painting on the Gein*, 1906
Pencil drawing taken from a sketchbook
Gemeentemuseum, The Hague

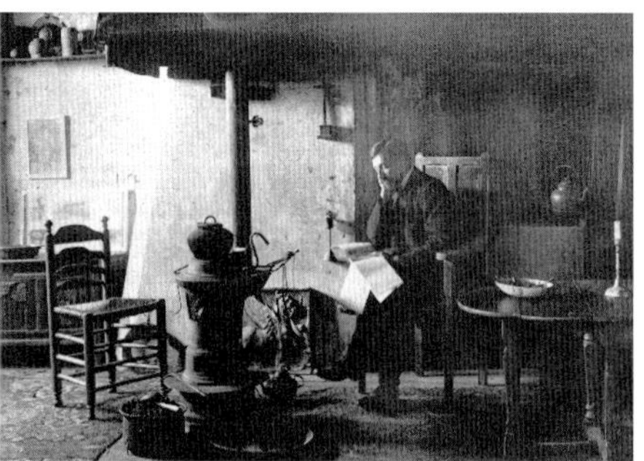

Fig. 29
Mondrian in his studio on the Rembrandtplein examining sketches
Gemeentemuseum, The Hague

vision. Significantly, it was at this time that Mondrian must have painted his studio white–a new studio on the Rembrandtplein, located on the top floor of the building that housed the Saint Lucas society (fig. 29).

With *Oostzijdse Mill on the Gein* (cat. 49), *The Gein: Trees along the Water* (cat. 50), and *Geinrust Farm in the Haze* (cat. 51), Mondrian experimented once again with the possibilities of oil painting.[92] Around 1906–7, he did not delve into this area as deeply as he did into drawing; his drawings were much more elaborate and precise. He relied on his virtuosity, which did not allow him immediately to attain the serenity that characterized his works on paper. It is tempting to see, in the perpendicularity and the verticality of the windmill's blades–just as in the repetition of the grove of trees–the seed of his nonfigurative art of the future. The rapport between the play of horizontal and vertical elements in the painting and ideas developed by the founder of the De Stijl group is easy to establish. In 1906–7, however, Mondrian was a long way away from what he would eventually become.

Through his concepts and his technique, he wisely remained centered within the limits of received knowledge. Only with *Geinrust Farm in the Haze* does one see Mondrian exploring something entirely new. In order to represent the farm surrounded by a grove of trees, he boldly limits himself to the use of a gray heightened by red, yellow, and blue in all areas but the foreground, where a small band of green evokes the naturalist mode. The farm is nestled behind the trees, which form a sort of vault or cocoon above it, adding to the serene character of the work.

With *Evening Mood on the Amstel (Omval)* (cat. 52) and *Open Landscape* (cat. 53) Mondrian exploits, in a more insistent manner, the formal as well as technical possibilities of a tonality that recalls his Brabant period. The contrasts are restrained, and only accents of green, red, blue, and yellow lend brightness to the work. In

92. These three works also show the characteristic holes made by tacks and, on the edges of the stretchers, a continuation of what was represented in the paintings. The same applies to *Farm at Duivendrecht* (cat. 38).

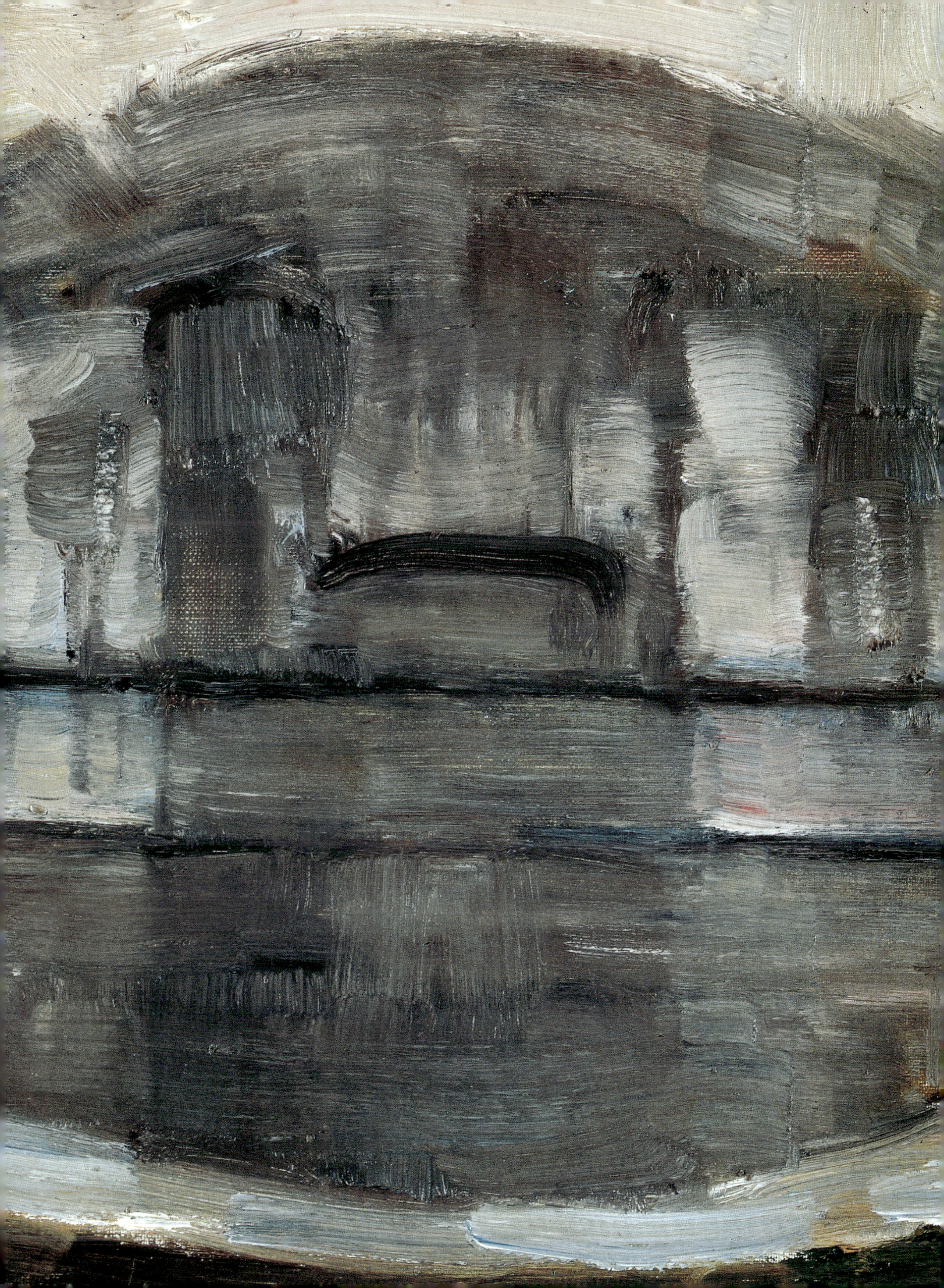

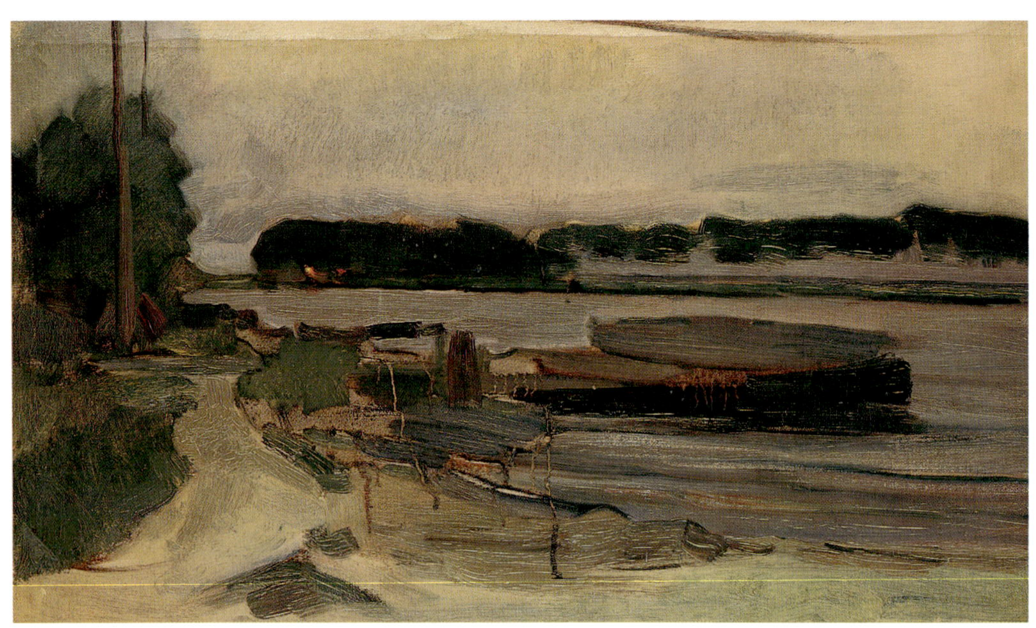
52

Cat. 52 *Evening Mood on the Amstel* (*Omval*), 1906–7
Oil on canvas
16.5 x 29.5 in. (42 x 75 cm)
Not signed
Gemeentemuseum, The Hague, bequest of
Salomon B. Slijper, 1971, inv. S 112–1971 (A 528)

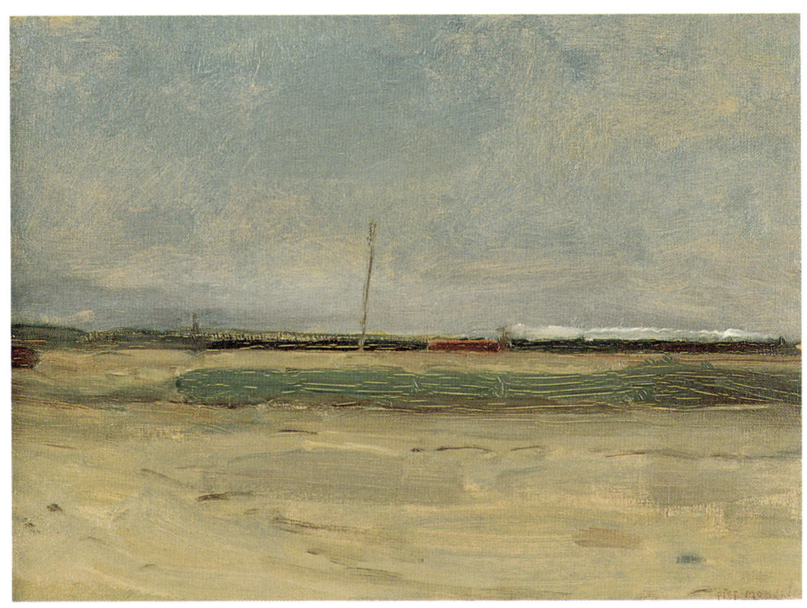

53

Cat. 53 *Open Landscape*, c. 1907
Oil on canvas
14 x 19.7 in. (35.5 x 50 cm)
Signed lower right: PIET MONDRIAAN
Musée d'Orsay, Paris, anonymous life-interest gift accepted by the State, 2000, inv. RF 2000–20 (A 515)

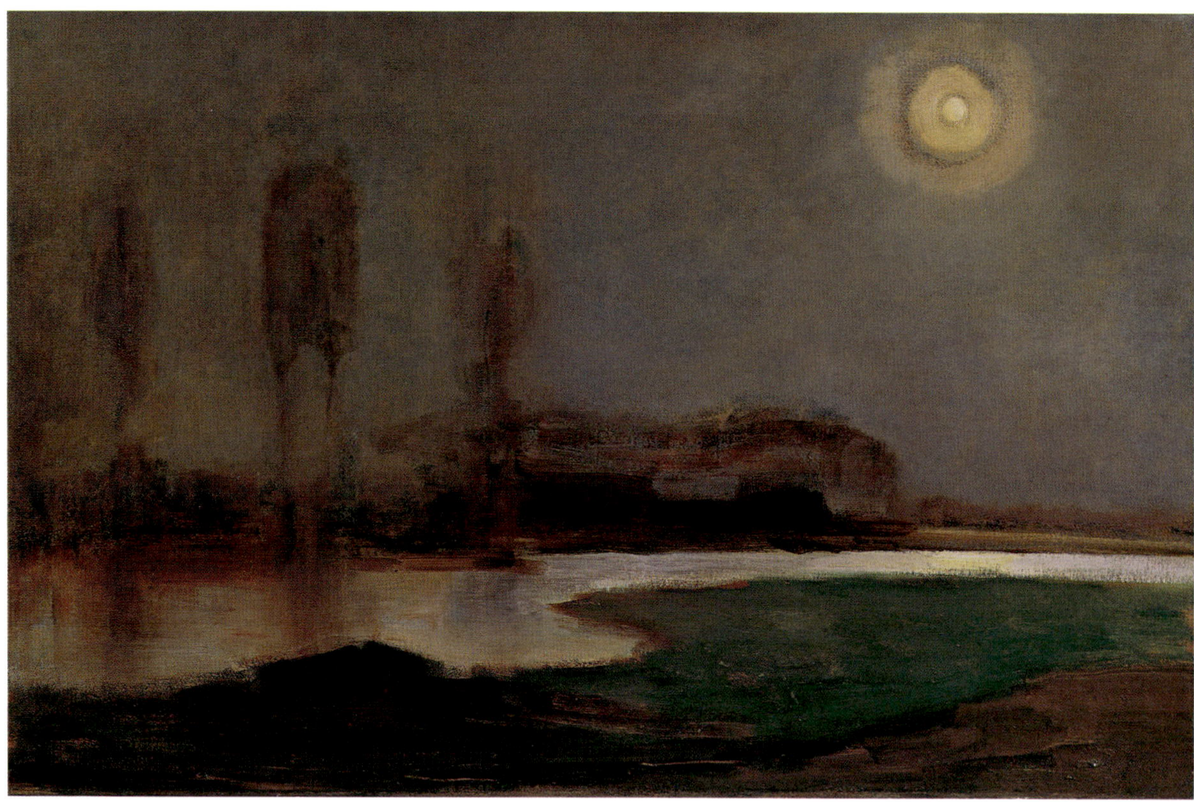

55

Evening Mood on the Amstel (Omval), the sky is brushed in with vertical strokes while the river and its boats are essentially rendered in horizontals. There are no indications that these works were ever exhibited. Until 1907, Mondrian's contributions to exhibitions remained limited to quite traditional still lifes, with which he was winning prizes (fig. 31)!

He was still utterly removed from artistic developments taking place elsewhere, especially those in Paris. It seems that even the comprehensive Vincent van Gogh exhibition that took place at the Stedelijk Museum in 1905, where, in addition to the early work, a large part of the painter's French period was represented, was completely wasted on Mondrian and his colleagues. Etha Fles had made it known as early as 1892 that Van Gogh marked a real rupture in everything the Dutch tradition valued and cherished. It is important not to underestimate how stubborn tradition can be.[93]

At the Arti exhibition in April 1907, the critic of *De Telegraaf*, Conrad Kikkert (1882–1965), was full of praise for *Zomernacht* (*Summer Night*) (cat. 55). He wrote: "Piet Mondrian (painting frightfully badly hung): a dream of a 'Summer Night.' A misty moon above a tall tree on the water's edge. In silvery tones of a violet white. The hole in the clouds–dark violet around the gilded moon–clashes, and has no form, no depth."[94] The lyrical language Kikkert uses testifies to a need to understand the art of Mondrian otherwise than through the customary jargon of the nineteenth-century critic. But his approach could not do

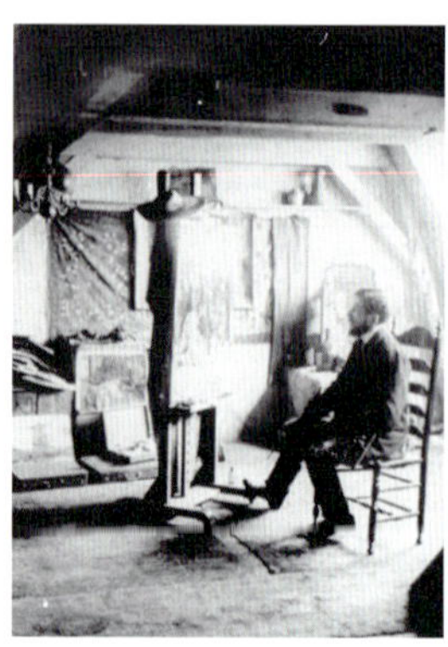

Fig. 31
Mondrian in his studio on the Rembrandtplein, in front of the still life [A 264] that won him the Willink van Collen Prize in 1906. Gemeentemuseum, The Hague

93. Etha Fles, "Vincent van Gogh, 1853–1890," *Algemeen Handelsblad*, December 23, 1892.
94. Conrad Kikkert, "Feuilleton Arti et Amicitiae," *De Telegraaf*, April 13, 1907. The first of Kikkert's critiques to which we referred was published on March 1, 1907, in the daily *De Telegraaf*. It concerns Gust van de Wall Perné, a friend and colleague of Mondrian. Kikkert had previously written articles of general criticism under the pseudonym C. A. Méléon.

Cat. 55 *Zomernacht* (*Summer Night*), 1907
Oil on canvas
28 x 43.5 in. (71 x 110. 5 cm)
Not signed
Gemeentemuseum, The Hague,
inv. S 3–1967 (A 523)

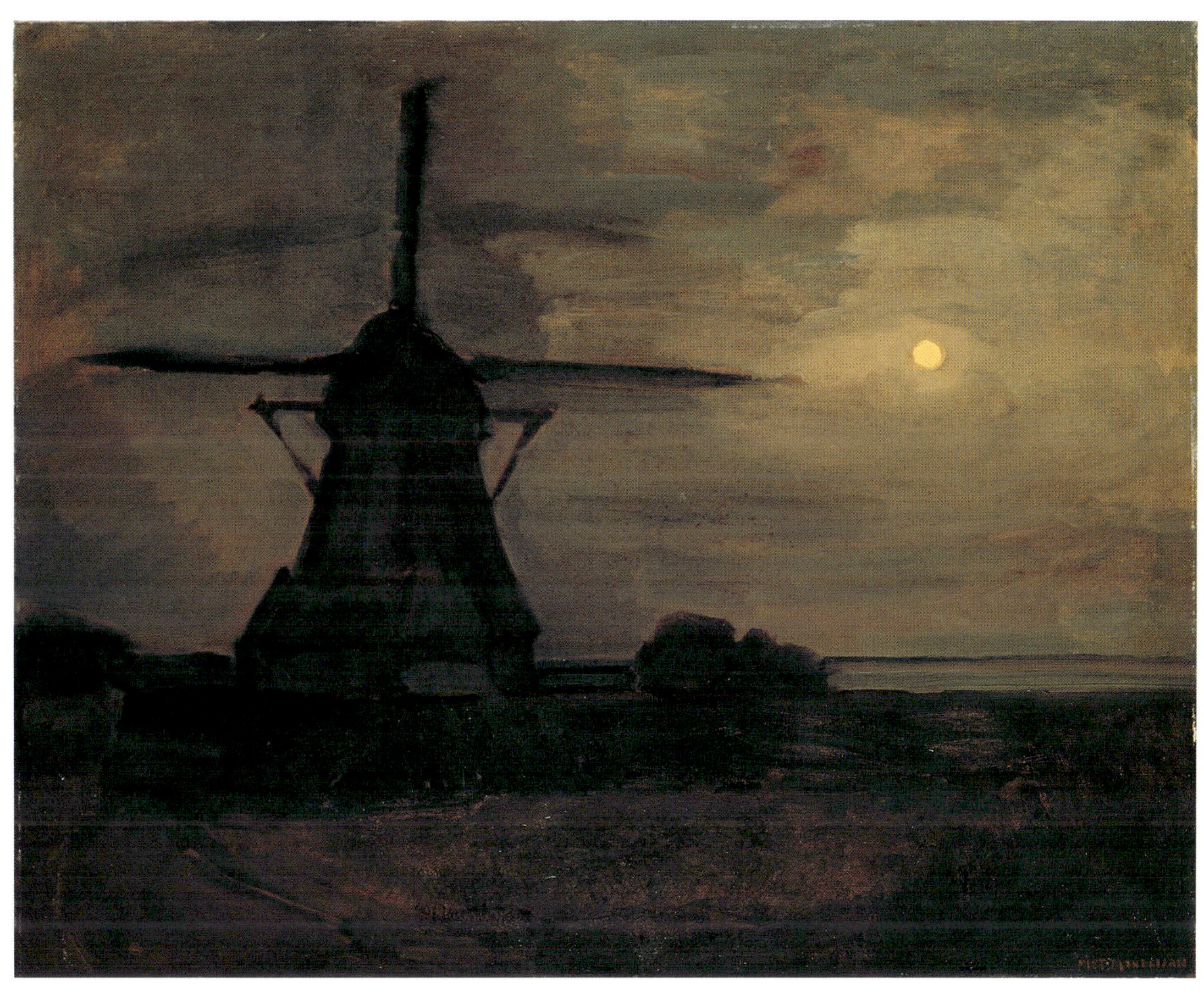
54

Cat. 54 *Oostzijdse Mill in Moonlight*, 1907
Oil on canvas
39.2 x 49.4 in. (99.5 x 125.5 cm)
Signed lower right: PI ET MONDRIAAN
Gemeentemuseum, The Hague, bequest of Salomon B. Slijper, 1971, inv. S 20–1939 (A 420)

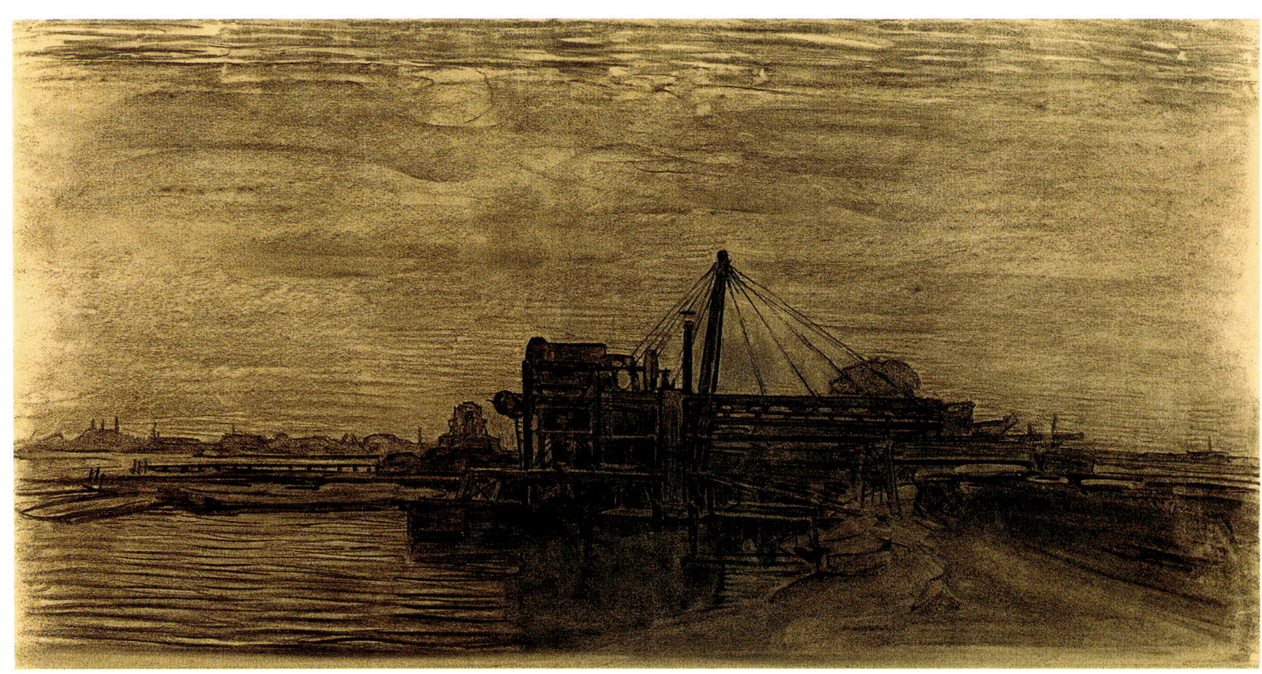
56

justice to the systematic vision that Mondrian had developed. In *Oostzijdse Mill in Moonlight* (cat. 54), the somber silhouette of the windmill hovers over a landscape of browns and greens. Mondrian creates volume by placing the nocturnal landscape in a basin-shaped foreground. Elsewhere, the image is flat, without depth, and full of subtle contrasts. The inward curve captures the eye, and leads it into the world of the painting. The highly detailed character of *Dredge* (cat. 56) and of *Amstel* (cat. 57) contradicts the theory that Mondrian conceived his designs on paper as final studies before the execution of versions in oil. Here again, we have autonomous works, as substantiated by the fact that Mondrian sold them soon after he had produced them. In *Fen near Saasveld* (cat. 58), the horizontal format reinforces the impression of serenity and splendor. It is one of the largest paintings Mondrian had produced up to that time, but the exact purpose of the venture remains obscure.

Toward 1906, Mondrian's philosophical reflections on his art must have become more profound, based on conclusions to which his work had led him. One conclusion must have been the need to think of the representation of nature as a mental transformation process brought about through the use of the materials of art. This was a thought that he had glimpsed in Goethe, Charles Blanc, and other theoreticians he encountered in the National Academy. Charles Blanc imagined nature as feminine–fortuitous and capricious– awaiting the entry into action of Spirit, which he imagined as masculine. The artist's task was to penetrate the Essence, to attain the ideal, that is, the permanent. He would thus escape individualism and materialism, both inherent in imitation, and rise to reign over the truly collective and universal.[95] Much more important, Mondrian had in fact come across these kinds of concepts in the subjects and the materials of his own work. It is also possible that, as early as 1906, he had met, through the Saint Lucas society, a group of artists who gained in importance in the following years, and who were to be close witnesses of his evolution toward a

95. Herbert Henkels was the first to establish the relationship between Mondrian's ideas and those of Charles Blanc, without suggesting, however, when Mondrian might have come into contact with Blanc's ideas. See Henkels 1980–81.

Cat. 56 *Dredge*, 1906–7
Charcoal and crayon on paper
22.4 x 44.2 in. (57 x 112 cm)
Not signed
Gemeentemuseum, The Hague, bequest of Salomon B. Slijper, 1971, inv. T 46–1971 (A 534)

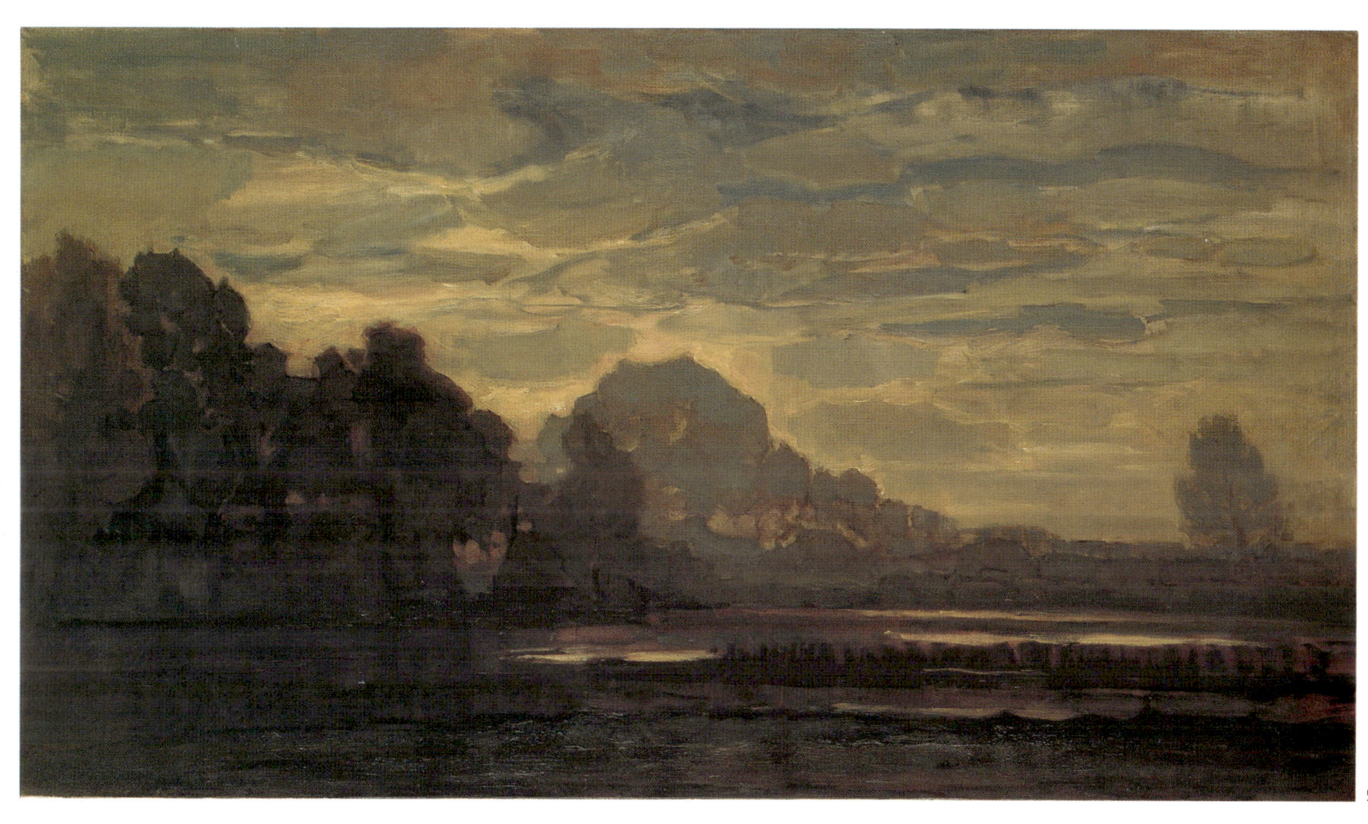

58

Cat. 58 *Fen near Saasveld,* 1907
Oil on canvas
40.1 x 71.1 in. (102 x 180.5 cm)
Signed lower left: *Piet Mondriaan.*
Gemeentemuseum, The Hague, bequest of Salomon
B. Slijper, 1971, inv. S 110–1971 (A 554)

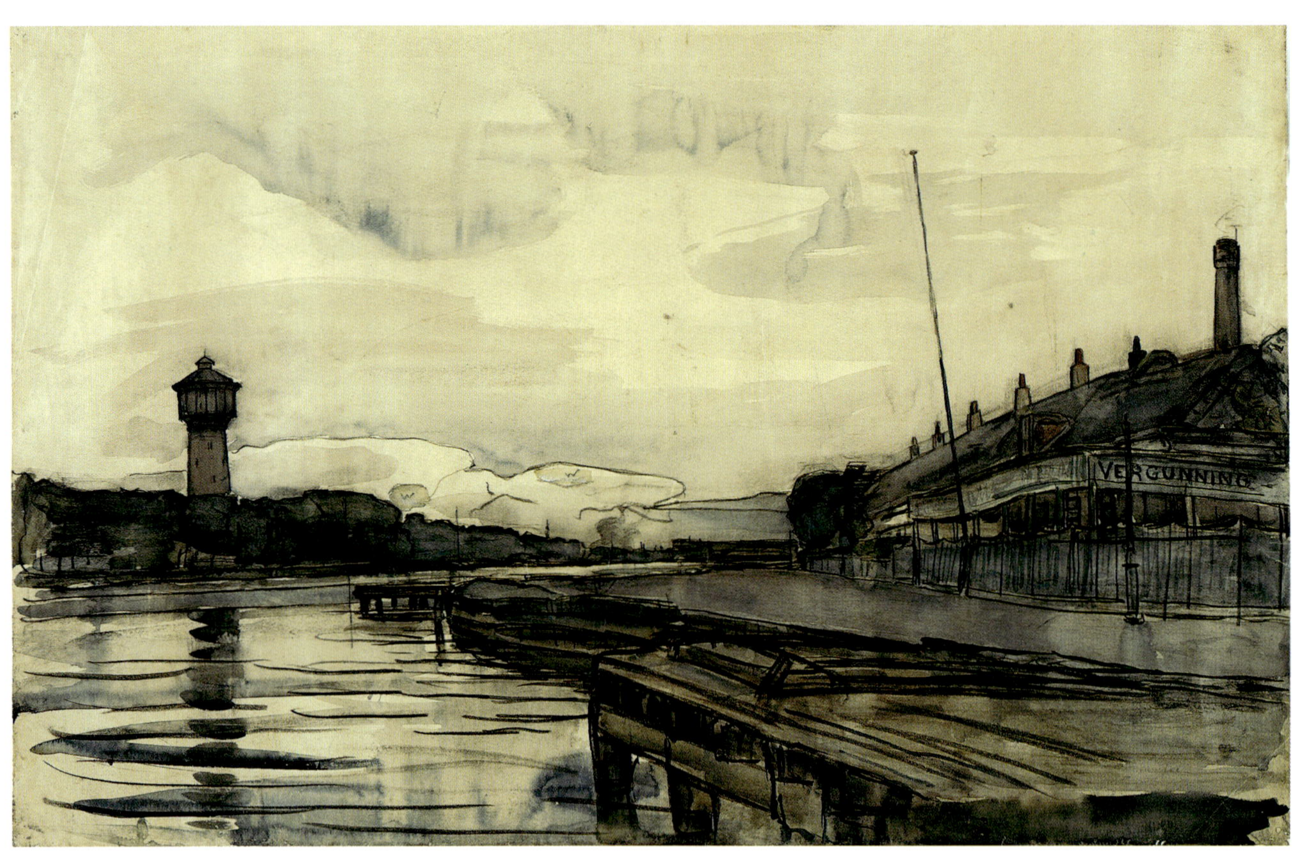

57

Cat. 57 *Amstel,* 1907
Charcoal and watercolor on paper
27.2 x 43.3 in. (69 x 110 cm) (image); 43.2 x 77 in. (109.8 x 195.6 cm) (support).
Not signed
The Museum of Modern Art, New York, gift of Sheldon H. Solow, bequest of Lillie P. Bliss (by exchange), inv. 388–84 (A 535)

Fig. 32
Photograph of Mondrian taken by Jacob Vetter, reproduced in Onze moderne meesters (Our Modern Masters), *by the critic F. M. Lurasco*
Work published by Chr. Veldt, 1907
Gemeentemuseum, The Hague

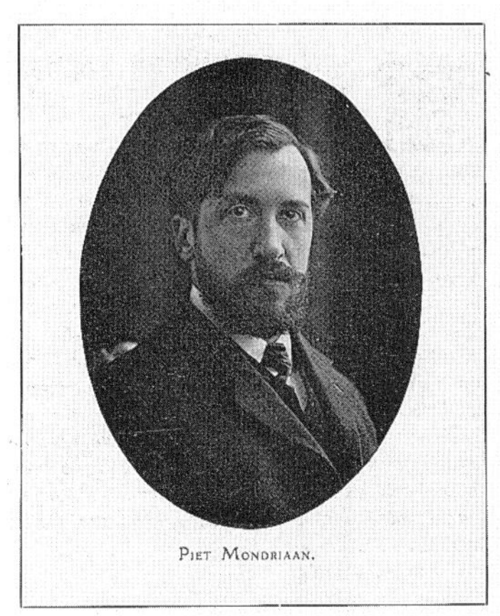

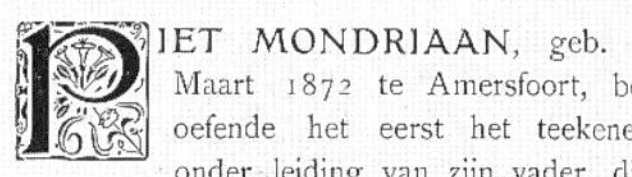

PIET MONDRIAAN, geb. 7 Maart 1872 te Amersfoort, beoefende het eerst het teekenen onder leiding van zijn vader, die er veel aan deed, toen ging hij op veertienjarigen leeftijd aan 't schilderen onder leiding van zijn oom, Frits Mondriaan uit Den Haag, te Winterswijk, waar deze kwam om buiten te schilderen, haalde de lagere en middelbare acte handteekenen, studeerde nog wat bij Joh. Braedt van Uberfeldt en ging dan voor drie jaar naar de Academie te Amsterdam. Toen arbeidde hij zelfstandig, maakte eerst figuur en landschap, later landschap alleen en had succes, zoowel op exposities als door verkoop.

Woonplaats Amsterdam.

more spiritual art: Cornelis Spoor (1867–1928), Jacoba van Heemskerck (1876–1923), and Gust van de Wall Perné (1877–1911). The fact that Mondrian and these artists sent works to Dresden together in 1905, and submitted others at the instigation of the art dealer Emil Richter, for the official visit of Queen Wilhelmina, leads us to believe that they already knew each other—and perhaps Jan Sluijters as well.[96]

The year 1907 was a year of scandals and rupture in the history of Dutch art. It started with an exhibition of the work of Jan Sluijters, produced in Paris with the money from his Prix de Rome, and showing the definite influence of Divisionism and Fauvism, styles completely contrary to the Dutch spirit. Critics, thirsting for sensationalism, began to create ripples in the peaceful waters of the Dutch art world. Jan Toorop moved to Amsterdam, which gave the city a new opportunity to become acquainted with artistic developments abroad. In Amsterdam in June, Toorop showed some of his new, divisionist works, mostly smaller drawings; and at Saint Lucas, one could see the work of Ferdinand Hodler (1853–1918), which was mostly early work. Kees van Dongen (1877–1968) also arrived in Amsterdam, sent by Parisian art dealers to look into the possibility of organizing an exhibition on van Gogh in Paris. He failed, but art circles in Amsterdam discovered his anarchic work, which they had only read about in the newspapers. Mondrian remained imperturbable for the moment. His contribution to the Saint Lucas exhibits no longer consisted of mere still lifes, but the critics were still not convinced: ". . . this is a very sensitive and extremely gifted artist who does not cheat, but who, alone against all the others, will not weather the storm."[97]

When, at last, he entered *Amstel* (cat. 57) in an Arti exhibition, he was told with contempt that it was above all in recognition of his good will that the work was accepted. The critics seemed impatient. Mondrian was a painter with a reputation, as much in Saint Lucas as in Arti, and he was known for his demanding art-philosophical bent. The work that he presented did not correspond to this image. At that moment, in his studio on the Albert Cuypstraat, however, he was occupied by something completely different from what he showed in public demonstrations and exhibitions. At least this is what his submission to a commission headed by Willem Maris for the Royal Subsidy competition at the beginning of April leads us to believe. When Simon, Maris's son, asked what the reaction of the commission was, his father's judgment was damning: "Bah! It was mediocre; if [Mondrian] intends to compete again next year, he will have to present a more important entry and at least five works. He should submit studies

96. See the information provided by the daily *De Telegraaf*, October 11, 1906 (evening edition). It is not exactly known what Mondrian contributed. Since 1901, Cornelis Spoor had been a voting member of the Saint Lucas society; Jacoba van Heemskerck was certainly an associate member from 1908, and Gust van de Wall Perné was a voting member from 1904, as Jan Sluijters had been since 1903.

97. Conrad Kikkert, "Schilderkunst.: De Stedelijke Vierjaarlijksche, 3" ("Painting: The Stedelijk Quadrennial, 3"), *De Telegraaf*, September 15, 1907 (second leaflet).

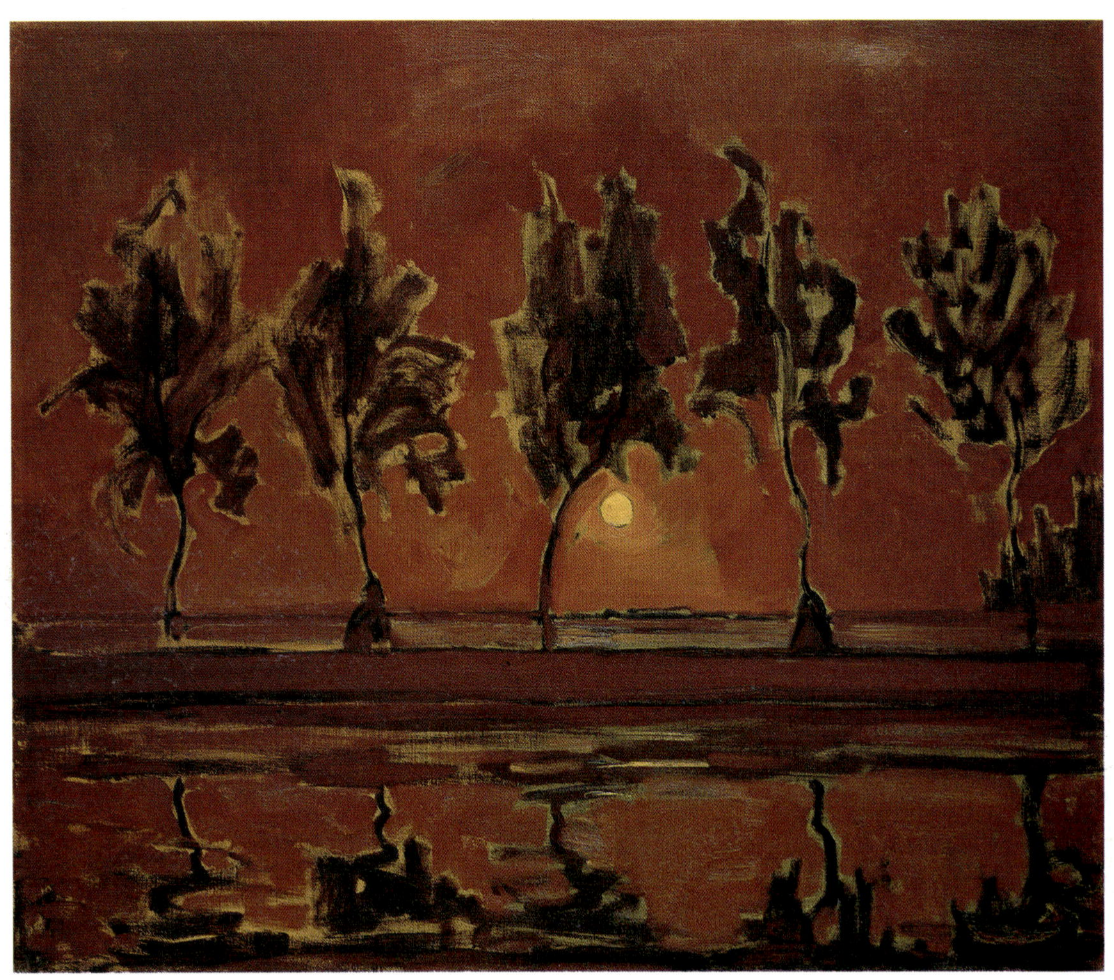

59

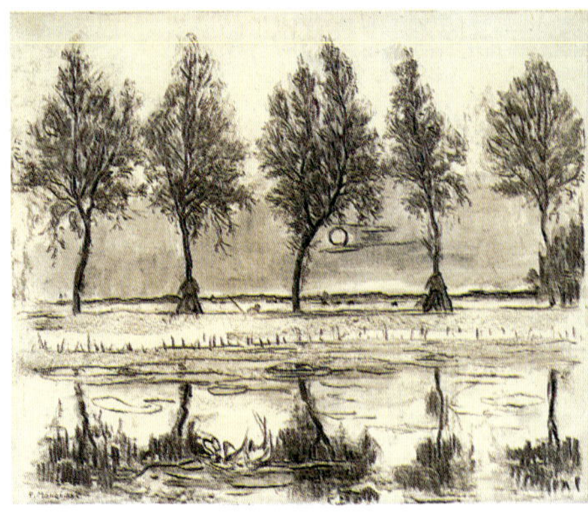

Fig. 33
Piet Mondrian, *Trees on the Gein: Moonrise*, 1907
Pencil on paper
Gemeentemuseum, The Hague (A 659)

Cat. 59 *Trees on the Gein: Moonrise*, 1907
Oil on canvas
31.1 x 36.4 in. (79 x 92.5 cm)
Not signed
Gemeentemuseum, The Hague, gift of Albert van den Briel, inv. S 59–1956 (A 660)

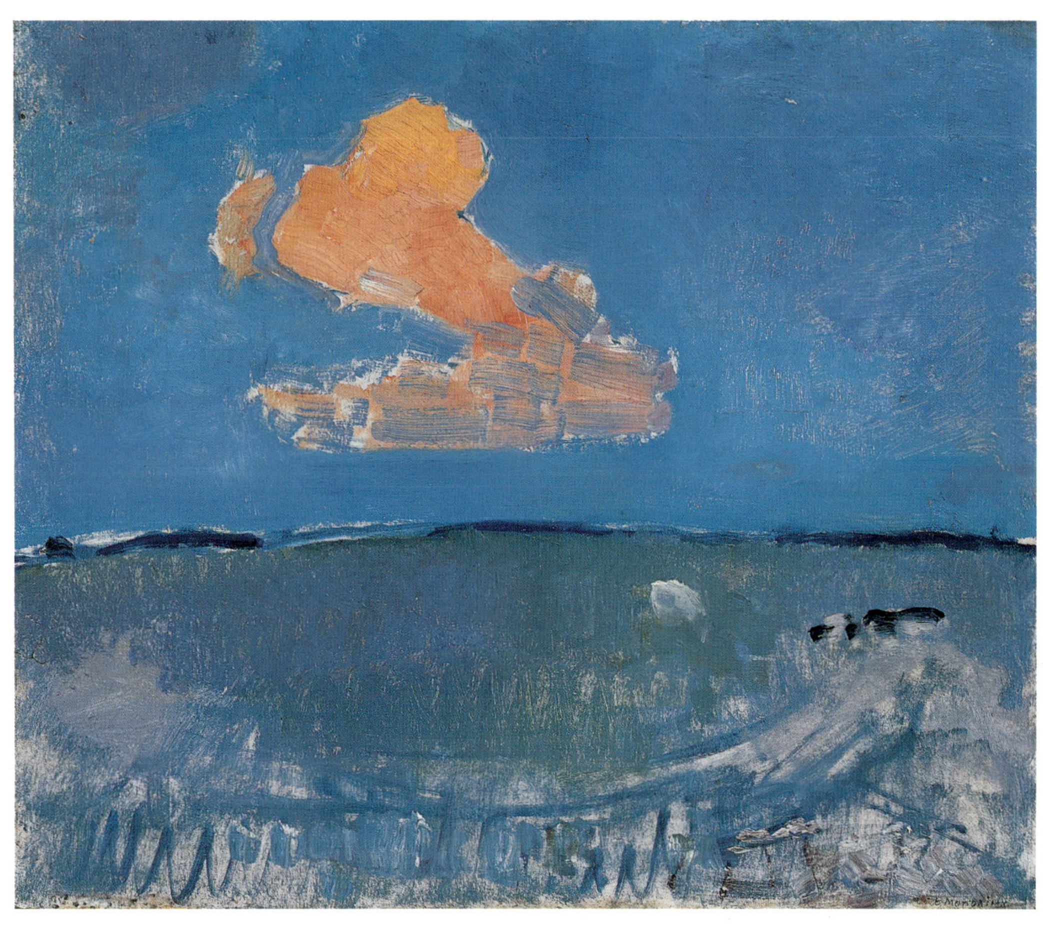
60

painted in a more detailed fashion or accomplished paintings. What he submitted was not appreciated by anyone."[98]

It was probably around this time (1907) that Mondrian painted *Trees on the Gein: Moonrise* (cat. 59), *The Red Cloud* (cat. 60), and *Oak Trees at Dusk* (cat. 61), oils that bear, in different ways, the characteristics of sketches, the fleeting qualities. *Trees on the Gein: Moonrise* appears to have been painted on raw canvas, all in one session: the golden yellow, the green, the brown, and the black applied in the beginning melted together completely naturally to obtain the nuances of the final red brown. The little trees that give rhythm to the painting were a particularly prized and poetic component of the landscape along the banks of the Gein. Mondrian also made a detailed chalk drawing of them (fig. 33)–once again, this is more than a study and could be considered an independent drawing–in which the linear qualities of the motif are more minutely examined than in the painting. The human presence is completely missing in the painting, and the qualities of the brushstroke are replaced by modeling. Moonlight has attained the stature of a subject in its own right.

Cat. 60 *The Red Cloud*, 1907
Oil on paper mounted on panel
25.2 x 29.5 in. (64 x 75 cm)
Signed lower right: *Piet MonDRI AAn*
Gemeentemuseum, The Hague, gift of Albert van den Briel, inv. S 23–1956 (A 569)

98. Letter from Willem Maris to his son Simon of March 15, 1908. Simon Maris Archives, RKD, The Hague. The prize was ultimately awarded to A. Briët. See *De Telegraaf*, April 16, 1908 (morning edition).

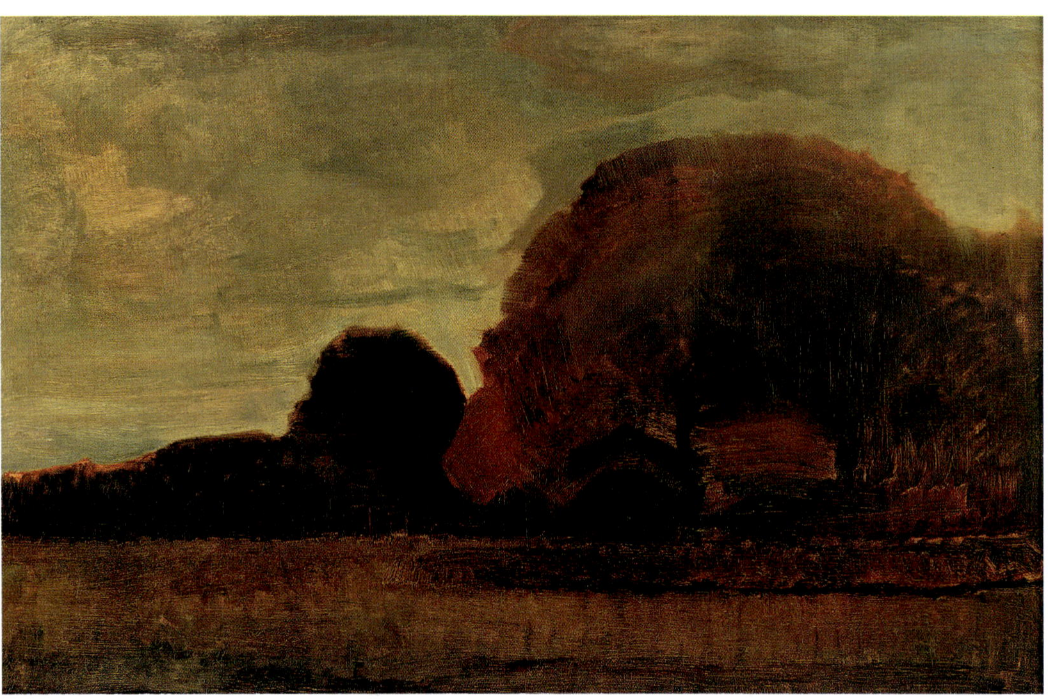
61

The Red Cloud (cat. 60) and *Oak Trees at Dusk* (cat. 61) are equally rapidly painted, apparently in one session. While this latter work is compact and dense, painted in sallow tones, and without depth, there exists a meticulously drawn and very detailed version that exploits in full the possibilities of space. It leaves no doubt that Mondrian, seeking the limits of perception, was once again determined in these works to oppose the absence of tonal relief with the clear and profound affirmation of lines. In *The Red Cloud* this research led him to another apogee of his art. The landscape is constructed of a blue applied with brio and lightness of touch over a greenish prairie; the brushstroke, lively and zigzagging, follows the original dark blue outline, still visible here and there. The horizon line, curved slightly, is painted with several heavy strokes of a dark blue. The sky is a vivid blue. The cloud is above all given space by the curved form of the landscape, which spreads out below, a device already used in *Oostzijdse Mill in Moonlight* (cat. 54). The bright, complementary orange of the cloud is like a breath of air across the image and counterbalances the brief notation of the cattle below.

The reasons for the sudden appearance of this new aesthetic in Mondrian's work are not entirely clear. It appears that he broke radically at this time with his earlier "twilight landscapes" and converted to an expressive style intended to convey an impression. It is generally agreed, following the opinion of Aleid Loosjes-Terpstra, that this turnabout is tied to two discoveries: that of the modernist, arbitrary use of colors in the work of Sluijters, and that of the drawings of Van Dongen, exhibited in July and August in Amsterdam at the galleries of C. M. van Gogh. The Ferdinand Hodler exhibition that took place in July 1907 at Saint Lucas has also been mentioned. None of these events was ever

Cat. 61 *Oak Trees at Dusk*, 1907
Oil on canvas
36.6 x 57.1 in. (93 x 145 cm)
Not signed
Private collection (A 590)

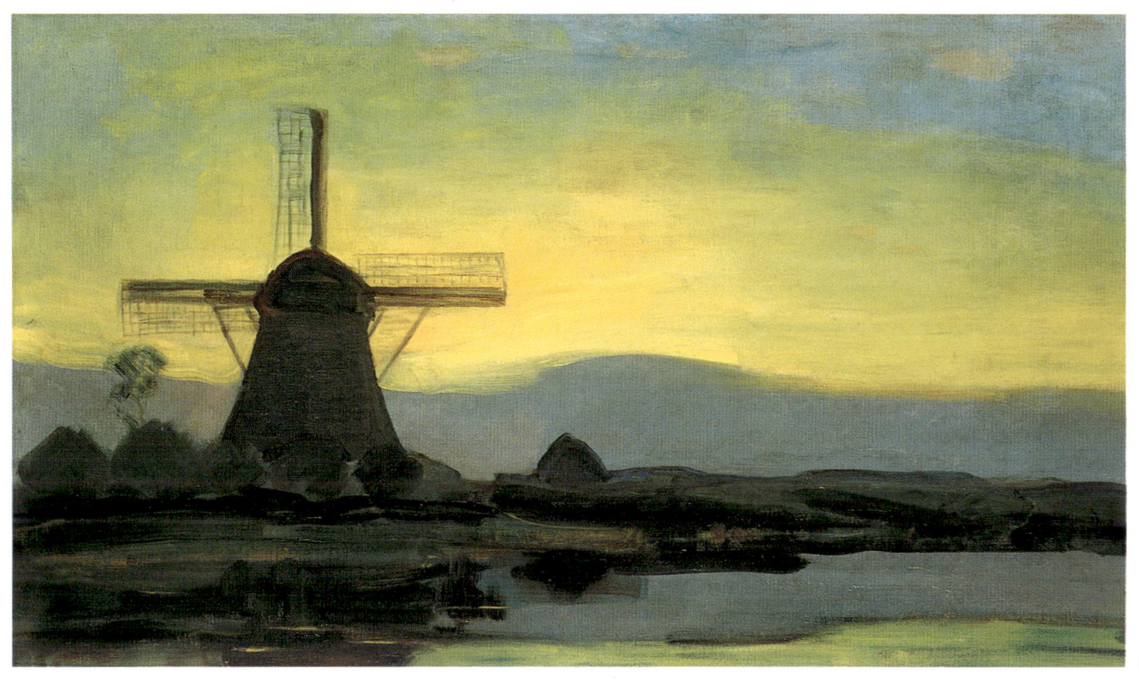

62

Cat. 62 *Mill in the Evening*, 1907–8
Oil on canvas
26.6 x 46.3 in. (67.5 x 117.5 cm)
Signed lower left: PIET MONDRIAAN.
Gemeentemuseum, The Hague, bequest of Salomon B. Slijper, 1971, inv. S 75–1971 (A 411)

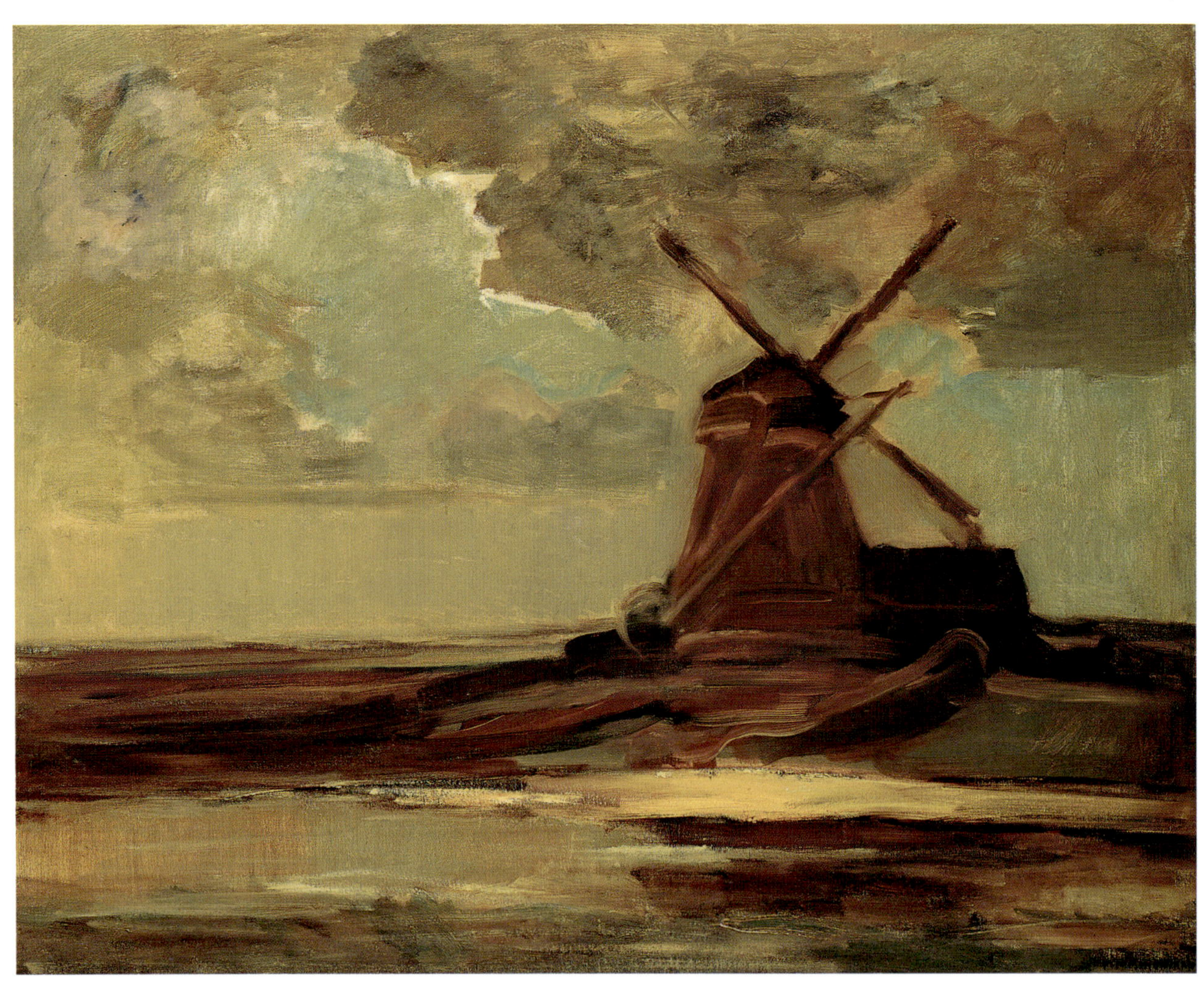
64

Cat. 64 *Oostzijdse Mill*, 1908
Oil on canvas
39 x 47.2 in. (99 x 120 cm)
Signed lower right: PIET MONDRIAAN.
Private collection (A 418)
Fort Worth only

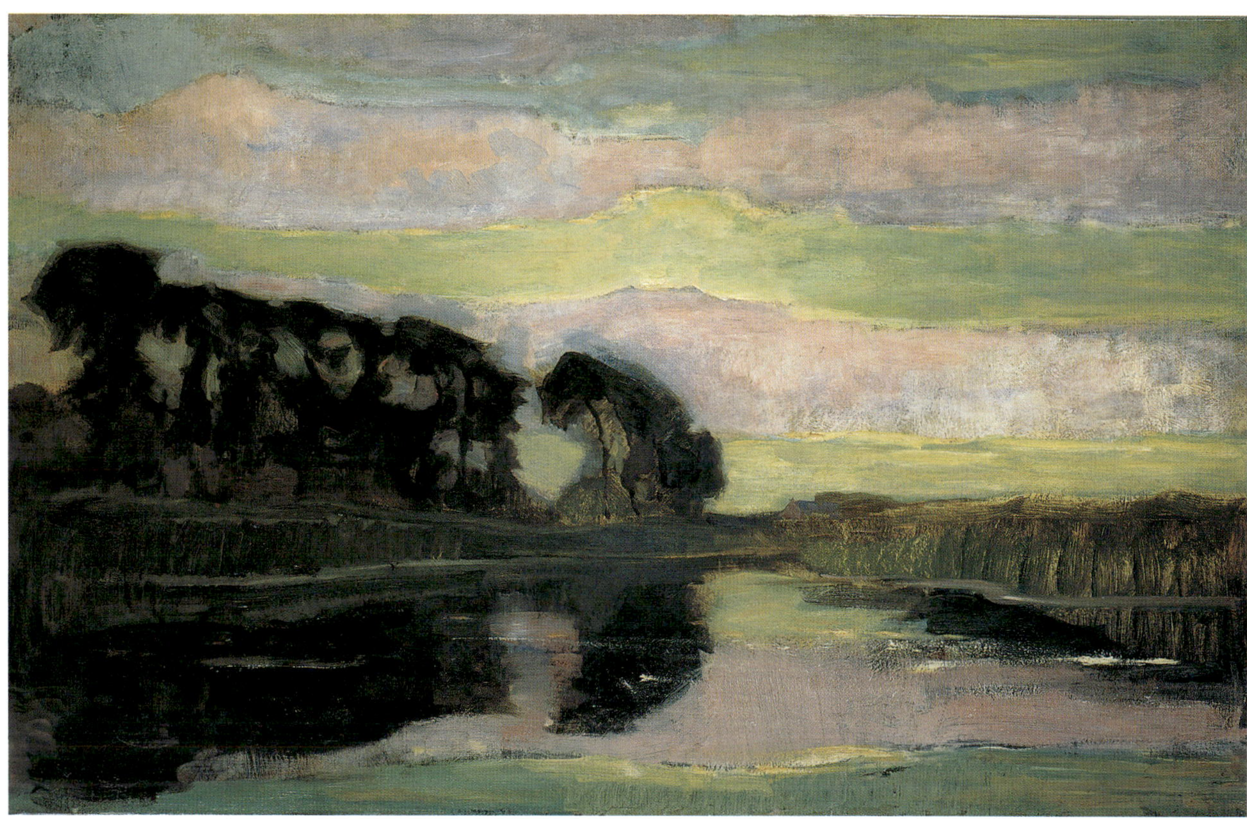

63

referred to by Mondrian himself, however, and it is perfectly possible, even most plausible, that the works in question were experiments made in the intimacy of the studio by an artist who, for years, had worked systematically to explore the potentialities of certain means of expression. In the case of *The Red Cloud*–for which, fairly characteristically, no drawings are known–we are dealing with the results of experiments made in Twente.[99] It is an oil sketch like those Mondrian made so often, and it illustrates perfectly the words of van den Briel:

Mondrian painted like Mondrian, because he could not paint otherwise. . . And always this instinct for self-derision, when, suddenly, he began to work in a different manner, carried away as if by a wave, and the need to begin to understand what happened himself, because this new condition implied a denunciation of his earlier work.[100]

The artist must not have shown any of these paintings before the major exhibition that he organized with Spoor and Sluijters in 1909 at the Stedelijk Museum.

Mondrian disclosed certain aspects of his new style for the first time in 1908, when he entered *Avond* (*Evening*) (cat. 65) in the Arti exhibition of April, and then, shortly afterward, in the Saint

Cat. 63 *Large Landscape*, 1907–8
Oil on canvas
29.5 x 47.2 in. (75 x 120 cm)
Not signed
Gemeentemuseum, The Hague, bequest of
Salomon B. Slijper, 1971, inv. S 111–1971 (A 497)

99. The painting is on cardboard and identical in format to a group of sketches that Mondrian made on the same material—which he acquired specially and brought with him to the Twente in the period 1906–8.
100. Henkels 1988, 46–47.

Lucas exhibit. The paintings *Oostzijdse Mill* (cat. 64), *Zomerdag* (*Summer Day*) (cat. 66), *Mill in the Evening* (cat. 62), and *Large Landscape* (cat. 63) are all treated in the same style. When Mondrian wrote in 1942, "I forsook natural color for pure color. I had come to feel that the colors of nature could not be reproduced on canvas. Instinctively, I felt that painting had to find a new way to express the beauty of nature,"[101] his statement applied to this group of paintings.

Certain critics thought that Mondrian had temporarily lost his mind and that he was more "the man of grays and refined hues" than a Hercules of color.[102] Others were of the opinion that he was trying to command support through the sensationalist–and therefore disturbing–modernism of a painter such as Sluijters.[103] The crucial question was always whether Mondrian could have seen things this way in nature, or not. Only the change in his use of color was commented on. Nobody noticed the equally thorough schematization in the use of paint.

The May 1908 Saint Lucas exhibition was an important moment. Conrad Kikkert described the works shown by Toorop—eleven of his latest paintings, remarkable for their "fierce touch of luminous color";[104] by Sluijters; and by Mondrian as a new aspiring to "another light; to open air; to atmospheres of a different color; to a more liberated, more exuberant, more passionate rendering of style; to making an appeal on the technical level to the decomposition of color; to a rapid, direct touch; to a very particular, personal line."[105] "Dutch Luminism," as the movement was quickly baptized, has always been traced back to French influences, notably Fauvism. Kees van Dongen, who lived in Paris, has been considered the link, along with Sluijters, who had also lived there for a while. But it is important to emphasize that the Luminism of Amsterdam was not a cohesive movement, endowed with a clearly defined program. Mondrian, from the beginning, had very little in common with Sluijters, who deliberately drowned himself in color.[106] It is quite possible that Mondrian admired Van Dongen's approach–he even mentions him in his autobiographical statement of 1941–but he had had only a single, relatively short meeting with him, as he pointed out later in a letter to van Doesburg.[107] Again, it is essential not to lose sight of the solid tradition from which Mondrian emerged. Even more than Sluijters–who, until 1906, was enthusiastic for the work of Böcklin, von Stuck, and the Pre-Raphaelites–Mondrian had his feet solidly anchored in the Dutch tradition of landscape painting. Mondrian, as we have demonstrated above, found his roots not just in the Hague school of painting, but further back, in Dutch realism of the seventeenth-century.[108] Perception, the concentrated observation of the timeless and unchanging by way of the specific, lay at the heart of this realism. Light played a crucial role here, creating space and rendering visible the Divine perspective.[109]

101. Mondrian 1942.
102. Conrad Kikkert, "Saint Lucas," *De Telegraaf*, May 7, 1908.
103. Willem Steenhoff, "Tentoonstelling van Saint Lucas, 3," *Der Amsterdammer Weekblad*, June 7, 1908.
104. Kikkert 1908, 239–40.
105. Ibid.
106. See the letters of Jan Sluijters to Kees Spoor in van Ginneken and Joosten 1970, 207, 263–65, and from Mondrian to Simon Maris, in Gorter, van Burkom, and Joosten 1998–99, no. 3, 40–41.
107. Letter from Piet Mondrian to Theo van Doesburg, April 4, 1922. Van Doesbug Archives, RKD, The Hague.
108. Streng 1994, 236–50.
109. Bakker 1993, 97–115, and Leeflang 1994, 18–32.

Chapter Six

1908–1910

"It seems to me that clarity of thought should be accompanied by clarity of technique."[110]

Hans Janssen and Joop M. Joosten

The evening landscapes, of which *Evening (Avond)* (cat. 65) is a fine example, inspire a feeling of timelessness and transcendence associated with the light at the end of the day. The paintings *Woods near Oele* (cat. 67), *Devotion* (cat. 68), and *Mill in Sunlight* (cat. 69) all have a profusion of light as their subject. Through their subjects they evoke the "radiance" seen as a principle of composition for the first time in *Village Church* (cat. 15), in 1898. This principle served to render symbolic content visible. In *Woods near Oele,* rays of sunlight piercing the clouds set the woods ablaze. In *Devotion,* the glow is linked to the meandering design, a transformation of paint into devotedness, and in *Mill in Sunlight,* it results from a frontal blow to the eye, a pitiless effect of backlighting, the most physical manner of making radiance visible.

The strange and rough character of *Woods near Oele* takes us by surprise. Like *Devotion,* it has been often likened to the work of the Norwegian painter Edvard Munch. The similarity is based on the elongated strokes of paint that seem to exist independently from what is represented and to reinforce the evocation of spiritual meanings. However, Mondrian could never have encountered the work of Munch, who was not discovered in Holland until much later, and who had never even been the object of a review or description, let alone any kind of reproduction. Even more

110 Querido 1910, as translated in Welsh and Joosten 1969, 10.

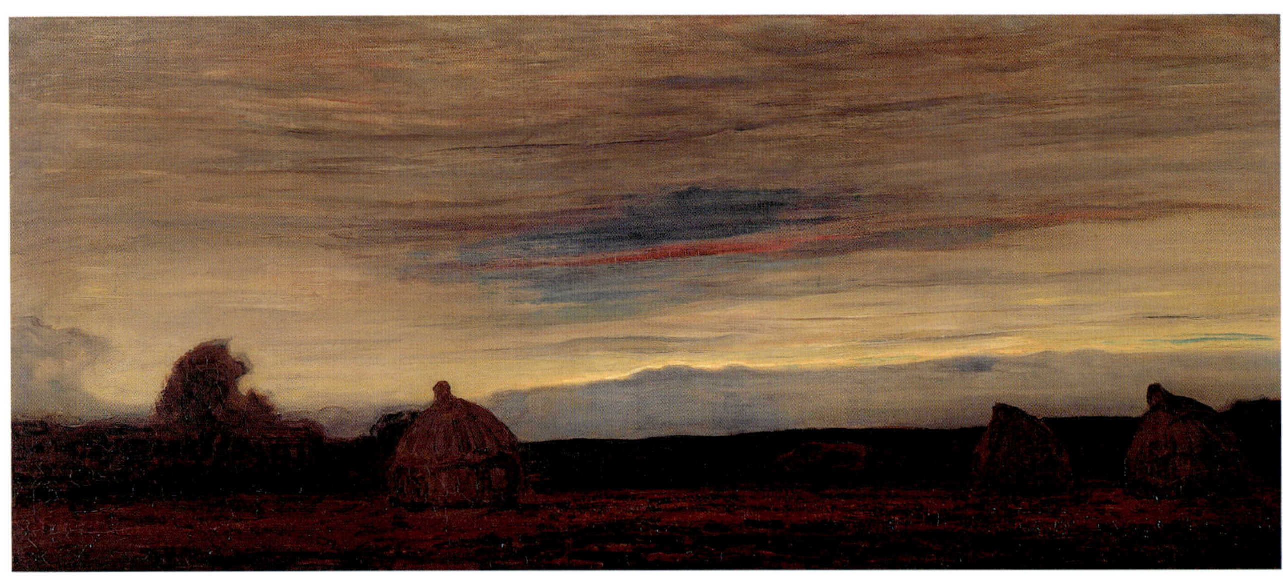
65

than the facture, the striking correspondence between this Mondrian and the work of Munch is the rather premature decision, as in *The Red Cloud,* to consider the work finished. Mondrian always outlined his paintings in a very thin paint wash, with which he drew on the canvas. Then, over that sketch, he laid in his surfaces and, if necessary, worked in the details. In *Woods near Oele,* this process is combined with partially finished, scattered painting in which touches of color are placed next to each other without mixing.

Devotion goes even further. The fluid trace of the first drawing was completed not by surfaces of color but by an abundant flow of lines, reminiscent of the shorter hatching found in the last works of van Gogh, some of which were shown in Amsterdam in September and October 1908 at the galleries of C. M. van Gogh.

In *Mill in Sunlight* (cat. 69) one again senses van Gogh in the staccato rhythm of little brushstrokes and in the red and blue graphic traces that describe the windmill. The repetitive use of the palette knife, notably for the yellow and blue sky, again evokes Toorop. In the 1880s, Toorop had learned from Guillaume Vogels, his teacher in Brussels, that it was possible to evoke the spiritual by mastering the use of the palette knife to suggest the play of shadows and light. Mondrian and Toorop almost certainly discussed this topic

Cat. 65 *Avond* (*Evening*), 1908
Oil on canvas
32.3 x 76 in. (82 x 193 cm)
Signed lower left: *Piet Mondriaan'08*
Private collection (A 561)
Fort Worth only

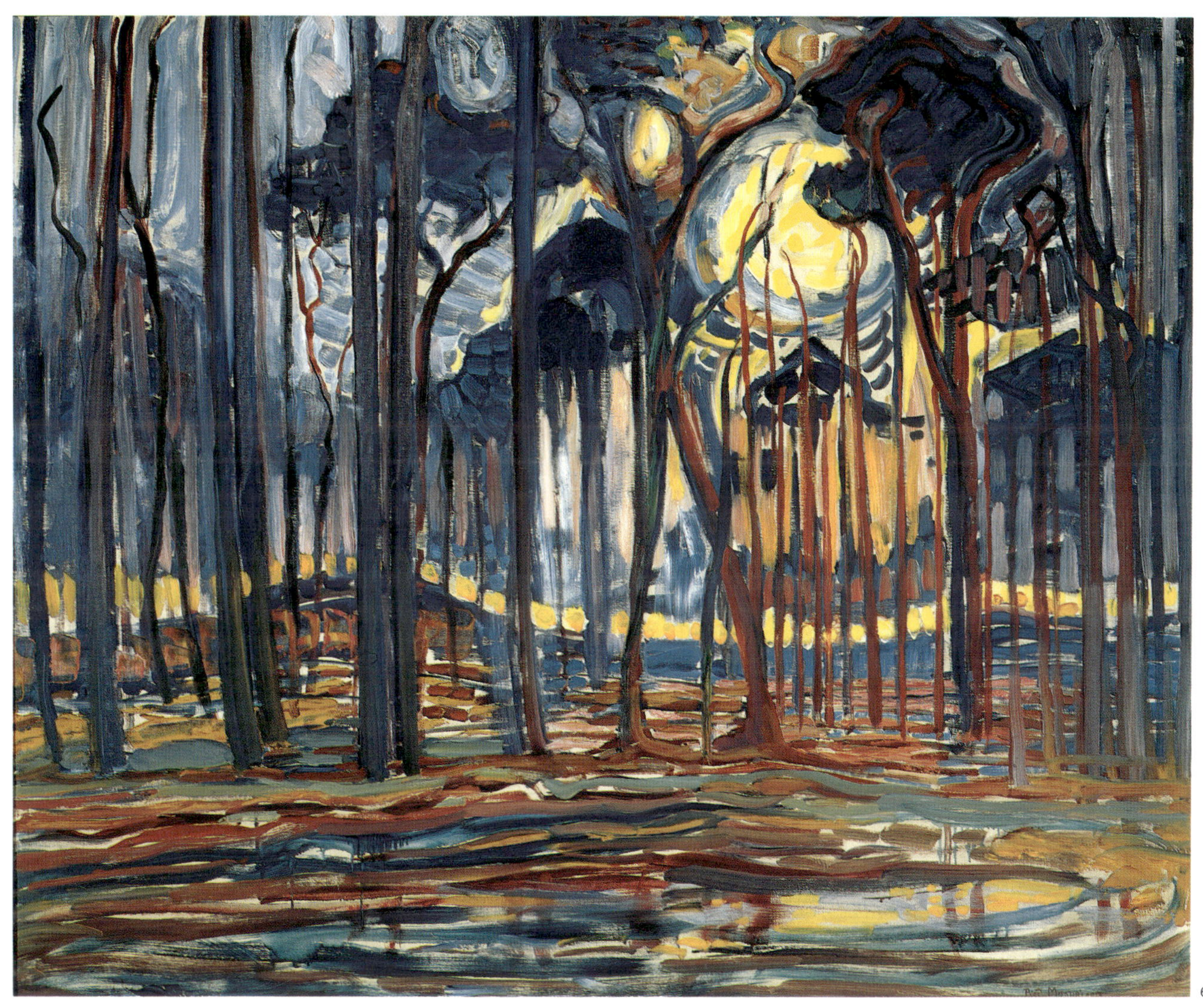
67

Cat. 67 Bosch (*Woods near Oele*), 1908
Oil on canvas
50.4 x 62.2 in. (128 x 158 cm)
Signed lower right: *PI ET MONDRIAAN.*
Gemeentemuseum, The Hague, bequest of Salomon
B. Slijper, 1971, inv. S 126–1971 (A 593)

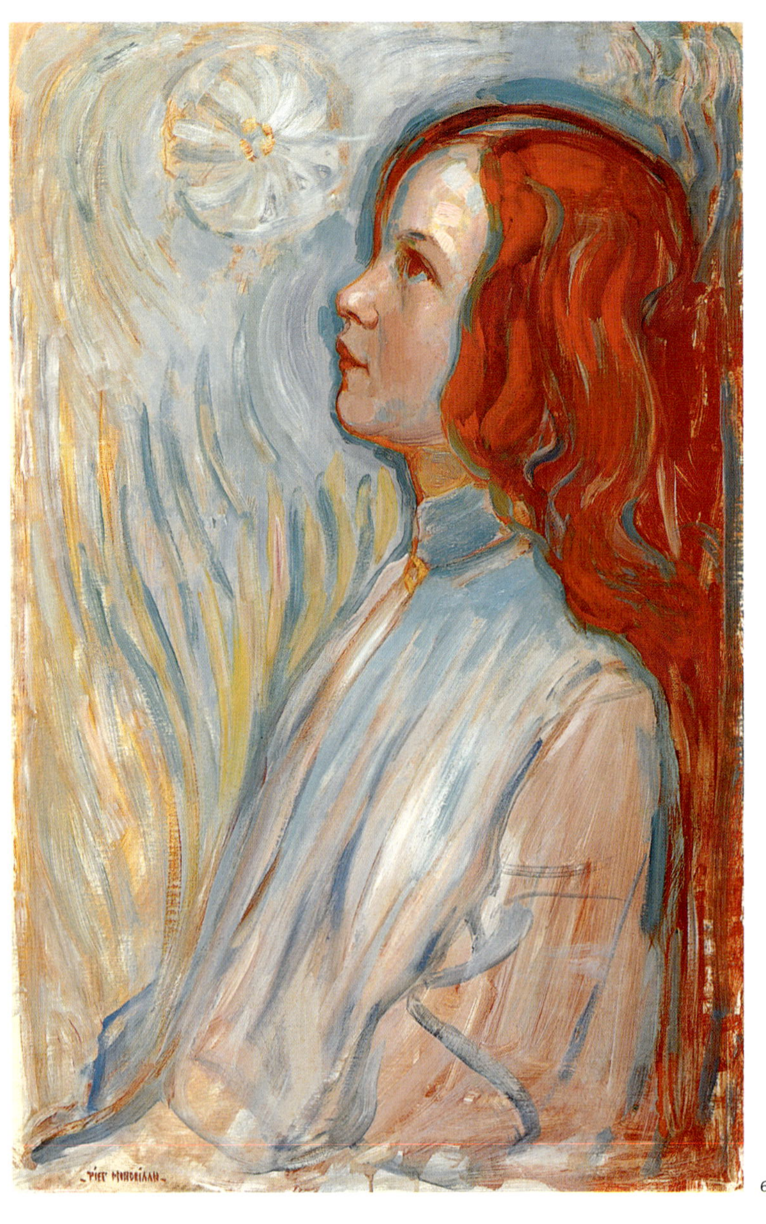

68

Cat. 68 *Devotie* (*Devotion*), 1908
Oil on canvas
37 x 24 in. (94 x 61 cm)
Signed lower left: - PIET MONDRIAAN -
Gemeentemuseum, The Hague, bequest of Salomon B. Slijper, 1971, inv. S 128–1971 (A 642)

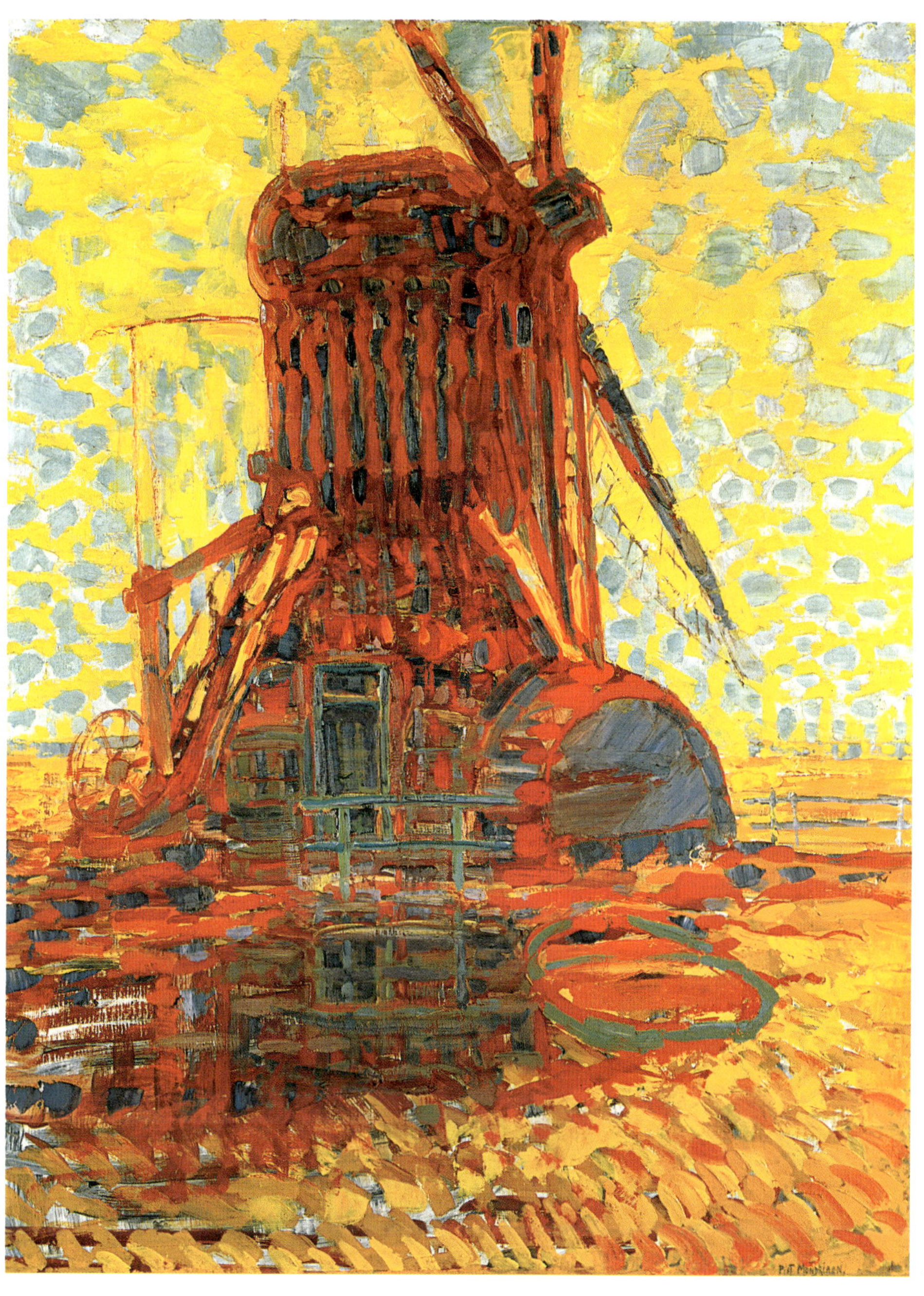
69

Cat. 69 *Mill in Sunlight*, 1908
Oil on canvas
44.9 x 34.3 in. (114 x 87 cm)
Signed lower right: *Pi eT Mondriaan.*
Gemeentemuseum, The Hague, bequest of Salomon B. Slijper, 1971, inv. S 130–1971 (A 654)

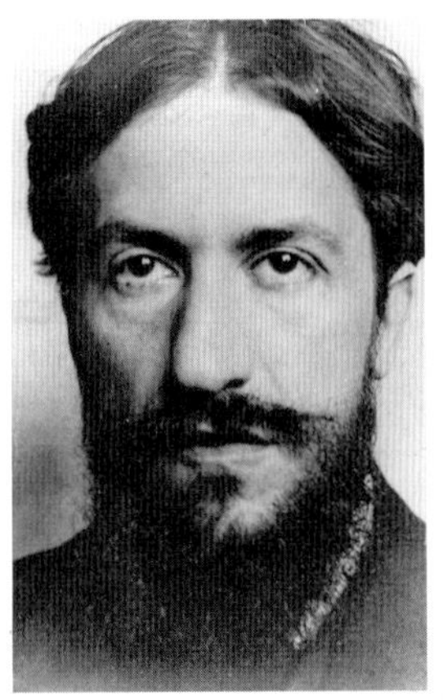

Fig. 34
Mondrian, hair parted in the middle, wearing a beard and a chain, c. 1908
Gemeentemuseum, The Hague

during their stay in the late summer of 1908 at the seaside resort of Domburg, where Toorop spent all his summers beginning in 1903. There was surely an immediate understanding between them. Toorop, who had converted to Catholicism in 1905, found in Mondrian a partner with whom he could discuss spiritual questions.[111]

However, the influence of van Gogh was even more important than that of Toorop. In 1908, for the first time, Mondrian considered himself to be veritably—and ostensibly—a modern artist of the first rank. "I knew little of the modern art movement. When I first saw the work of the Impressionists, van Gogh, van Dongen, and the Fauves, I admired it. But I had to seek the true way alone."[112] This remark reminds us of the primacy of observation in the Dutch tradition, a primacy that, with the painter's complicity, generates all development. Art historians have written on Dutch Luminism as an originally French trend that embellished upon Impressionism, Pointillism, and Fauvism, but this is really only applicable in the particular case of Mondrian.

Mondrian had much to learn from van Gogh with regard to color as a means of symbolic expression freed from traditional notions of locality, gradation by shades, and direct observation. According to the critic Israel Querido (1872–1932), who became acquainted with Mondrian around 1908–9, van Gogh's great strength resided in what he discovered through experimentation, through the study of light and relations between colors on the canvas, and through following his intuition. The process led to the "revelation of the enigmatic secrets of life."[113] During this time, Mondrian completed paintings that could be related to the theosophical theory of evolution, according to which the disappearance of a life form is considered to be a positive change, the passage from one stage to another superior one. Color plays an important role here. The paintings *Haystacks II* (cat. 71), *Dying Sunflower I* (cat. 73), and *Dying Sunflower II* (cat. 74) show (in the words later used by Mondrian) the different evolutionary stages from "natural color" to "pure color." Here he used for the first time a palette of full, vibrant, and intense colors that would become characteristic of the period until 1910.

In January 1909, Mondrian, Cees Spoor, and Jan Sluijters organized a spectacular retrospective at the Stedelijk Museum in Amsterdam (fig. 35). The three artists realized that it was not possible to show the development of their art through ordinary channels. For that reason, they asked the city council to be good enough to put a certain number of rooms at their disposal in the Stedelijk. Analysis of the documents and reviews indicates that Mondrian had three galleries in the right wing on the first floor for his paintings.[114] In the first gallery, he showed "too many" landscape sketches,[115] "unpleasantly" presented, and "in rough, scarcely planed, white wood frames, as if he himself felt that his hallucinatory landscapes

111. See the letter from Mondrian to C. Spoor, circa October 3, 1909, in van Ginneken and Joosten 1970, 262–63.
112. Mondrian 1942, in Holtzman and James 1986, 38.
113. Querido 1910, 184–272 (written about the great exhibition in Amsterdam of 1909, at the art galleries of the Larensche Kunsthandel).
114 Gio. [Jan Kalff], "Kunst en Wetenschappen: C. Spoor, P. Mondriaan, J. Sluijters" (Art and Sciences: C. Spoor, P. Mondrian, J. Sluijters"), *Algemeen Handelsblad*, January 14, 1909.
115 Ibid.

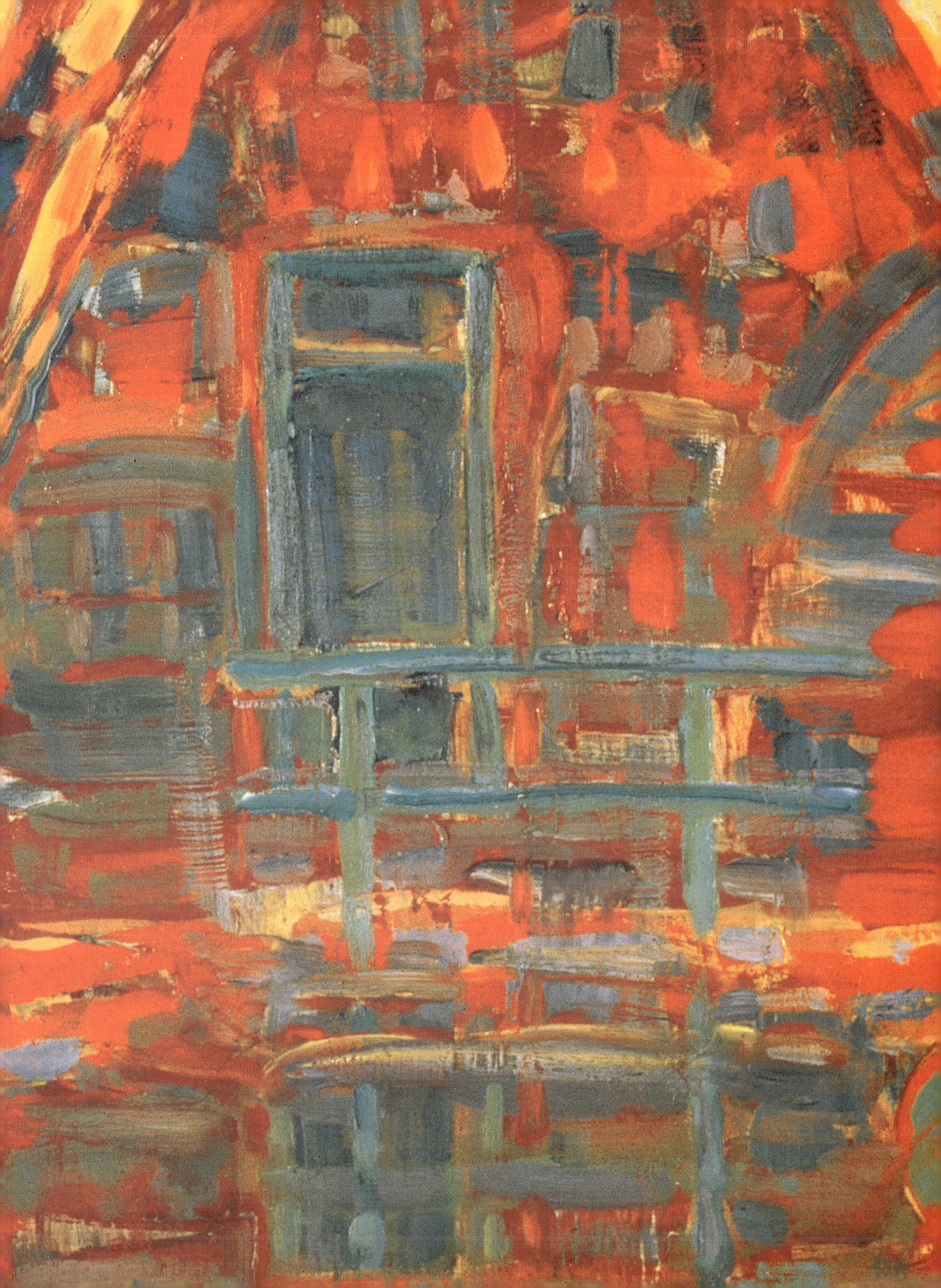

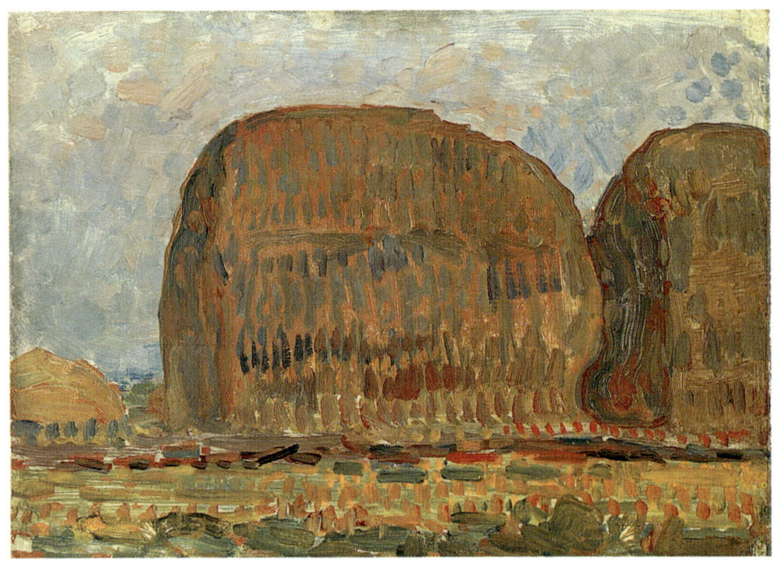

71

73

Cat. 71 *Haystacks II,* 1908
Oil on canvas mounted on cardboard
13.6 x 17 in. (34.5 x 43.2 cm)
Monogrammed lower right: PM
Sidney Janis Family Collection (A 656)

Cat. 73 *Dying Sunflower I,* 1908
Oil on canvas
24.8 x 12.2 in. (63 x 31 cm)
Signed lower right: PIET MONDRIAAN
Gemeentemuseum, The Hague, bequest of Salomon B. Slijper, 1971, inv. S 123–1971 (A 596)

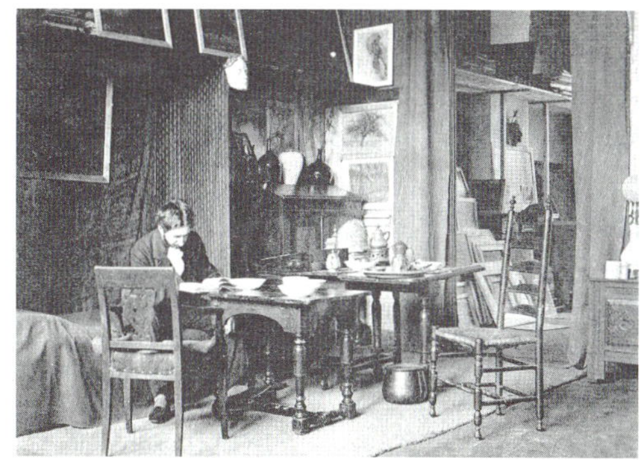

Fig. 35
R. Denktraan, *Mondrian's studio/apartment, 42 Sarphatipark,* late 1908
In the adjoining room, it is possible to see the framed paintings ready for the January 1909 exhibition that he organized with Spoor and Sluijters at the Stedelijk Museum.
Gemeentemuseum, The Hague

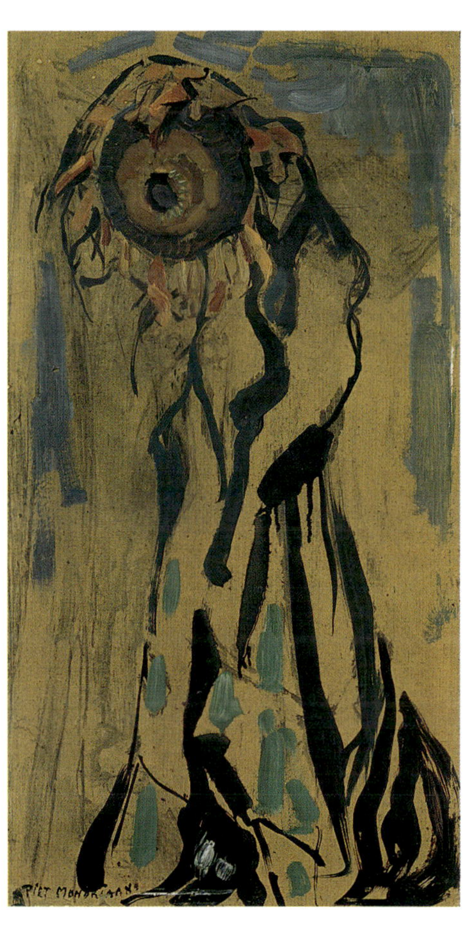

74

Cat. 74 *Dying Sunflower II*, 1908
Oil on cardboard
26.8 x 13.4 in. (65 x 34 cm)
Signed lower left: PIET MONDRIAAN.
Gemeentemuseum, The Hague, bequest of Salomon B. Slijper, 1971, inv. S 124–1971 (A 597)

[were] still quite crude, and [could] at most be considered as interesting attempts to break the ground–with a roar—for a future neo-Romanticism."[116] These frames, also judged to be "garish" and "shabby," were the simple, flat wooden frames that even today surround many of the first works of Mondrian, sometimes still with their original paint, sometimes (as with *The Royal Wax Candle Factory* [cat. 20]) painted by later owners. "[The framing] related well to the objects, the unfinished studies, impressions, and atmospheres, sometimes just barely washes—that are in reality sublimated representations of landscapes. Our typical Dutch landscape," remarked the director of the Rijskmuseum, Willem Steenhoff.[117] In this gallery, one could see, among others works, *Dorpskerk* (*Village Church*) (cat. 15), *Forest* (cat. 16), *Evening on the Weesperzijde* (cat. 26), and *Cows in an Orchard* (cat. 33). The last gallery displayed a selection of evening landscapes from all periods. These reassured most of the critics, who were at least forced to recognize Mondrian's technical talents. The second room was the "central" gallery but, as it was situated in an angle, it should not be confused with the Gallery of Honor, located in the center of that floor.[118] In his "central" gallery, Mondrian showed his recent works, the "visions of an insane individual":[119] two large self-portraits

116. Willem Steenhoff, "Tentoonstelling C. Spoor, Piet Mondrian, J. Sluijters in het Stedelijk Museum, 2" ("The Exhibition of C. Spoor, P. Mondrian, and J. Sluijters at the Stedelijk Museum, 2"), *De Amsterdammer Weekblad*, January 17, 1909, 7; and Frits Lapidoth, "Kunst in de Hoofdstad, 1: Het Stedelijk" ("Art in the Capital: The Stedelijk Museum"), *De Nieuwe Courant*, January 30, 1909, 10.
117. Willem Steenhoff, op. cit., January 31, 1909, 10.
118. H. L. Berckenhoff, "C. Spoor/ P. Mondriaan / J. Sluijters, 3," *Nieuwe Rotterdamsche Courant*, June 11, 1909, evening edition, leaflet B.
119. C. L. Dake, "Schilderkunst: Drie avonturiers in het Stedelijk Museum" ("Painting: Three Adventurers in the Stedelijk Museum"), *De Telegraaf*, January 8, 1909.

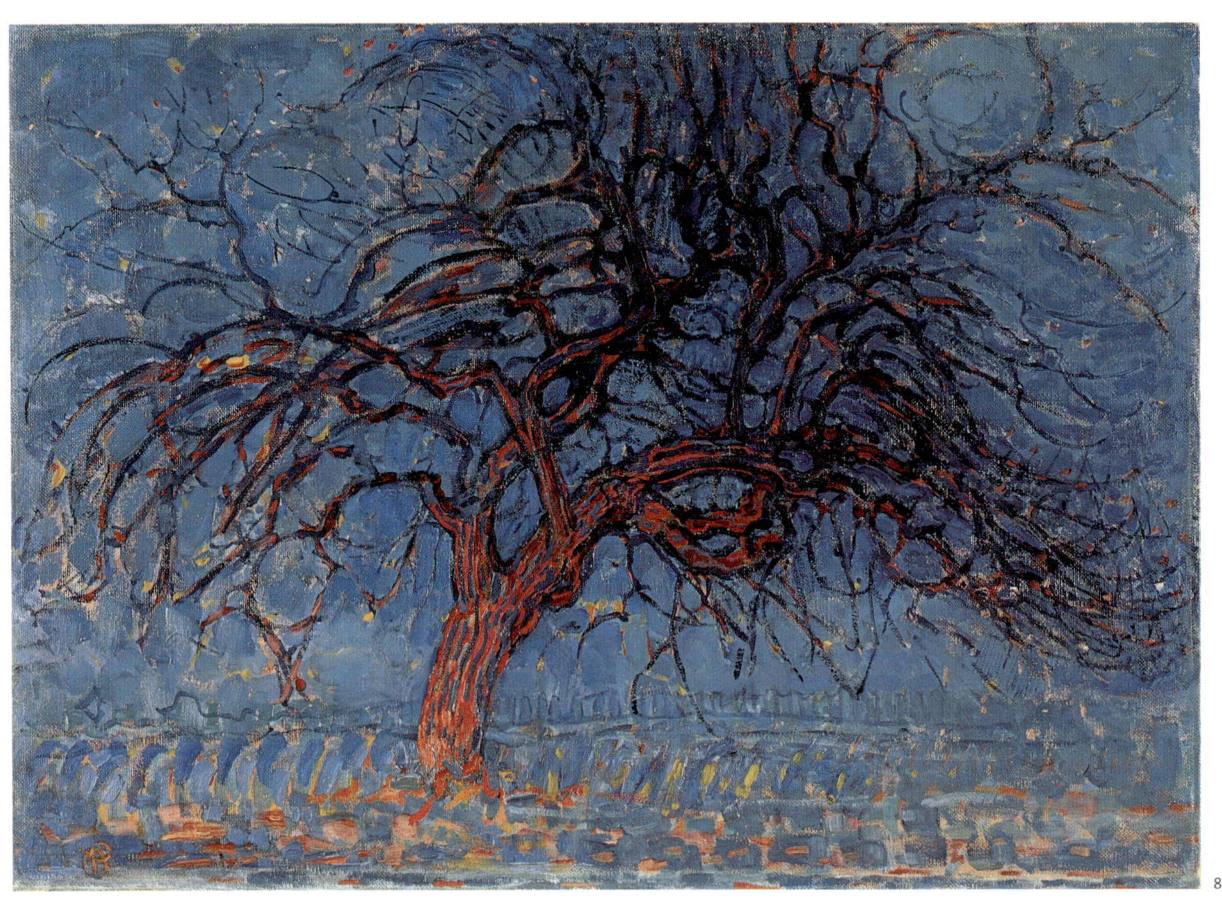

85

Cat. 85 *Avond (Red Tree),* 1908–10
Oil on canvas
27.6 x 39 in. (70 x 99 cm)
Monogrammed lower left: PM
Gemeentemuseum, The Hague, inv. T 17–1933 (A 671)

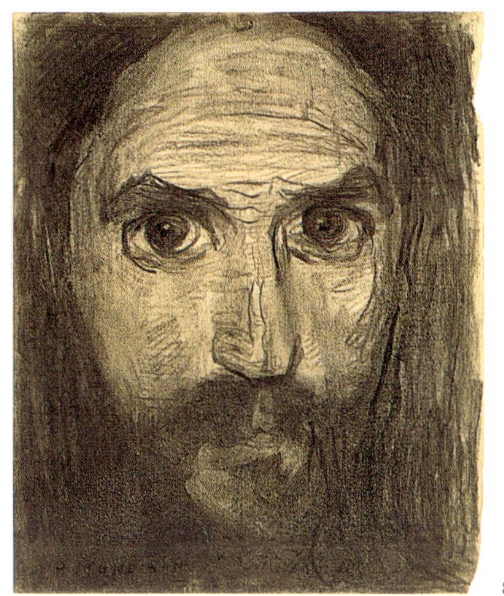

86

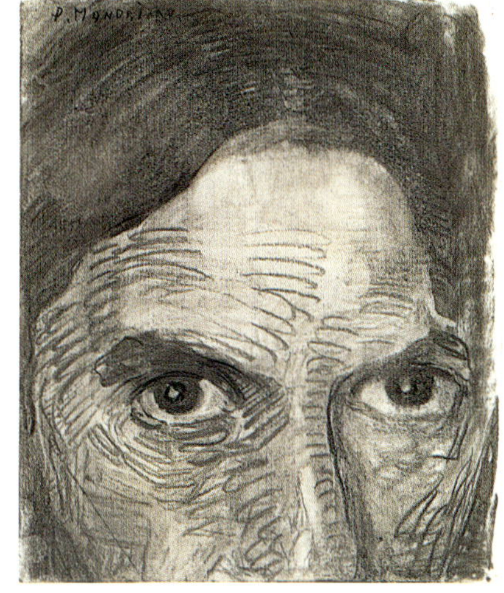

87

Cat. 86 *Self-Portrait,* 1908
Crayon on paper
11.8 x 10.0 in. (30 x 25.5 cm)
Signed lower left: P. Mondriaan
Gemeentemuseum, The Hague, bequest of Salomon B. Slijper, 1971, inv. T 53–1971 (A 639)
Paris only

Cat. 87 *Self-Portrait,* 1908
Crayon on paper
11.8 x 9.6 in. (30 x 24.5 cm)
Signed lower left: P. Mondiaan *[sic]*
Gemeentemuseum, The Hague, bequest of Salomon B. Slijper, 1971, inv. T 52–1971 (A 638)
Paris only

flanking a tree painted blue (cat. 85, 86, 87, and fig. 36a, b, and c) on one wall. On another wall hung an entirely blue landscape; across the way was a multicolored landscape, *Zomerdag (Summer Day)* (cat. 66); a *Mill in Sunlight* (cat. 69); and, farther away, were three *Haystacks* (including cat. 71), sunflowers (cat. 73 and 74), some blue trees (cat. 70, 76, and 77), *The Red Cloud* (cat. 60), and *Devotie* (*Devotion*) (cat. 68). According to the critical reviews, Mondrian was not alone in presenting "cycles."[120] Cees Spoor showed flowers in the light of morning, noon, and night: "a plastic vision: the nascent flower as it bursts open, then resplendent with life, and then finally fading, all bathed in a feeling of eternity, at first subterranean, then emerging . . . With Spoor, the symbolic has melted into the object itself."[121]

From March 4 through 8, 1908, Rudolf Steiner had given a series of lectures before the Dutch Theosophical Association. A year later, Mondrian became a member of the association. His candidacy was supported by Cees Spoor. It is certainly possible to consider the painting *Metamorphosis* (cat. 75), as well as the cycles mentioned above, as being the symbolic representation of theosophical ideas about life and death. In order to exploit completely the symbolic potential of a motif, Mondrian was careful to remove it from its context, and the flowers and the haystacks prove the value of this practice. He may already have far advanced his development of symbolic form in September 1908 while visiting Jan Toorop and Cees Spoor at their vacation house at Domburg in Zeeland. In the works he made there, he treated the motif of a tree or a church tower separately and as an autonomous focus of significance. This was the first time, breaking with his earlier landscapes, that he devoted himself to motifs detached from their natural environment that rose to the level of independent signs. *Lighthouse at Westkapelle* (cat. 72) is painted in the style of *Woods at Oele* (cat. 67) and rises like a massive stone over the flat landscape of Walcheren. Jan Toorop had already represented this lighthouse in a drawing as a symbol of unwavering faith. In Mondrian's painting, the colors are schematic, expressive, and tense. The tension persists in a series that Mondrian would later call "my special period (in blue),"[122] in which he took as his motif the isolated tree. *Apple Tree in Blue* (cat. 70) and the two versions of *Blue Tree* (cat. 76 and 77) seem to arise from a style of drawing that explicitly recalls van Gogh. There is also much to be said, however, for

120. Carel Blotkamp has already confirmed that Mondrian exhibited several "cycles" in Amsterdam in 1909 (along with some *Haystacks* and *Dying Sunflowers*). A more precise analysis of the reports confirms this opinion. See Blotkamp 1994, 46–7.

121. "C. Spoor: Een schilderstudie" ("C. Spoor: Study of a painter"), in Querido 1912, 91. Querido describes three paintings of flowers that combine light red and vivid blue, dark red, periwinkle, purple, and dark blue.

122. Letter from Mondrian to Salomon Slijper, March 8, 1922, Slijper Archives, RKD, The Hague.

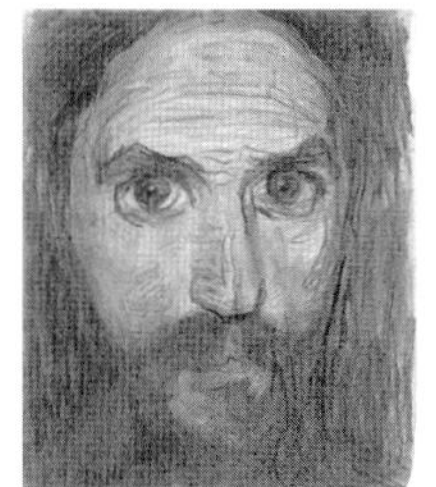

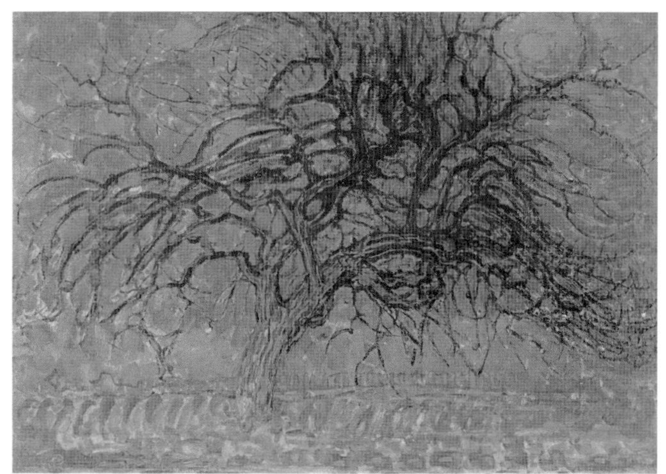

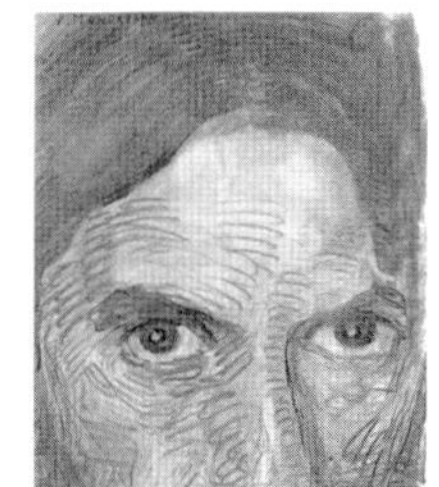

Fig. 36a, b, and c
Reconstruction of the placement of Avond (Evening), *chosen by Mondrian for the 1909 exhibition.*
Gemeentemuseum, The Hague

66 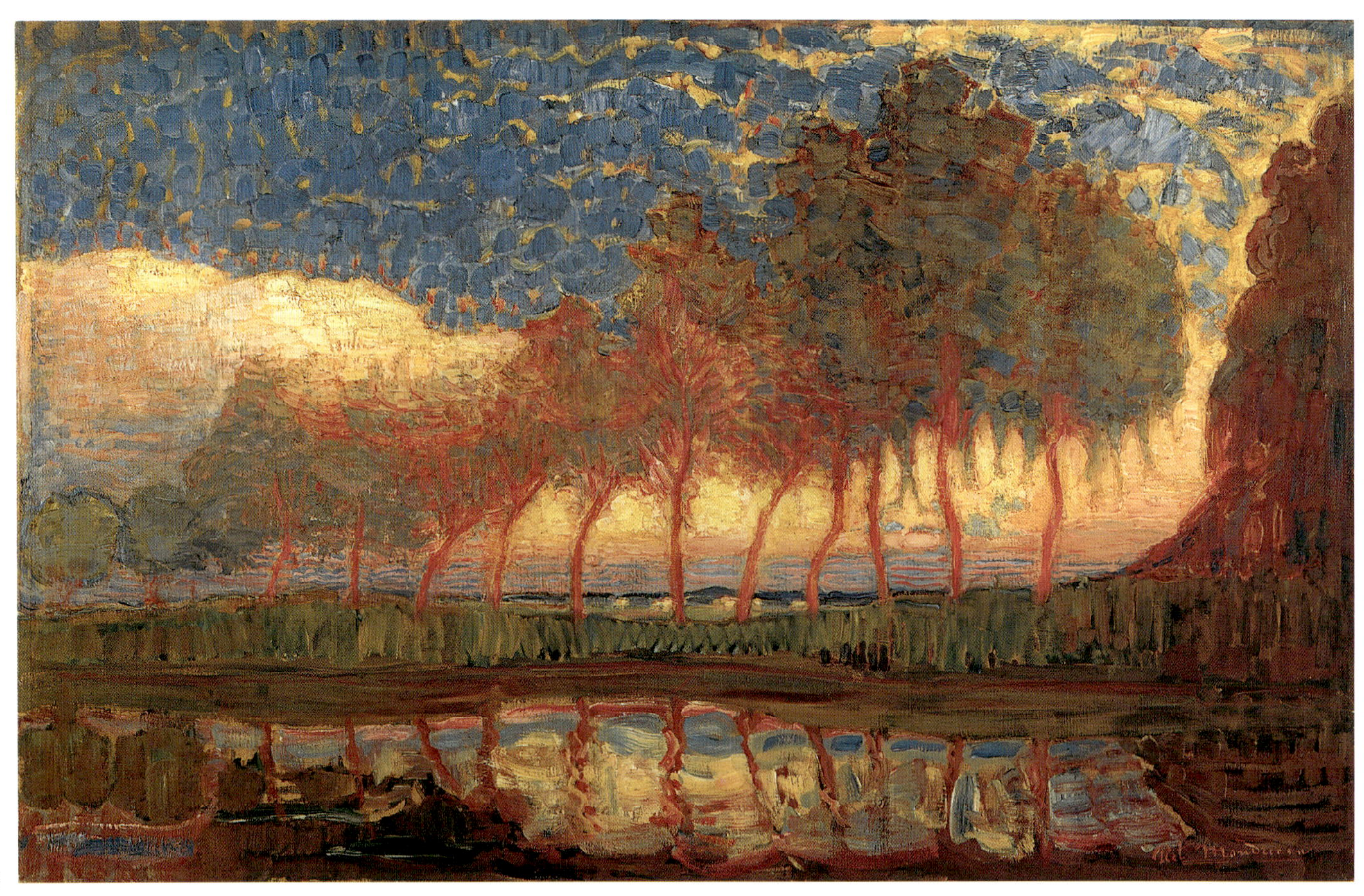

Cat. 66 *Zomerdag (Summer Day)*, 1908
Oil on canvas
27.1 x 44.1 in. (69 x 112 cm)
Signed lower right: *Piet Mondriaan.*
Stichting Hannema-de Stuers Foundation, Heino/Wijhe, inv. 178 (A 658)
Paris only

Cat. 75 *Metamorphose* (*Metamorphosis*), 1908
Oil on canvas
33.3 x 21.3 in. (84.5 x 54 cm)
Signed lower left: PIET MONDRIAAN.
Gemeentemuseum, The Hague, bequest of Salomon B. Slijper, 1971, inv. S 125–1971 (A 601)

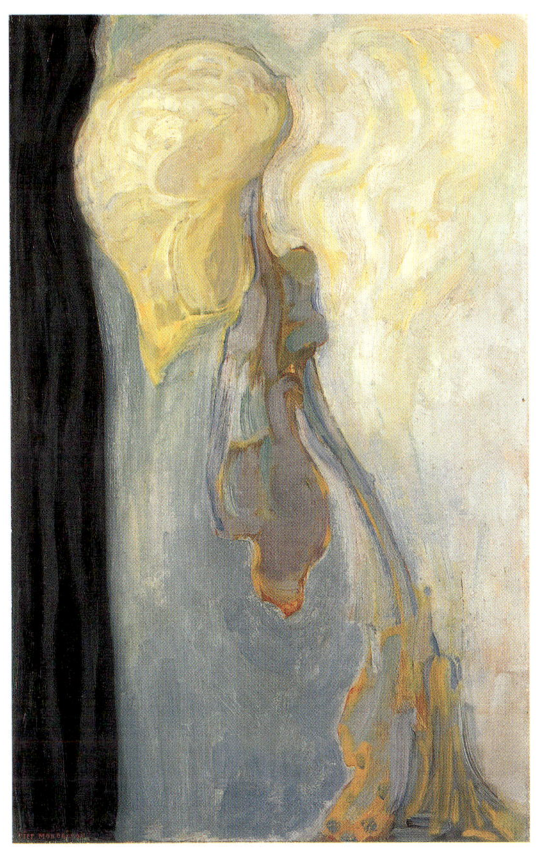

75

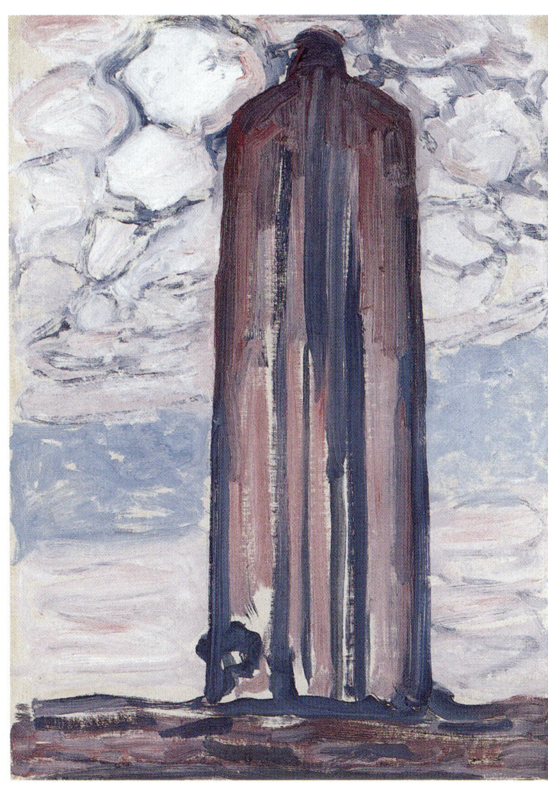

72

a suggestion made by Israel Querido. In the vibrant blue palette, the use of full and unmixed colors, and the total conjuring away of all differentiation between shadow and light, Querido saw a rapport with Giovanni Segantini, especially with his alpine prairies, one of which had just been exhibited in Amsterdam.[123]
In the reviews of the exhibition of January 1909 at the Stedelijk Museum, the recurring discussion of meaning in relation to technique shows that Mondrian was speaking about the decisive role of technique in his work to whoever was willing to listen. Conrad Kikkert lamented that, "Mondrian makes it his duty to produce this work when it is opposed to his most profound being—a sweet nature."[124] Willem Steenhoff summed up the situation this way: " Mondrian's work, seen from the most technical angle—we refer to the rapport between form and content. Good intentions, as far as we can understand them, should also be endowed with effective means to express themselves."[125] In a letter to Israel Querido, published in October 1909, Mondrian himself elucidated the rapport, so important to him, between form and technique, as well as the relationship between art and philosophy:

I believe that color and line can do much towards this end; moreover, I should not wish to do without line (regarding this I certainly must have expressed myself incorrectly). It is precisely the essential lines of any object that I find fundamentally important and, also, the color. . . . I find the work of the great masters of the past very beautiful and very grand, but you will agree with me, that everything done in our own time must be expressed very differently,

Cat. 72 *Lighthouse at Westkapelle*, c. 1908
Oil on canvas
28 x 20.5 in. (71 x 52 cm)
Signed lower left: P. MONDRIAAN.
Gemeentemuseum, The Hague, bequest of Salomon B. Slijper, 1971, inv. S 127–1971 (A 682)

123. Querido 1910, 248. The text that precedes the passage on Segantini, which treats the symbolic potentialities of painting and of the tragic–claiming genesis, development, denouement–is fully applicable to the works of Mondrian in this period.
124. Kikkert 1909, 98.
125. W. Steenhoff, op. cit. January 31, 1909, 10.

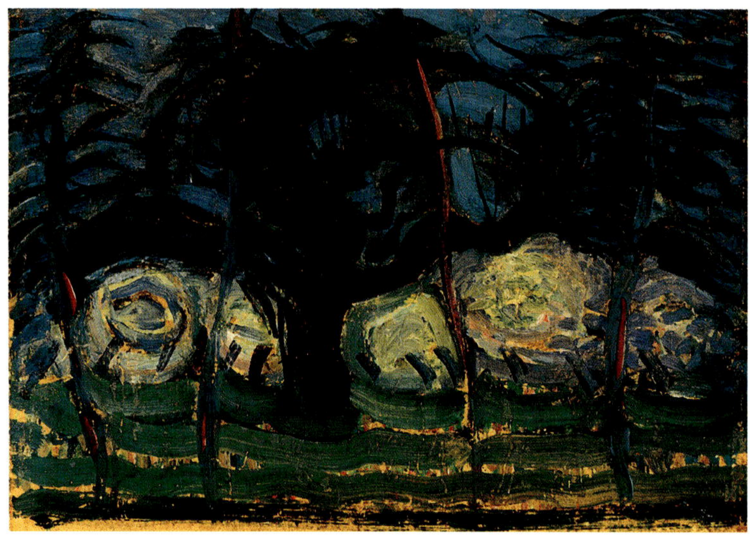

70

even through a different use of technique. I believe that in our period it is definitely necessary that, as far as possible, the paint is applied in pure colors set next to each other in a pointillist or diffused manner. This is stated strongly, and yet it relates to the thought that is the basis of meaningful expression in form as I see it. It seems to me that clarity of thought should be accompanied by clarity of technique. . . . It seems to me that you too recognize the important relationship between philosophy and art, and it is exactly this relationship which most painters deny. The great masters grasp it unconsciously, but I believe that a painter's conscious spiritual knowledge will have a much greater influence upon his art, and that it is merely weakness in him–or a lack of genius–should this spiritual knowledge be harmful to his art. Should a painter progress so far that he attains definite first-hand knowledge of his finer regions through development of the finer senses, then perhaps his art will become incomprehensible to mankind, which as yet has not come to know these finer regions. And you wish to warn me against this danger.[126]

Mondrian wrote this letter during his stay in Domburg. He had returned there in June 1909, in the company of Cees Spoor, and stayed there, with a few interruptions, until the second week in October. He received a visit from his friend Albert van den Briel, who was present when he painted *Sea after Sunset* (cat. 80). "This sea [at Domburg] was painted very late in the day, when it was already rather dark, from the Hooge Hil [a dune near Domburg]. I was there, and I saw it being born in the darkness."[127] The first layers were light and in "natural colors"; those following were increasingly somber and "purer," to use

Cat. 70 *Apple Tree in Blue*, c. 1908
Oil on paper mounted on canvas
10.7 x 15.1 in. (27.2 x 38.4 cm)
Not signed
Zeeuws Museum, Middelburg, inv. M 94–008 (A 666)

126. Querido 1909–10.
127. Letter from Albert van den Briel to Rudi Oxenaar, January 1, 1955. Archives of the Gemeentemuseum, The Hague.

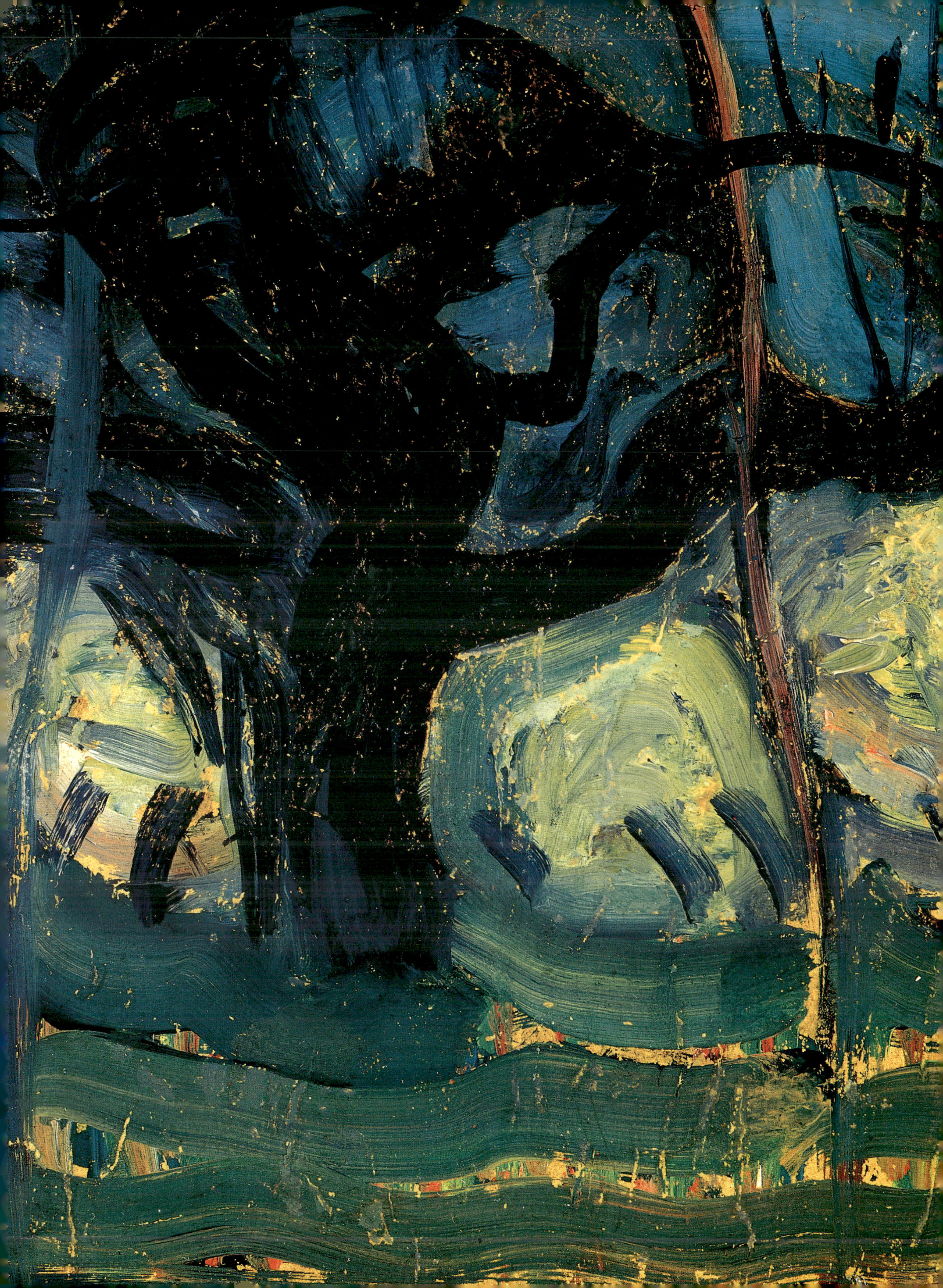

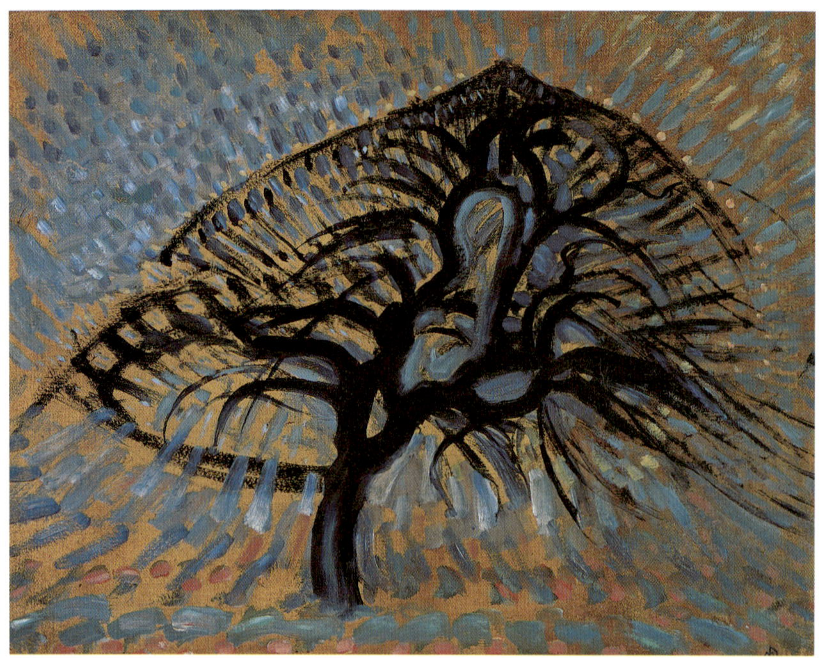

76

Mondrian's terminology. The wide strokes of blue in the foreground and all along the lower edge of the painting were applied in the dark, more or less blindly. They are the expression of an interior concentration more than visual perception. This anecdotal account of its creation reveals *Sea after Sunset* to be a particular variation on the theme of the evening landscape.

Besides this painting, Mondrian made many sketches in Domburg and in the area of Walcheren. Van den Briel was struck by "Toorop's almost envious admiration of Mondrian's work... He was especially impressed by the technical aspect of Mondrian's work and by his use of color. He sensed the power in this 'palette,' and its difference from his own work."[128] But Mondrian also had much to learn from Toorop. The older artist had, since 1903, established close contacts with several groups of painters in Switzerland and southern Germany, among whom were Giovanni Giacometti, Ferdinand Hodler, and Ernst Würtemberger.[129] These were the champions of emulsion painting—oil paint mixed with albumen of animal origin—which, in addition to drying rapidly, permitted the artist to obtain a beautiful, matte surface. Over and above these aesthetic effects, emulsion paint gives an intense brightness to color and accentuates the materiality of its components. There was yet another reason to convert to emulsion. It was said that the technique came from early Flemish and Italian painters such as van Eyck, Mantegna, and

Cat. 76 *Blue Tree*, 1908–9
Oil on cardboard
22.4 x 29.5 in. (56.8 x 75 cm)
Monogrammed lower right: PM
Dallas Museum of Art, Foundation of the Arts Collection, gift of the James H. and Lillian Clark Foundation, inv. 1982–26 FA (A 673)

128. Henkels 1988, 24 and 88.
129. See, for what follows, Janssen and Tabak 1998, 20–21.

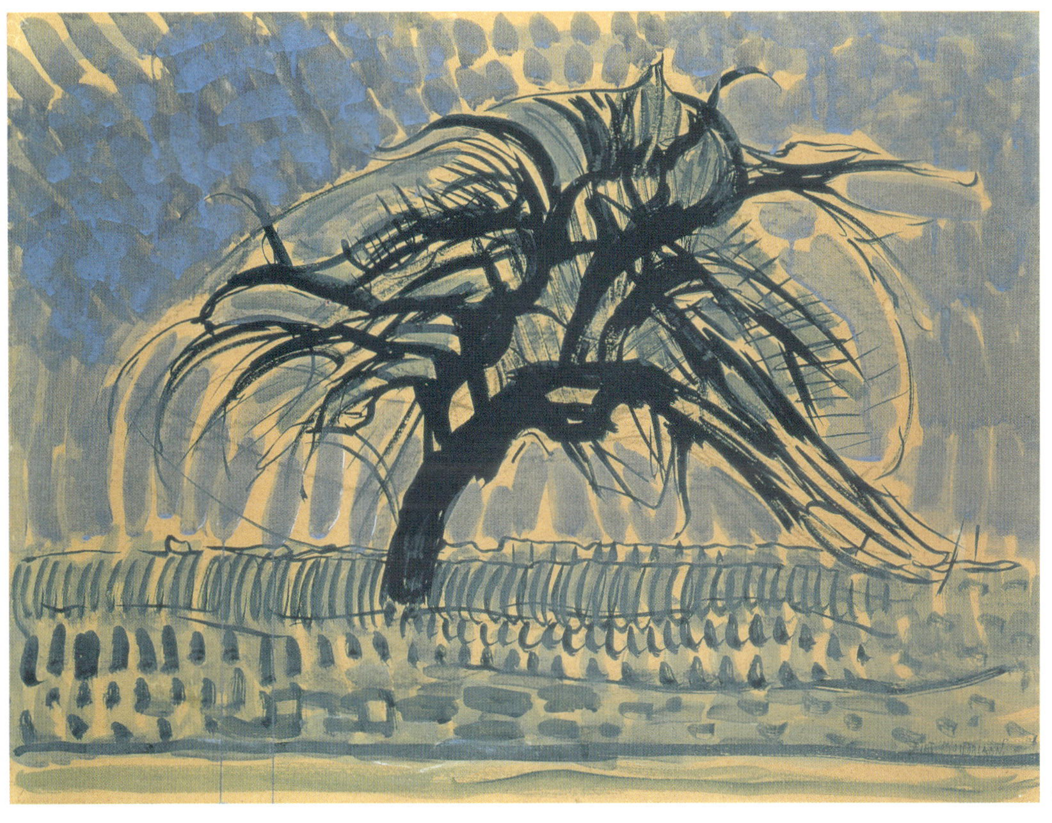

77

Cat. 77 *Blue Tree,* c. 1909
Tempera on cardboard
29.7 x 39.2 in. (75.5 x 99.5 cm)
Signed lower right: PIET MONDRIAAN.
Gemeentemuseum, The Hague, gift of Conrad Kikkert, inv. T 99–1934 (A 672)

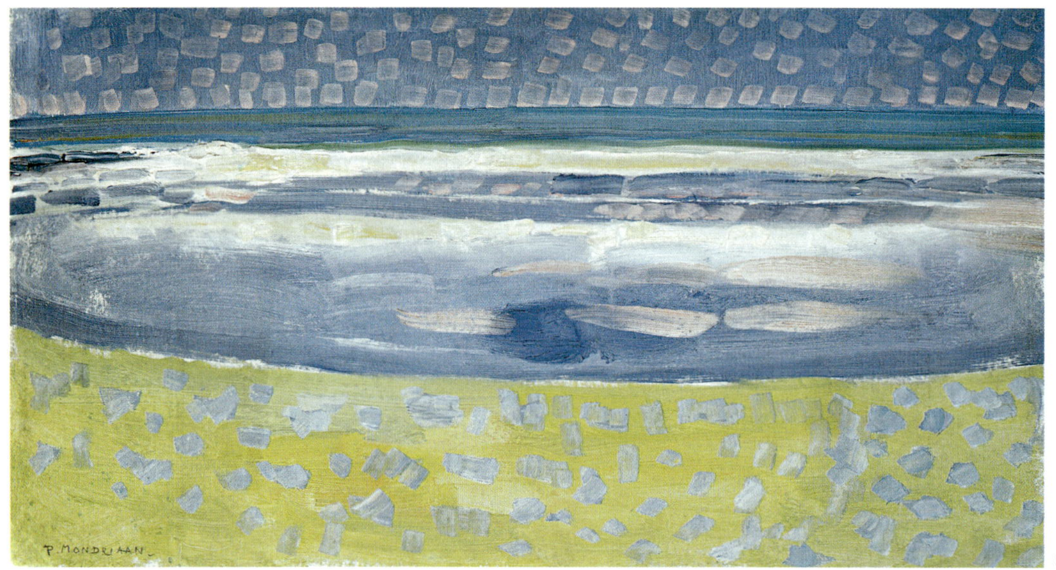
80

Cat. 80 *Sea after Sunset*, 1909
Oil on cardboard
16.1 x 29.9 in. (41 x 76 cm)
Signed lower left: P. MONDRIAAN.
Gemeentemuseum, The Hague, bequest of Salomon B. Slijper, 1971, inv. S 131–1971 (A 694)

Dürer, who used it in the service of spiritual meaning. In this sense the use of emulsion was explicitly opposed to the French tradition which, with the exception of the Nabis, maintained a preference for pure oil.[130]

Mondrian, too, would begin to paint in this medium at the time he experimented with tempera in *Blue Tree* (cat. 77). The often quoted passage from the letter that Mondrian wrote to Israel Querido in 1909, in which he discusses the link between "clarity of thought" and "clarity of technique," thus appears in a new light. Clearly there was a close relationship between divisionist inclinations and spiritual aspirations, developed in the heart of Swiss artistic circles in those years, and the relationship established itself in Mondrian through the intermediary of Toorop. During his prolonged stay in Domburg, from the end of the summer to the end of October 1909, Mondrian made great use of emulsion.[131] He worked *en plein air*, taking advantage of the paste's qualities of quick drying, matte finish, and absorption of light to suggest the intense luminosity of the peninsula. In a letter of autumn 1909 to a violinist friend, Aletta de Iongh (1887–1975), he wrote that he had spent six weeks all alone in the dunes, where calm reigned, "a great calm, favorable to work."[132] His mood of looking inward into himself and of meditation, described by Albert van den Briel and others, engendered splendid paintings, in which oppositions were studied and perfected in the course of continuous experimentation. In his lighthouses and dunes it is certainly possible to find affinities to Monet's series—haystacks and church portals—whose motifs serve the sole function of giving full play to light. But Mondrian differed fundamentally from the French Impressionist. In diverse versions of a motif, he did not seek to render different moments or

130. Mauner 1991, 20–21 Since the Impressionists, French artists had also shown a preference for painting with a matte, dry surface, but they obtained it by using a very thin paint and applying it over an absorbent base. For the Impressionist technique, see especially Bomford, Kirby, Leighton, and Roy 1990, 72–75; Callen 1988, 24; and H. Travers Newton, "Observations on Gauguin's Painting Technique and Materials," in Hoyle, Peres, and van Tilborgh 1991, 103–9.

131. Even though albumens of animal origin had been discovered in works of 1908, among them *Devotion* (cat. 69).

132. Letter from Mondrian to Aletta de Iongh, with the note "Friday night."

different qualities of light as such; he was not so concerned with the "effect" as Monet. His goal was to explore, in a most empirical manner, the expressive possibilities of various compositions and techniques. This desire was the sole reason Mondrian repeated a motif, as he had previously done with the Gein. While the version of *Lighthouse at Westkapelle* (cat. 72) exploits the use of line–with *Woods at Oele* [cat. 67] as a prototype–in *Lighthouse at Westkapelle* (cat. 78), Mondrian strives to make the sunlight vibrate with heavy touches of blue, pink, and ocher applied over the thinly painted first sketch, so that the pink and violet of the lighthouse stand out harshly in relation to the blue of the sky. With three strokes of white he evokes some clouds, which give a sudden effect of depth behind the lighthouse. Likewise in *Sea after Sunset* (cat. 79 and 80), *Dune I* (cat. 81), *Dune II* (cat. 82), and *Dune IV* (cat. 83), he develops different versions by the same process, varying the placement of colors, forms, and strokes.

Although each of these works, through its dynamism and expressive force, gives the impression of having been made in a single painting session, the process of their completion in fact suffered many interruptions. It is even possible that they were not finished until after Mondrian's return to Amsterdam in November 1909; he wrote at that time, in a letter to Aletta de Iongh: "I am speeding up work on several small things I brought back from Zeeland, which I do completely according to my intentions."[133]

Is it possible to draw a connection between the systematic and entirely structured conception of these works Mondrian brought back to Amsterdam, and the showing of works by Cézanne in the Rijksmuseum in December 1909? The director of the Rijksmuseum, Willem Steenhoff, had eleven Cézannes and seven van Goghs that he had received on loan two years earlier hanging in the building's newly completed south wing. The Cézannes had come from the Hoogendijk collection and the van Goghs from Johanna Bonger's collection. Israel Querido later related his memories of the extraordinary event: "I remember that one day, Spoor, overwhelmed with excitement, came to find me to suggest that we go see several never before shown van Gogh still lifes at Steenhoff's, at the Rijksmuseum. He led me there. His admiration was nothing less than joy, happiness, and uncontrollable delight at seeing so much beauty. Never have I seen an artist more sincere in his enthusiasm. . . . However, never—absolutely never—did the work imitate or copy the tragic grandeur that permeated van Gogh's entire life."[134] Van Gogh's art must have impressed Mondrian as well. Unlike Querido and his friends, however, he might have been moved even more by the works of Cézanne, in which color and form worked together, because that partnership is what he himself had never ceased working to create through the systematic character of his work, during the course of his last stay in Domburg. In a letter of September 1909 to Aletta de Iongh, Mondrian described this aspect

133. Letter from Mondrian to Aletta de Iongh, with the note "Sunday night" (January–beginning of February 1910). Archives of the Kröller-Müller Museum, Otterlo.

134. "Cees Spoor: Een Schilderstudie" ("C. Spoor: Study of a Painter") in Querido 1912, 76–108.

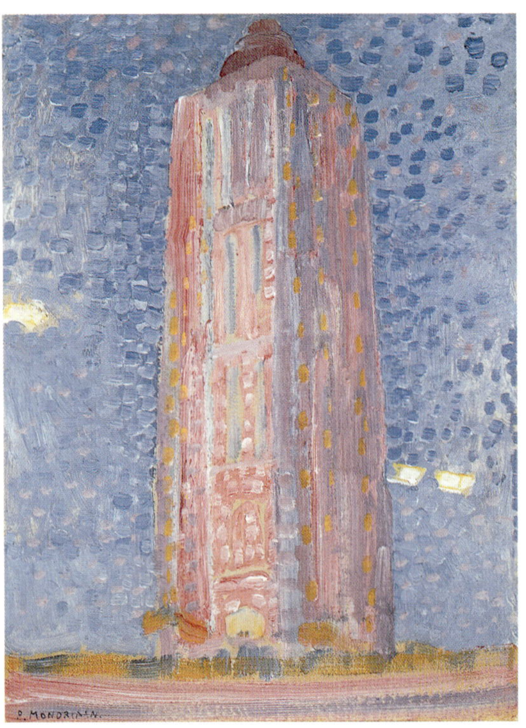
78

of his research: "It is very beautiful here; also in the woods; and the bare poplars. But because I must leave so soon, I have no more time to appreciate all that. I have worked mostly on the dunes and churches. If one did not concentrate on a few things, it would not be possible to produce anything among all this beauty, would it?"

The systematic analysis of color and form is also visible in *Lighthouse at Westkapelle* (cat. 84). Again, the full and harsh light of Westkapelle is essential, but Mondrian, preferring to use almost pure primary colors for the lighthouse, while emphasizing lines in the style of *Woods near Oele* (cat. 67) and modeling with a generously filled, wide brush and a palette knife, acquires an intense expressiveness. It seems quite possible that Mondrian also returned to work on two paintings around this time, *Avond* (*Red Tree)* (cat. 85) and *Zon, Kerk in Zeeland* (*Sun, Church in Zeeland*) (cat. 88). Under the top layer of paint of both works is hidden another state that Mondrian altered to obtain harsh contrasts between blue and red and blue and orange, contrasts that then dominate the final images. In *Red Tree*, long brushstrokes dominate. The opposite is true with *Zon, Kerk in Zeeland* (*Sun, Church in Zeeland*), in which short strokes are placed one on top of the other, forming a gradation from thin to fat, from fine to thick. In *Duinen bij Domburg* (*Dunes at Domburg)* (cat. 89), this form of expressivity gives way to fine, vertical brushstrokes high in the sky opposing the lazier, strongly horizontal brushstrokes reserved for the dunes. This variation of facture is comparable to what Mondrian had created in *Evening Mood on the Amstel (Omval)* (cat. 52), as well as other earlier paintings and studies.

In April 1910, Mondrian showed these last works,

Cat. 78 *Lighthouse at Westkapelle*, 1909
Oil on cardboard
15.4 x 10.2 in. (39 x 29.5 cm)
Signed lower left: P. MONDRIAAN.
Gemeentemuseum, The Hague, bequest of Salomon B. Slijper, 1971, inv. S 137–1971 (A 684)

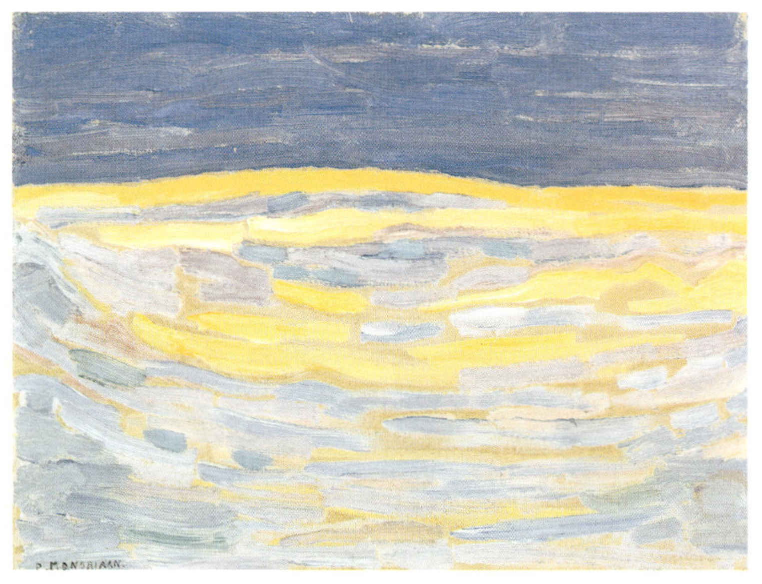

81

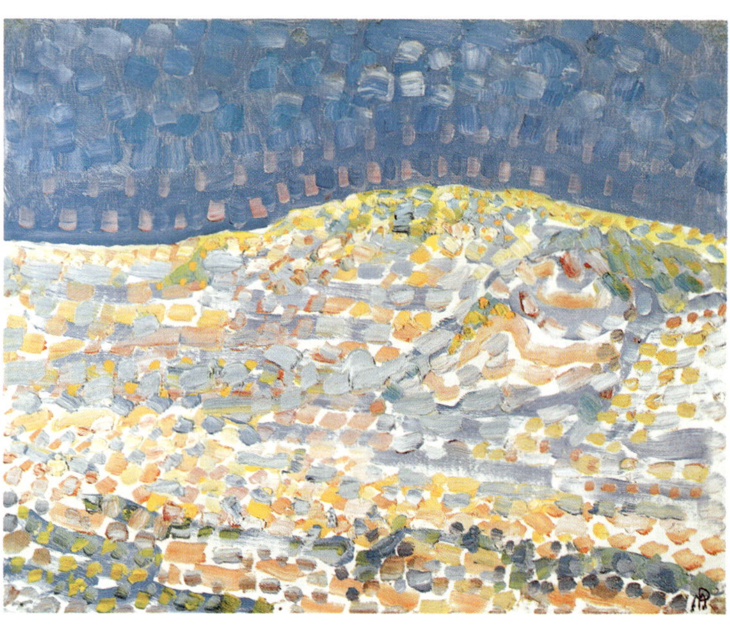
82

Cat. 81 *Dune I,* 1909
Oil on cardboard
11.8 x 15.7 in. (30 x 40 cm)
Signed lower left: P. MONDRIAAN.
Gemeentemuseum, The Hague, bequest of Salomon B. Slijper, 1971, inv. S 133–1971 (A 701)

Cat. 82 *Dune II,* 1909
Oil on canvas
14.8 x 18.3 in. (37.5 x 46.5 cm)
Monogrammed lower right: PM
Gemeentemuseum, The Hague, bequest of Salomon B. Slijper, 1971, inv. S 134–1971 (A 704)

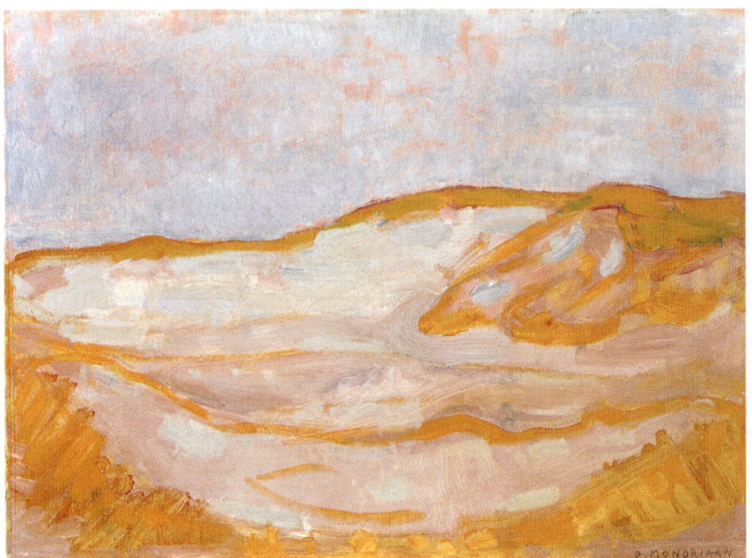

83

Cat. 83 *Dune IV*, 1909
Oil on cardboard
13 x 18.1 in. (33 x 46 cm)
Signed lower right: P. MONDRIAAN
Gemeentemuseum, The Hague, bequest of Salomon B. Slijper, 1971, inv. S 144–1971 (A 707)

and another entitled *Rhododendrons* (fig. 37), at the Saint Lucas exhibition, which became known as the "triumph of Domburg." *Rhododendrons* (fig. 38) is a version in pastel and charcoal of the original–about which until a short time ago, we knew only that it had disappeared during a fire in the United States (see fig. 37.)[135] The exact circumstances of the event remained unknown. A small catalogue found recently in a private collection, in combination with the archives of the American Immigration and Naturalization Service, reveals that the painter Dirk Smorenberg (1883–1960) had taken a trip to the United States in October 1910, supported by the collectors and financial sponsors J. F. and T. G. Fredricks. He traveled with the journalist Henri de Hoog. Smorenberg carried in his baggage a great number of paintings from the Saint Lucas spring 1910 exhibition. Among these were two of Mondrian's flower pieces; these were exhibited at the Morgan Hotel in New York and one of them was definitely sold.[136]

To a greater height even . . . in the ideal regions of art, runs the painter-poet-idealist Mondriaan, the taciturn man about whom everyone is speaking. If it be true what philosophers say–that it is not quite easy for a talkative man to think and the reverse, that a thinking man has a difficulty in speaking–then, thinking, reflecting, pondering is the real essence of Mr. Mondriaan. And in his ideal world he sees things differently and in a more brilliant light than we do in our world of speech and groping. The ideal flower blossoming on the spiritual side of life–and represented by every flower here on earth–may not be clearly seen by us. Mondriaan sees it, and his artist's hands reproduce the ray of heavenly light, which

135. See Louis Saalborn, "Herinneringen aan Mondriaan" ("Memories of Mondrian"), *De Telegraaf*, March 17, 1955.

136. *Catalogue: Exhibition of Dutch Masters, of Fredriks Bros. from Holland.* A single example of the catalogue (private collection) has been preserved. I thank Jan de Ruijter for this discovery and for his help in assembling the information. Mondrian was shown in New York with Robert Graafland, Maurits de Groot, Dirk Filarski, and Dirk Smorenberg, who, as the organizer, had furnished the greatest number of works. Mondrian exhibited *Amaryllis* (A 626 [?]) and *Rhododendrons* (see fig. 37).

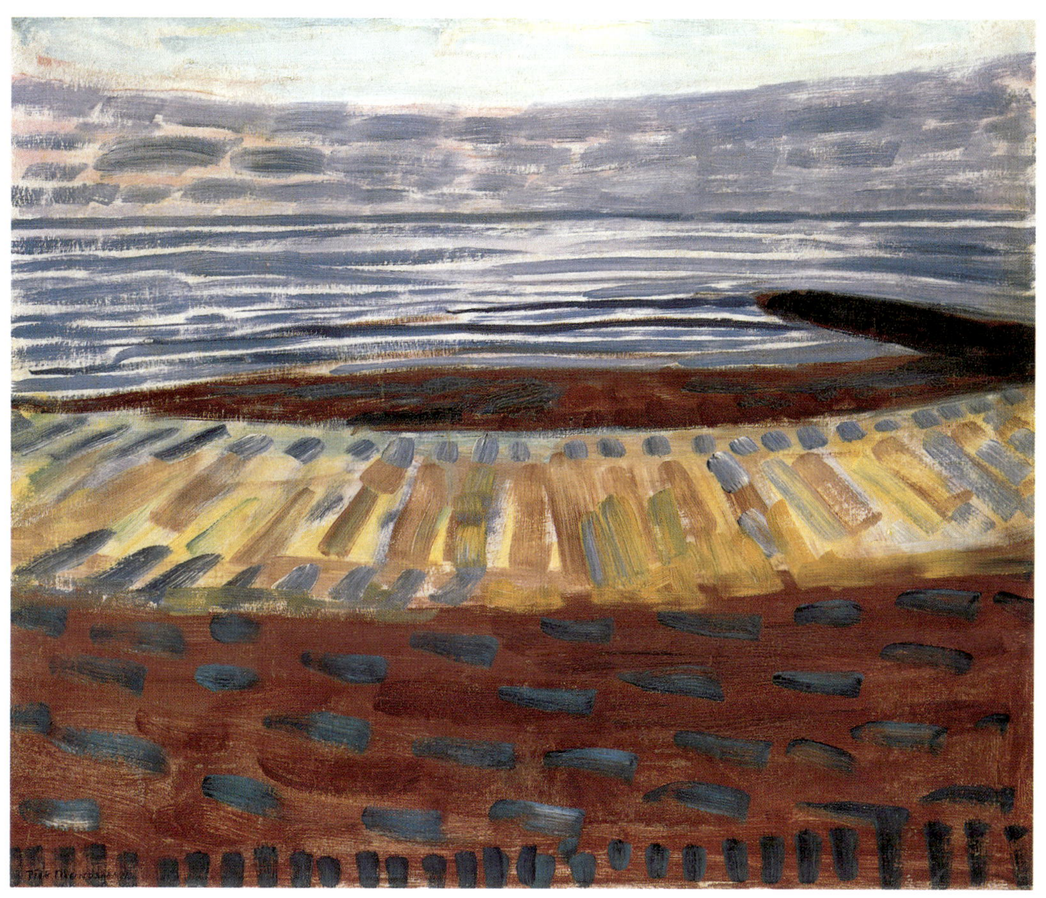
79

Cat. 79 *Sea after Sunset,* 1909
Oil on cardboard mounted on panel
24.6 x 29.3 in. (62.5 x 74.5 cm)
Signed lower left: *Piet Mondriaan.*
Gemeentemuseum, The Hague, gift of Albert van den Briel, 1963, inv. S 47–1963 (A 693)

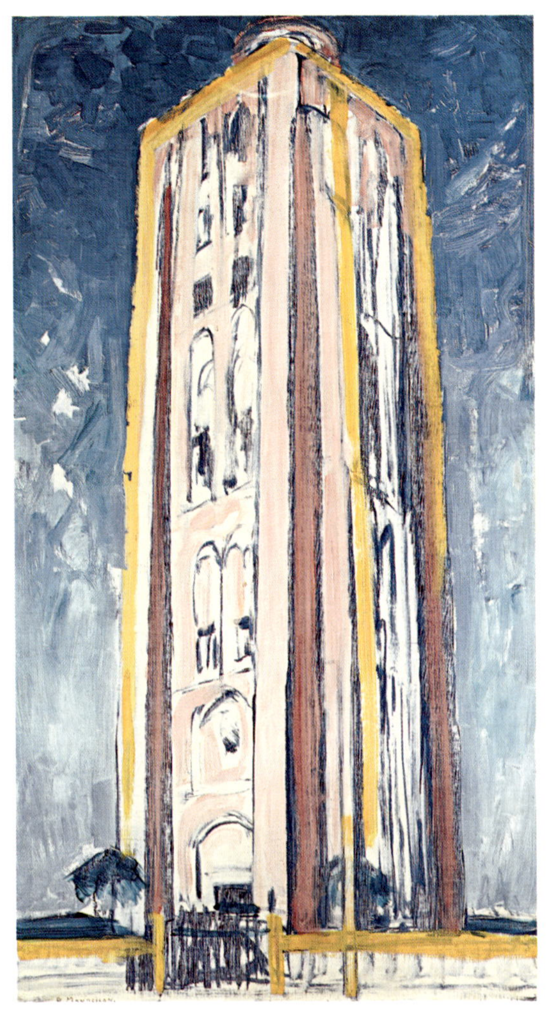
84

he should happen to behold with his prophet's eyes. In a shape of intimacy he carries the celestial down to us. It has been said that the highest fame was never reached except by those whose eyes were directed towards something higher, and also that fame is nothing but love. Should this be so, the highest fame has been reserved for Mondriaan, because his aspirations reach higher than to fame, and his love of art is extremely great.[137]

137. Ibid.

Cat. 84 *Lighthouse at Westkapelle*, c. 1910
Oil on canvas
53 x 29.5 in. (135 x 75 cm)
Signed lower left: P. MONDRIAAN.
Gemeentemuseum, The Hague, bequest of Salomon B. Slijper, 1971, inv. S 143–1971 (A 687)

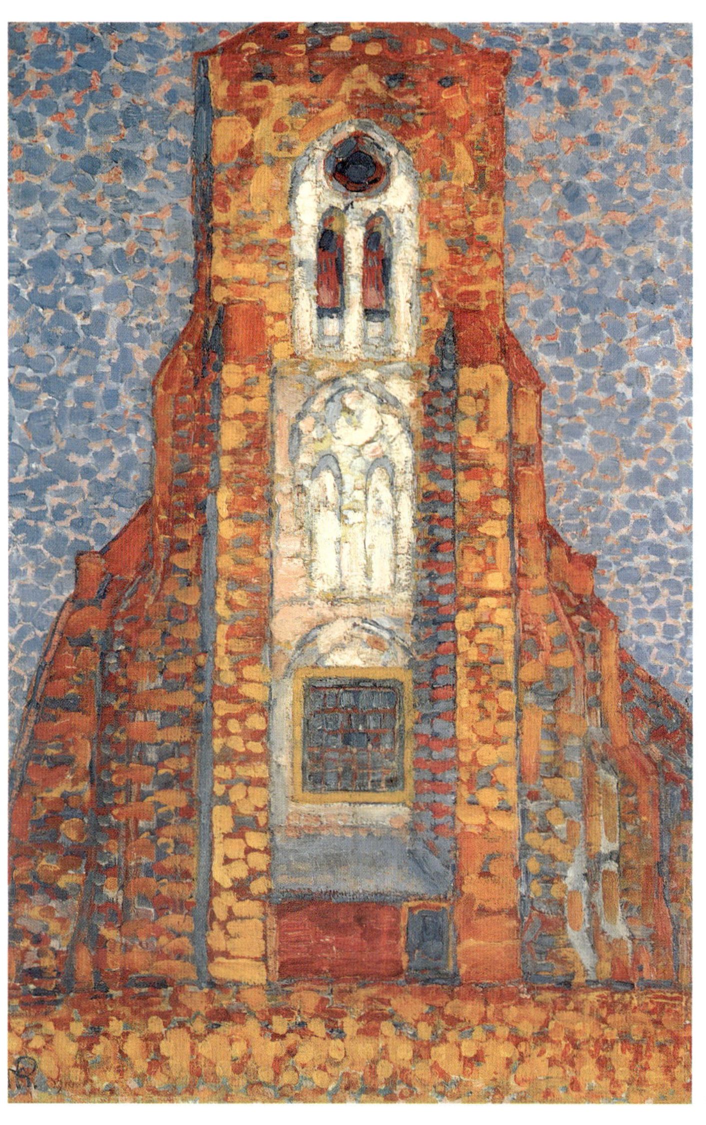

88

Cat. 88 *Zon, Kerk in Zeeland* (*Sun, Church in Zeeland*), c. 1910
Oil on canvas
35 x 24 in. (88.9 x 61 cm)
Monogrammed and dated lower left: PM. 1910.
Tate Gallery, London, purchased with the assistance of the National Lottery for The Heritage Lottery Fund, The Kreitman Foundation, The National Art Collections Fund, and The Society of Friends of the Tate Gallery, 1997, T 07328 (A 689)

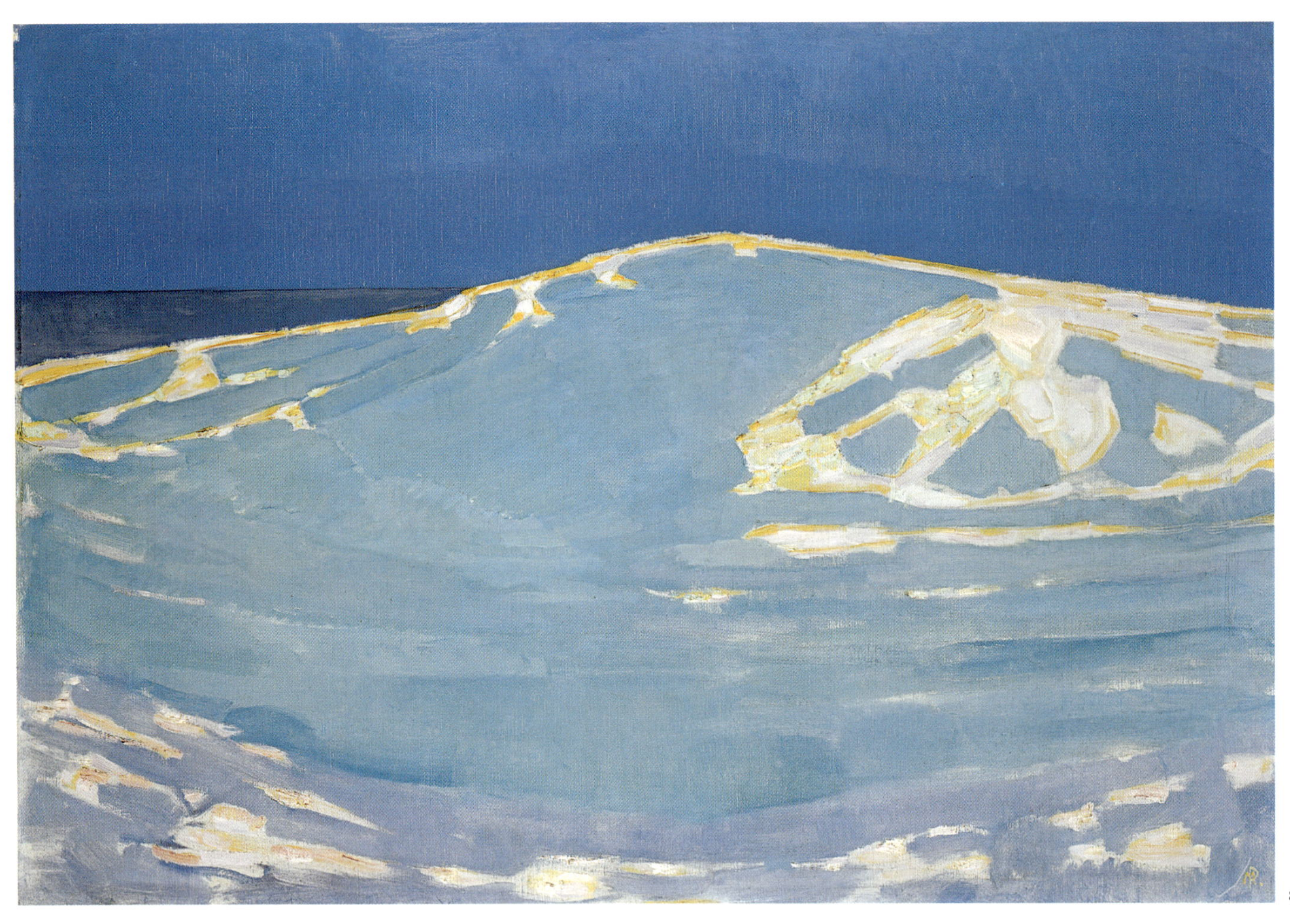
89

Cat. 89 *Duinen bij Domburg* (*Dunes at Domburg*), c. 1910
Oil on canvas
25.8 x 37.8 in. (65.5 x 96 cm)
Monogrammed lower right: PM.
Gemeentemuseum, The Hague, inv. S 83–1957 (A 709)

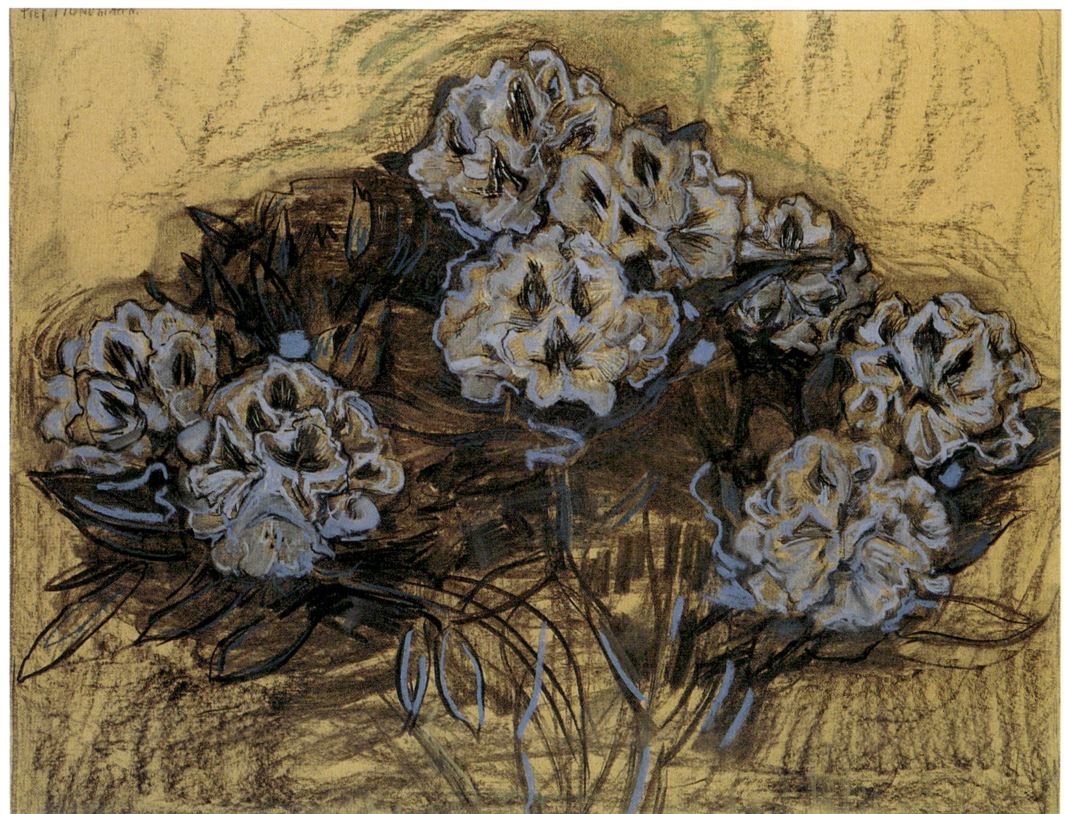

Fig. 38
Piet Mondrian, *Rhododendrons*, 1909–10
Charcoal and pastel on paper
Gemeentemuseum, The Hague (A 617)

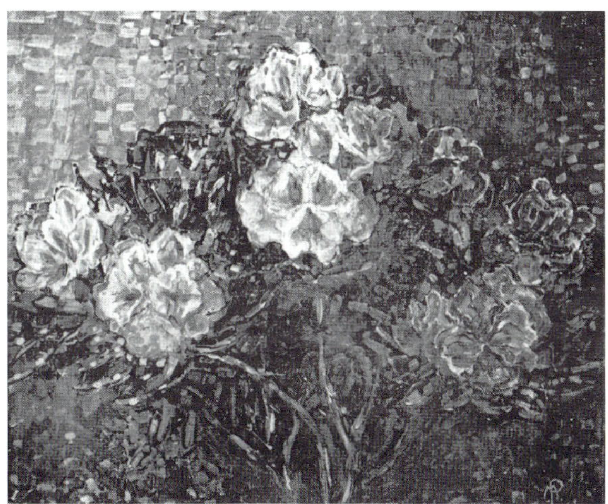

Fig. 37
Piet Mondrian, *Rhododendrons*, 1909–10
Oil on canvas
The Work disappeared after being exhibited in October 1910 at the Hotel Morgan, 355 West 11th Street, New York.
Photograph taken from the exhibition catalogue
Present location unknown (A 618)

Chapter Seven

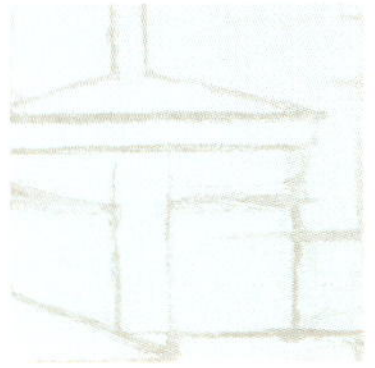

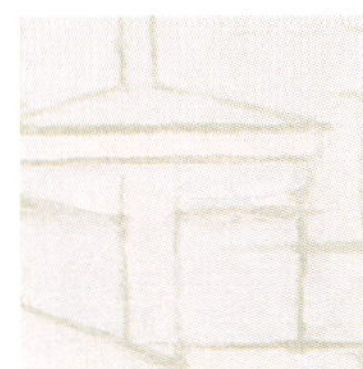

1910–1912

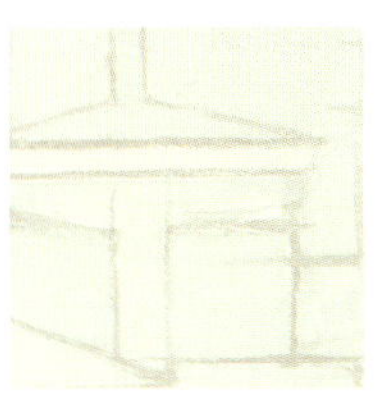

"Accordingly, I observe my work attaining greater consciousness and that it loses all that is vague."[138]

Joop M. Joosten

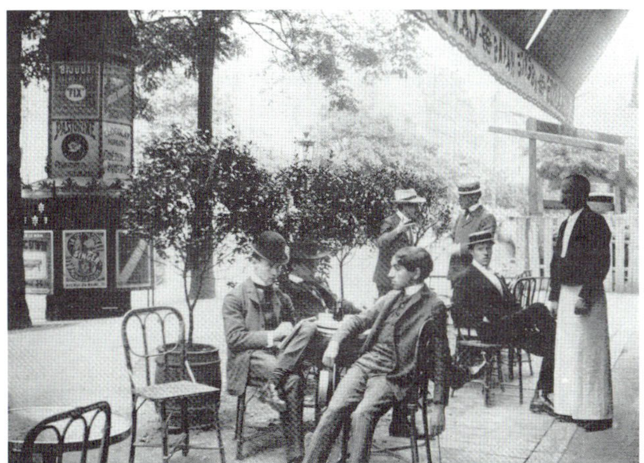

Fig. 39
On the terrace of the café Le Dôme, *in Paris,* summer 1907
From left to right, seated: G. Wiegels, Conrad Kikkert, Jules Pascin, and Lodewijk Schelfhout; standing, the art dealer Alfred Flechtheim and Rudolf Levy.
(Photo W. Uhde, *Von Bismarck bis Picasso,* 1938, p. 161.)
RKD, The Hague

In May 1911, Mondrian traveled to Paris for the first time. He went as a representative of the *Moderne Kunst Kring* (Modern Art Circle), an association founded six months earlier by Conrad Kikkert. The goal of this society was to organize an annual autumn salon in Amsterdam, after the example of the Salon d'Automne in Paris. The plan was also to create a forum by which the Dutch public, and artists in particular, could be informed about the most important new currents in the visual arts, not only in Holland, but also–and especially–abroad. After his stay in Domburg from August to October 1910 and until his trip to Paris, Mondrian had been forced to spend his time making drawings of microscopic slides for a friend of his,

138. Querido 1909–10

a professor of biology at the University of Leiden, in order to make ends meet.

Through his activities as a critic, and thanks to his friendship with the artist Lodewijk Schelfhout (1881–1943) who had lived in Paris for years, Kikkert had been able to learn much about the latest developments in the Parisian art world. Schelfhout's contacts among the circles of young German painters who gathered at the Café du Dôme on the Boulevard Montparnasse were also especially helpful (fig. 39). These artists were interested above all in French Impressionism, Neo-Impressionism, and Fauvism, of which Henri Matisse was the central figure. Kikkert's initial idea, in the spring of 1911, was therefore to draw the attention of the Dutch to Matisse and the painters around him. As the most recent developments in Dutch art clearly followed similar paths as these artists, Kikkert could count on the approval he needed. Soon after the founding of the Moderne Kunst Kring, in November 1910, he came however into contact with the newest French trend, namely Cubism. His participation in the Tuesday evening meetings organized by Paul Fort at the Closerie des Lilas, just a little farther down the Boulevard Montparnasse, to which he was introduced in early 1911, allowed Kikkert to become acquainted with some of the leading Cubists of the Left Bank: Le Fauconnier, Delaunay, Gleizes, Metzinger, and Léger. During this same period, he had probably also come into contact, through Wilhelm Uhde (1874–1947), the German art dealer and collector living in Paris, with the work of the Right Bank Cubists, in particular that of Braque and Picasso.

The nearly total ignorance of Cubism at this time in Holland, even among the members of the board of the Moderne Kunst Kring, made Kikkert realize the necessity of bringing them to Paris so that they could see and appreciate for themselves the importance of these new artistic developments. In this way he hoped to obtain their consent to present works of the Cubists at the next Amsterdam exhibition, instead of those of Matisse and his followers.

This trip was Mondrian's first art-related voyage abroad. He had gone to London twice, probably both times on the occasion of a visit to Cornwall, which he related later,[139] and in 1903, when, as mentioned above, he had gone with two friends by boat to the northern coast of Spain. But in all probability, he participated in few if any art activities or questions during these two trips. It is not known if he made any other trips abroad.

Nevertheless, we must not think that it was only in 1911 that he set his sights on Paris and France! In 1910, probably encouraged by Schelfhout during a visit of the latter to Holland, and at the time they were introduced, Mondrian had contacted the Société des Artistes Indepéndants (Society of Independent Artists) and the organizers of the Salon d'Automne, seeking to gain access to at least one of the two Parisian salons.

As early as July 1910, he had duly obtained his membership in the Société des Artistes Indépendents, and was permitted, even before coming to Paris, to enter the exhibition at Nantes organized for January 1911 by the Société des Amis des Arts (Society of the Friends of Art). The catalogue mentions Mondrian's name, and those of Kikkert, Schelfhout, and Jan Sluijters, as well as the titles of their contributions. From this, we know that Mondrian sent *Soleil de Printemps* (*Spring Sun*) and *Matin d'été* (*Summer Morning*), paintings he had shown in Amsterdam in April under their Dutch titles, *Lentezon* (A 651) and *Zomermorgen* (*Summer Morning*)(A 688).

Mondrian was thirty-nine years old when he arrived in Paris. He was fortunate that his visit coincided with the Salon des Indépendants. That year, 1911, the Left Bank Cubists, Delaunay, Gleizes, Le Fauconnier, Léger, and Metzinger, as

139. Letter from Mondrian to Til Brugman of Ocober 10, 1921, "You went to London, did you? A long time ago, I went there twice for several days. I found that it was a grandiose and beautiful city and I saw that life there was completely different and better than it is at home. But I find that Paris, once I had arrived, is in fact what suits me best. But all you have described to me and that I noticed also attracts me." Jaffé Archives, RKD, The Hague

well as the Neo-Impressionists headed by Paul Signac, were allowed to exhibit their works in specially designated galleries, a privilege that signaled the official recognition of their art.

This was the first Paris salon in which Mondrian participated. He showed one work, *Soleil*–probably the *Spring Sun* shown in Nantes–although one cannot rule out the possibility that it might have been *Zon, Kerk in Zeeland* (*Sun, Church in Zeeland*) (cat. 88). It must have felt odd for Mondrian to see a painting like *Zon, Kerk in Zeeland (Sun, Church in Zeeland)*, exhibited in Paris. A year earlier, in April 1910, it had been part of a series of fourteen "Luminist" paintings exhibited in Amsterdam, which gained Mondrian the reputation of leader of the Dutch avant-garde. The situation was just the opposite in Paris. He was only one painter among many, and here he was not thought of as avant-garde at all.

But Mondrian had himself also abandoned Luminism. The works that were in progress when he came to Paris were of a completely different style and broke with all that he had produced up to that moment. Combinations of light, scintillating colors–harmonizing or contrasting–in which the reflection of the sunlight conditioned by the hour of the day or the season, so characteristic of the work exhibited in April 1910, had given way to monumental compositions whose large surfaces were clearly defined by sharp and strongly contrasting colors, generally reds and blues, but also greens, yellows, and grays, applied partially in parallel lines. Among these works were *Evolutie* (*Evolution*) (cat. 91), *Zeeuwsche Kerktoren* (*Zeeland Churchtower*) (A 691), *Molen* (*Mill*) (cat. 90), *Duinlandschap* (*Dune Landscape*) (cat. 92), and yet another version, since disappeared, of rhododendrons (fig. 37), entitled *Bloemen* (*Flowers*) (U 1).

In his account of the historical antecedents of Neo-Plasticism, included in his first great essay of 1917, "De Nieuwe Beelding in de schilderkunst" ("The Neo-Plasticism in Painting"), published in *De Stijl*, Mondrian describes this evolution:

Throughout modern painting we see a trend to the straight line and planar, primary color. Shortly before Cubism we see the broad contours emphasized as strongly as possible and the colors within them made flat and intense (Van Gogh and others). The technique of painting was correspondingly transformed: the work took on a new appearance, although the inner impulse came from the same source.... At the same time, the ideas that Cézanne had already established (that everything has a geometric basis, that painting consists solely of color oppositions, etc.) were increasingly stressed and cleared the way for Cubism.[140]

As mentioned, the work of these two precursors, van Gogh and Cézanne, was not unknown to Mondrian while he was making his change of course. Van Gogh, in particular his late works, was regularly exhibited in Holland, and had been the subject, in relation to Mondrian, of two important landmarks, both in Amsterdam: the 1905 retrospective at the Stedelijk Museum, and a small exhibition, entirely devoted to the last period, at the galleries of C. M. van Gogh in September 1908. At the opening of the "Drucker" extension–the present South Wing of the Rijksmuseum in December 1909–eleven Cézannes of the period 1880–1900 were displayed in the lower galleries. They were from the collection of C. Hoogendijk of The Hague, and had been on loan to the Rijksmuseum since 1907. This exhibition occasioned lively critiques, not only on the works shown, but also on Cézanne's ideas published by Emile Bernard in his 1907 essay, "Souvenirs sur Paul Cézanne" ("Souvenirs of Paul Cézanne").

140. Mondrian 1917–18, 130; as translated in Holtzman and James 1986, 63.

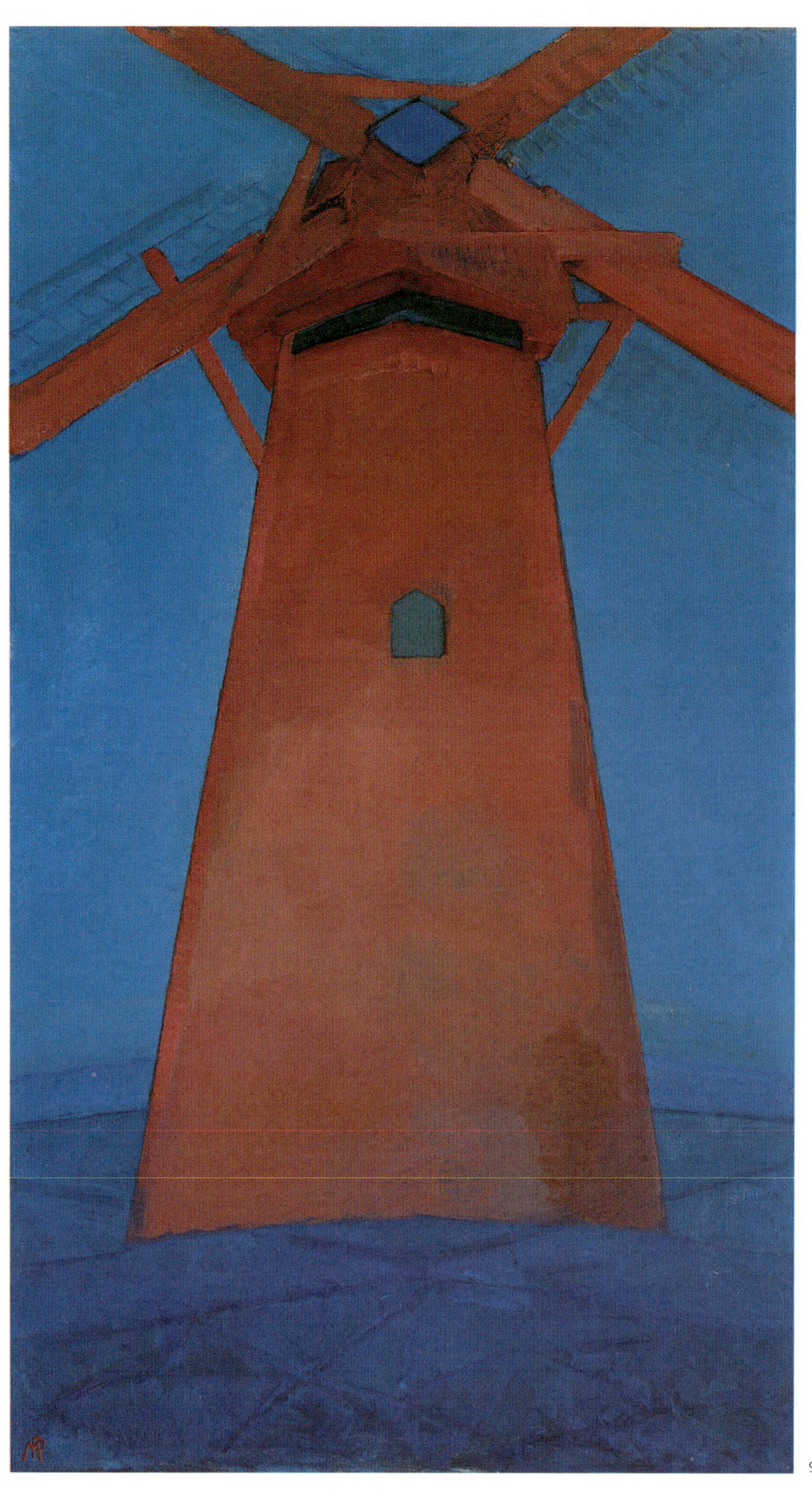

90

Cat. 90 *Molen* (*Red Mill*), 1910
Oil on canvas
59.1 x 33.9 in. (150 x 86 cm)
Monogrammed lower left: PM
Gemeentemuseum, The Hague, bequest of Salomon B. Slijper, 1971, inv. S 147–1971 (A 692)

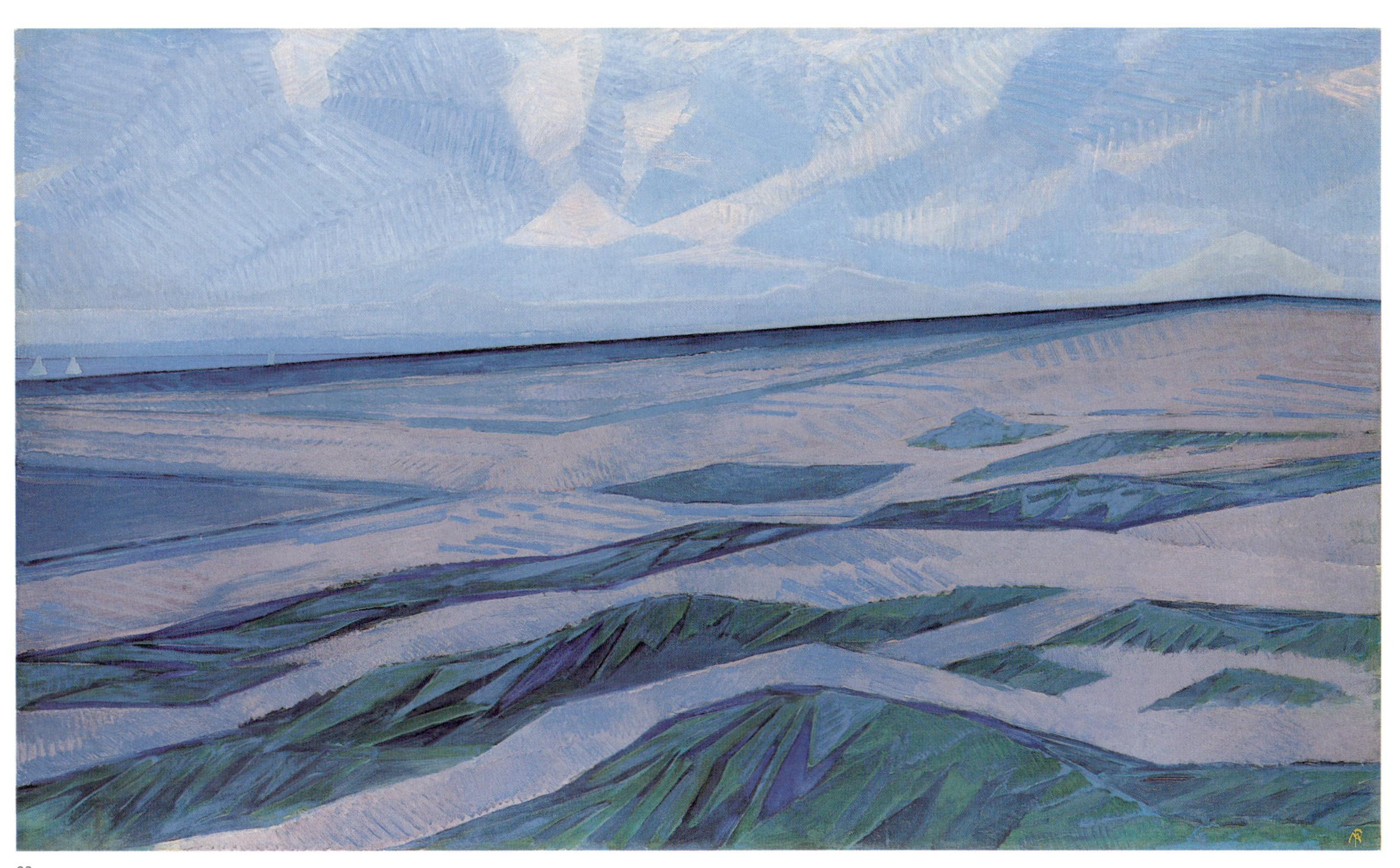

92

Cat. 92 *Duinlandschap* (*Dune Landscape*), 1911
Oil on canvas
55.5 x 94.1 in. (141 x 239 cm)
Monogrammed lower left: PM
Gemeentemuseum, The Hague, bequest of Salomon
B. Slijper, 1971, inv. S 149–1971 (B 1)

The appearance of Cézanne's works along with seven paintings from van Gogh's French period, coming in part from the Hoogendijk loan and in part from a loan made for the occasion by Johanna van Gogh-Bonger, surely led to the feeling that the contribution of either of these two artists to the development of modern art could not be dissociated from that of the other.
Would the impact of the fundamental formal innovations introduced by these two precursors of modern art have been as strong on Mondrian if, during the same period, he was not deeply involved in the study of Theosophy? This is doubtful: Even if he had been able to see and study Cézanne's work more thoroughly, this would not have sufficed to enable him to fathom its meaning for the further development of painting, or, more particularly, to learn from the way Cézanne valued the peculiarities of color and brushstroke–each in its own right–and deploy them as the principal tools of visual expression.
In October 1909, in a letter from Domburg to Aletta de Iongh, Mondrian had written this surprising remark:

So, you found me so changed? Well, yes, it is only an appearance; I am still the same, with just a little more equilibrium, if I am not mistaken. The study of Theosophy has had much to do with it. I owe much to this kind of knowledge; it is truly a guide in the development of the awareness of oneself.

to which was added this postscript, "I did not find you changed; with me it is the disappearance of my beard that looks strange!"[141] Mondrian's remarks leave no doubt that his friend was not referring to changes in his physical appearance, but to the fact that she had sensed in him that "little more equilibrium," that "development of awareness," to which "the study of Theosophy" had led.

Several months earlier, in May 1909, Mondrian had become a member of the Amsterdam section of the Theosophical Society. This membership gave him the opportunity to attend conferences and assemblies organized by the society, and to have access to its library. The study of this doctrine certainly encouraged him to research even more deeply the fundamental principles and foundations of art and its meaning. Through Theosophy, Mondrian was able to lay the groundwork for his very logically constructed, future reflections on art, but, above all, Theosophy must have stimulated his quest to know the essence of painting and therefore helped him to understand the significance of the formal innovations of van Gogh and Cézanne. At the same time, Mondrian wrote, still from Domburg, the letter to Israel Querido already mentioned. If we often quote from this letter, it is because Mondrian's theosophical preoccupations appear very clearly in it, without the word "Theosophy" ever being mentioned. What interests us, is Mondrian's response to a remark from Querido:

And further you write at the end that what I have achieved was obtained through my talent as a painter etc., and you consider my work like that of others, who do the same. And yet I know that, despite much similarity, there is a great difference. It seems to me that you too recognise the important relationship between philosophy and art, and it is exactly this relationship which most painters deny. The great masters grasp it unconsciously, but I believe that a painter's conscious spiritual knowledge will have a much greater influence upon his art, and that it is merely a weakness in him–or a lack of genius–should this spiritual knowledge be harmful to his art. . . . Accordingly, I observe my work attaining greater consciousness and that it loses all that is vague.[142]

141. Unpublished letter, Aletta de Iongh Archives, Kröller-Müller Museum, Otterlo.
142. Querido 1909–10, as translated in Welsh and Joosten 1969

A year later, in 1910, Mondrian subscribed to a new weekly paper *Eenheid: weekblad voor maatschappelijke en geestelijke stroomingen* (*Unity: Weekly Magazine of Social and Spiritual Movements*). Independent of any religious affiliation, it offered him a broader viewpoint as well as wider information about society. Its influence can be found in his future writings.

We are grateful to Jozien Knap, the daughter of the painter Gerrit Knap (1873–1931), who occupied the studio above Mondrian's at 42 Sarphatipark in Amsterdam, for this souvenir of a visit to Mondrian's studio, which he had then drastically refurnished: "Above the wainscoting, everything was white; the floor was black, and on the easel stood a canvas of an immaculate white."[143] Mondrian's protégé at the time, the painter Loe Saalborn (1891–1957), also described this arrangement, but several years later:

When I stepped for the first time into the large white studio on Sarphatipark–in which there reigned an order that rhymed, with magic effect, the rare pieces of furniture and radiant paintings on white easels–I was seized by a sublime sensation of spiritual happiness and celestial peace.[144]

In a letter to Aletta de Iongh from May 1909, Mondrian gives the news first hand: "Because I darkened a wall of the studio with coal tar, it smells so much of bitumen that you could get a headache, and I had to get out. I thought that the odor would quickly go away. . . ."[145] He begged her to postpone her visit to the studio.[146]

This drastic rearrangement of Mondrian's studio, and the fact that he shaved his beard, can only be interpreted as a definitive rejection of the idea of artistic genius—until that time respected and strongly supported by tradition—and the adoption of a position in favor of new ideas about nature and the essence of the work of art.

In "The New Plastic in Painting," Mondrian expressed himself this way several paragraphs before the one cited above:

Until the modern era, the plastic means of all painting was rather the natural appearance of objects than natural form and color. Natural appearance was transformed by the prevailing sense of style but always in such a way that the natural remained recognizable. Thus we can understand the astonishment and even anger aroused in recent times when form and color began to be used autonomously and natural appearances were no longer recognizable. One was confronted with the necessity of accepting a new way of seeing. A more conscious vision, which saw form and color as means in themselves, resulted from the conscious perception of what was previously perceived unconsciously: that beauty in art is created not by the objects of representation but by the relationships of line and color (Cézanne). Despite its greater consciousness, the new era was slow to accept this, so deeply rooted was naturalistic vision.[147]

It is possible that the process of realization mentioned in this text had been such an intimate experience for Mondrian that he had wanted to render it plastically. In the triptych *Evolutie* (*Evolution*) (cat. 91), on the left, Life is seen unaware of herself; in the center, the moment when Awareness is born; and, on the right, Life achieving Awareness. Once in the Salon des Indépendants, Mondrian must have realized that there was little chance that the work he was exhibiting would be noticed.[148] It would be fascinating to know how he would have measured the development of Cubism, such as it was seen in this Salon, against the most recent evolution of

143. Scherphuis 1994, 74
144. Loe Saalborn, "Mondriaan zag in mij de schilder" ("Mondrian Saw the Painter in Me"), *De Telegraaf*, March 12, 1955.
145. Unpublished letter, Aletta de Iongh Archives, Kröller-Müller Archives. Otterlo.
146. There exists a remarkable letter as well from R. F. E. Schweizer of October 9, 1986, to H. Henkels, in which a conversation between Mondrian and Sluijters is reported: JAN: Pieter, if I understand you correctly, you want to paint an entirely white painting. PIET: Yes, Jan, you are right, but, only it's so difficult!" Archives of the Gemeentemuseum, The Hague.
147. Mondrian 1917–18, 129; Holtzman and James 1986, 63.
148. Pierre Cabanne writes, in *L'Epopée du cubisme* (*The Epic of Cubism*), Paris, 1963, 139, without indicating the source, "Delaunay is equally very interested in a *Soleil* (*Sun*) by the Dutch painter, Piet Mondrian, who has also been influenced by Cubism, but will not delay in abandoning it for successive abstractions, preludes to the horizontal-vertical order."

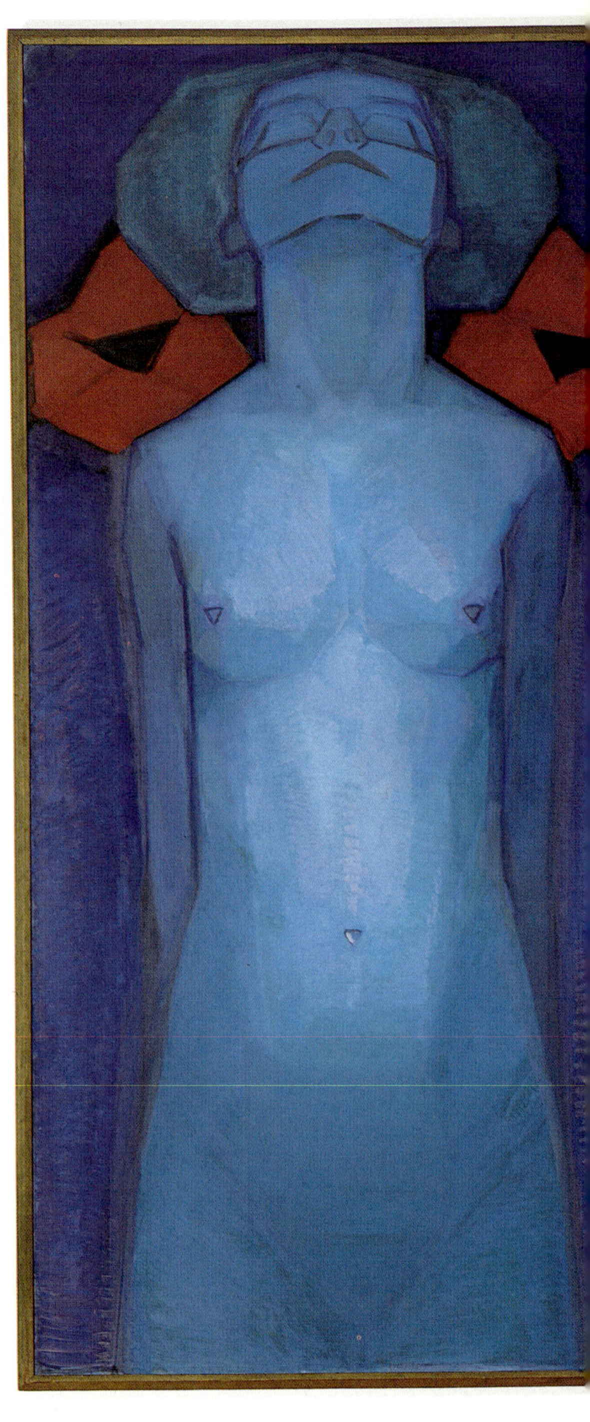

Cat. 91 *Evolutie* (*Evolution*), 1910
Oil on canvas (triptych)
70.1 x 33.5 in. (178 x 85 cm) (side panels); 72 x 33.5 in. (183 x 87.5 cm) (center panel)
Each panel is monogrammed lower right: PM
Original frames
Gemeentemuseum, The Hague, bequest of Salomon B. Slijper, 1971, inv. S 148–1971 (A 647)

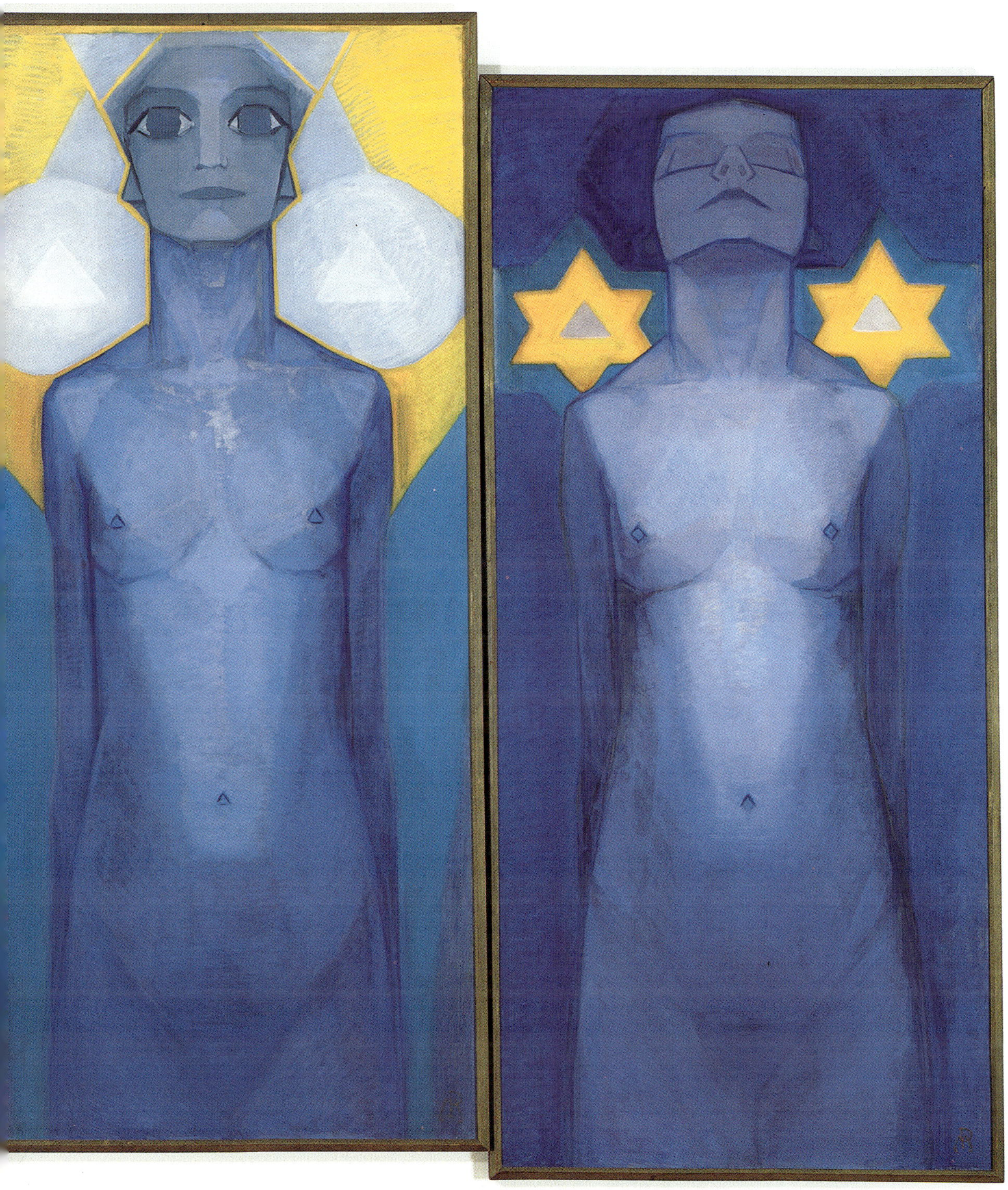

91

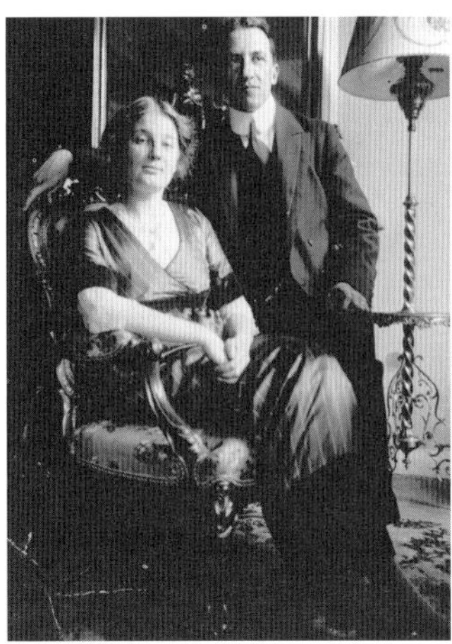

Fig. 40
Engagement photograph: Greta Heijbroek and Piet Mondrian, in Laren, October 1911
Gemeentemuseum, The Hague

his own work. All that comes to us from him about his voyage and his life in Paris is contained in a few words written on a postcard, addressed during his stay to his friend Simon Maris, "I am having a very good time here. Everything is grand and grandiose."[149]

Because the goal of the trip was to see (and to come to terms with) Cubism, we can suppose that he studied deeply, gauging and judging the works of the pioneers—Delaunay, Gleizes, Le Fauconnier, Léger, and Metzinger—gathered again for the Salon. In gallery 45 were Delaunay's *The Eiffel Tower*, a painting that disappeared in 1945, and *La Ville number 2*, currently at the National Museum of Modern Art in Paris; Gleizes's *The Woman with Phlox*, now at the Museum of Fine Arts, Houston, and *Paris Landscape*, sold at auction in New York in 1999; Le Fauconnier's *Abundance*, now at the Gemeentemuseum in The Hague, and *Portrait of Paul Castiaux*, formerly in the collection of W. Beffie; Léger's *Nudes in the Forest*, now in the Kröller-Müller Museum in Otterlo; and a *Landscape*, with two nudes against a background of trees, by Metzinger. Elsewhere in the exhibition was *The Cuirassier* by de La Fresnaye, now in the National Museum of Modern Art in Paris.

We can presume also that Kikkert introduced Mondrian to the art dealers D. H. Kahnweiler, Clovis Sagot, and Wilhelm Uhde, to see works by Braque and Picasso, and that from this Mondrian would have been able to form a clear idea about their production. It is even possible that he attended a party given by Le Fauconnier, again introduced by Kikkert, and then became aware of Le Fauconnier's proclamation "Oeuvre d'art" (Work of Art), the content of which might have seemed to him both too naturalistic and too theoretical.

Back in Holland again after his ten-day visit to France, Mondrian worked on putting the finishing touches to the works he wanted to show in the first exhibition of the Moderne Kunst Kring, scheduled for October at the Stedelijk Museum in Amsterdam.

At the end of July and beginning of August 1911, he spent several days in Domburg, on the occasion of the opening of the first exhibition of works by the painters active in Zeeland, in which he participated. He left afterward to see his father in Arnhem. On August 14 and 21, he signed in at the Rijksmuseum to copy paintings there, always motivated by worries over his poor financial situation. Finally, preparations for the celebration of his official engagement to Greta Heijbroek (1884–1964), which was to take place in October, must have absorbed him for the greater part of August and September (fig. 40).

On Friday, October 6, 1911, at the Stedelijk Museum in Amsterdam, the Exposition Internationale d'Art Moderne (International Exhibition

149. Gorter, van Burkom, and Joosten 1998, no. 3, 36.

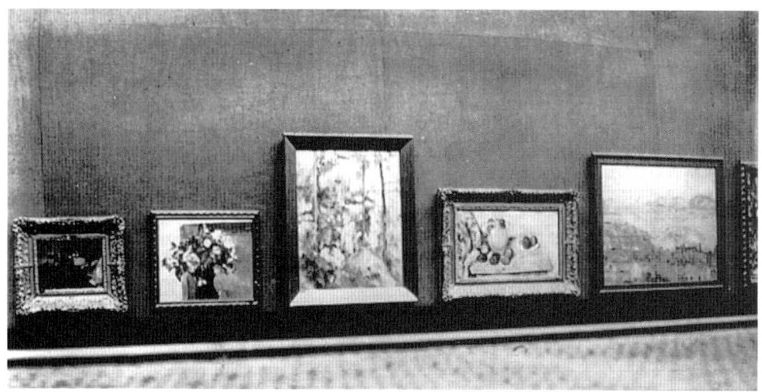

Fig. 41a, b, and c
The International Exhibition of Modern Art,
October 1911
An homage to Cézanne opened the first exhibition of the Moderne Kunst Kring (Modern Art Circle) at the Stedelijk Museum, Amsterdam.
RKD, The Hague

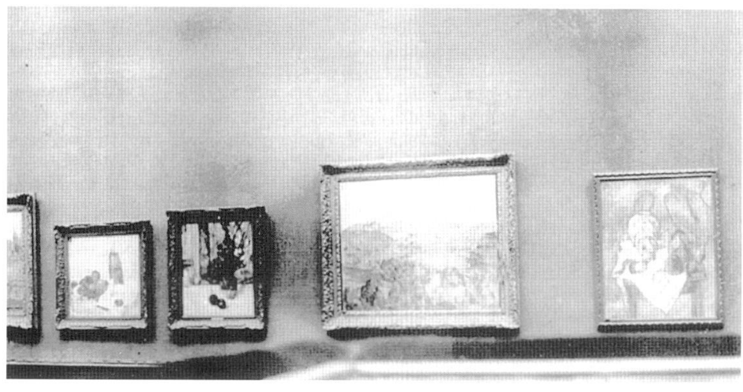

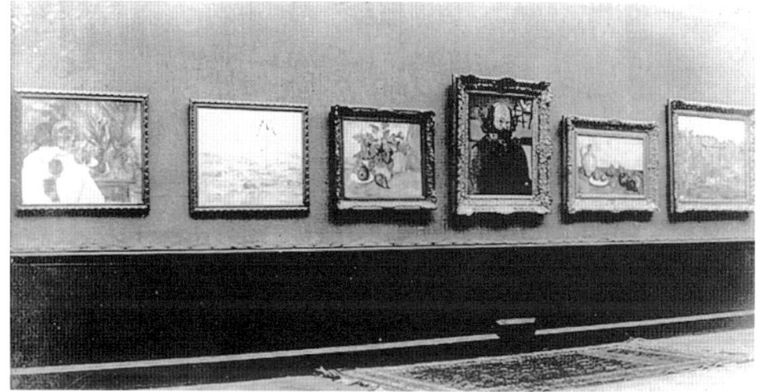

of Modern Art) opened with a speech by Jan Toorop, president of the Moderne Kunst Kring and dean of the defenders of the new art to which the Circle was devoted.

The exhibition began with a homage to Paul Cézanne, "the great Cézanne" as Toorop referred to him, adding, "[He] was the father in France and even, dare I say it, in all of this brave Europe of painting, the precursor of the modern school; the laborer; the profound, subtle, and majestic tonalist; precursor, after Manet, of this modern school."[150] Twenty-eight of the thirty-three works by Cézanne that composed the Hoogendijk Collection were on exhibit (fig. 41a, b, c).

Among the foreign contributors were the Parisian Cubists Braque and Picasso and the painters close to them, such as Derain, Dufy, Herbin, and Puy. Le Fauconnier, Rudolf Levy, Hermann Lismann, and Schelfhout, of the Montparnasse group, were there as well. Other French painters represented

150. Review of the opening. *De Tijd,* October 7, 1911.

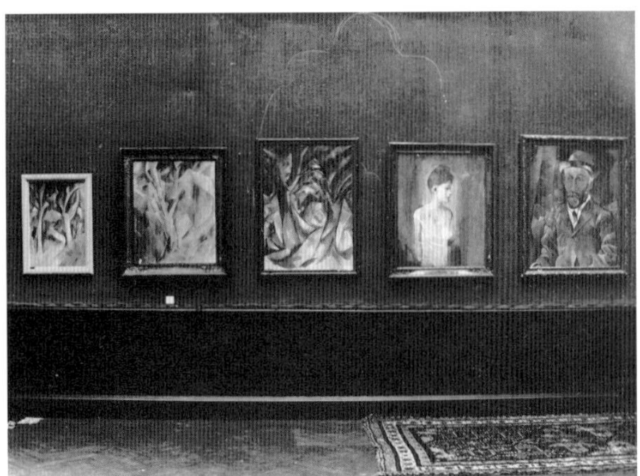

Fig. 42
The International Exhibition of Modern Art, October 1911
The works of Georges Braque and Pablo Picasso were exhibited beside those of Cézanne during the first exhibition of the Moderne Kunst Kring (Modern Art Circle) at the Stedelijk Museum, Amsterdam.
RKD, The Hague

were J. L. Chaillé, Denis, O. Friesz, H. Manguin, Redon, Vlaminck, and van Dongen, who had shown several times in Holland during the preceding years, causing much excitement.

A great restraint regarding modernity prevailed in the choice of works. With Braque and Picasso, the chosen paintings were from 1908 and 1909 and earlier, that is to say, works in which the object represented was still clearly identifiable (fig. 42). This last observation was equally true for the selection of paintings by Le Fauconnier, Levy, Lismann, and Schelfhout, who all contributed recent works. Did Kikkert alone make the selections? Or was it the work of the collective decision of the board? Were they trying not to shock the Amsterdam public? Or was the selection perhaps even chosen to complement the work of Cézanne?

Mondrian showed the five works described above, characterized by large surfaces of contrasting colors, comparable to those of the Cloisonnists in the 1890s: *Evolutie (Evolution)* (cat. 91), *Zeeuwsche Kerktoren* (*Zeeland Church Tower*) (fig. 43), *Molen (Mill)* (cat. 90), *Duinlandschap (Dune Landscape)* (cat. 92), and *Bloemen* (*Flowers*) (U 1), since disappeared. He also showed the 1910 painting mentioned first in the catalogue of Saint Lucas, *Zomer, Duin in Zeeland* (*Summer, Dune in Zeeland*) (A 708). In most of the critical reviews of the exhibition, the work of Mondrian, especially *Flowers*, and *Dune Landscape*, was defined as Cubist or considered strongly influenced by Cubism. Also, the reviews consistently referred to the well-defined, especially triangular, geometric surfaces. This particular borrowing from Cubism had already been mentioned in Toorop's inaugural lecture, in which, addressing himself to the artists, he exhorted them to move toward a great simplification of style, "in verticals and horizontals rectilinear or gently curving . . . in triangles, as in the very interesting research of the

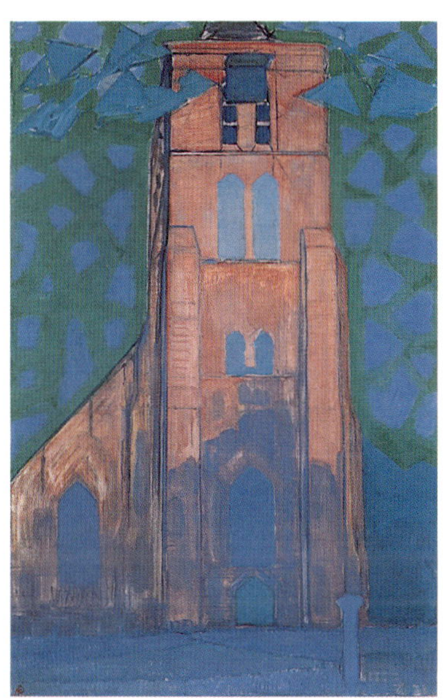

Fig. 43
Piet Mondrian, *Clocktower in Zeeland*, 1911
Oil on canvas
Gemeentemuseum, The Hague (A 691)

young French Cubists of these last few years."[151]
The most obvious explanation of this interpretation of Cubism as founded on the triangle is that it had as a starting point the general impression given by the exhibited Cubist paintings themselves. The presence of Le Fauconnier's *Portrait of Paul Castiaux* suggests that the theoretical approach of LeFauconnier, still strongly shared at that moment by his less original disciples Levy, Lissmann, and Schelfhout, played an important if not decisive role both in this characterization of Cubism and in the interpretation of Mondrian's work. It is a pity that *Flowers* has disappeared. The fact that this painting, together with *Dune Landscape,* was mentioned first in the catalogue could indicate that they were the most recent works Mondrian sent to the exhibition. The triangular forms in the lower half of *Dune Landscape* are particularly striking, and the painting *Flowers* was perhaps even more disturbing. That could well have been the reason for the disappearance of this work, which was far too dependent on a form of Cubism that later proved to have produced rather dubious results.
Unlike the balance sheet of sales for the Saint Lucas society's exhibition of 1910, there are no mentions of any sales at all for Mondrian in 1911. The new turn that his work had taken was obviously too abrupt and too radical.
What, if anything, did this exhibition teach Mondrian? In the catalogue assembled in 1964 by Blok of Mondrian's works in the Gemeentemuseum in The Hague, Blok noted that Mondrian's friend Van den Briel had recounted how, before Mondrian's departure for Paris, the painter had sent to Van den Briel the gingerpot and some other accessories represented in *Still Life with Gingerpot I* (cat. 93). This act indicates that the work must date from before his departure for Paris—where Mondrian was planning to move in 1912. At first sight, the painting evokes the most complex of Cézanne's still lifes. Even if it cannot be ruled out that Mondrian had seen and studied similar still lifes during his visit to Paris, it is more logical to think that it was the paintings of the Hoogendijk Collection that influenced him. However, the most complex still lifes of this collection were not included in the Rijksmuseum catalogue of 1911, and cannot, therefore, have been included in the permanent installation after December 1909. It must therefore have been during the nearly complete presentation of the Hoogendijk Collection at this first exhibition of the Moderne Kunst Kring that Mondrian was able to see these still lifes. He would then have been able to study them for a sufficiently long time to memorize their specific characteristics, on both the structural and pictorial levels; to understand the importance these elements carried in the ensemble of the painting; and to be able to

151. Ibid

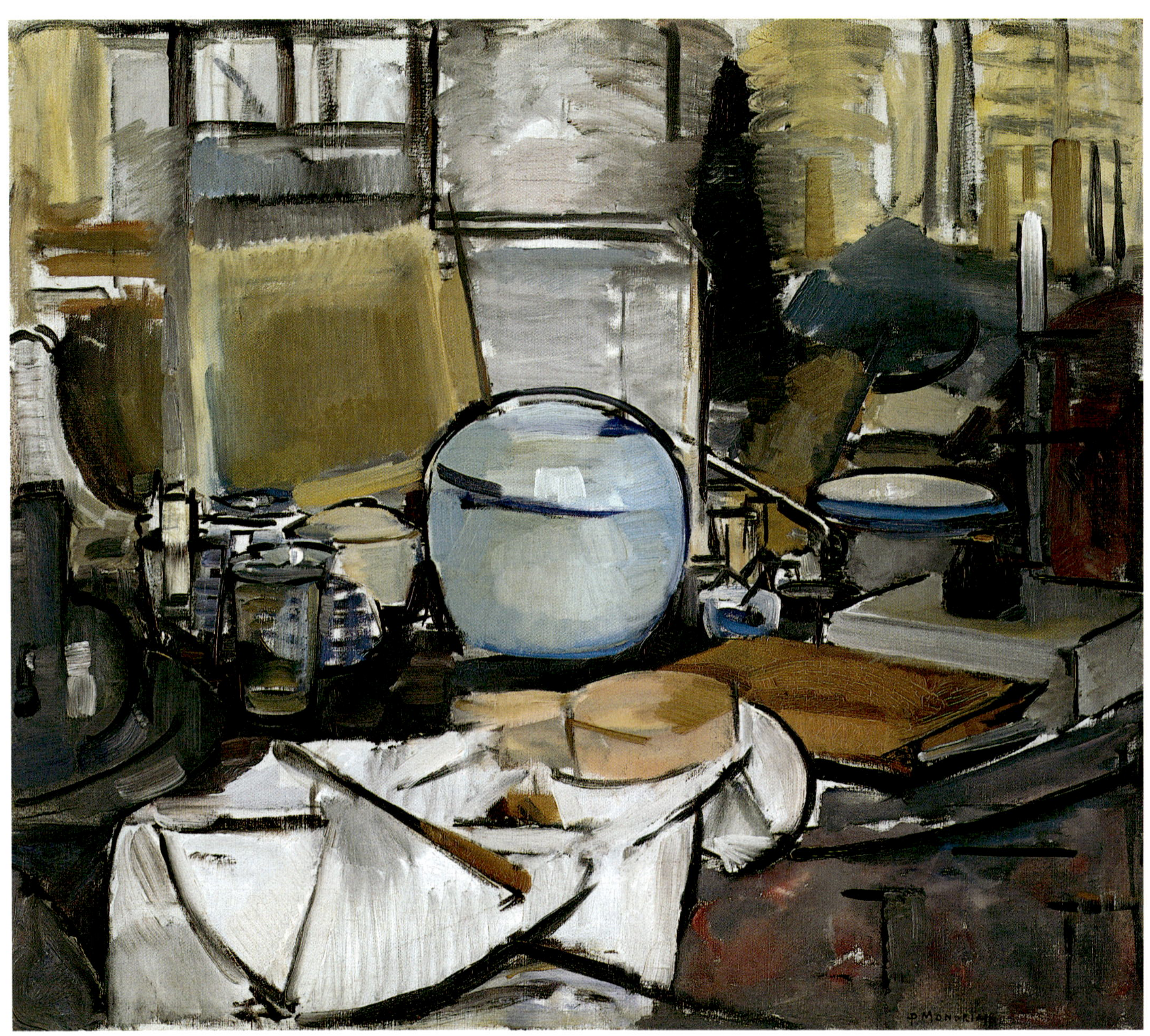

93

Cat. 93 *Still Life with Gingerpot I*, 1911
Oil on canvas
26.1 x 29.5 in. (66.5 x 75 cm)
Signed lower right: P MONDRIAN.
The Solomon R. Guggenheim Museum, New York, inv. 295.76
(B 2)

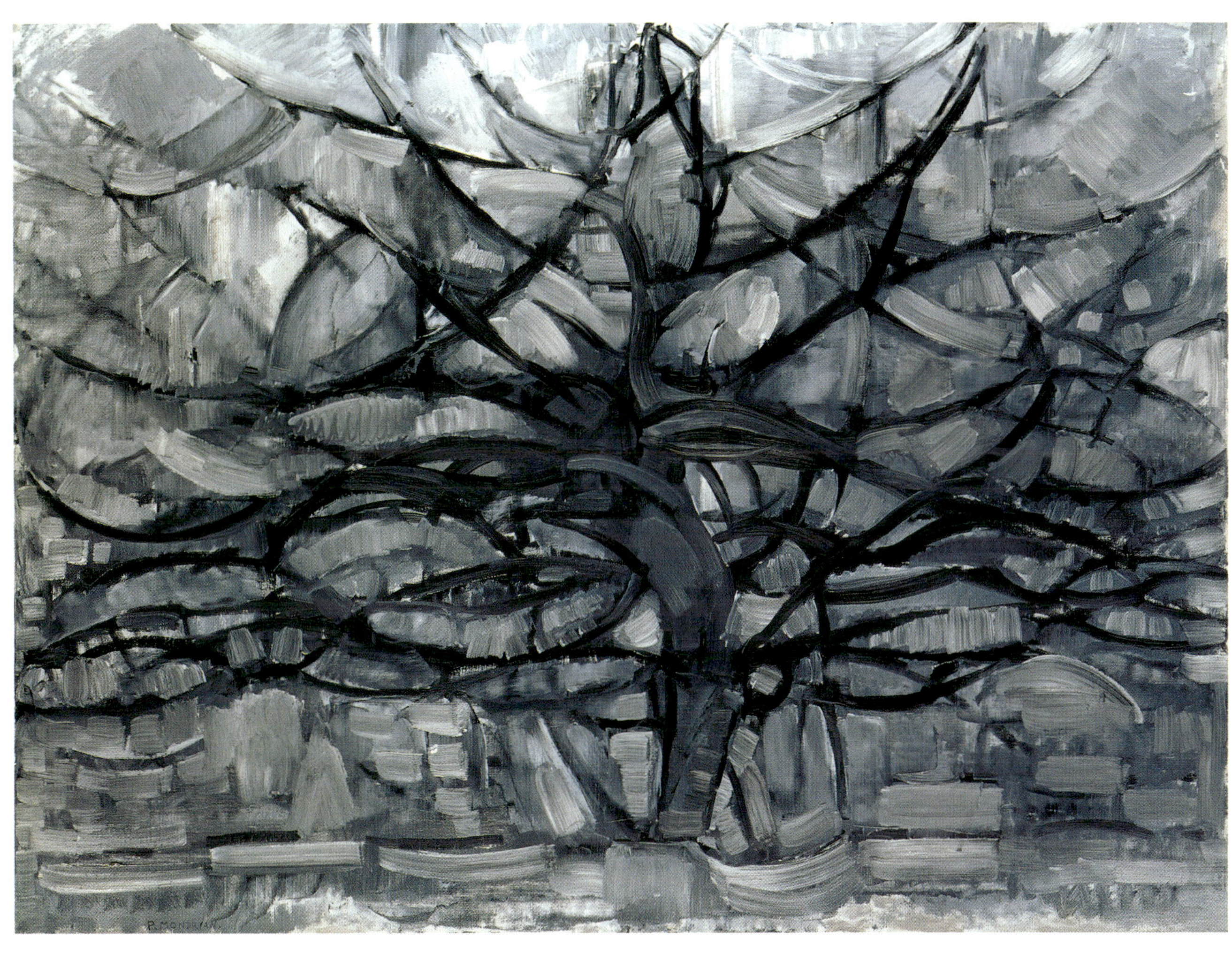

94

Cat. 94 *The Gray Tree,* c. 1911–12
Oil on canvas
31.4 x 43 in. (79.7 x 109.1 cm)
Signed lower left: P. MONDRIAN.
Gemeentemuseum, The Hague, bequest of Salomon B. Slijper, 1971, inv. S 156–1971 (B 4)

remember what he had learned when turning to a similar composition in his studio, made with appropriate objects that he had at hand, borrowed from his friend Van den Briel.

If one considers what Mondrian produced in the twelve months following the exhibition of October 1911, only one conclusion is likely: the lessons that he drew from it came much more from the study of Cézanne's work, so extensively represented, than from the Cubist painters shown. In this context, it is necessary, in my opinion, to make a place for Mondrian's painting *The Gray Tree* (cat. 94). This work recalls Cézanne's canvas entitled *Sous-bois provençal* (*In a Provençal Forest*; The Museum of Modern Art, New York), that figured in the Moderne Kunst Kring exhibition. In *The Gray Tree*, Mondrian borrowed the technique so characteristic of the late work of Cézanne, whatever the subject, in which the particular character of the brushstroke is never sacrificed to the reproduction of the exterior appearance, as clearly demonstrated by the drawing of the trunk and the branches, and the laying on of the colors stroke by parallel stroke. However, where Mondrian clearly and explicitly stands apart from Cézanne's style is in the way he directs his brushstrokes. Contrary to Cézanne, whose strokes generally follow the dominant directions in the painting, Mondrian always chooses oppositions, as here in the orientation of the gray and white strokes vis-à-vis the darker lines of the trunk and branches. This effect is of a visual field conceived as two-dimensional, a concept absolutely foreign to Cézanne, but one that is the key, not only to the early, but also to Mondrian's future work. There are no indications that allow us to date *The Gray Tree*; probably, though, it was painted between October 1911 and July 1912.

It is not really so strange that Mondrian was able to execute only one painting during the last quarter of the year 1911, if one considers that, during this time, he became officially engaged to Greta Heijbroek; that he was preparing for their marriage, only to break off their engagement shortly before the ceremony; and that, having decided to move to Paris, he had, at this same time, to settle his affairs in Amsterdam (see fig. 40).

Except for two photographs, only two documents have so far come to light mentioning the engagement, the plan for marriage, and the break-up with Greta Heijbroek. The first is the announcement made by Jan Toorop to his daughter Charley in a letter from Domburg dated October 26, 1911: "Mondrian, who just became engaged, will probably come and introduce his friend to us at Nijmegen. He is going to be married soon. I met his fiancée at the opening of the exhibition. Mondrian asked me to tell you. He sends you fond regards."[152] The second document comes from Paris, in a letter—Mondrian's last—to Aletta de Iongh, written when he had moved in to one of the "studio-residences" on the Avenue du Maine. He wrote:

You have certainly heard also that I was almost married this last fall, but that I fortunately saw in time that it was nothing but an illusion, all that beauty. Although I have always lived for my art, even so, in life the beautiful is tempting, and that is why I do things that sometime seem strange for me.[153]

We know very little about Greta Heijbroek, twelve years younger than Mondrian, the younger sister of M. J. Heijbroek, who worked in a bank in Amsterdam and had bought some of Mondrian's works. She also painted and was Mondrian's student.

As for Mondrian's settling his affairs, in a letter from November 1945 to Slijper, Van den Briel writes that Mondrian sold everything he could to raise money, as he had done three years earlier at the time of his exhibition with Jan Sluijters and

152. Unpublished letter, Archives Jan Toorop, Koninklijke Bibliotheek, The Hague.
153. Unpublished letter, Aletta de Iongh Archives, Kröller-Müller Museum, Otterlo. Gorter, van Burkom, and Joosten 1998, 47.

Cornelis Spoor at the Stedelijk Museum in January 1909. He gave Van den Briel what he considered to be the best of his work that he had not sold. In addition, a cashbook belonging to Simon Maris that has survived shows that on November 29, 1911, Maris paid 130 florins for a "collection of paintings and sketches of P. Mondrian."[154] This amount does not suggest that important works were involved. It is known, however, that Mondrian left his four latest paintings with Anna Bruin (1871–1931), who lived in The Hague and regularly bought his work while she still lived in Amsterdam.

On December 20, 1911, Mondrian had his name removed from the civil registry of the city of Amsterdam. Faithful to his habits, he surely spent the Christmas holidays at his father's house and did not leave the country until the New Year, when he departed for Paris.

Mondrian probably found his first lodgings in Paris through the offices of the French section of the Theosophical Society. In any case, well before mid-March he had moved into one of the studio-residences on 33 avenue du Maine, where Kikkert and Schelfhout had lived and worked since before October 1911. His last letter to Aletta de Iongh written from this address, tells us that his beginnings in Paris had been difficult:

. . . the unknown, the studio to furnish . . . [but] here I am almost exactly as I was on Sarphatipark in Amsterdam. I have only one little room, but the studio is every bit as big. It does not cost more than in Amsterdam, and one learns much more here, you see. In a great metropolis it is crazy how one feels.[155]

Unfortunately, it is not known whether Mondrian also painted this studio white. Mondrian could not have made a better debut than to participate in the second Salon des Indépendants, which opened on March 19, 1912. The works he showed, like Schelfhout's, were placed in gallery 20, proclaimed the "Realm of the Cubists" by André Salmon in *Paris-Journal* of March 20, and designated by Apollinaire as being "perhaps the most important gallery of the Salon," in *L'Intransigeant* of April 3.

Among the other works on display were *Les Baigneuses (The Bathers*) by Gleizes, today in the National Museum of Modern Art in Paris; *Le Chasseur (The Hunter*) by Le Fauconnier, now in the Gemeentemuseum in The Hague; Léger's *Composition avec Personnages* (*Composition with Figures*), known as *La Noce* (*The Wedding*), now in the National Museum of Modern Art in Paris; and *Le Port* (*The Port*) and *La Femme au cheval* (*The Woman with a Horse*) by Metzinger.

The catalogue mentions three works by Mondrian—*Dans le jardin* (*In the Garden*), *Dans la forêt* (*In the Forest*), and *La Fruitière* (*The Fruit Seller*). Although a fair number of critics mentioned his name, only Salmon gives his opinion on these works:

Mondrian makes Cubism blindly, in complete ignorance of the laws of volumes, and his inspiration comes from van Dongen! Such newcomers, alas! will drive critics [l'opinion] to distraction, will lead opinion astray for a long time. The writers of 1885 suffered from this kind of confusion.[156]

Unfortunately these three works have not been identified with certainty.

In the Garden, which was exhibited a few months later in Nijmegen as *In den tuin*, should, if one can rely on the descriptions furnished by the reviews of this last exhibition, be considered lost. *In the Forest*, whose original stretcher was used in 1913 for *Composition No. II* (B 42), judging by its dimensions, is also lost. *La Fruitière* (*The Fruit* Seller) could well be *Large Nude* (fig. 44), assuming that the white is an apron, and the red shapes in the foreground are fruit.

154. Gorter, van Burkom, and Joosten 1998, 47
155. Unpublished letter, Aletta de Iongh Archives, Kröller-Müller Museum, Otterlo
156. André Salmon, "Le Salon des Indépendants," *Paris Journal*, March 20, 1912.

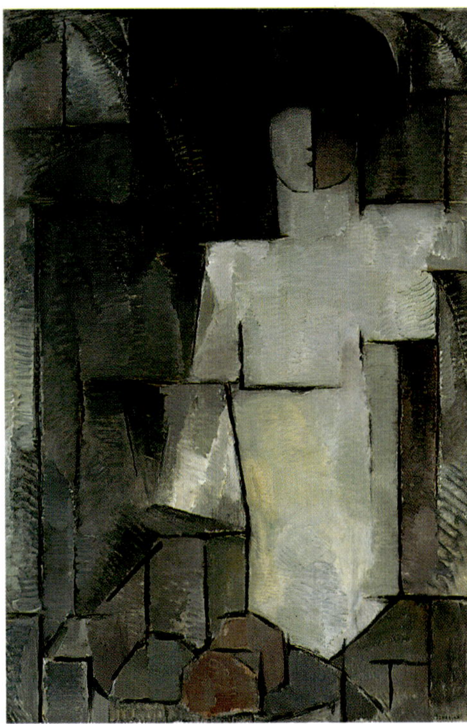

Fig. 44
Piet Mondrian, *Large Nude*, 1912
Oil on canvas
Gemeentemuseum, The Hague (B 7)

No doubt *Large Nude* was painted before June 1912, as was *Landscape with Trees* (cat. 95). Analogies exist with *Still Life with Gingerpot I* (cat. 93), but unlike the latter, these two works are rather flat, the lines are more pronounced, the brushstroke is more rigid, and the colors are restrained and attenuated. As in *The Gray Tree* (cat. 94), the painter is above all working to render the structure visible.

It was not until May 11, 1912, that Mondrian registered officially with the police as living at 26 rue du Départ, a new block of studio-residences destined to replace that of 33 avenue du Maine, which was being razed to permit the extension of the Montparnasse train station.[157] Mondrian and Schelfhout occupied a studio on the top floor, Kikkert one on a lower level. After he had installed the studio, it became urgent for Mondrian to think about earning a living. He obtained authorization from the Louvre to paint copies in the museum, from June 1, 1912, until the end of the year. It is not known what he copied; but on July 20, he completed work on a copy so that he could leave the next day to go to Holland for several weeks. He was planning to stay until the end of July with his father in Arnhem and to spend the first ten days of August in Domburg—in fact, he stayed thirteen days—and, finally, to go to Amsterdam for several days before returning to Paris. He described this plan to W. J. Steenhoff in a postcard.

In Domburg he was able to use the studio of Jacoba van Heemskerck. *The Sea* (fig.45) and *Landscape* (cat. 96), which he showed in the second exhibition of the Moderne Kunst Kring in October 1912 as *Marine (esquisse)*, and *Arbres (esquisse)*, as well as a third painting, *Sur les Dunes (esquisse)* (U 6), which is lost, were certainly painted during his visit. In addition, twenty-four sketches from two sketchbooks are known to us; their subject and style lead us to think that they too were made in Domburg during the summer of 1912, along with two large drawings, *Study of Trees* (fig. 53) and *Forest* (B 11), *Study for "The Trees"* (cat. 99).

157. Postma 1995, 36–9.

In *The Sea* (fig. 45), Mondrian has succeeded remarkably, with great sobriety of means: black horizontal, slightly curved lines and, in between, ranges of white, gray and blue gray vertically hatched strokes that evoke the waves rolling in over a long distance. They are bordered by a foam bathed with light, the horizon in the upper half of the canvas, and the blue sky above. All these effects are created without any attempt to represent the sand, the water, and the spray or the sky. This same style, which evokes without representing, also characterizes *Landscape* (cat. 96), which was, because of this, once titled *Brugstudie* (*Study of a Bridge*). Here again the flat landscape is represented only by lines and brushstrokes with the two trees bending toward the middle in the foreground, and the sky and the light behind and above (fig. 46).

Back in Paris, Mondrian announced to Kikkert, in a letter dated August 26, 1912, that he had indeed arrived and was beginning a "still life" which he believed would be very good.[158] On Monday, September 20, he announced to Mies Elout-Drabbe (1875–1956) in Domburg that this work was finished, "Thank God!," and that he was not unhappy, especially with several works that he referred to as *Trees*, but that "the still life" did not correspond to what he had had in mind. "If, when hanging it in Amsterdam, things do not go too badly, it will be the first time that I will be 'a little pleased with myself,'"[159] he added. That same day, he informed Steenhoff that he would not be able to meet him on Wednesday, but only on Thursday. All signs indicate that on October 1, Mondrian left for Amsterdam to attend the meeting of the jury and to attend the opening of the second exhibition of the Moderne Kunst Kring on Sunday, October 6, at the Stedelijk Museum.

A display of thirty-three canvases by Le Fauconnier, dating from 1907 to 1912, almost all works of importance, were the major event of this exhibition. Mondrian's essay "Modern Sensitivity and Painting" was also published in the catalogue.

158. Joosten 1968, 210.
159. Van Vloten 1990, 36–7.

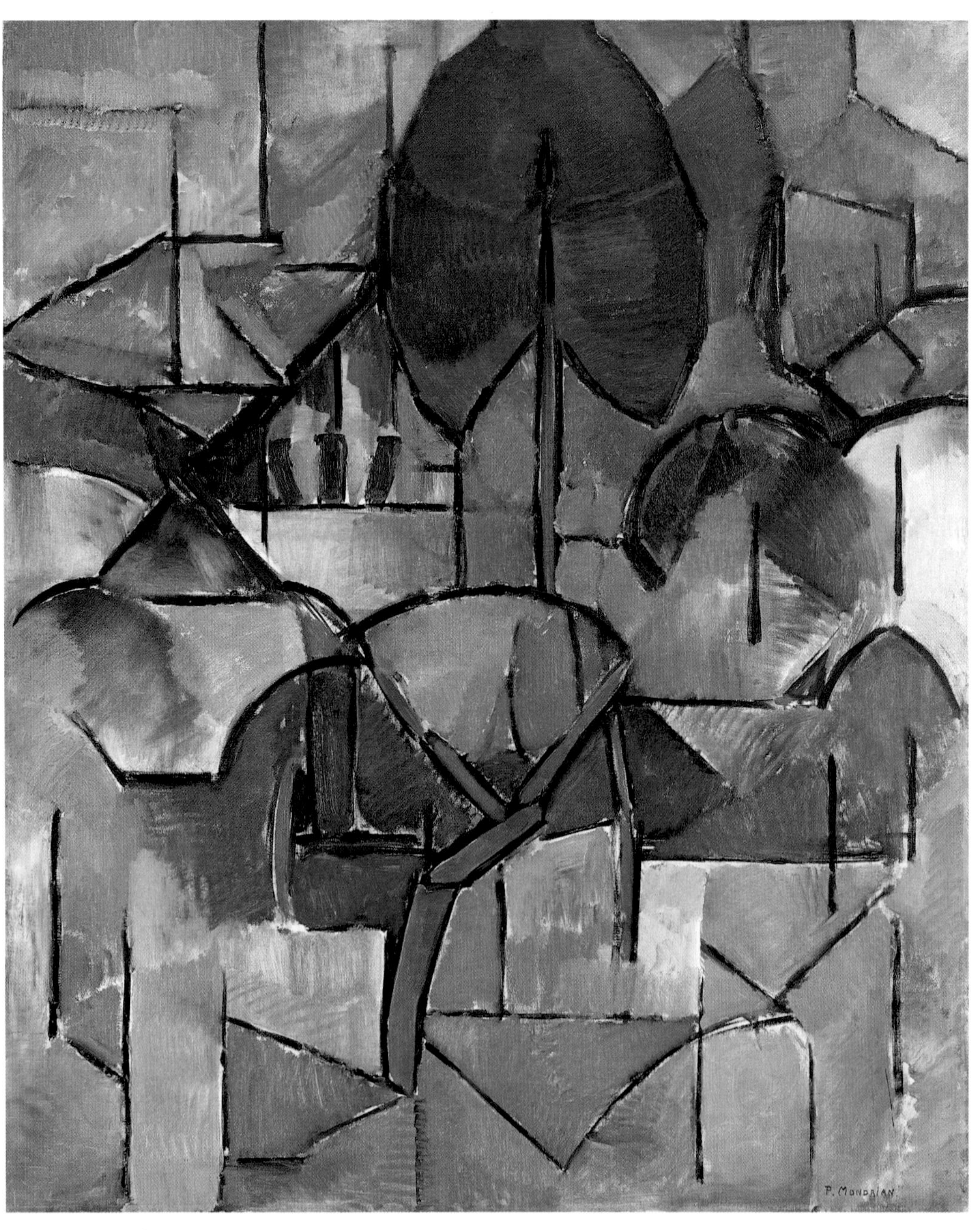

95

Cat. 95 *Landschap met bomen* (*Landscape with Trees*), 1912
Oil on canvas
47.2 x 39 in. (120 x 100 cm)
Signed lower right: P. MONDRIAN.
Gemeentemuseum, The Hague, bequest of Salomon B. Slijper, 1971, inv. S 151–1971 (B 6)

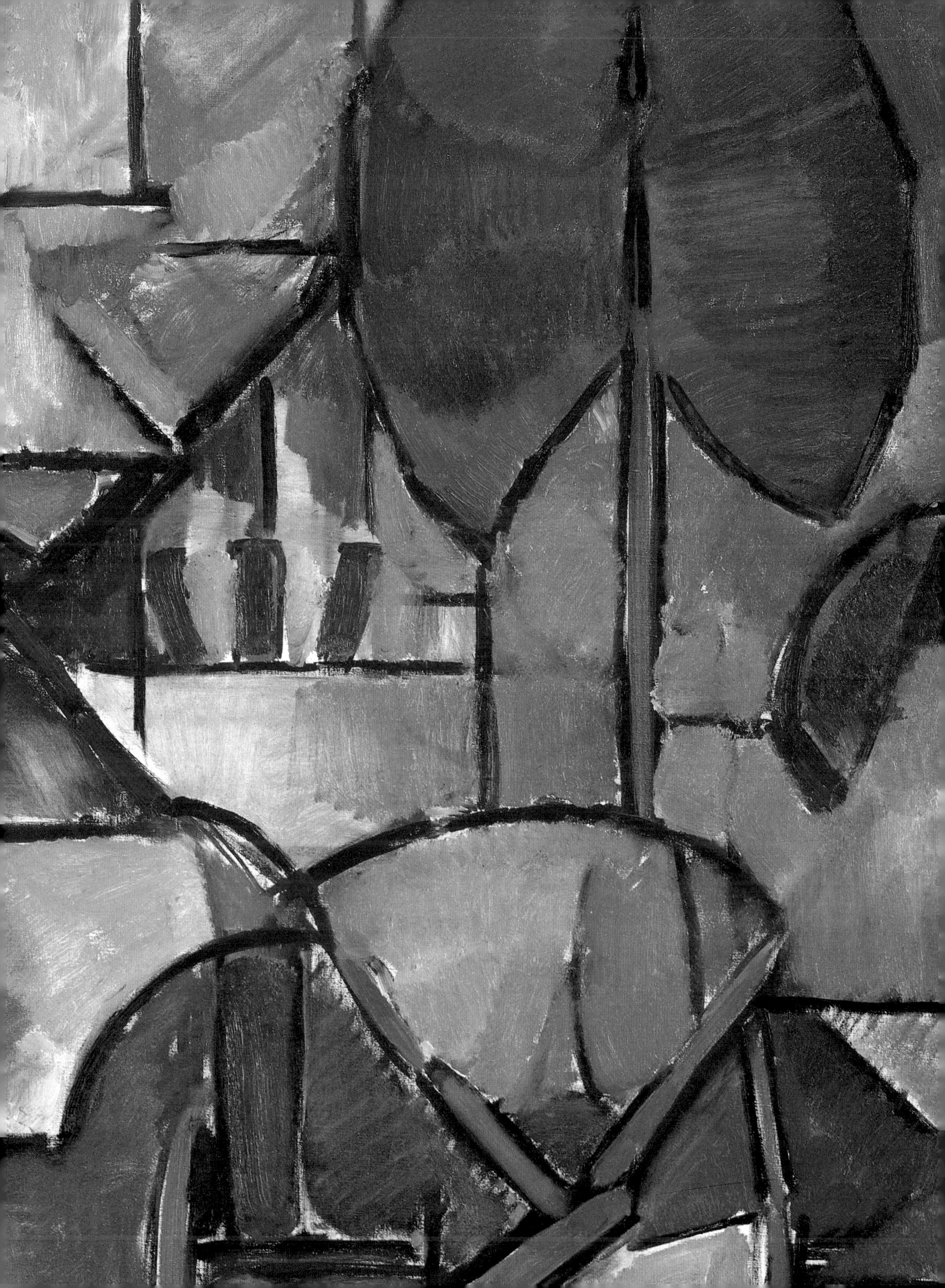

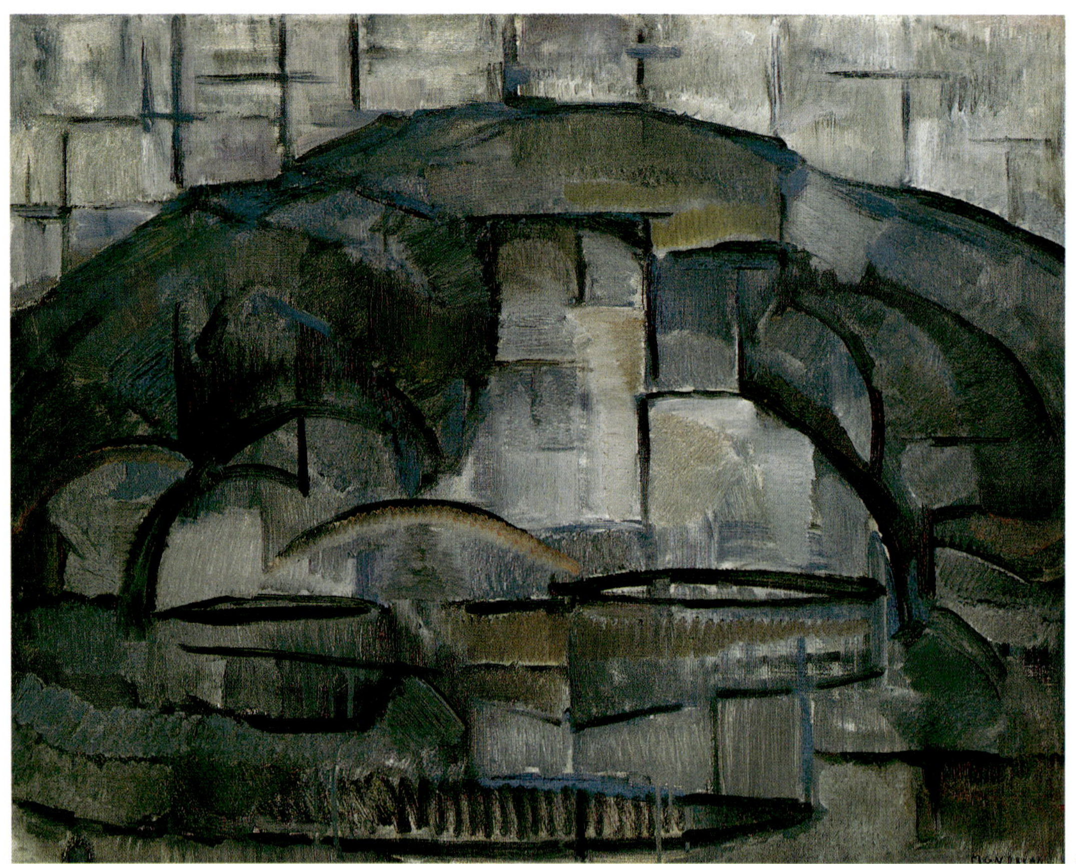

96

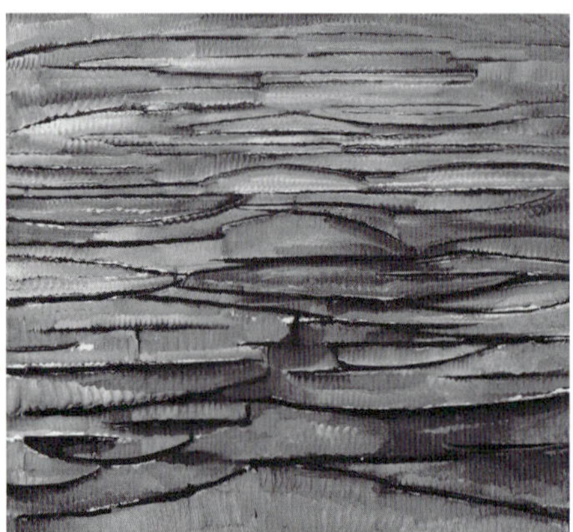

Fig. 45
Piet Mondrian, *The Sea,* Domburg, August 1912
Oil on canvas
Private collection (B 17)

Cat. 96 *Landscape,* 1912
Oil on canvas
24.7 x 30.7 in. (63 x 78 cm)
Signed lower right: MONDRIAN.
Gemeentemuseum, The Hague, bequest of Salomon B. Slijper, 1971, inv. S 150–1971 (B 16)

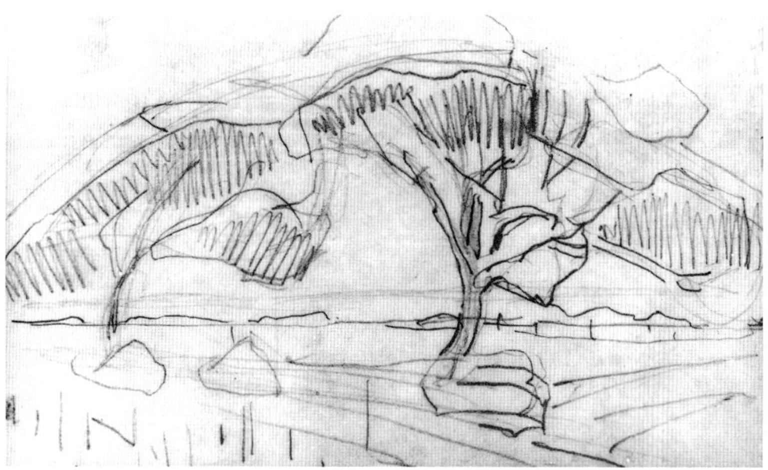

Fig. 46
Piet Mondrian, *Two Trees*, Domburg, August 1912
Pencil
Preparatory study for *Landscape* (cat. 96)
Private collection (B 380)

In comparison with the first exhibition, Cubism was now much more strongly represented. Recent analytical works by Braque and Picasso were shown: for Picasso, seven out of a total of twelve works, including *Man with a Pipe*, an oval composition now belonging to the Kimbell Art Museum, Fort Worth, and *Mandolin Player*, now belonging to the Beyeler Foundation in Basel (fig. 47); and two or perhaps three out of a total of six works for Braque. Also figuring again in the exhibition were works by Gleizes, Metzinger, and Léger (among others, *Nudes in a Landscape* and *Study for Three Portraits*, two *Still Lifes*, one *Landscape*, and eight drawings).

Mondrian had sent seven paintings: the three conceived during his visit to Domburg, discussed above, and those sent from Paris, one "still life" and three "trees," which were discussed in a letter to Mies Elout-Drabbe. The catalogue mentions them under the titles *Nature morte*, *Arbres*, *Pommier à fleurs*, and *Arbres en fleurs*, which correspond to *Still Life with Gingerpot 2* (cat. 97), *Trees* (cat. 99), *Bloeiende Appelbloom* (*Flowering Apple Tree*) (cat. 98), and *Bloeiende Bomen* (*Flowering Trees*) (B 20).

The first and third painting have their origin in *Still Life with Gingerpot 1* (cat. 93) and *The Gray Tree* (cat. 94) respectively. *Trees* (cat. 99) goes back to the drawing mentioned above, entitled *Forest* (B 11). The beginning of *Bloeiende Bomen (Flowering Trees)* lies in one of the two sketchbooks in which Mondrian made a preliminary study of an orchard.

Even though he was not satisfied with it, closer investigation indicates clearly that *Still Life with Gingerpot 2* (cat. 97) was a crucial work for Mondrian. In this painting, the artist assembles conclusively all that he had experimented with and allowed to mellow during the past year and a half. Thus what determines the representation in *Still Life with Gingerpot 1* (cat. 93) has completely lost its figurative function. This task has been

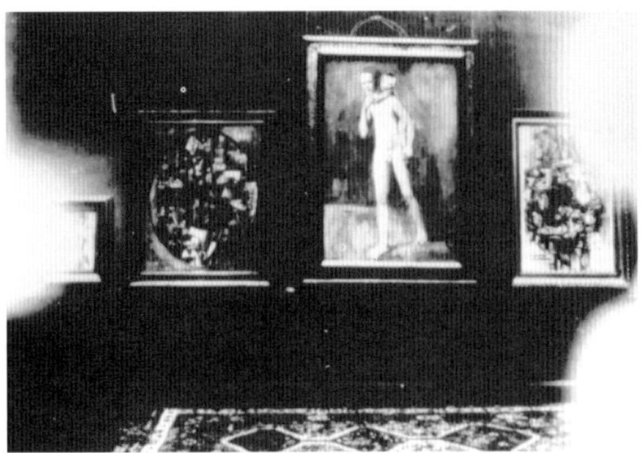

Fig. 47
Three works by Picasso shown in the second exhibition of the Moderne Kunst Kring (Modern Art Circle) at the Stedelijk Museum, Amsterdam, October 1912
From left to right: *Man with a Pipe,* 1911; *Two Brothers,* 1906; and *Mandolin Player,* 1911.
Gemeentemuseum, The Hague

delegated instead to the pictorial means: line, color, and the texture of the brushstrokes. What we see from this moment on is the structure of *Still Life with Gingerpot 1,* in a balanced interplay of essentially horizontal and vertical lines. This is accompanied by an equally dynamic interplay of the three primary colors. These are toned down to intermediary colors with the help of white, gray, and black, serving to oppose light and dark. The carefully counterposed lines are mostly horizontal in the lower half of the painting, where they are coupled with vertical brushstrokes, and essentially vertical in the upper part, where they are coupled with horizontal brushstrokes. In total opposition to this subtle play that Mondrian would later call "universal plastic means," stands the spherical turquoise gingerpot, whose brown contours and focal point of reflected light, are still represented according to the traditional rules of naturalistic painting. This radical opposition can mean only one thing, the swan song of the naturalistic style before its final abandonment. It makes way for an art founded on the use—exclusive, systematic, and composed of oppositions—of an inherently technical visual means, and which can be justly called "abstract": line, texture, color. This last element is brought back to the three primaries, red, yellow, blue–which a few brushstrokes distribute on the cover and upper edge of the pot sketched to the right of the gingerpot—and the tonalities of light and dark.

Contrary to *Still Life with Gingerpot 2,* the curved line dominates once again in the three paintings of trees. As for color, Mondrian distances himself from the naturalistic style so well that line as well as color can here equally be qualified as "abstract." Thus, in *Bloeiende Appelboom (Flowering Apple Tree)* (cat. 98), the style of *The Gray Tree* (cat. 94), that made such a clear reference to Cézanne, gives way to the purely abstract style of *Still Life with Gingerpot 2* (cat. 97).

The variations of light of *Bloeiende Bomen* (*Flowering Trees*), under the trees, in the crests and above, are sensitively rendered by varying the

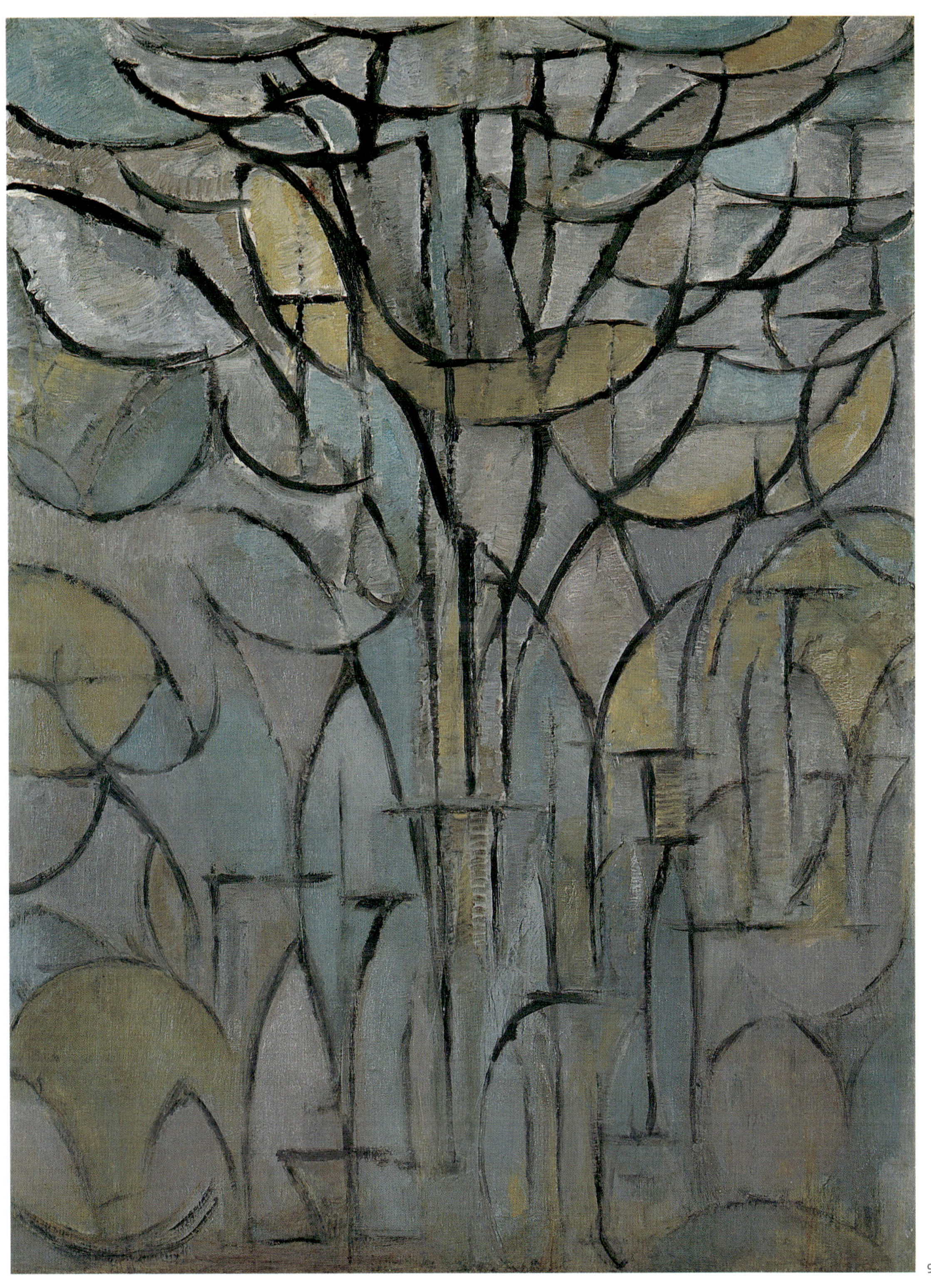

99

Cat. 99 *Trees*, c. 1912
Oil on canvas
37 x 27.2 in. (94 x 69.8 cm)
Not signed
The Carnegie Museum of Art, Pittsburgh, Patrons Art Fund, 1961, inv. 61–1 (B 21)

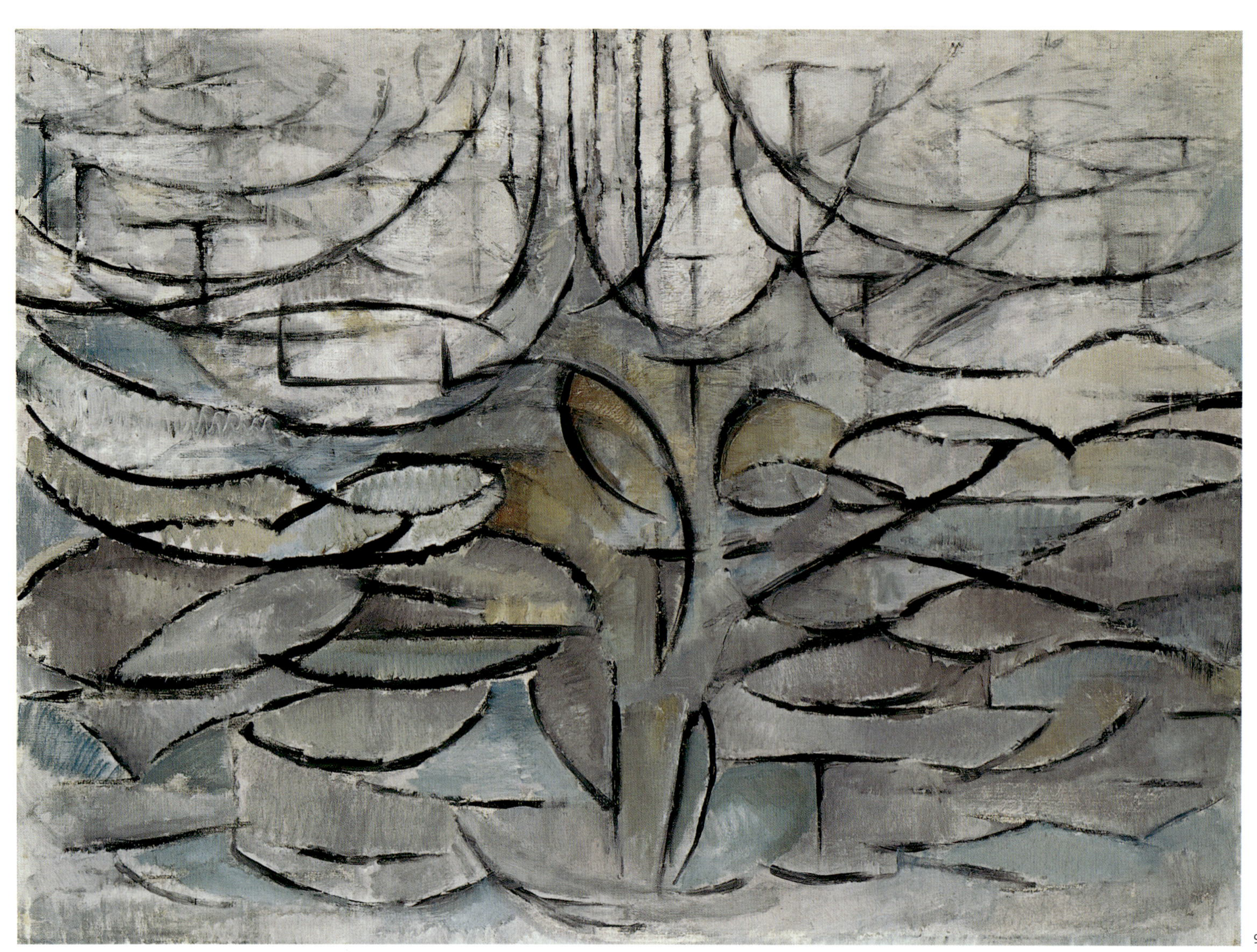
98

Cat. 98 *Bloeiende Appelboom* (*Flowering Apple Tree*), 1912
Oil on canvas
31 x 42.3 in. (78.5 x 107.5 cm)
Not signed
Gemeentemuseum, The Hague, gift of Conrad Kikkert, 1934,
inv. S 55–1934 (B 19)

paint mixture to white or gray. The flowers become almost palpable through the texture of the paint, without anything at all figurative (fig. 48).

From old photographs, we know that the four paintings had a wooden strip as frame, mounted on the sides of the stretched canvas. While this anticipates the type of frame Mondrian would use for his later works, here it was certainly a temporary expedient, chosen for lack of time. These four works were, furthermore, originally not signed.

Four of Mondrian's paintings were sold: *Trees* (cat. 99), *Bloeiende Bomen* (*Flowering Trees*), the lost sketch *Sur les Dunes (On the Dunes)* and *Paysage* (*Landscape*) (cat. 96.)

Upon his return to Paris, Mondrian encountered two manifestations of a rapidly evolving, multidirectional Cubism. One was the Salon d'Automne, in which Léger showed *La Femme en bleu* (*Woman in Blue*), now in the Kunstmuseum Basel. The other was the Salon de "La Section d'Or" (Golden Section). It would be interesting to know if Mondrian attended the lectures given by Apollinaire, Maurice Raynal, and René Blum during this event.

In 1977, the Dutch artist Jan van Deene (1886–1977), at that time ninety-one years old, recounted the following reminiscence of his visit to Mondrian during his stay in Paris from the fall of 1911 to December 1912, with his colleague Jacob Bendien (1890–1993):

Another of our friends, a little older, was Piet Mondrian. I remember him as a simple and charming man without pretensions. He really wanted to be seen and for that reason he attended all the openings. Bendien, because of this particularity, had surnamed him Piet-zie-je-me-niet ["Piet-have-you-seen-me"]. I much enjoyed his cheerful company. He was forty years old; I was twenty-seven, Bendien was younger, and it is true that age makes a big difference. One day we went, all three of us, to a carnival. Mondrian, who was not at all a hermit, danced on Quatorze juillet, the French national holiday, at

160. van Deene 1977, 79.

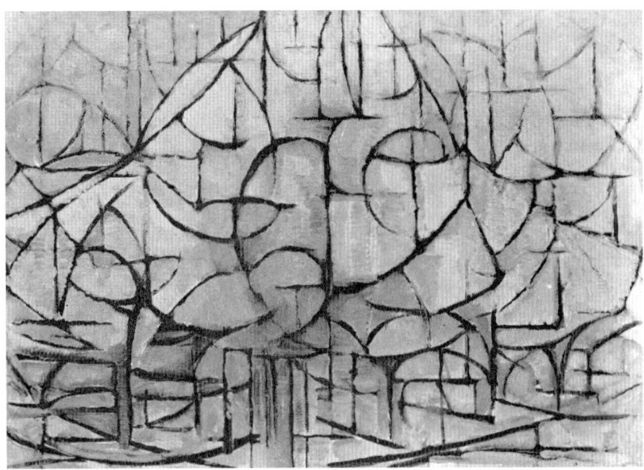

Fig. 48
Piet Mondrian, *Flowering Trees*, Paris, September 1912
Oil on canvas
Judith Rothschild Foundation, New York (B 20)

the local street dance, merry and relaxed, with the working-class girls.[160]

Another reminiscence related to the end of 1912/beginning 1913 comes from the composer Jakob van Domselaer (1890–1960), who was in Paris for his work during this period, and had numerous contacts with Mondrian. He recalled that the painter was then occupied with "trees," and that he lived very much by himself. "Solitude was vital for Mondrian. . . . to be unexpectedly disturbed was extremely disagreeable for him, and he never failed to comment on it, and everyone was afraid of him because of that."[161]

161. van Domselaer-Middelkoop 1959–60, 270–71.

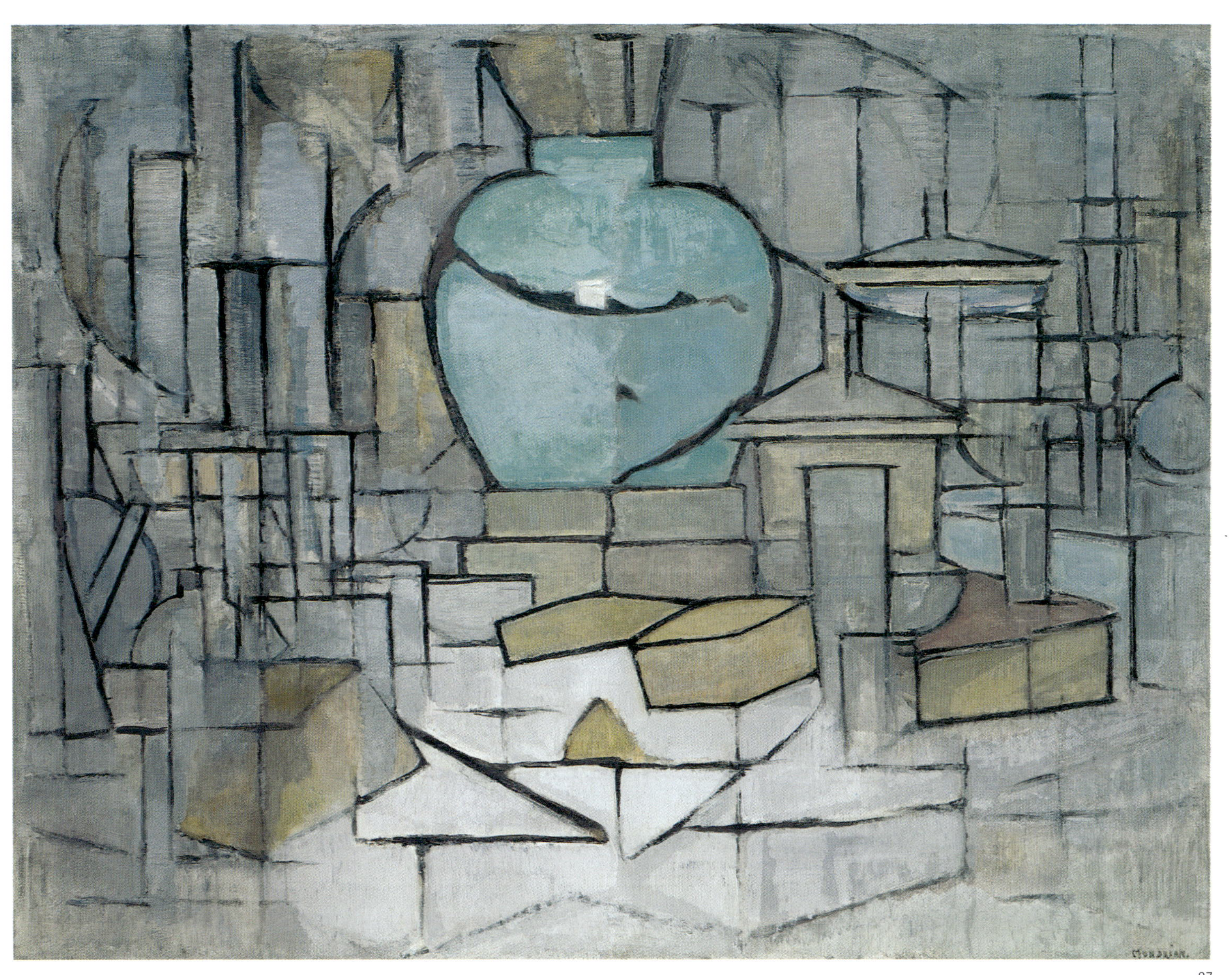

97

Cat. 97 *Still life with Gingerpot 2*, 1912
Oil on canvas
36 x 47.2 in. (91.5 x 120 cm)
Signed lower right: MONDRIAN.
The Solomon R. Guggenheim Museum, New York, inv. 294–76 (B 18)

Chapter Eight

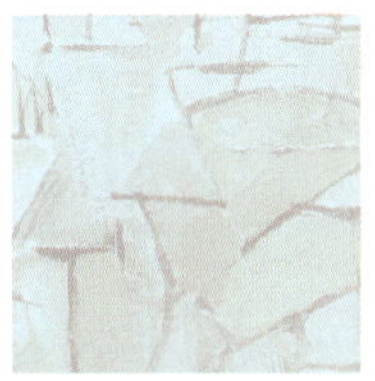
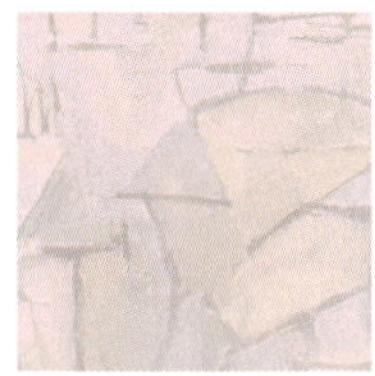

1912–1914

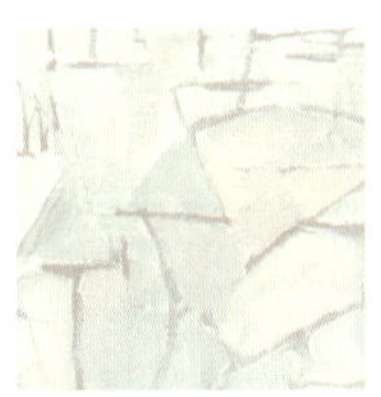

"I felt that only the Cubists had discovered the right path; and, for a time, I was much influenced by them."[162]

Joop M. Joosten

In March 1913, Mondrian participated again in the Salon des Indépendants. Through Kikkert's efforts, there was a kind of "Dutch gallery," Gallery 43, which brought together works by Mondrian, Peter Alma (1886–1969), Jacoba van Heemskerck, Otto van Rees (1884–1957), and Lodewijk Schelfhout, among others.

The catalogue mentions three paintings by Mondrian: *Arbre* (*Tree*), *Arbre en fleurs* (*Flowering Tree*), and *Femme* (*Woman*). Apollinaire recommended seeing the work of Mondrian in his reviews of the Salon that appeared in *L'Intransigeant* and in *Montjoie!* on March 18, 1913. In his introduction to the article in *L'Intransigeant,* Apollinaire counted Mondrian's "trees" among "the most noticed works" in the exhibition, along with Delaunay's *L'Equipe de Cardiff* (*Cardiff Team*), today in the National Museum of Modern Art in Paris; Léger's *Femme nue* (*Nude Woman*), in the collection of the Solomon R. Guggenheim Museum in New York; Marie Laurencin's *Le Bal élégant* (*The Elegant Ball*); Gleize's *Les Joueurs de football* (*The Soccer Players*); and Metzinger's *L'Oiseau bleu* (*The Blue Bird*), today in the National Museum of Modern Art, Paris. He analyzed the "Dutch gallery" in great detail, remarking of Mondrian's work, "Let us mention the highly abstract painting of Mondrian. His *Trees* and his *Portrait of a Woman* are of great interest."[163]

162. Mondrian 1942.
163. Apollinaire 1960, 294, as translated in Apollinaire 1972, 287.

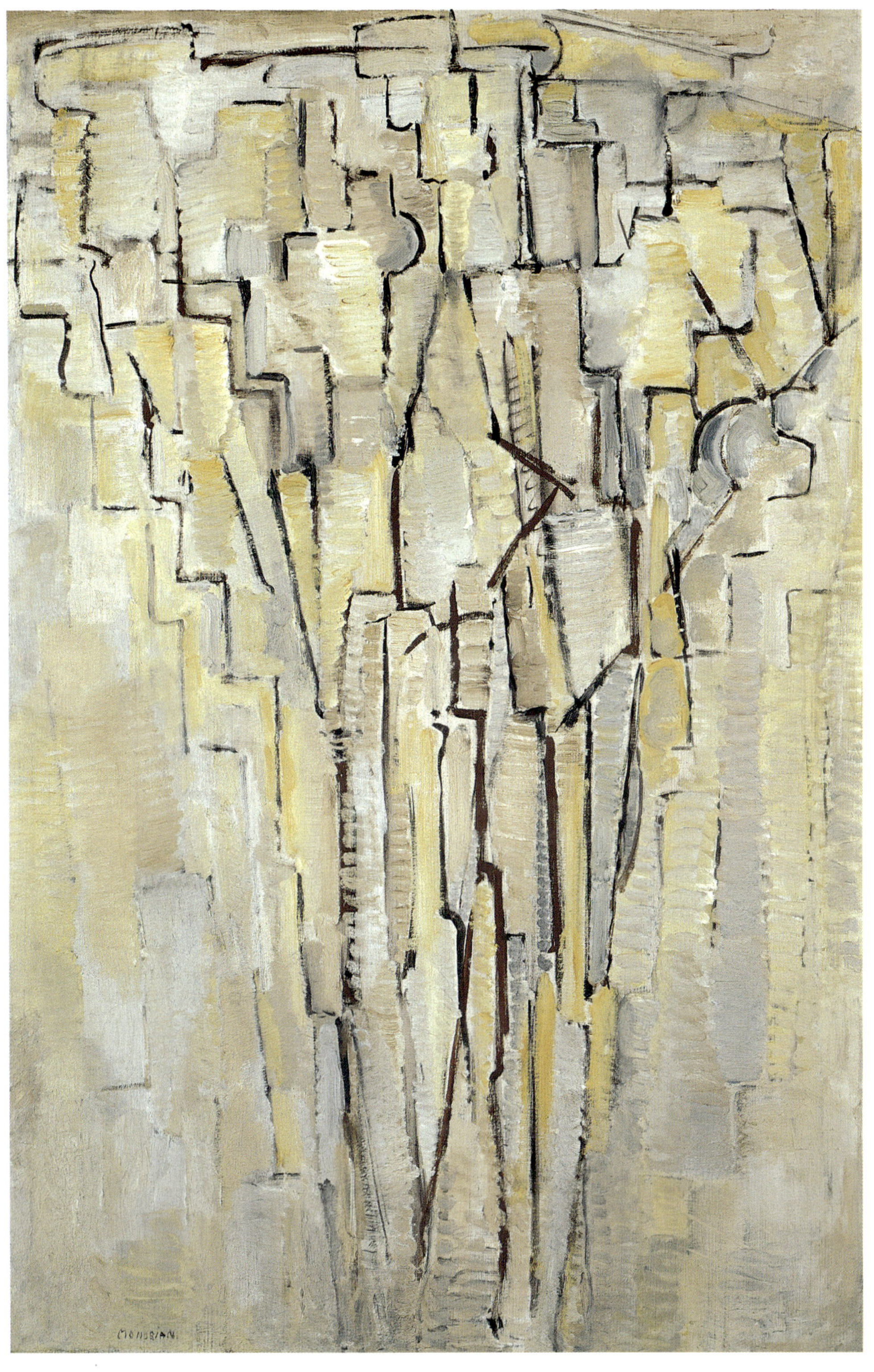

102

Cat. 102 *Tree A*, 1913
Oil on canvas
39.3 x 26.5 in. (100.2 x 67.2 cm)
Signed lower left: MONDRIAN.
Tate Gallery, London, 1977, inv. T 0 2211 (B 30)

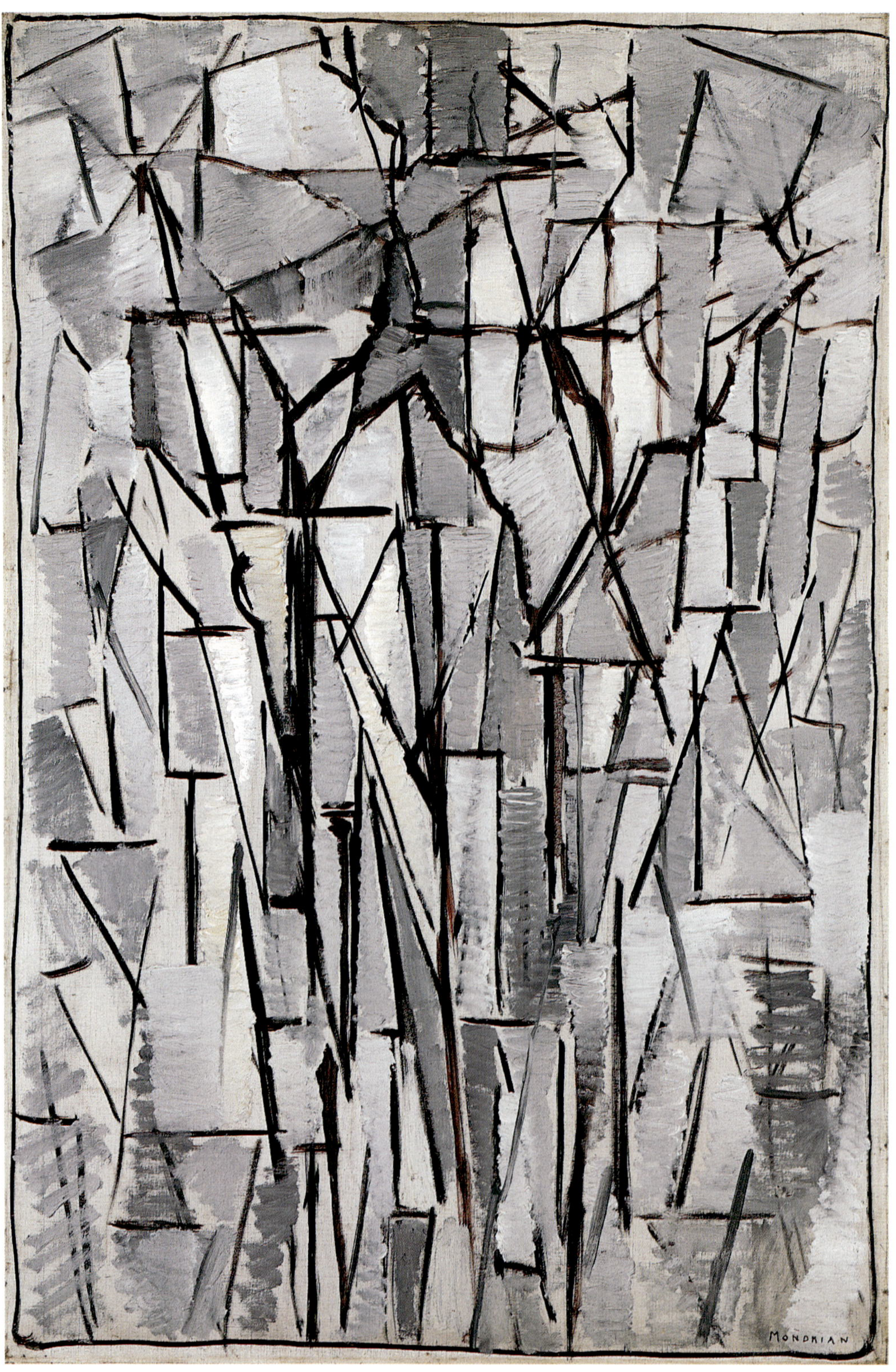

100

Cat. 100 *Composition: Trees 2*, c. 1912–13
Oil on canvas
38.6 x 25.6 in. (98 x 65 cm)
Signed lower right: *MONDRIAN*
Gemeentemuseum, The Hague, bequest Salomon
B. Slijper, 1971, inv. S 158–1971 (B 24)

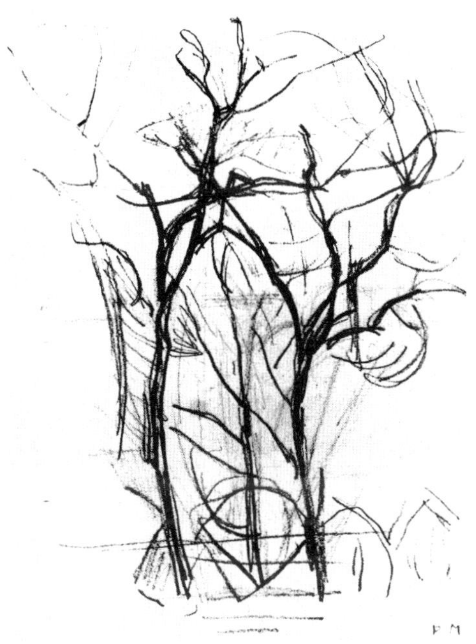

Fig. 49
Piet Mondrian, *Trees*, Domburg, August 1912
Pencil
Private collection (B 394)

In the March 18 edition of *Montjoie!*, he went into greater detail:

The highly abstract Cubism of Mondrian, a Dutchman–we know that Cubism has penetrated the museum in Amsterdam; while in France our young painters are being ridiculed, [in Amsterdam] they are exhibiting the works of Georges Braque, Picasso, etc., next to those of Rembrandt–Mondrian, an offshoot of the Cubists, is certainly not their imitator. He seems to have been influenced by Picasso above all, but his personality remains wholly his own. His trees and his portrait of a woman reveal an intellectual sensibility. This kind of Cubism is heading in a direction different from that currently pursued by Braque and Picasso, whose experiments with materials are proving extremely interesting.[164]

The title given by Apollinaire ("Portrait of a Woman") and the reference insisting on Picasso's influence makes it possible to identify with near certainty the works sent by Mondrian. *Arbre* is surely the painting now titled *Tree A.* (cat. 102); *Arbre en fleurs* is to be identified as *Tableau No. 4* (*Painting no. 4*) (cat. 101), and *Femme* is *Composition No. XI* (B 31). Closer scrutiny shows that the numbering is not chronological. The earliest of the three works is probably *Tableau No. 4*, characterized by its multiplicity of mostly straight lines in vertical, horizontal and oblique positions, in which one still clearly recognizes the skeleton of the curved convex and concave lines of *Bloeiende Appelboom* (*Flowering Apple Tree)* (cat. 98). The difference stems from the opposition between the "portrait" format of *Tableau No. 4* and the "landscape" format of *Bloeiende Appelboom* (*Flowering Apple Tree*). The first (vertical) format results in a more balanced and more compact composition.

The same abundance of lines is found in *Composition: Trees 2* (cat. 100). This canvas recalls, through its sketch *Composition: Trees 1* (B 23), other sketches of trees made in Domburg in August 1912 (fig. 49). Thanks to this last work, it is easy to see that the multiplicity of mostly straight lines in *Composition: Trees 2* was obtained by stretching out and fragmenting the lines that were still drawn from nature in the sketches made in Domburg. It is this same operation of lengthening and fragmenting the curved lines that led to *Tableau No. 4*.

For Mondrian, "breaking up lines and shapes" was synonymous with Cubism, more precisely the analytical Cubism advocated by Picasso, as can be discerned in the historical position ascribed to Neo-Plasticism in his essay "De Nieuwe Beelding

164. Ibid., 300–301, translated in Apollinaire 1972, 289.

in de schilderkunst" ("The New Plastic in Painting"):

The Cubist plasticism is no longer naturalistic: it still seeks the volume, and volume above all, but in an entirely new way. Cubism still represents particular things, but no longer in their traditional perspective appearance. Cubism breaks form, omits parts, and interjects other lines and forms: it even introduces the straight line where it is not directly seen in the object. . . . Cubism broke the closed line, the contour that delimits individual form; but because it also represents this breaking, it falls short of pure unity. While it achieves greater unity than the old art, because its composition has strong plastic expression, Cubism loses unity due to the fragmented character of the natural appearance of things. For objects remain objects despite their fragmentation.[165]

Works representing this analytical Cubism in the second exhibition of the Moderne Kunst Kring in 1912, which certainly did not escape Mondrian's attention, have been mentioned above. It is possible that he saw other analytical Cubist works later in Paris, but in the absence of proof to the contrary, we may assume that he had already recognized the message contained for him in this kind of painting, comparing his most recent works in Amsterdam with those of Braque and, especially, Picasso.

It is remarkable to see Mondrian making continual reference to Picasso and his work in his writings and his letters when discussing Cubism and its significance for his own work. On the other hand, he never refers in this way to Braque. In a letter of January 29, 1914, to H. P. Bremmer, where he describes in detail his latest paintings, he refers to Picasso:

Finally, I must tell you that I was influenced upon seeing Picasso's work, which I admire very much. I am not ashamed to speak of this influence, because I think it nobler to accept the fact that one can improve oneself than to be satisfied with an imperfection once developed, and to believe oneself to be authentic! As so many painters believe they are! And furthermore, I am sure to be completely different from Picasso, as it is said currently.[166]

The two most recent works of Mondrian in the Salon des Indépendants of 1913, *Tree A.* (cat. 102) and *Composition No. XI* (B 31), allow us to see a marked difference in structure that is tied to the position of the lines, vis-à-vis *Tableau No. 4* (cat. 101). If one could still speak in the latter work of a certain equilibrium between vertical, horizontal, and oblique lines, it is now the vertical and horizontal lines that predominate–more precisely, long verticals and short horizontals intertwining at times in stair-step fashion. Mondrian explained in his essay "Het bepaalde en het onbepaalde" (The Determinate and the Indeterminate) that appeared in the revue *De Stijl* in December 1918, what he was aiming for:

Accentuating the plastic of relationship led to the exaggeration of this expression, to abstraction from the natural (Pointillism, Divisionism, Expressionism, Cubism), and finally to the plastic of plasticism of sheer relationships (Neo-Plasticism). Seeing the gradual development of the plasticism of sheer relationships out of naturalistic painting by the successive schools, we also see its evolution in the development of the founders of the Neo-Plasticism. . . . Was it by chance that they were attracted to straightness and–to the distress of ordinary vision–dared to represent a wood simply by a few vertical tree trunks? Was it surprising that, once they had

165. Mondrian 1917–18, 130–31, as translated in Holtzman and James 1986, 63–64.
166. Joosten 1968, 211.

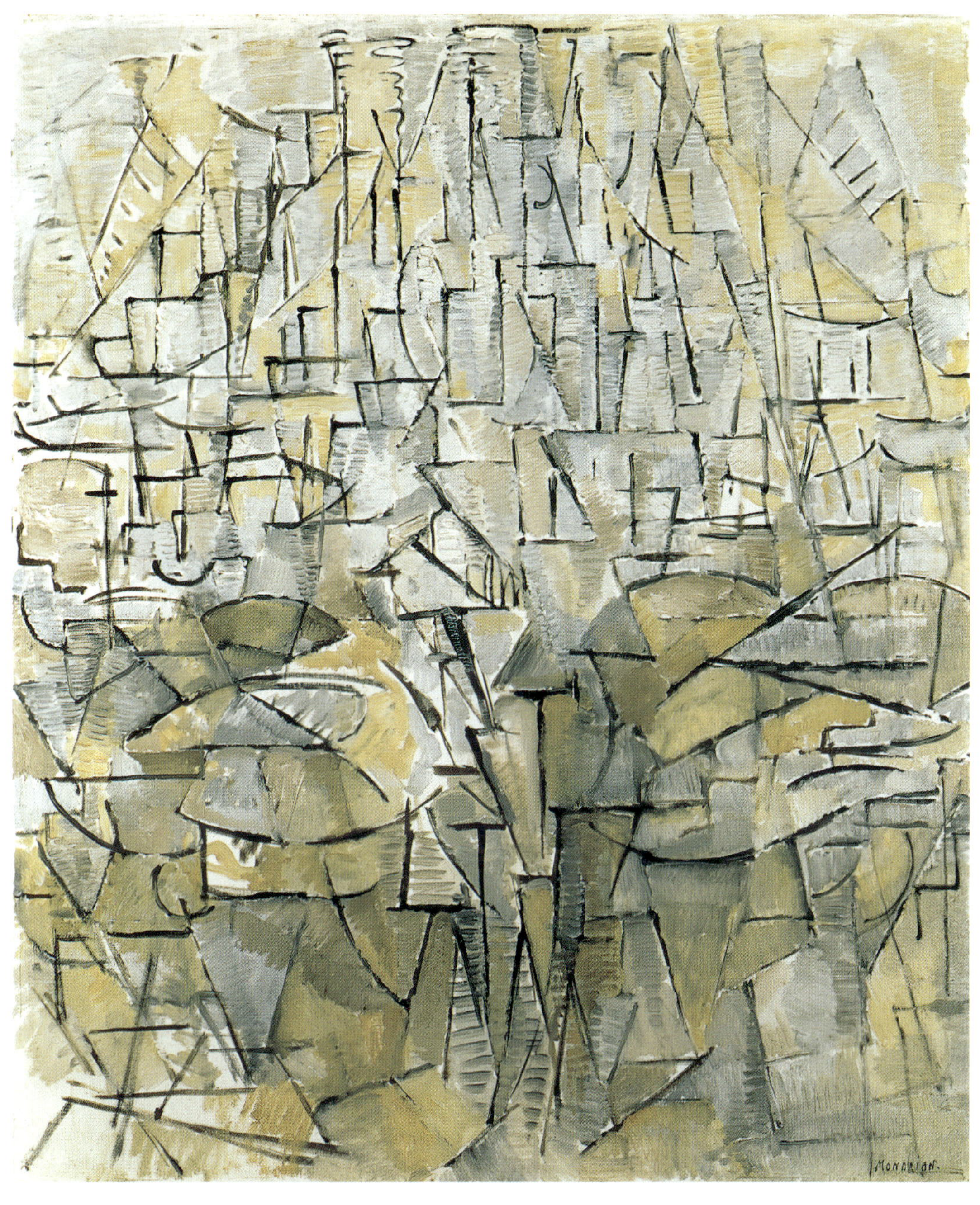

101

Cat. 101 *Tableau No. 4/Composition No. VIII/Compostie 3*, 1913
Oil on canvas
37.5 x 31.5 in. (95 x 80 cm)
Signed lower right: MONDRIAN.
Gemeentemuseum, The Hague, bequest Salomon B. Slijper, 1971, inv. S 159–1971 (B 27)

abstracted these trunks to lines or planes, they spontaneously came to express the horizontal–barely visible in nature–thus creating equilibrium with the vertical? . . . Did they do more than exaggerate what all painting has always done?[167]

This exaggeration of plastic expression is also one of the characteristics of *Tableau No. 3* (cat. 103), which evokes *Tableau No. 4* (cat. 101), which, in turn, evokes *Bloeiende Appelboom* (*Flowering Apple Tree*) (cat. 98).

It is interesting to note that Mondrian, probably following Picasso, here chose the oval shape for his canvas so as to prevent the painting becoming dispersed into the corners. But, contrary to the practice of Picasso and Braque, Mondrian remains faithful to the rectangularity of the surface of the painting and has completely covered the exterior of the oval and the frame in a unified bronze color.

After *Tableau No. 3*, seven paintings were completed in 1913, of which six are dominated by an irregular web of paired and parallel verticals and horizontals of varying lengths. Four of these paintings comprise two pairs, entitled respectively *Gemälde No. I* (B 38 and B 40) and *Gemälde No. II* (B 39 and B36). A third pair was entitled *Tableau No. 1* (cat. 104) and *Tableau No. 2/Composition No. V* (cat. 106).

In the *Erster Deutscher Herbstsalon*–the First German Autumn Salon, opened on September 10, 1913, and organized in Berlin by Herwarth Walden, editor of the avant-garde journal *Der Sturm*–Mondrian, according to the catalogue, was represented by two works, designated *Gemälde 1* and *Gemälde 2*. These names refer

167. Mondrian 1918–19, 17, as translated in Holtzman and James 1986, 73.

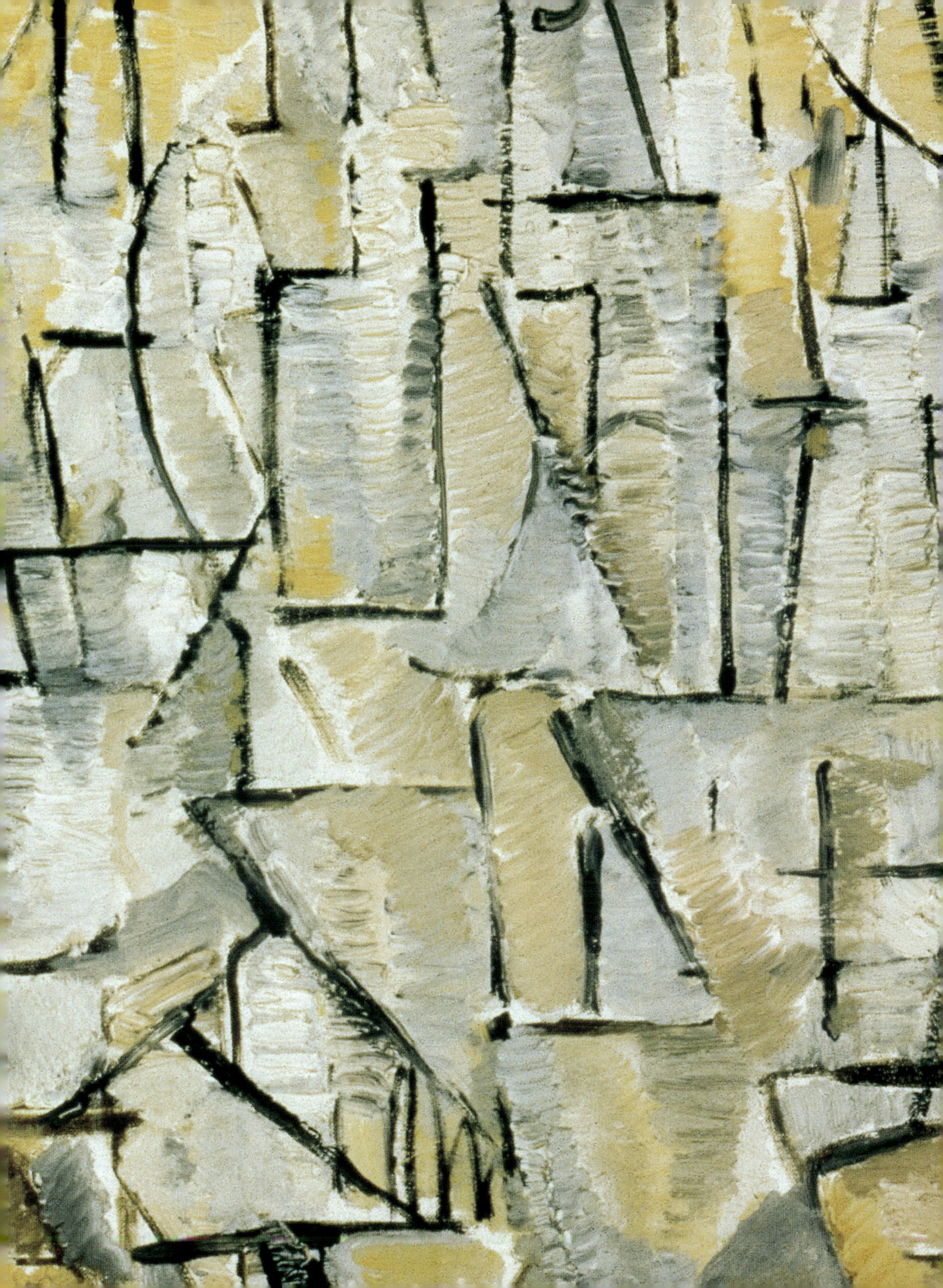

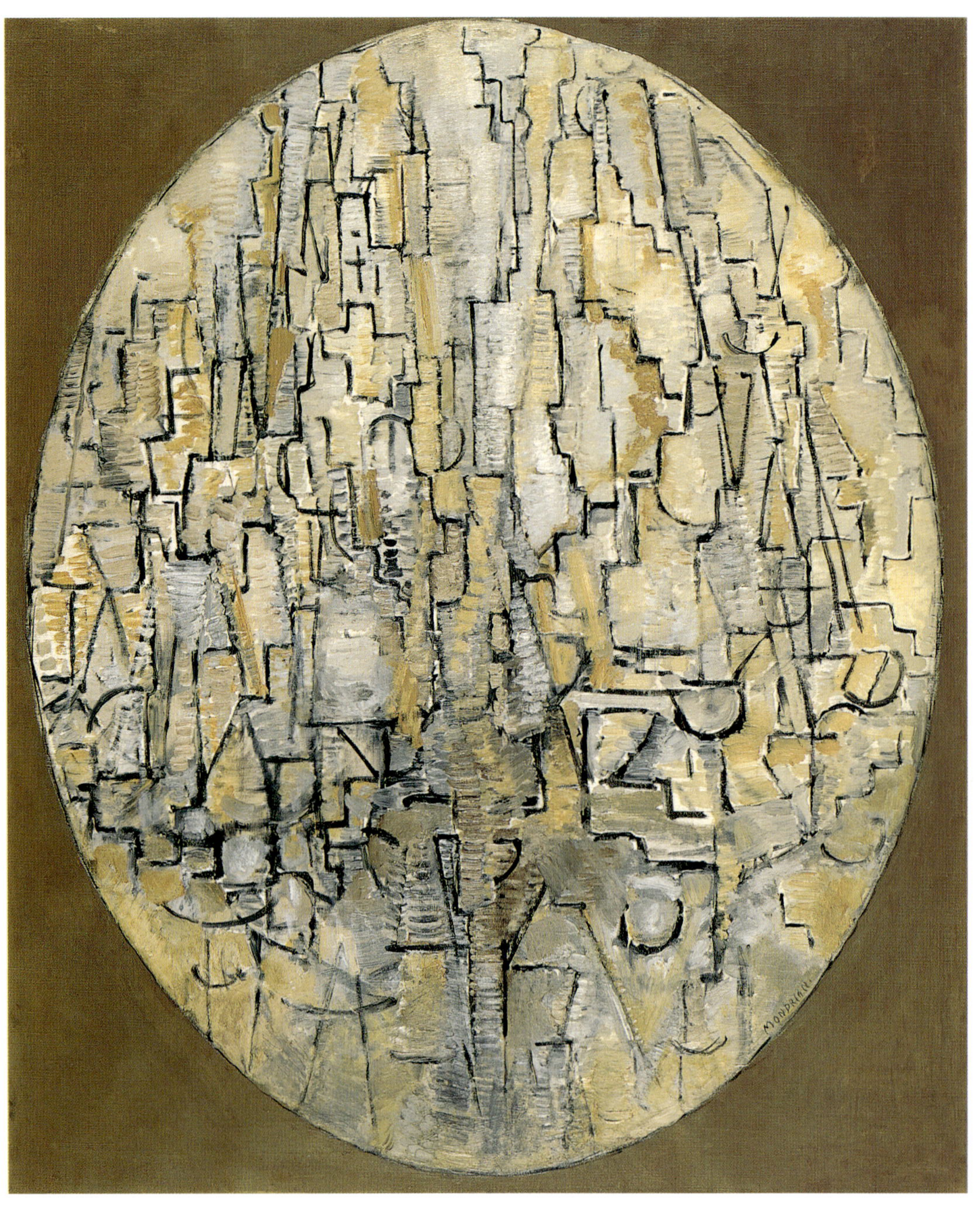

103

Cat. 103 *Tableau No. 3*, 1913
Oil on canvas
37 x 30.7 in. (94 x 78 cm)
Signed lower right : *MONDRIAN.*
Stedelijk Museum, Amsterdam, inv. A 6043 (B 33)

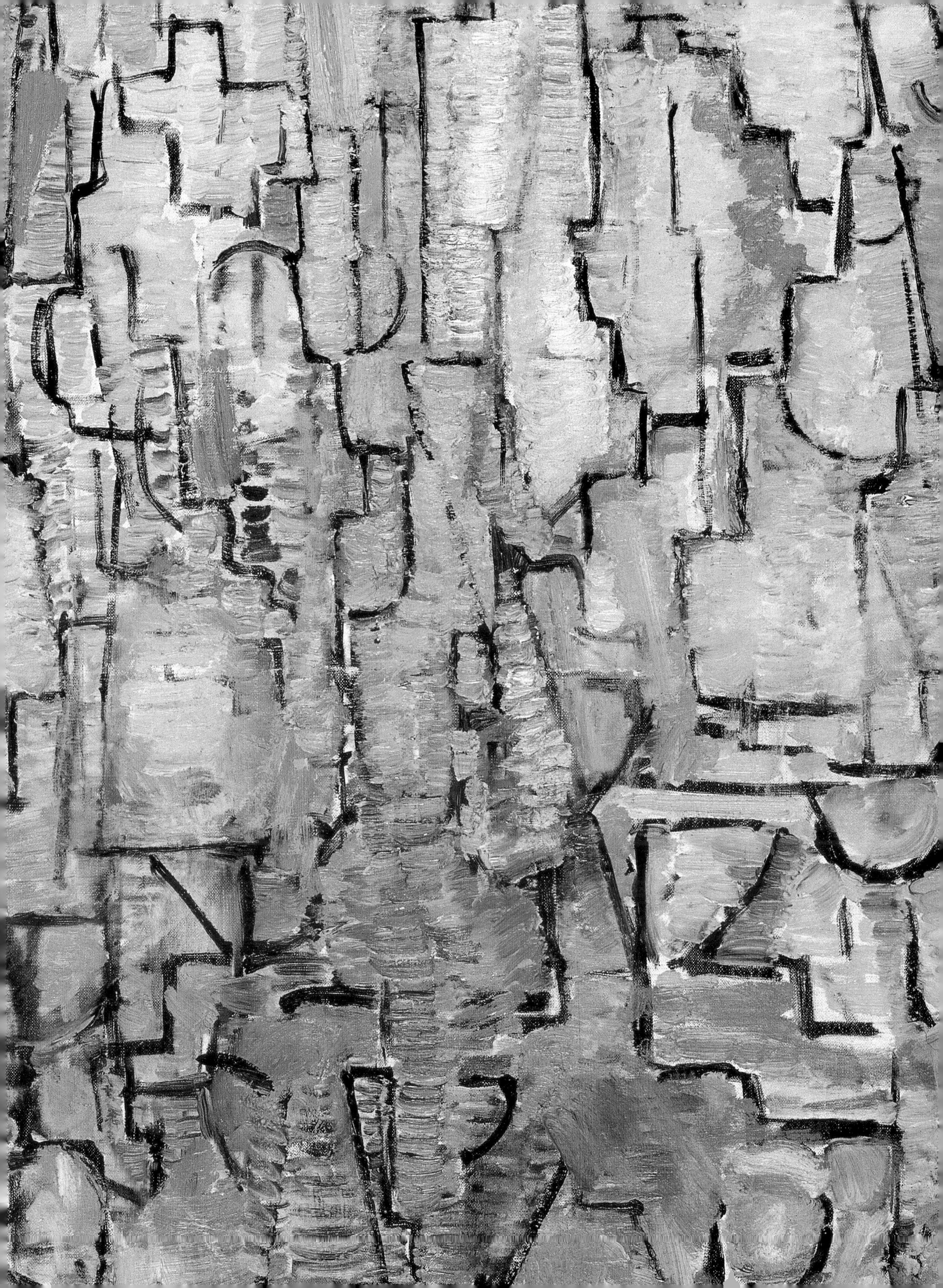

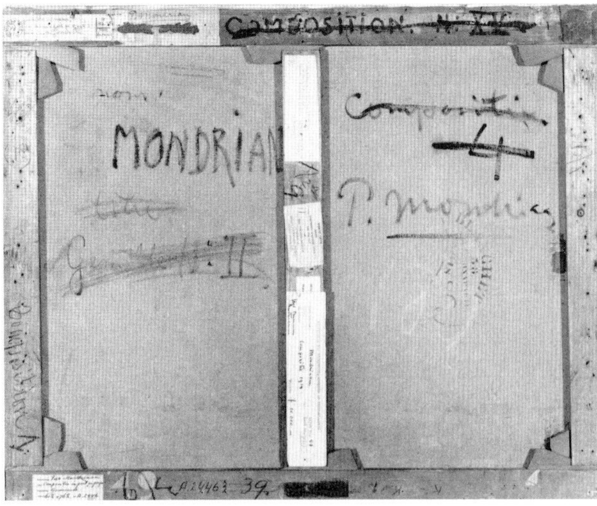

Fig. 50
Writing on the back of a painting: Gemälde No. II /Composition No. XV/Compositie 4, 1913
Oil on canvas
Stedelijk Museum, Amsterdam (B 39)

probably to one of the pairs mentioned above. In the absence of more precise information, it is not possible to determine which pair was exhibited, or where the other pair might have been shown.
The works numbered *Tableau No. 1* (cat. 104) and *Tableau No. 2/ Composition No. VII* (B 35), were sent by Mondrian to the third exhibition of the Moderne Kunst Kring, which opened November 7, 1913, at the Stedelijk Museum in Amsterdam, together with *Tableau No. 3* (cat. 103) and *Tableau No. 4* (cat. 101). The latter two works were classed in this new numbering system only on this occasion, to link them to the works numbered 1 and 2.
Mondrian had never shown much interest in titles. Only works that were sent to exhibitions were given a title, and that was probably for the sole reason that they needed to have one. Rarely are the titles given in catalogues found on the works themselves. If so, the titles are most often found on the exhibition label still glued to the back of the canvas. In the logic of this practice of not naming his works, Mondrian chose from this time on the principle of numbering, choosing a specific numbering for each exhibition. Even more remarkably, from this time on, he systematically wrote the numbers on the back of the canvases.
The figures were variously written in Arabic or Roman numbers, in capital letters or in lower case, beginning each time with 1 or I, a or A. Mondrian preceded each of these signs by an indication of the type of object or work, in the language of the country to which he was sending the work: *Tableau, Gemälde, Schilderij, Picture,* or *Composition, Compositie, Komposition.* Consequently, a painting conserved in its original state might carry many numbers, the frequency of which equals the number of exhibitions to which Mondrian had sent it (fig. 50). Conversely, works that he never exhibited have no numbers.
What we have characterized above as an irregular, moving network of verticals and horizontals, of longer or shorter length, often in parallel pairs, reveals that a radical transformation in Mondrian's choice of motifs came about in 1913. Once he was well integrated into Paris life, Mondrian began to see the metropolis:

as abstract life given form: it is closer to him than nature and it will more easily stir aesthetic emotion in him. For in the metropolis nature is already tensed, ordered by the human spirit. The relationships and rhythm of plane and line in its architecture will move man more directly than the capriciousness of nature. In the metropolis, beauty is expressed more mathematically; it is here that the mathematical artistic temperament of the future will develop–here the New Style will emerge.[168]

168. Mondrian 1917–18, 132, note 8, as translated in Holtzman and James 1986, 59.

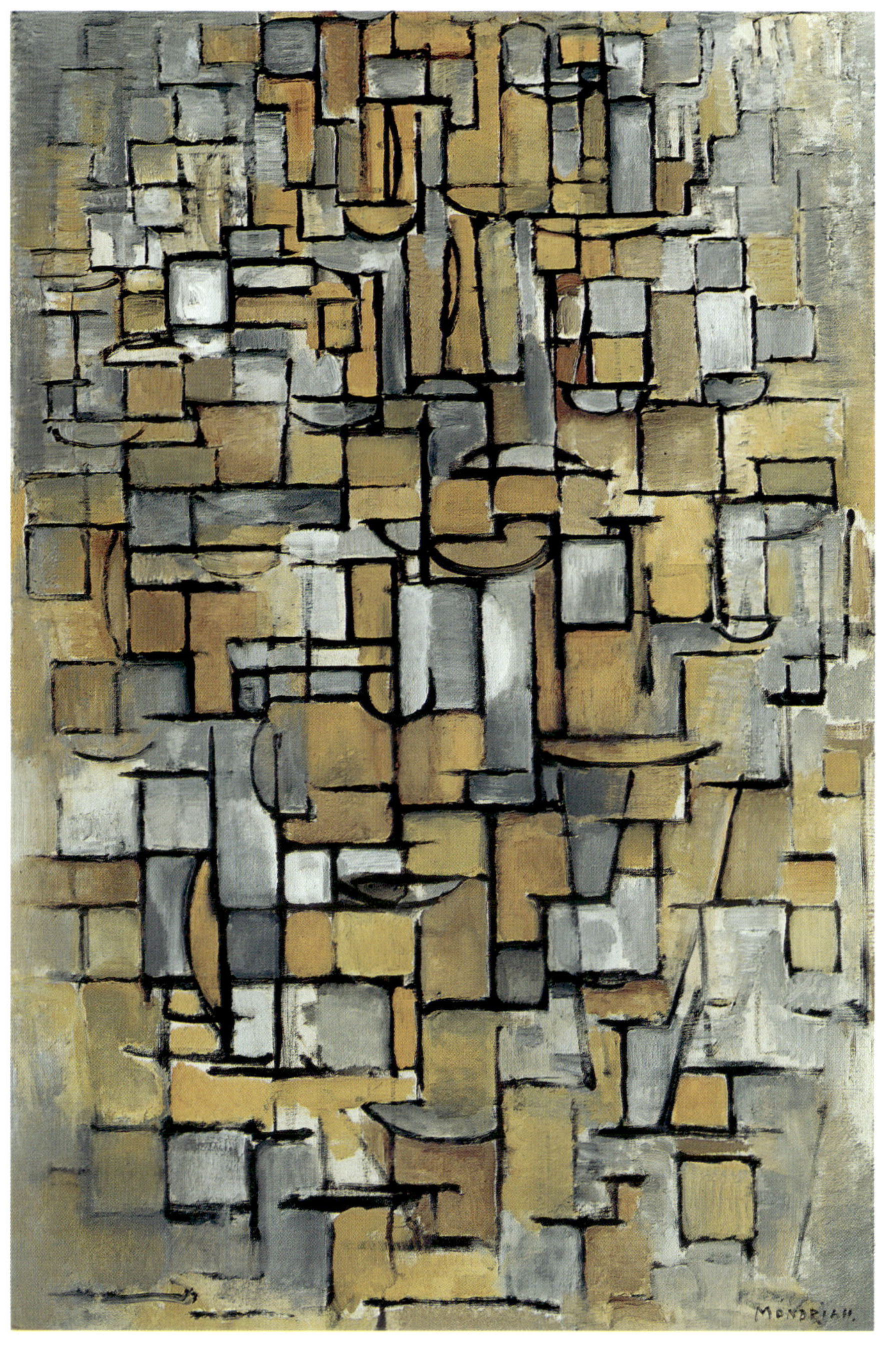

104

Cat. 104 *Tableau No. 1*, 1913
Oil on canvas
37.8 x 25. 2 in (96 x 64 cm)
Signed lower right: MONDRIAN.
Kröller-Müller Museum, Otterlo, inv. 531–13 (B 37)

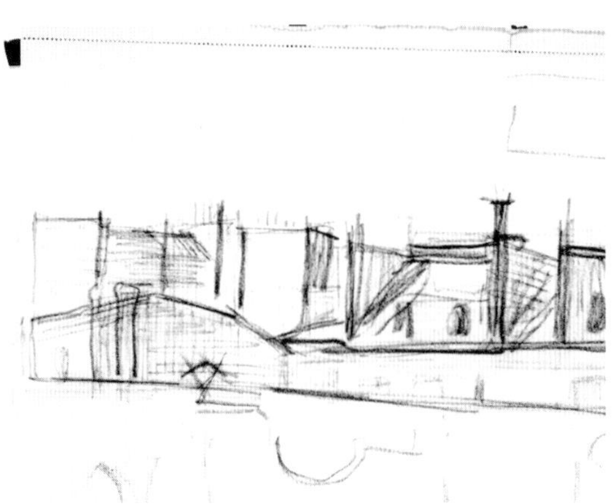

Fig. 51
Piet Mondrian, *Façades of Paris buildings*, 1914
Pencil drawing taken from a sketchbook
Private collection (B 410)

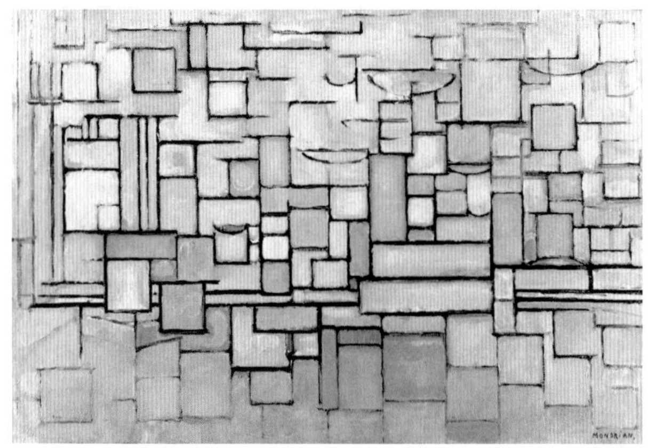

Fig. 52
Piet Mondrian, *Gemälde No. 1/Composition No. XII*, 1913
Oil on canvas
Private collection (B 40)

In Mondrian's estate there are a great many sketches of Paris buildings representing facades and their rears, conserved loose or in a little sketchbook. In these sketches the "relationships and rhythm of plane and line" and the "mathematical artistic temperament" are perfectly visualized (fig. 51). *Gemälde No. 1* (fig. 52) is based unquestionably on the sketch reproduced here. And *Gemälde No. 2* (B 39) likewise originated in a view of the railroad tracks of the Montparnasse station seen from the studio on the rue du Départ.

As one can see, Mondrian does not abandon nature. *Tableau No. 2* (fig. 54) and *Tableau No. 1* (cat. 104) originate from the study of a tree, as do *Tableau No. 4* (cat. 101) and *Tableau No. 3* (cat. 103), which date earlier. But the tree is of another type than the one in the "Compositions," which was the object of a mathematical interpretation (fig. 53 and 54).

Mondrian had not been able to devote all his time to his art in 1913. At the end of May he wrote to Schelfhout that he was working on a copy that had been commissioned from him. In the registry of the Rijksmuseum, his name appears on the date July 29, 1913, for making a copy of an 1851 portrait. He spent a period from late July to early August in Holland. Did he attend the selection of the Dutch paintings for the third exhibition of the Moderne Kunst Kring in November 1913? Probably not.

Mondrian was no doubt satisfied with the works he had sent to that third exhibition. His contribution attracted the attention of H. P. Bremmer (1871–1956), the extremely influential connoisseur and advisor of the most important modern art collector in Holland, Helene Kröller-Müller (1869–1939). Bremmer bought two works, one for her, *Tableau No. 1*, and one for himself, *Tableau No. 3*. Bremmer soon revealed himself to be more than a simple buyer.

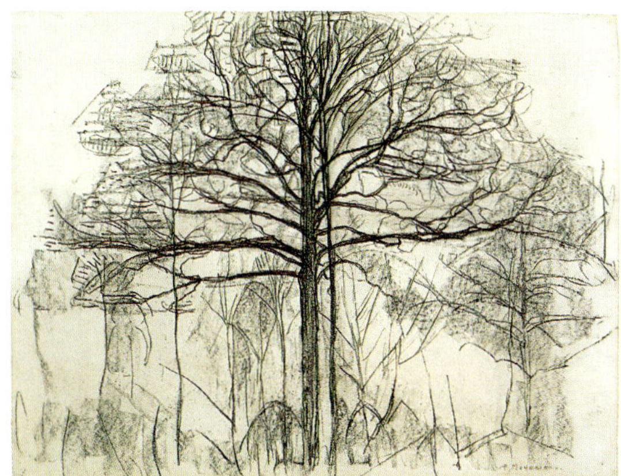

Fig. 53
Piet Mondrian, *Study of a Tree 1*, 1912–13
Charcoal on paper
Gemeentemuseum, The Hague (B 10)

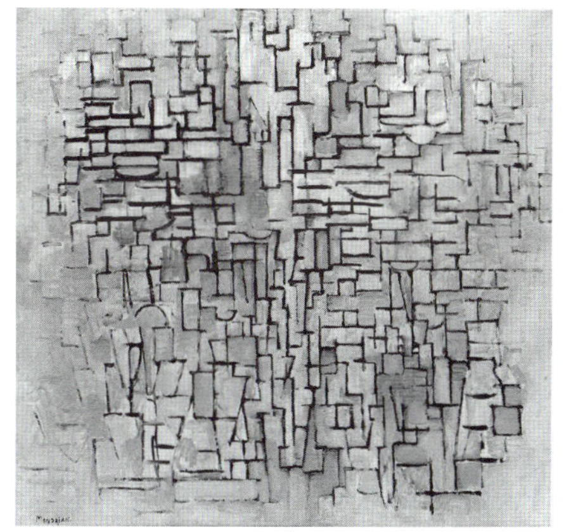

Fig. 54
Piet Mondrian, *Tableau No. 2/Composition No. VII*, 1913
Oil on canvas
The Solomon R. Guggenheim Museum, New York (B 35)

Mondrian spent the end of the year writing his first essay on art, "Art and Theosophy," at the request of the Theosophical Society. He submitted it in May 1914, but it was refused. "It was too revolutionary for those people," he wrote to Schelfhout.[169] The manuscript must be considered lost.

His seventh work of 1913, the last of the year—it was only in June 1914 that Mondrian wrote the date 1913 on the painting—marks the beginning of a new evolution, evident in the more attenuated construction of the web of verticals and horizontals and the return to color. An analysis of the composition shows that the artist was inspired by an earlier landscape motif, the view toward the Geinrust farm from the opposite bank of the river. A painting, two pastels, and two watercolors with this motif are known to us. The only work Mondrian might have been able to use at that time for the execution of *Composition No. II* is the most schematic of the two watercolors, which belongs today to the Gemeentemuseum in The Hague: *Geinrust Farm and Young Trees* (fig. 55). It is this watercolor that best corresponds to the construction of *Composition No. II* (fig. 56). The likelihood of working from a sketch may explain the assurance and serenity that emanate from the painting. This assurance opened the way for a return to color. A request by Bremmer for authorization to reproduce the two works he had bought at the exhibition of the Moderne Kunst Kring in an article in his monthly *Beeldende Kunst* (*Visual Arts*), gave Mondrian the chance to explain in writing the principles underlying his work. *Composition No. II* (fig. 56) had been recently finished, and the manner in which he explores his intentions makes it seem that Mondrian had the painting in front of him. "The public finds my work rather vague. . . ." So begins the account written in his letter of January 29, 1914:

169. Joosten 1968, 215.

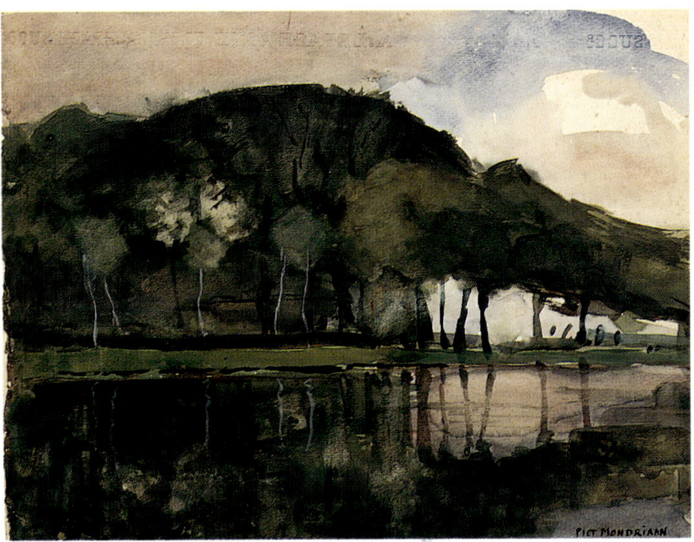

Fig. 55
Piet Mondrian, *Geinrust Farm and Young Trees,*
1905–7
Gouache sketch
Gemeentemuseum, The Hague (A 447)

at best, they find that it makes them think a great deal about music. Frankly, I have nothing against that, except when one pursues the thought by asserting that in this way my work abandons the domain of the visual arts.
For I construct lines and combinations of colors on a flat surface with the goal of representing universal beauty as conscientiously as possible. Nature (or what I see) inspires me, gives me, as it gives all painters, the emotion that brings forth creative élan, but I am seeking to approach truth as closely as possible, and to abstract everything from it until I reach the foundations (always visible foundations!) of things. That is for me a truth: while not wanting to say anything determinate, one pronounces precisely what there is that is most determinate, truth (which is of great comprehensiveness).
I consider ancient architecture the greatest art. I estimate that it is possible, through the use of horizontal and vertical lines, conscientiously constructed–not in a calculated way—but guided by a profound intuition and in harmony and in rhythm, I estimate that it is possible to be able to achieve, thanks to these archetypes of beauty, completed if necessary, by other lines, in other positions, or even by curved lines, a work of art just as strong as it is true.
For him who sees more deeply, nothing is vague; the vague does not exist except for him who sees nature superficially. And one must guard against chance as much as against calculation. It seems to me also that it is constantly necessary to break the horizontal or vertical line, because when these axes are not opposed to others, then they will begin again to represent something "intended" and therefore something human. It is exactly when one strives not to tell or say

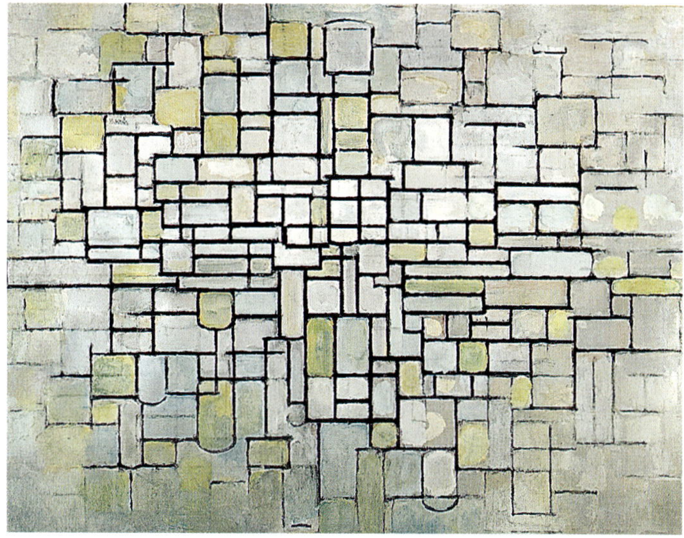

Fig. 56
Piet Mondrian, *Composition No. II*, 1913
Oil on canvas
Kröller Müller Museum, Otterlo (B 42)

anything human, when one forgets oneself completely, that the work of art emerges, which is a monument of Beauty: it appears above all that is human and is, in its depth and its universality, still the best of what is human! I am sure and certain that here lies the art of the future. Futurism, even if it is progress over naturalism, worries too much about human sensation. Cubism (whose content is still well founded in aesthetic creations of the past and which for that reason is less in step with its time than Futurism), Cubism took the decisive step toward abstraction and that is why it is still of our time and of future times, therefore not modern by its content, but very modern by its action.
For my part, I count myself among neither of the two, but I feel the spirit of the times in both, as in myself.[170]

170. Joosten 1968, 211.

Chapter Nine

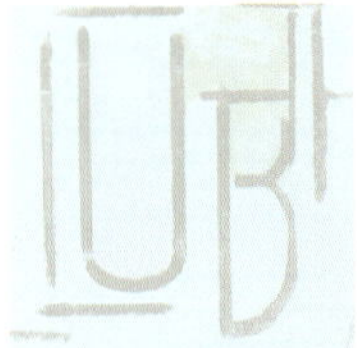

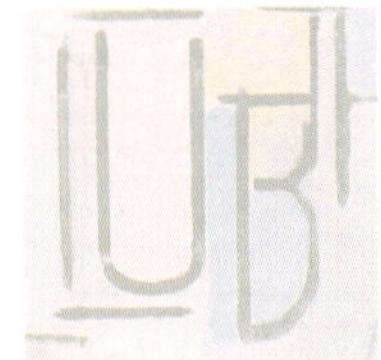

1914

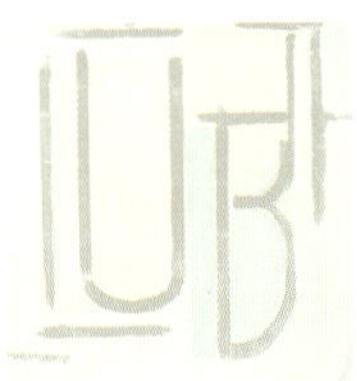

"Gradually, I became aware that Cubism did not accept the logical consequences of its own discoveries." [171]

Joop M. Joosten

At the end of February 1914, Mondrian sent only two works to the Salon des Indépendants, which was to open the first of March. In both works, *Tableau No. 1/ Composition No. 1* (cat. 105) and *Tableau No. 2/Composition No. V* (cat. 106), the systematized plasticism of relationships, already visible in *Composition No. II,* is carried further, due most notably to the mathematical character of the façades of Paris buildings, which Mondrian chose as his starting point. *Tableau No. 1* appears to have been inspired by a sketch of the rear of a building. It is possible that the scene is a view from Mondrian's studio. *Tableau No. 2* apparently evokes a view of gables rising up above an unidentified construction site. This view served equally as the foundation for *Gemälde No. I* (B 40), for which we again have a preparatory study (see fig. 51 and 52).

Once again, Mondrian's paintings did not leave the critics indifferent. Apollinaire limited himself, in *L'Intransigeant* of March 3, to an ". . . I cite Mondrian," while Salmon, in the March issue of *Montjoie!* wrote, "The paths—so brief—through the virgin and perfectly equatorial forest of the *Indépendants* have left me no time for rest, which is so necessary, it seems to me, to penetrate the meaning of the completely new art of M. Mondrian and the Youth of Holland."

To frame these paintings, Mondrian used only straight, flat strips of wood, which were painted

171. Mondrian, 1942.

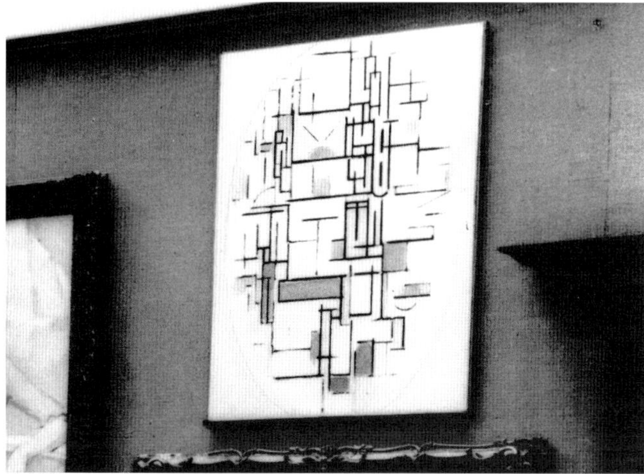

Fig. 57a
Composition in Oval with Color Planes 1, with its original frame, 1914
Photograph taken during the exhibition, *Modern Dutch Art*, Brighton, England, Public Art Galleries

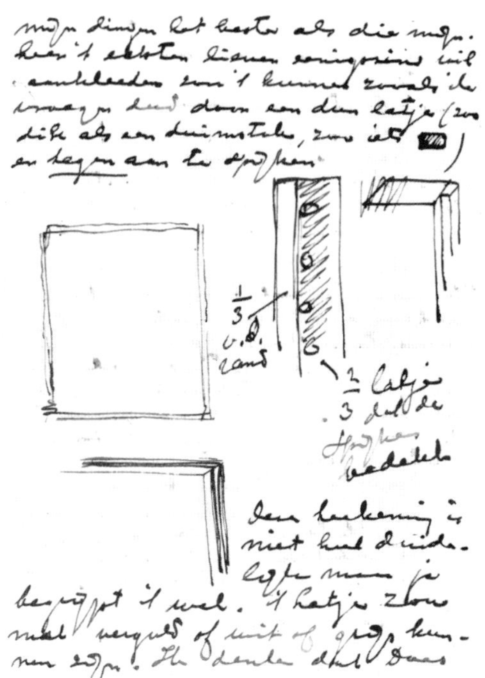

Fig. 57b
Page of a letter from Mondrian to the architect J. J. P. Oud, dated March 31, 1921, explaining the placement of the pieces of wood for the frame.
Netherlands Institute, Paris

bronze and applied to the edges without overlapping the painted surface. Since he would organize his composition over the complete surface of the painting, he had probably decided–more and more consciously–that standard overlapping frames were an insult to his works, and thus arrived at this drastic and highly unusual solution (fig. 57a and b).

After the exhibit he was no longer very satisfied with his entry, as he confided to Bremmer and Schelfhout in letters dated May 5 and June 6 respectively, telling them about his intention to rework the canvases. The cause for this vexation is reflected in one of his first letters to Theo van Doesburg, in November 1915, in which he describes these paintings, as well as two other analogous works, as "too dogmatic," "too absolute," and "incomprehensible." Apparently a response from van Doesburg led him to answer as follows, in a second letter dated November 20, 1915:

As far as dogmatism etc. is concerned, you did not understand me, because I was too succinct, too incomplete. In my book,[172] *I explain myself clearly. You have understood that I, like you, do not take into consideration what people think; but I have the conviction that even we—and consequently, I, even though as far as I know, I am one of those for whom art most expresses the*

172. Published two years later, "De Nieuwe Beelding in de schilderskunst ("The New Plastic in Painting") in *De Stijl*. 1917–18.

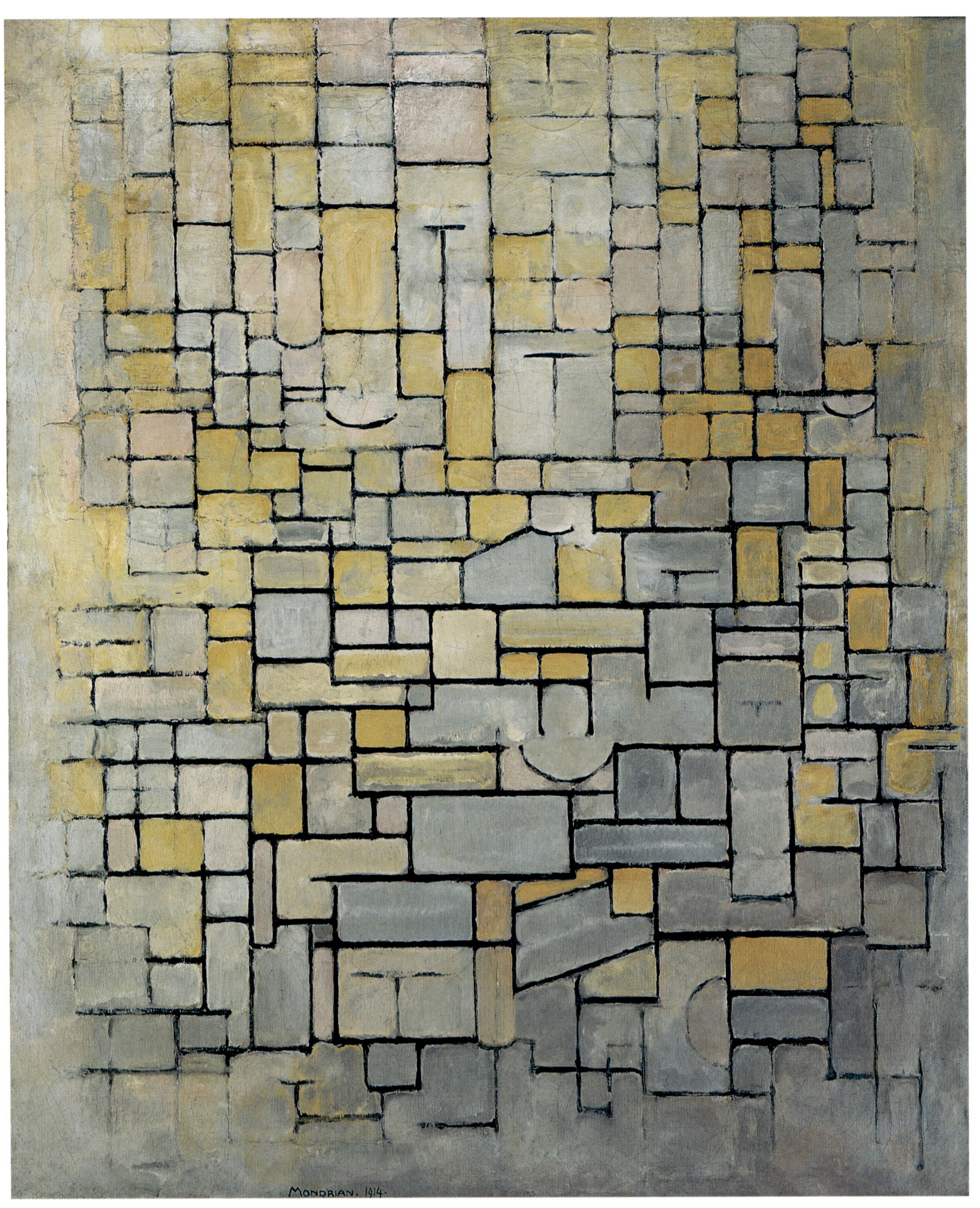

105

Cat. 105 *Tableau No. 1/Composition No. I/Compositie 7*, 1914
Oil on canvas
47.5 x 40.4 in. (120.6 x 101.3 cm)
Signed and dated: MONDRIAN. 1914.
Kimbell Art Museum, Fort Worth, Gift of The Burnett Foundation of Fort Worth in memory of Anne Burnett Tandy, 1983, inv. Apg 1983.03 (B 44)

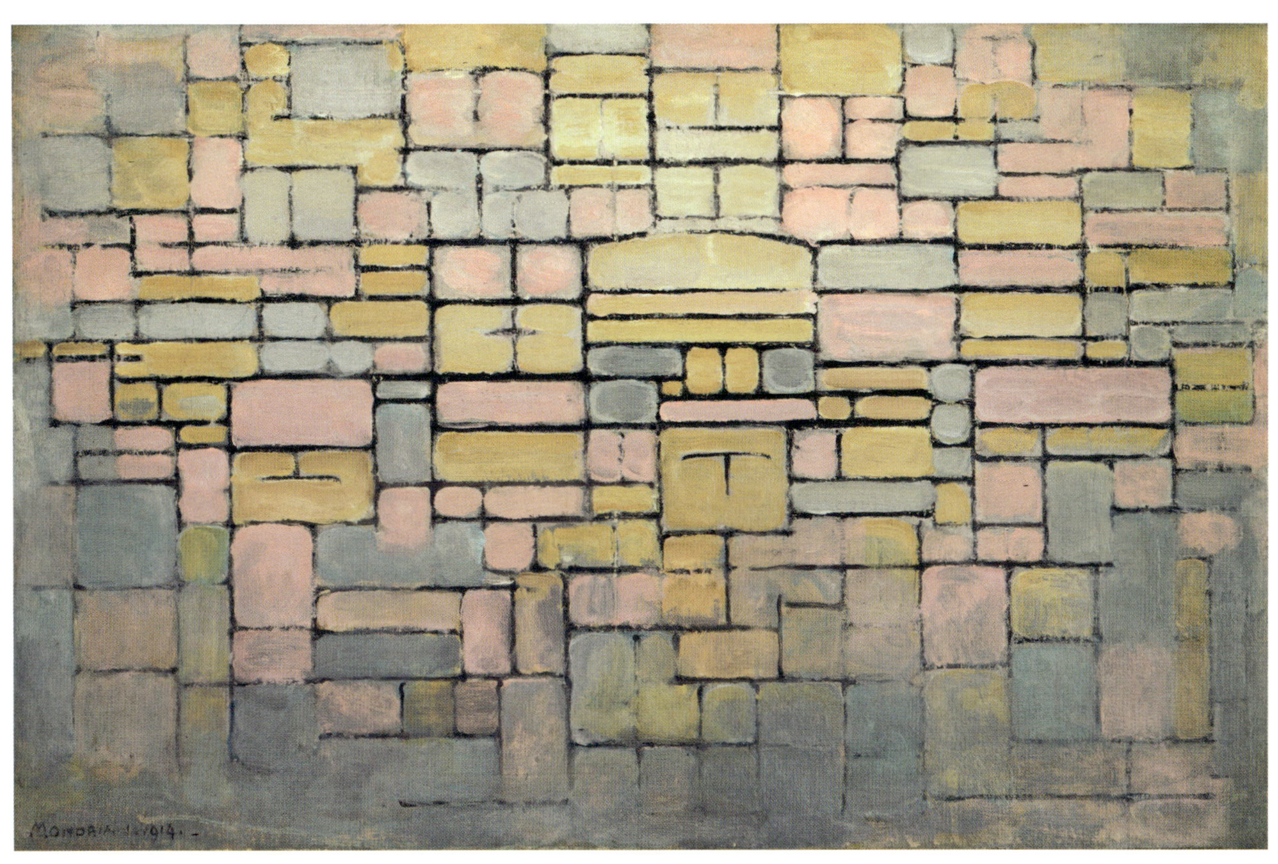

106

Cat. 106 *Tableau No. 2/Composition No. V*, 1914
Oil on canvas
21.6 x 33.6 in. (54.8 x 85.3 cm)
Signed and dated lower left: MONDRIAN. 1914.
The Museum of Modern Art, New York, The Sidney and Harriet Janis Collection (B 45)

absolute–we are still so far from this absolute that, when we create an absolute form, we feel or we perceive that, for us (and as a consequence for the people who are the most advanced among laymen), this form has something dogmatic about it. In brief, the absolute must be represented under the appearance of the relative until a new order arises. I discovered that my closed rectangular form, for example, was too absolute. We'll get to this, but later.[173]

On July 7, 1914, Mondrian informed Schelfhout that he had made yet more "effective headway" since the Salon des Indépendants, and had sent fifteen paintings from the last eighteen months, as well as "a sketch done just recently," to The Hague for an exhibition that Bremmer was instrumental in organizing. In response to an urgent request from Mondrian, asking him to help find clients likely to purchase or order copies, Bremmer had contacted the art dealer W. Walrecht in The Hague, who was very willing to organize an exhibition. One may presume that this exhibition was intended to promote buying among Bremmer's disciples.

The exhibition ran from approximately June 15 to July 31. The sixteen works that Mondrian sent formed a numbered series, running from "Composition No. I" to "Composition No. XVI." The numbers I to VI were his latest works, of which the earliest was *Composition No. II*, of 1913, which we have already discussed (fig. 56). The latest was the "sketch done just recently," *Composition No. VI* (cat. 109). The works bearing numbers I and V were those mentioned above under their earlier numbers: *Tableau No.1* (cat. 105) and *Tableau No. 2* (cat. 106). There remain Compositions III and IV, identifiable as *Composition No. III/Compositie 8* (B 47) and *Composition No. IV/Compositie 6* (cat. 107).

These six works exhibit two innovations: in the first place, they are dated. Until that time Mondrian had dated his paintings only very sporadically; henceforth he would always do so, with perhaps some rare exceptions. Secondly, all six works are furnished with the simple frame described above. It is placed identically for numbers I, II, and V. In the case of numbers III, IV, and VI, the frame was set back from the edge of the canvas, thus completely revealing the complete painted surface. The narrow band of canvas on the side that was not covered by the frame was painted the same bronze color as the frame. Mondrian used this last type of framing until 1937, but replacing the bronze color with white in 1917.

The lack of correspondence between numbering and chronology illustrated by these six works is even more noticeable in the other ten paintings.

In the "sketch done just recently," *Composition No. VI*, the compact image of "closed rectangular forms" is broken up to the point of disintegration. Sketchbook drawings demonstrate that Mondrian had gone on to another motif. What we see here is the schematic representation of the side wall of a building showing the remains of an adjacent demolished apartment house. It seems likely that these sketches represent one of the four side walls with traces of the demolished buildings at the two ends of the lengthened rue

173. Unpublished letter, Van Doesburg Archives, RKD, The Hague.

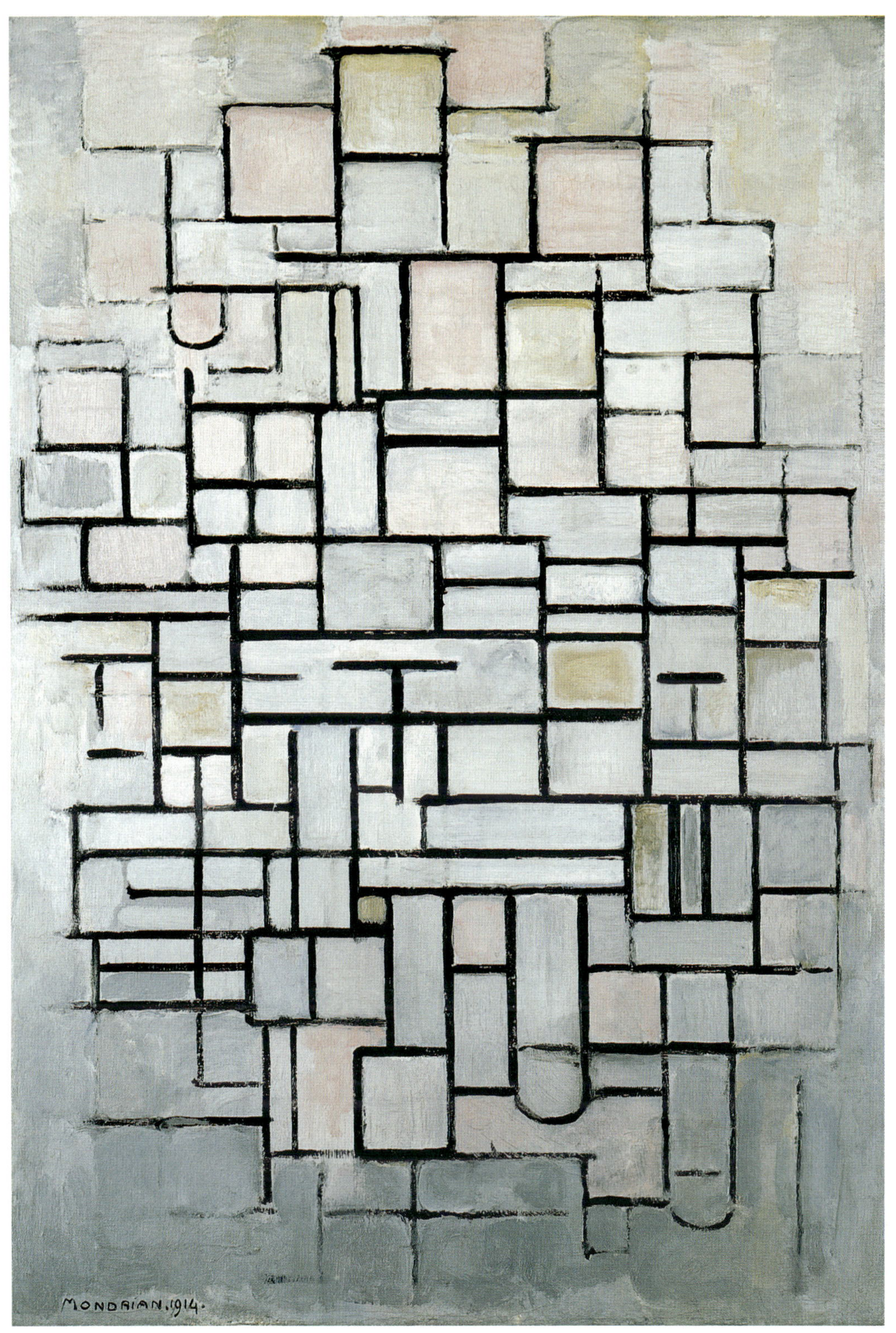

107

Cat. 107 *Composition No. IV/Compositie 6*, 1914
Oil on canvas
34.6 x 24 in. (88 x 61 cm)
Signed and dated lower left: MONDRIAN. 1914.
Gemeentemuseum, The Hague, bequest Salomon
B. Slijper, 1971 (B 46)

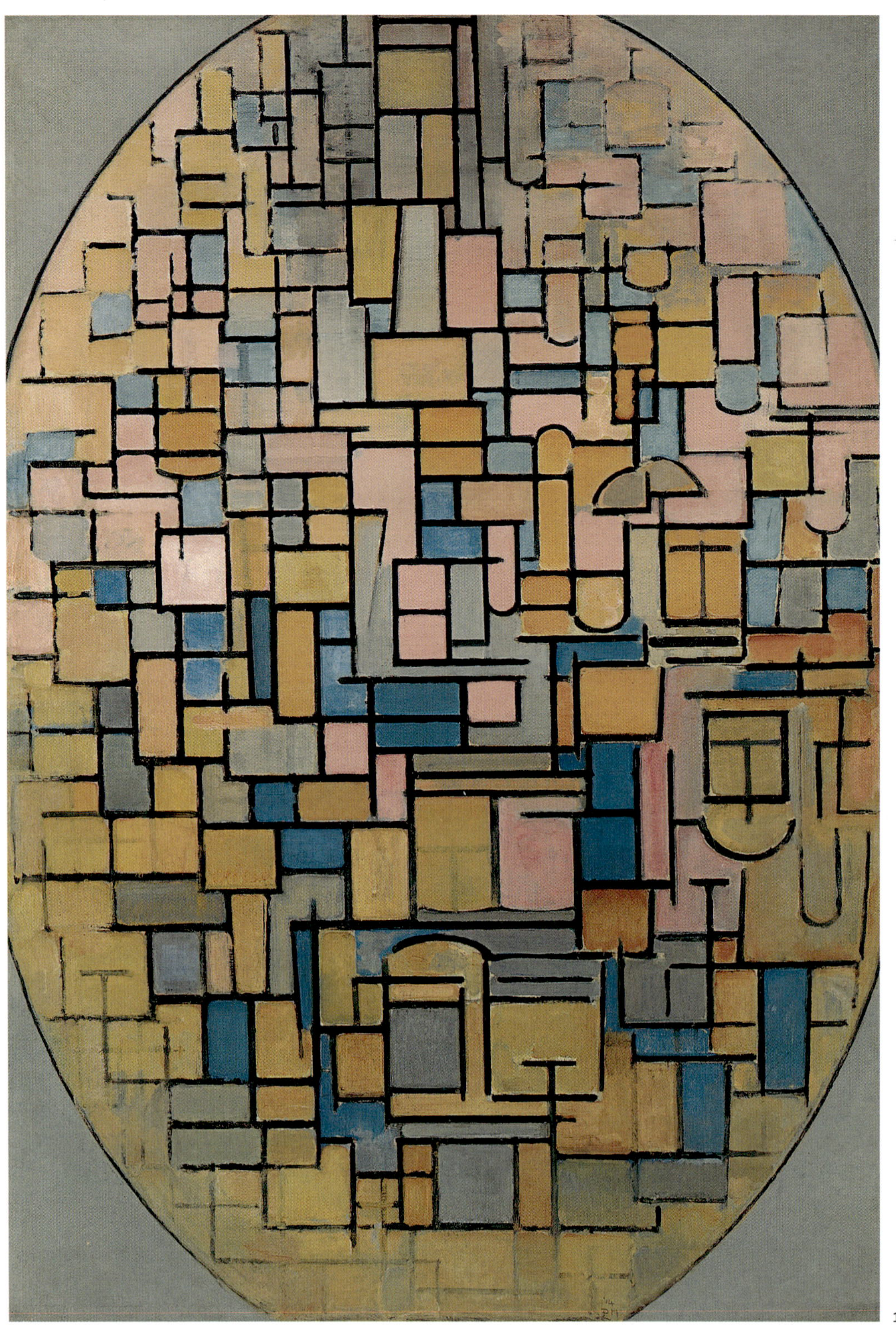

108

Cat. 108 *Tableau III*, 1914
Oil on canvas
55.1 x 39.8 in. (140 x 101 cm)
Monogrammed and dated lower right: '14 PM
Stedelijk Museum, Amsterdam, inv. A 24589 (B 49)

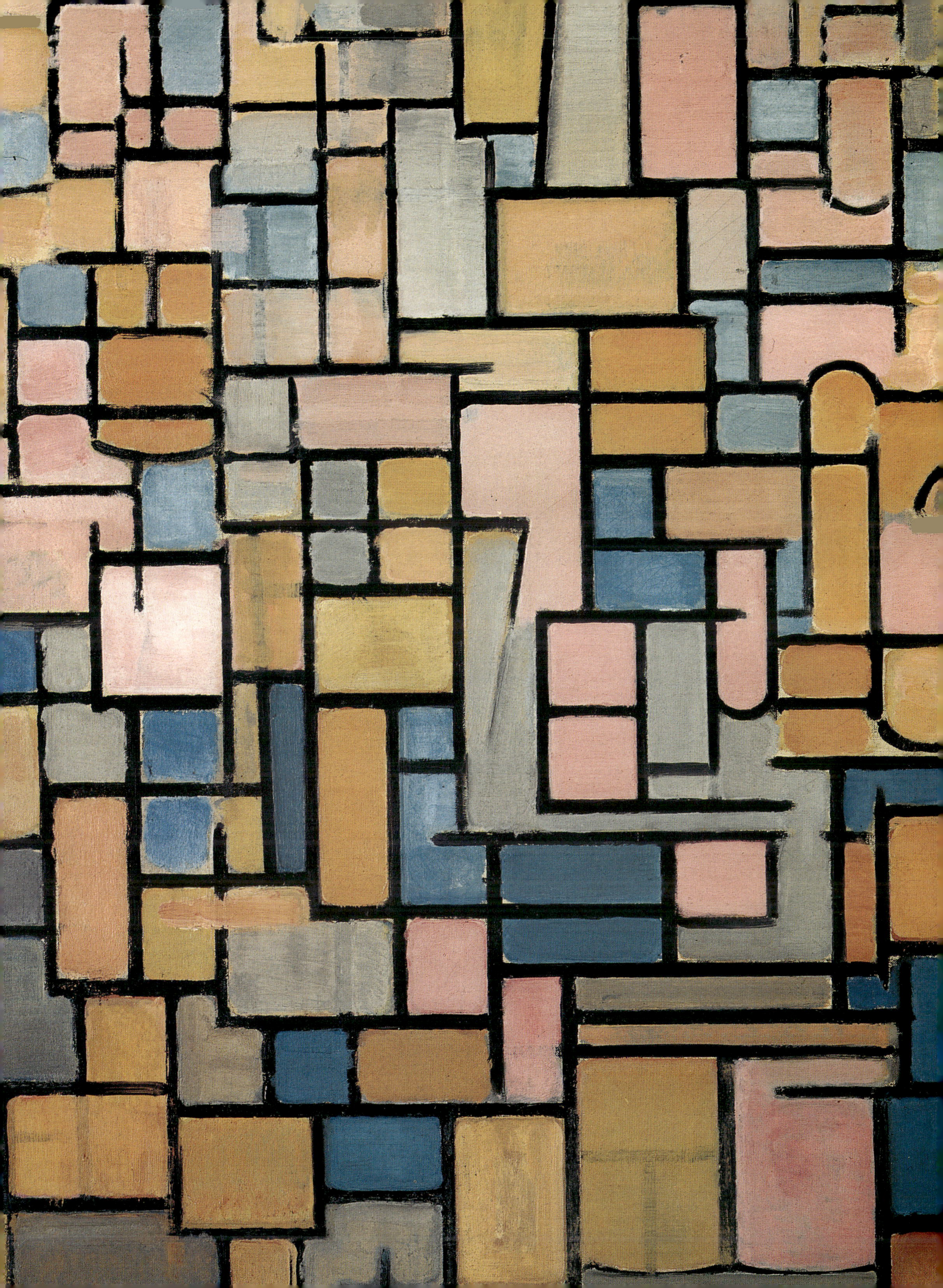

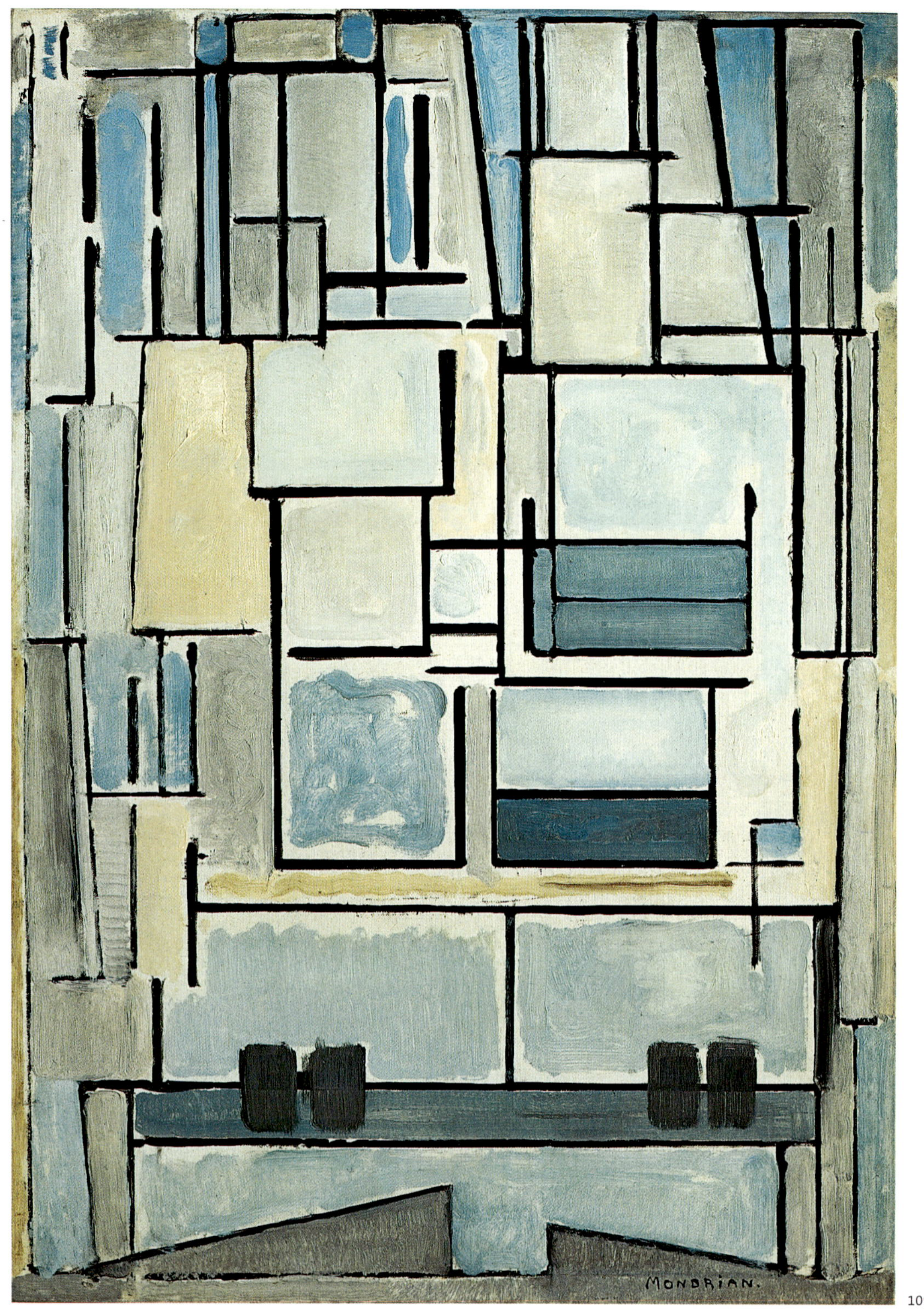

109

Cat. 109 *Compositie No. VI/Compositie 9,* 1914
Oil on canvas
37.5 x 26.6 in. (95.2 x 67.6 cm)
Signed lower right: MONDRIAN.
Beyeler Collection, Basel, (B 50)

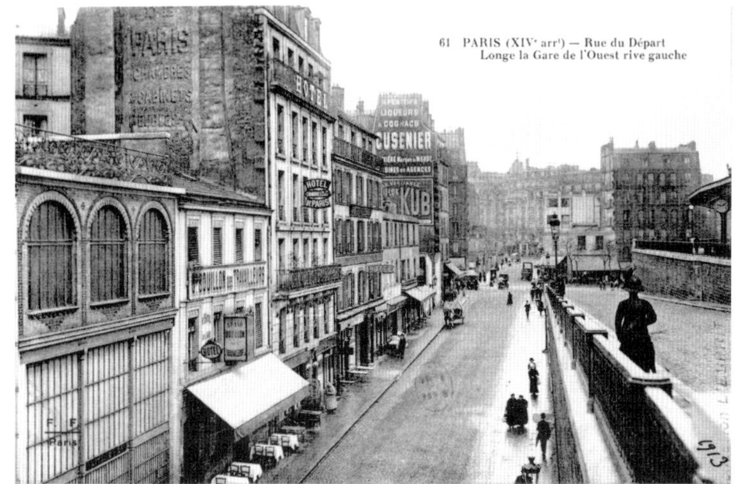

Fig. 58
Postcard, *Paris (XIVe arrondissement): Rue du Départ along the Gare de l'Ouest (West Station) on the Right Bank*, c. 1913
It is possible to see the raised walkway at the beginning of the rue du Départ and the side of the building at the corner of the rue du Départ and boulevard Edgar-Quinet, with the billboard for KUB-brand bouillon. On the right, toward the end of the walkway, is Mondrian's studio/apartment, at 26 rue du Départ.
Musée Carnavalet, Paris

du Départ, where the painter had his studio (fig. 58).

Mondrian had earlier remarked how in a metropolis "the natural is already ordered, controlled by the human spirit"; how "beauty is expressed more mathematically"; and that in the metropolis "the mathematical artistic temperament of the future will develop." These side walls taught him that this man of the future, this same human spirit, also destroyed blow-by-blow the mathematical ordering by destroying the original architecture, or by adding new architectural elements, colors, lines, etc. In this way, future man added to this mathematical ordering the element of relativity that Mondrian was looking for himself.

This knowledge, this experience, and this awareness of relativity are expressed in the purity and monumentality of *Composition No. VI* (cat. 109) and the three following paintings, the last ones he painted in Paris before World War I.

On Saturday July 25, 1914, Mondrian returned to Holland to see his father, then his friends in Domburg and Amsterdam. It is possible that he saw the exhibition organized by W. Walrecht in The Hague, and perhaps even brought the painting *Composition with Color Planes* (B 51) to add it to the works exhibited. It was sold shortly thereafter to one of the disciples of Bremmer.

With the outbreak of World War I, Mondrian decided to delay his return to Paris until the end of the hostilities. As did so many, he thought that he would not have long to wait. He was forced to wait five years. Firmly resolved to return to Paris, he maintained his studio in spite of the occasional difficulties in paying his rent during these years.

He had left three recent works in Paris, all painted in an oval format on a rectangular support. The canvas entitled *Tableau III* (cat. 108), probably completed at the time of the exhibition in The Hague, might also have been sent, but its large size perhaps made its shipment impossible. Its composition recalls a drawing representing a building shored up by scaffolding. The two paintings *Oval Composition with Color Planes 1* (B 53) and *Composition in Oval* (cat. 110) must have been completed just before his departure. The sketch that was the source of the first painting, a wall being demolished, still exists. The second painting relates to the rough sketches of a well-known view that one finds on postcards of the era, showing the side exit from the Gare Montparnasse onto the rue du Départ (fig. 58, 59, and 60). The complex image of the setbacks and sides of buildings surmounted by the double advertising sign, which so blatantly opposes the

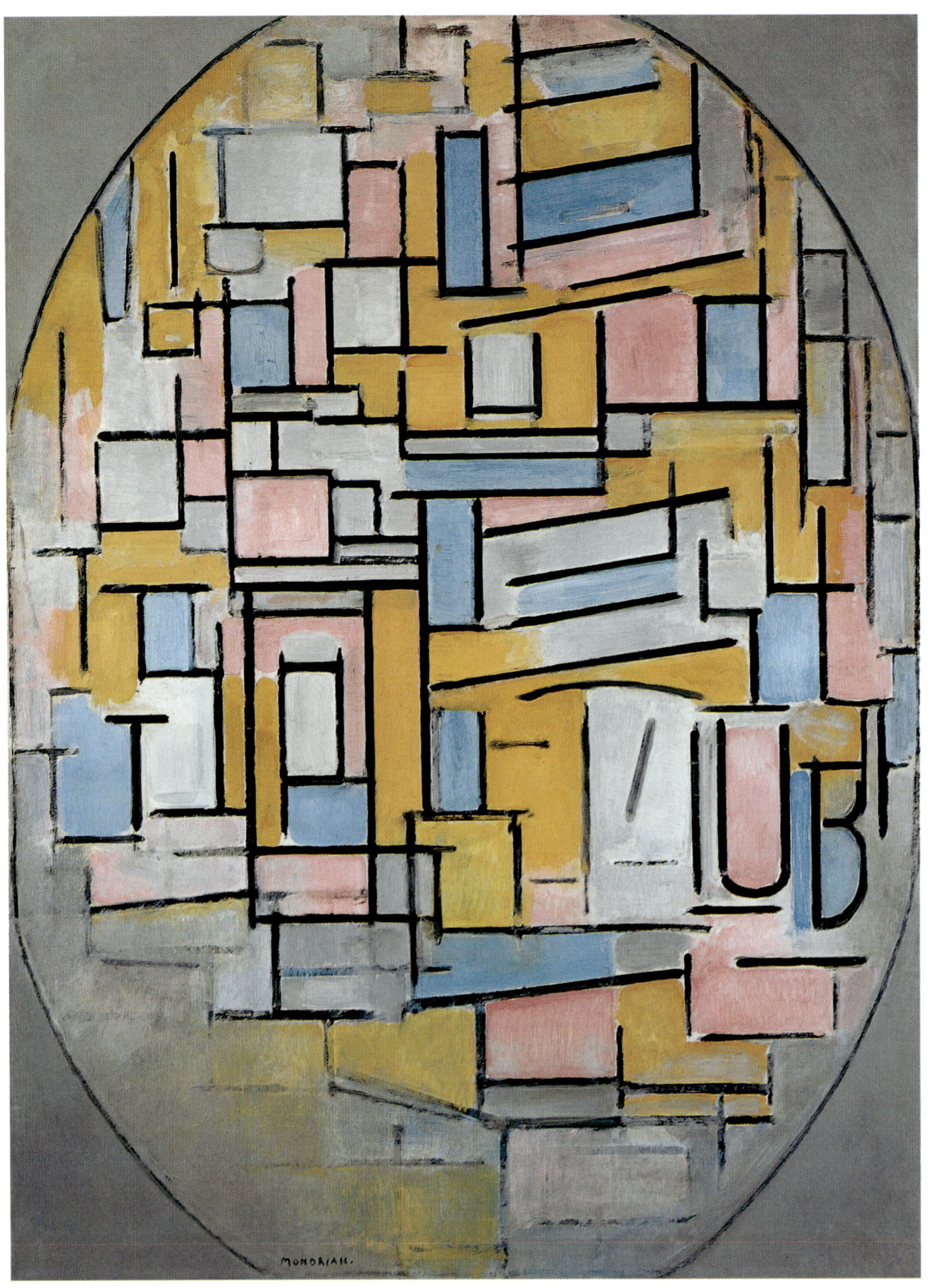

110

Cat. 110 *Composition in Oval*, 1914
Oil on canvas
44.5 x 33.25 in. (113 x 84.5 cm)
Signed lower left: MONDRIAN.
Gemeentemuseum, The Hague, bequest Salomon B. Slijper, 1971,
inv. S 160–1971 (B 55)

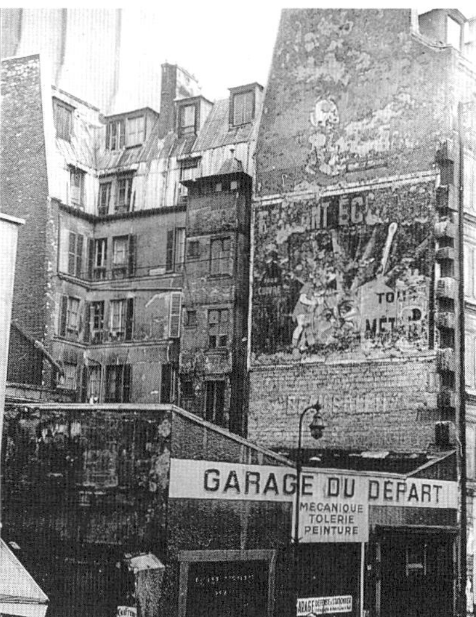

Fig. 59
Buildings along the boulevard Edgar-Quinet, seen from the rue du Départ, 1914
Gemeentemuseum, The Hague

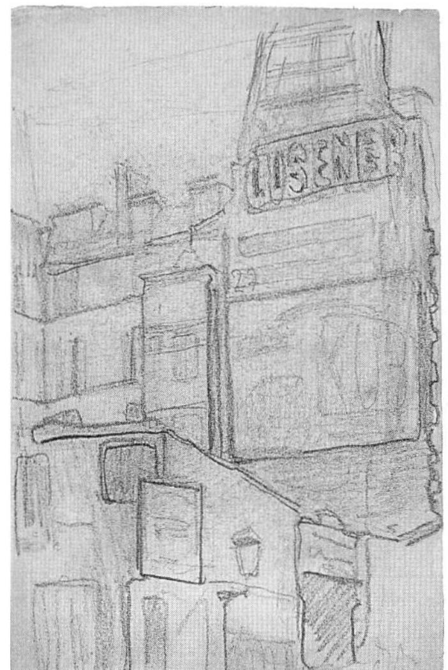

Fig. 60
Piet Mondrian, *Parisian façades*, 1914
Buildings on the boulevard Edgar-Quinet, seen from the rue du Départ.
Pencil. Drawing taken from a sketchbook
Private collection (B 405)

construction forms, must have appealed to Mondrian. A chance encounter made this *Composition in Oval* the last work of his first stay in Paris. He found the opportunity, without having looked for it, to integrate the famous pun of Braque and Picasso from the popular advertisement for bouillon cubes. The position of the "(K) UB" in the lower right area of the painting—looking as if it is ready to escape—seems to evoke a goodbye to Cubism, and in particular to the Cubism of Picasso, which had meant so much to him, teaching him to fragment form and, thus, representation—from then on banished from his work—and showing him the path to what he would later name "abstract-real" painting. For the last stop of his voyage, upon his return to Holland, Mondrian found himself, relying upon himself alone, pursuing experiments with newly discovered means of expression: lines and their internal relationships in rectangular blocks, and primary colors: red, blue, and yellow, as well as the colors of light and darkness: white, gray, and black.

Archives Cited

RKD: Rijksbureau voor Kunsthistorische Documentatie, The Hague

Aletta de Iongh Archives:
Letters of Aletta de Iongh, Kröller-Müller Museum, Otterlo

Jaffé Archives:
H. L. C. Jaffé Archives, Rijksbureau voor Kunsthistorische Documentatie, The Hague

Simon Maris Archives, Rijksbureau voor Kunsthistorische Documentatie, The Hague

Slijper Archives:
Salomon B. Slijper Archives, Rijksbureau voor Kunsthistorische Documentatie, The Hague

Van Doesburg Archives
Theo van Doesburg Archives, Rijksbureau voor Kunsthistorische Documentatie, The Hague

Bibliography

Alpers 1983
Alpers, Svetlana. *The Art of Describing: Dutch Art in the Seventeenth Century.* Chicago: University of Chicago Press, 1983.

Apollinaire 1960
Apollinaire, Guillaume. *Guillaume Apollinaire: Chroniques d'Art (1902–1918).* Paris: Gallimard, 1960.

Apollinaire 1972
Apollinaire, Guillaume. *Apollinaire en Art: Essays and Reviews, 1902–1918.* London: Thames and Hudson, and New York: The Viking Press.

Baar 1994
Baar, Peter-Paul. "Mondrian aan de Amstel." *Ons Amsterdam* 46, no. 2 (February 1994).

Bakker 1993
Bakker, Boudewijn. "Levenspelgrimage of vrome Wandeling? Claes Jansz. Visscher en zijn serie 'Plaisante Plaetsen.'" *Oud Holland,* no. 107 (1993).

Bakker 2000
Bakker, Boudewijn. "De stad in beeld. 't Was of 'k mijzelven vond. Het stadsgezicht als spiegel van de tijd." *Amsterdam in de tweede Gouden Eeuw.* Amsterdam: Gemeentearchief, 2000.

Bakker, Bax, and Welsh 1994
Bakker, Boudewijn, Marty Bax, and Robert P. Welsh. *Mondrian aan de Amstel, 1892–1912.* Exh. cat. Amsterdam: Gemeentearchief, 1994.

Blotkamp 1991
Blotkamp, Carel. "Kunstenaars als critici: Kunstrkritiek in Nederland 1880–1895." *De Schilders van Tachtig: Nederlandse Schilderkunst, 1880–1895.* Exh. cat. Amsterdam: Rijksmuseum Vincent van Gogh, 1991.

Blotkamp 1994
Blotkamp, Carel. *Destructie als kunst,* Zwolle: Waanders, 1994.

Bois 1994
Yve-Alain Bois. "The Iconoclast." In *Piet Mondrian: 1872–1944.* Exh. cat. The Hague, Gemeentemuseum; Washington, National Gallery of Art; New York, The Museum of Modern Art, 1994–96, 313–72.

Bomford, Kirby, Leighton, and Roy 1990
Bomford, David, Jo Kirby, John Leighton, and Ashok Roy. *Art in the Making: Impressionism.* Exh. cat. London and New Haven: Yale University Press, 1990.

Bradley 1944
Bradley, Jay. "Piet Mondrian, 1872–1944: Greatest Dutch Painter of Our Times." *Knickerbocker Weekly,* no. 51 (February 1944).

Cabanne 1963
Cabanne, Pierre. *L'Epopée du cubisme.* Paris: La Table ronde, 1963.

Callen 1988
Callen, Anthea. *Techniques of the Impressionists.* London: 1988.

Cooper 2001
Cooper, Harry. "Looking into the Transatlantic Paintings." In *Mondrian: The Transatlantic Paintings.* Exh. cat. Cambridge: Harvard University Art Museums: 2001.

Coplans 1968
Coplans, John. "Serial Imagery: Piet Mondrian." In *Serial Imagery.* Exh. cat. Pasadena and Santa Barbara: Pasadena Art Museum, 1968–69.

De Meester-Obreen 1915
A. O. [Augusta de Meester-Obreen]. "Piet Mondriaan." *Elsevier's Geïllustreerd Maandschrift,* 25th year, vol. 50, no. 11 (November 1915).

Gorter, Van Burkom, and Joosten 1998
Gorter, Paul, Frans Van Burkom, and Joop M. Joosten. "Mies Maris'vergeten Mondriana." *Jong Holland,* vol. 14, no. 2: 22–35 and no. 3: 35–47 (1998).

Henkels 1980–81
Henkels, Herbert. "Mondrian in seinem atelier/Mondriaan in zijn atelier/Mondrian in his studio: Een essay over Mondriaan's kunstenaarschap." In *Mondrian Zeichnungen, Aquarellen, New Yorker Bilder.* Exh. cat. Stuttgart: Staatsgalerie, and The Hague: Gemeentemuseum, 1980–81.

Henkels 1988
Henkels, Herbert. "'t Is alles een groote eenheid, Bert. Piet Mondriaan, Albert van den Briel en hun vriendschap aan de hand van brieven, documenten en fragmenten." *Bezorgd en van een nawoord voorzien door Herbert Henkels.* Haarlem: Joh. Enschedé en Zonen, 1988.

Herwerden, 1927
Herwerden, C. van. "M. W. van der Valk als Leeraar." *Elsevier's Geïllustreerd Maandschrift,* 37th year (1927), vol. 74: 381–82.

Holtzman and James 1986
Holtzman, Harry, and Martin S. James. *The New Art–The New Life: The Collected Writings of Piet Mondrian.* Boston: G. K. Hall, 1986.

Hoyle, Peres, and Van Tilborgh 1991
Hoyle, Michael, Cornelia Peres, and Louis Van Tilborgh. "A Closer Look: Technical and Art-Historical Studies on Works by van Gogh and Gauguin." *Cahiers Vincent,* no. 3, Amsterdam: Rijksmuseum Vincent van Gogh, and Zwolle: Waanders, 1991.

Janssen and Tabak 1998
Janssen, Hans, and Ida Tabak. "Kunnen niet eens groote Franschen gevraagd worden? Mondrian, Holder en de introductie van het modernisme in Nederland." *Jong Holland,* 14th year, vol. 4 (1998): 20–37.

Joosten 1968
Joosten, Joop M. "26 brieven van Piet Mondriaan aan Lod. Schelfhout et H. P. Bremmer, 1910–1918." *Museumjournaal,* no. 4 (August 1968), no. 5 (October 1968), no. 6 (December 1968).

Joosten and Welsh 1998
Joosten, Joop M., and Robert P. Welsh, *Piet Mondrian: Catalogue Raisonné,* 3 vols. New York: Harry N. Abrams, 1998. [vol. 1: Welsh, *Catalogue Raisonné of the Naturalistic Works (until early 1911)*; vol. 2: Joosten, *Catalogue Raisonné of the Work of 1911–1944*; vol. 3: Joosten and Welsh, *Appendix*].

Kikkert 1908
Kikkert, Conrad. "Saint Lucas, werkende leden-tentoonstelling." *Onze Kunst,* 7th year (1908), vol. 13, no. 6.

Kikkert 1909
Kikkert, Conrad. "Piet Mondriaan, Jan Sluijters, en C. Spoor." *Onze Kunst,* 8th year (1909), vol. 15.

Leeflang 1994
Leeflang, Huigen. "Het landschap in boek en prent. Perceptie en interpretatie van vroeg zeventiende eeuwse Nederlandse landschapsprenten." In Boudewijn Bakker and Huigen Leeflang. *Nederland naar't leven: landschapsprenten uit de Gouden Eeuw.* Exh. cat. Amsterdam: Rembrandthuis, and Zwolle: Waanders, 1994.

Locher 1994
Locher, J. L. [Hans]. *Piet Mondriaan: Kleur, structuur en symboliek.* Amsterdam: Meulenhoff and Berne, and Berlin: Gachnang & Springer, 1994.

Loosjes-Terpstra 1959
Loosjes-Terpstra, A. B. [Aleid]. *Moderne kunst in Nederland, 1900–1914.* Utrecht: Haantjens, Dekker en Gumbert, 1959.

Lurasco 1907
Lurasco, F. M. [Frits]. *Onze moderne meesters.* Amsterdam: C. L. G. Veldt, 1907.

Mali, Booij, and Scholtz 1994
Mali, Anco, Bert Booij, and Wim Scholtz. *Pieter Cornelis Mondriaan Senior, 1839–1921. Een gedreven vader.* Amersfoort: Stichting Mondriaanhuis, and Winterswijk: Ver. Het Museum, 1994.

Mauner 1991
Mauner, Georg. *Cuno Amiet: Hoffnung und Vergänglichkeit.* Aarau-Baden: Aargauer Kunsthaus, 1991.

Mondrian 1917–18
Mondrian, Piet. "De nieuwe beelding als abstract-reëlle schilderkunst. Beeldingsmiddel en compositie." In "De Nieuwe Beelding in de schilderkunst." *De Stijl* 1 (1917–18).

Mondrian 1918–19
Mondrian, Piet. "Het Bepaalde en het Onbepaalde." In "De Nieuwe Beelding in de schilderkunst." *De Stijl* 2 (1918–19), no. 2 (December 1918).

Mondrian 1921–22
Mondrian, Piet. "Le Néoplasticisme: Sa réalisation dans la musique et au théâtre futur." *La Vie des Lettres et des Arts* 8 (August 1922), 1921–22, no. 11.

Mondrian 1942
Mondrian, Piet. *Toward the True Vision of Reality.* New York: Valentine Gallery, 1942. In Harry Holtzman and Martin S. James. *The New Art—The New Life: The Collected Writings of Piet Mondrian.* Boston: G. K. Hall, 1986.

Postma 1995
Postma, Frans Postma. *26 rue du Départ, Mondriaans atelier in Parijs, 1912–1936.* Berlin: Ernst & Sohn, 1995.

Querido 1909–10
Querido, Israel. "Een schilders-studie: Spoor, Mondriaan en Sluijters." *De Controleur,* vol. 20, no. 1004, 1909–10 (October 23, 1909).

Querido 1910
Querido, Israel. "Jan Toorop: Essay en critiek." *Van den Akker.* Amsterdam: L. J. Veen, 1910.

Querido 1912
Querido, Israel. *Geschreven portretten.* Amsterdam: L. J. Veen, 1912, 76–108.

Riley 1997
Riley, Bridget. "Mondrian Perceived." In *Mondrian: Nature to Abstraction.* Exh. cat. London: Tate Gallery, 1997.

Roland Holst 1928
Roland Holst, Richard. "August Allébé." In *Over kunst en kunstenaars. Beschouwingen en herdenkingen. Nieuwe bundel.* Amsterdam, 1928.

Ruskin 1904
Ruskin, John. *The Elements of Drawing.* In *The Works of Ruskin,* vol. 15. London: George Allen, and New York: Longmans, Green, 1904.

Scherphuis 1994
Scherphuis, Ageeth. "Vrienden over zijn vrouwen, zijn smaak, zijn armoede." *Vrij Nederland* 55, December 14, 1994.

Seitz 1956
Seitz, William. "Monet and Abstract Painting." *Art Journal* 6, no. 1 (Autumn 1956).

Streng 1994
Streng, Toos. "Het 'realisme" van de oud-Nederlandse schilderschool: Opkomst en ontwikkeling van de term 'realisme' in Nederland tussen, 1850–1875." *Oud Holland* 108 (1994), no. 4.

Streng 1995
Streng, Toos. *Realisme in de kunst—en literatuurbeschouwing in Nederland tot 1875.* Amsterdam: Amsterdam University Press, 1995.

Tempel 1999
Tempel, Benno. "'Such Absurdities Can Never Deserve the Name of Art': Impressionism in the Netherlands," *Van Gogh Museum Journaal*, 1999.

Van Adrichem-Ammerlaan 1993
Van Adrichem-Ammerlaan, C. R. M. [Corrie]. *Aan Hare Majesteit de Koningin-Regentes der Nederlanden ...* Amersfoort: Stichting Mondriaanjuis, 1993.

Van Adrichem-Ammerlaan 1994
Van Adrichem-Ammerlaan, C. R. M. *Mondriaan: Het begin van een schilderscarrière.* Amersfoort: Stichting Mondriaanhuis, 1994.

Van der Aa 1843
Van der Aa, A. J. *Aardrijkskundig woordenboek der Nederlanden.* Gorinchem: 1843.

Van Deene 1977
Van Deene, Jan. "Rechtvaardiging." *Mededelingen Centraal Museum Utrecht*, nos. 10–17 (March 1977).

Van Domselaer-Middelkoop 1959–60
Van Domselaer-Middelkoop, M. "Herinneringen aan Piet Mondriaan." *Maatstaf* 7, no. 5 (1959–1960).

Van Ginneken and Joosten 1970
Van Ginneken, Lily, and Joop M. Joosten. "Kunstenaarsbrieven aan Cees Spoor." *Museumjournaal* 15 (1970).

Van Vloten 1990
Van Vloten, Francisca. *Heimwee houdt ons gevangen: Kunstenaarsbrieven aan Mies Elout-Drabbe in Domburg.* Middelburg: S. B. K. Zeeland, 1990.

Van Westrheene 1856
Van Westrheene, Tobias. *Étude sur l'art en Hollande: Jan Steen.* The Hague: Martinus Nijhoff, 1856.

Wagner 1977
Wagner, Anna. *Jan Voerman: Ijsselschilder.* Wageningen: Zomer & Keuning, 1977.

Wagner 1994
Wagner, Anna. *Jan Voerman: Ijsselschilder.* Exh. cat. Laren: Singer Museum, and Zwolle: Waanders, 1994.

Welsh 1977
Welsh, Robert P. *Piet Mondrian's Early Career* (Ph. D. Dissertation, Princeton University, 1965). New York & London: Garland, 1977.

Welsh and Joosten 1969
Welsh, Robert P., and Joop M. Joosten. *Two Mondrian Sketchbooks, 1912–1914.* Preface by Harry Holtzman. 's-Gravenhage: Rijksbureau voor Kunsthistorische Documentatie, and Amsterdam: Meulenhoff International, 1969.

Works exhibited

Cat. 1 (illus. p. 31)
Stilleven (Still Life), 1893
Oil on canvas
26.2 x 30.5 in. (66.5 x 77.5 cm)
Signed and dated lower left
Stedelijk Museum, Amsterdam, inv. A 8756 (A 23)

Cat. 2 (illus. p. 32)
Country Road, 1893
Oil on cardboard
16.3 x 20.9 in. (41.5 x 53 cm)
Signed and dated lower right
Private collection (A -)

Cat. 3 (illus. p. 35)
Country Road and Farm, 1893
Oil on canvas
17.1 x 23.7 in. (43.4 x 60.2 cm)
Signed and dated lower right
Private collection (A -)

Cat. 4 (illus. p. 36)
Warmte (Warmth), c. 1893–94
Oil on canvas
25 x 29.5 in. (63.5 x 75 cm)
Signed and dated lower right
Private collection (A 20)

Cat. 5 (illus. p. 38)
Het Singel/Oud-Amsterdam (The Singel/Old Amsterdam), c. 1893–97
Oil on canvas
27.2 x 18.1 in. (69 x 46 cm)
Signed lower left
Gemeentemuseum, The Hague, bequest of Salomon B. Slijper, 1971, inv. S 98–1971 (A 30)

Cat. 6 (illus. p. 40)
Women Washing, 1894–95
Oil on canvas
11.3 x 9.4 in. (28.8 x 23.8 cm)
Signed lower left
Private collection (A 29)

Cat. 7 (illus. p. 41)
View of Schinkelbuurt, c. 1894–95
Oil on canvas
12.2 x 15.2 in. (31 x 38.5 cm)
Signed lower right
Gemeentemuseum, The Hague, bequest of Salomon B. Slijper, 1971, inv. S 86–1971 (A 186)

Cat. 8 (illus. p. 42)
Irrigation Ditch with Bridge, 1894–95
Oil on canvas mounted on cardboard
10.4 x 14.8 in.(26.5 x 37.5 cm)
Signed lower right
Gemeentemuseum, The Hague, bequest of Salomon B. Slijper, 1971, inv. S 58–1971 (A 37)

Cat. 9 (illus. p. 45)
Farmhouse with Clothesline, c. 1895
Oil on cardboard
12.4 x 14.8 in. (31.5 x 37.5 cm)
Signed lower right
Gemeentemuseum, The Hague, inv. S 27–1960 (A 171)

Cat. 10 (illus. p. 46)
Farmstead and Ditch, c. 1897
Oil on canvas mounted on panel
15.6 x 18.5 in. (39.5 x 47 cm)
Signed lower left
Gemeentemuseum, The Hague, purchase Chr. Veldt, 1956, inv. S 39–1956 (A 154)

Cat. 11 (illus. p. 47)
Country Road and Row of Houses, c. 1897
Oil on paper mounted on panel
15.3 x 11.6 in. (39 x 29.5 cm)
Signed lower right
Gemeentemuseum, The Hague, bequest of Salomon B. Slijper, 1971, inv. S 57–1971 (A 160)

Cat. 12 (illus. p. 52)
Tree Sketch for Dorpskerk, 1896–97
Charcoal and crayon on paper
19.7 x 14.2 in. (50 x 36 cm)
Not signed
Musée d'Orsay, Paris, anonymous life-interest gift accepted by the State, 2000, inv. RF 52 078 (A 57)

Cat. 13 (illus. p. 53)
Church, Winterswijk, 1897–98
Charcoal and crayon on paper
15.9 x 10 in. (40.5 x 25.5 cm)
Not signed
Winterswijk Museum (A 59)

Cat. 14 (illus. p. 54)
Church, Winterswijk, 1897–98
Charcoal and crayon on paper
8.3 x 4.7 in. (21 x 12 cm)
Signed lower right
Gemeentemuseum, The Hague, bequest of Salomon B. Slijper, 1971, inv. T 77–1971 (A 58)

Cat. 15 (illus. p. 50)
Dorpskerk (Village Church), 1897–98
Pencil, watercolor, gouache, crayon, and pastel on paper
29.5 x 19.7 in. (75 x 50 cm)
Signed lower left
Private collection (A 61)

Cat. 16 (illus. p. 56)
Forest, 1899
Watercolor and gouache on paper
17.9 x 22.4 in. (45.5 x 57 cm)
Signed lower left
Gemeentemuseum, The Hague, bequest of Salomon B. Slijper, 1971, inv. T 58–1971 (A 88)

Cat. 17 (illus. p. 57)
Forest, 1899
Lead pencil, colored pencils, and conte crayon on paper
12.1 x 15.9 in. (30.6 x 40.5 cm)
Not signed
Gemeentemuseum, The Hague, inv. T 34–1987 (A 87)
Fort Worth only

Cat. 18 (illus. p. 60)
Aan den arbeid/Op het land (*At Work/In the Fields*), c. 1898
Watercolor on paper
21.4 x 31 in. (54.4 x 78.7 cm)
Signed lower left
Signature partially painted over in lower right
Gemeentemuseum, The Hague, inv. T 66–1986 (A 85)

Cat. 19 (illus. p. 61)
Aan de Stadhouderskade te Amsterdam (*At the Stadhouderskade, Amsterdam*), 1898–99
Charcoal, watercolor, and pastel on cardboard
24.4 x 39.3 in. (62 x 100 cm)
Signed lower left
Musée d'Orsay, Paris, inv. RF 41 384 (A 196)

Cat. 20 (illus. p. 67)
The Royal Wax Candle Factory, c. 1899
Oil on canvas mounted on cardboard
13.8 x 18.9 in. (35 x 48 cm)
Not signed
Gemeentemuseum, The Hague, gift of Albert van den Briel, inv. S 7–1965 (A 190)

Cat. 21 (illus. p. 70)
Ditch near Landzicht Farm, c. 1900
Oil on canvas
9.3 x 14.8 in. (23.5 x 37.5 cm)
Signed lower right
Gemeentemuseum, The Hague, gift of Albert van den Briel, 1956, inv. S 25–1956 (A 212)

Cat. 22 (illus. p. 71)
Ditch near Landzicht Farm, 1900
Conte crayon on paper
15.3 x 24.3 in. (39.2 x 61.6 cm)
Signed lower right
Gemeentearchief, Amsterdam, inv. M 254–2 (A 215)

Cat. 23 (illus. p. 85)
Op het land (*In the Country*), 1902–3
Oil on cardboard
12.0 x 15 in. (30.5 x 38 cm)
Signed lower right
Gemeentemuseum, The Hague, gift of Albert van den Briel, inv. T 26–1956 (A 278)

Cat. 24 (illus. p. 73)
Bij Arnhem (*Near Arnheim*), 1901
Watercolor and gouache on paper
18.3 x 26 in. (46.5 x 66 cm)
Signed lower right
Private collection (A 285)

Cat. 25 (illus. p. 83)
Passiebloem (*Passion Flower*), c. 1901
Watercolor on paper
28.5 x 18.7 in. (72.5 x 47.5 cm)
Vertical inscription lower left
Signed on the vertical lower right
Gemeentemuseum, The Hague, gift of Albert van den Briel, inv. T 81–1957 (A 145)

Cat. 26 (illus. p. 84)
Avond aan de Weesperzijde (*Evening on the Weesperzijde*), 1901
Lead pencil, crayon, watercolor, and gouache on paper
21.7 x 26 in. (55 x 66 cm)
Signed lower left
Gemeentemuseum, The Hague, bequest of Salomon B. Slijper, 1971, inv. T 50–1971 (A 205)

Cat. 27 (illus. p. 74)
Bleekerij aan het Gein (*Bleachworks on the Gein*), c. 1901–2
Watercolor on paper
18.9 x 23.2 in. (48 x 59 cm)
Signed lower left
Private Collection (A 282)

Cat. 28 (illus. p. 75)
Bleachworks on the Gein, 1901
Oil on canvas mounted on cardboard
10 x 15.1 in. (25.5 x 38.5 cm)
Signed lower right
Gemeentemuseum, The Hague, bequest of Salomon B. Slijper, 1971, inv. S 114–1971 (A 296)

Cat. 29 (illus. p. 78)
Polder Landscape, c. 1900
Watercolor on paper
19.7 x 25.6 in. (50 x 65 cm)
Not signed
Musée d'Orsay, Paris, anonymous life-interest gift accepted by the State, 2000, inv. RF 52 079 (A 510)

Cat. 30 (illus. p. 79)
House on the Water with Woman, c. 1900–1902
Oil on canvas mounted on panel
8.9 x 10.8 in. (22.5 x 27.5 cm)
Not signed
Gemeentemuseum, The Hague, inv. S 29–1960 (A 254)

Cat. 31 (illus. p. 80)
Farmyard with Chickens, 1901
Oil on canvas
19.3 x 27 in. (49 x 68.5 cm)
Signed lower right
Gemeentemuseum, The Hague, bequest of Salomon B. Slijper, 1971, inv. S 66–1971 (A 330)

Cat. 32 (illus. p. 82)
Willowgrove on the Gein, c, 1902–3
Oil on canvas
21.3 x 24.8 in. (54 x 63 cm)
Signed lower left
Gemeentemuseum, The Hague, bequest of Salomon B. Slijper, 1971, inv. S 105–1971 (A 470)

Cat. 33 (illus. p. 81)
Cows in an Orchard, c. 1902–3
Oil on canvas
14.7 x 10.7 in. (37.4 x 27.1 cm)
Signed lower left
Private collection (A 46)

Cat. 34a (illus. p. 89)
Bij de Ossenstal (*Near the Oxstall*), 1904
Oil on cardboard mounted on panel
12 x 15 in. (30.5 x 38 cm)
Not signed
Gemeentemuseum, The Hague, gift of Albert van den Briel, inv. S 27–1956 (A 379)

Cat. 34b (illus. p. 88)
Oostzijdse Mill, c. 1903
Oil on cardboard
11.8 x 16.5 in. (30 x 42 cm)
Signed lower left
Fort Worth only

Cat. 35 (illus. p. 89)
Barn Interior, c. 1904
Oil on canvas
12.6 x 19.7 in. (32 x 50 cm)
Not signed
Gemeentemuseum, The Hague, bequest of Salomon B. Slijper, 1971, inv. S 52–1971 (A 357)

Cat. 36 (illus. p. 91)
Farmhouse, Brabant, 1904
Oil on paper mounted on cardboard
11.2 x 13.4 in. (28.5 x 34 cm)
Signed lower right
Gemeentemuseum, The Hague, bequest of Salomon B. Slijper, 1971, inv. S 85–1971 (A 362)

Cat. 37 (illus. p. 90)
Barns at Nistelrode, 1904
Oil on cardboard mounted on panel
13 x 16.9 in. (33 x 43 cm)
Not signed
Gemeentemuseum, The Hague, gift of Albert van den Briel, inv. S 29–1956 (A 365)

Cat. 38 (illus. p. 93)
Farm at Duivendrecht, c. 1905
Oil on canvas
18.1 x 23.2 in. (46 x 59 cm)
Signed lower right
Gemeentemuseum, The Hague, bequest of Salomon B. Slijper, 1971, inv. S 91–1971 (A 390)

Cat. 39 (illus. p. 94)
Farm at Duivendrecht, c. 1905
Chalk, watercolor, and gouache on paper
19.7 x 27.8 in. (50 x 65.5 cm)
Signed lower left
Frans Halsmuseum, Haarlem, inv. no. 702 (A 393)

Cat. 40 (illus. p. 95)
Farm at Duivendrecht, c. 1905
Charcoal, crayon, gouache, and pastel on assembled pieces of paper
17.4 x 30.1 in. (44 x 76.5 cm)
Signed lower left
Gemeentemuseum, The Hague, inv. T 80–1979 (A 395)

Cat. 41 (illus. p. 96)
In't Gein (*In the Gein*), c. 1905
Watercolor on paper
19.7 x 25 in. (50 x 63.5 cm)
Signed lower left
Private collection (A 431)

Cat. 42 (illus. p. 97)
Landzicht Farm, 1905
Watercolor on paper
15.2 x 24 in. (38.5 x 61 cm)
Signed and dated lower right
Gemeentemuseum, The Hague, gift of P. A. Scheen, inv. T 46–1960 (A 432)

Cat. 43 (illus. p. 98)
Geinrust Farm, 1905–6
Watercolor on paper
19.5 x 26 in. (49.5 x 66 cm)
Signed lower left
Private collection (A 448)

Cat. 44 (illus. p. 99)
Evening on the Gein, 1906
Oil on canvas
25.6 x 33.8 in. (65 x 86 cm)
Not signed
Gemeentemuseum, The Hague, gift of Albert van den Briel, inv. S 28–1956 (A 463)

Cat. 45 (illus. p. 100)
Isolated Tree on the Gein, c. 1906
Charcoal and crayon on assembled pieces of paper
22.1 x 32.9 in. (56.2 x 83.5 cm)
Not signed
Musée d'Orsay, Paris, anonymous life-interest gift accepted by the State, 2000, inv. RF 52 077 (A 455)

Cat. 46 (illus. p. 101)
Avond (*Evening*), 1906
Charcoal, crayon, and watercolor on paper
29.1 x 38.6 in. (74 x 98 cm)
Signed lower right
Gemeentemuseum, The Hague, bequest of Salomon B. Slijper, 1971, inv. T 51–1971 (A 545)

Cat. 47 (illus. p. 102)
Geinrust Farm, c. 1906
Crayon, sanguine, and pastel on paper
18.7 x 25.6 in. (47.5 x 65 cm)
Monogrammed lower left
Gemeentemuseum, The Hague, bequest of Salomon B. Slijper, 1971, inv. T 74–1971 (A 440)

Cat. 48 (illus. p. 103)
Geinrust Farm, c. 1906
Watercolor, crayon, and pastel on paper
19.1 x 26.5 in. (48.5 x 67.2 cm)
Signed lower right
Frans Halsmuseum, Haarlem, inv. no. 455 (A 441)

Cat. 49 (illus. p. 104)
Oostzijdse Mill on the Gein, c. 1906–7
Oil on canvas mounted on panel
13.6 x 17.5 in. (34.5 x 44.5 cm)
Signed lower right
Gemeentemuseum, The Hague, bequest of Salomon B. Slijper, 1971, inv. S 108–1971 (A 405)

Cat. 50 (illus. p. 104)
The Gein: Trees along the Water, 1906–7
Oil on canvas
17.7 x 26 in. (45 x 66 cm)
Not signed
Gemeentemuseum, The Hague, bequest of Salomon B. Slijper, 1971, inv. S 109–1971 (A 488)

Cat. 51 (illus. p. 105)
Geinrust Farm in the Haze, 1906–7
Oil on canvas
12.8 x 16.7 in. (32.5 x 42.5 cm)
Signed lower left
Gemeentemuseum, The Hague, bequest of Salomon B. Slijper, 1971, inv. S 122–1971 (A 444)

Cat. 52 (illus. p. 108)
Evening Mood on the Amstel (*Omval*), 1906–7
Oil on canvas
16.5 x 29.5 in. (42 x 75 cm)
Not signed
Gemeentemuseum, The Hague, bequest of Salomon B. Slijper, 1971, inv. S 112–1971 (A 528)

Cat. 53 (illus. p. 109)
Open Landscape, c. 1907
Oil on canvas
14 x 19.7 in. (35.5 x 50 cm)
Signed lower right
Musée d'Orsay, Paris, anonymous life-interest gift accepted by the State, 2000, inv. RF 2000–20 (A 515)

Cat. 54 (illus. p. 111)
Oostzijdse Mill in Moonlight, 1907
Oil on canvas
39.2 x 49.4 in. (99.5 x 125.5 cm)
Signed lower right
Gemeentemuseum, The Hague, bequest of Salomon B. Slijper, 1971, inv. S 20–1939 (A 420)

Cat. 55 (illus. p. 110)
Zomernacht (*Summer Night*), 1907
Oil on canvas
28 x 43.5 in. (71 x 110. 5 cm)
Not signed
Gemeentemuseum, The Hague, inv. S 3–1967 (A 523)

Cat. 56 (illus. p. 112)
Dredge, 1906–7
Charcoal and crayon on paper
22.4 x 44.2 in. (57 x 112 cm)
Not signed
Gemeentemuseum, The Hague, bequest of Salomon B. Slijper, 1971, inv. T 46–1971 (A 534)

Cat. 57 (illus. p. 114)
Amstel, 1907
Charcoal and watercolor on paper
27.2 x 43.3 in. (69 x 110 cm) (image); 43.2 x 77 in. (109.8 x 195.6 cm) (support)
Not signed
The Museum of Modern Art, New York, gift of Sheldon H. Solow, bequest of Lillie P. Bliss (by exchange), inv. 388–84 (A 535)

Cat. 58 (illus. p. 113)
Fen near Saasveld, 1907
Oil on canvas
40.1 x 71.1 in. (102 x 180.5 cm)
Signed lower left
Gemeentemuseum, The Hague, bequest of Salomon B. Slijper, 1971, inv. S 110–1971 (A 554)

Cat. 59 (illus. p. 116)
Trees on the Gein: Moonrise, 1907
Oil on canvas
31.1 x 36.4 in. (79 x 92.5 cm)
Not signed
Gemeentemuseum, The Hague, gift of Albert van den Briel, inv. S 59–1956 (A 660)

Cat. 60 (illus. p. 117)
The Red Cloud, 1907
Oil on paper mounted on panel
25.2 x 29.5 in. (64 x 75 cm)
Signed lower right
Gemeentemuseum, The Hague, gift of Albert van den Briel, inv. S 23–1956 (A 569)

Cat. 61 (illus. p. 118)
Oak Trees at Dusk, 1907
Oil on canvas
36.6 x 57.1 in. (93 x 145 cm)
Not signed
Private collection (A 590)

Cat. 62 (illus. p. 119)
Mill in the Evening, 1907–8
Oil on canvas
26.6 x 46.3 in. (67.5 x 117.5 cm)
Signed lower left
Gemeentemuseum, The Hague, bequest of Salomon B. Slijper, 1971, inv. S 75–1971 (A 411)

Cat. 63 (illus. p. 121)
Large Landscape, 1907–8
Oil on canvas
29.5 x 47.2 in. (75 x 120 cm)
Not signed
Gemeentemuseum, The Hague, bequest of Salomon B. Slijper, 1971, inv. S 111–1971 (A 497)

Cat. 64 (illus. p. 120)
Oostzijdse Mill, 1908
Oil on canvas
39 x 47.2 in. (99 x 120 cm)
Signed lower right
Private collection (A 418)
Fort Worth only

Cat. 65 (illus. p. 124)
Avond (Evening), 1908
Oil on canvas
32.3 x 76 in. (82 x 193 cm)
Signed lower left
Private collection (A 561)
Fort Worth only

Cat. 66 (illus. p. 136)
Zomerdag (Summer Day), 1908
Oil on canvas
27.1 x 44.1 in. (69 x 112 cm)
Signed lower right
Stichting Hannema-de Stuers Foundation, Heino/Wijhe, inv. 178 (A 658)
Paris only

Cat. 67 (illus. p. 125)
Woods near Oele, 1908
Oil on canvas
50.4 x 62.2 in. (128 x 158 cm)
Signed lower right
Gemeentemuseum, The Hague, bequest of Salomon B. Slijper, 1971, inv. S 126–1971 (A 593)

Cat. 68 (illus. p. 126)
Devotion, 1908
Oil on canvas
37 x 24 in. (94 x 61 cm)
Signed lower left
Gemeentemuseum, The Hague, bequest of Salomon B. Slijper, 1971, inv. S 128–1971 (A 642)

Cat. 69 (illus. p. 127)
Mill in Sunlight, 1908
Oil on canvas
44.9 x 34.3 in. (114 x 87 cm)
Signed lower right
Gemeentemuseum, The Hague, bequest of Salomon B. Slijper, 1971, inv. S 130–1971 (A 654)

Cat. 70 (illus. p. 138)
Apple Tree in Blue, c. 1908
Oil on paper mounted on canvas
10.7 x 15.1 in. (27.2 x 38.4 cm)
Not signed
Zeeuws Museum, Middelburg, inv. M 94–008 (A 666)

Cat. 71 (illus. p. 130)
Haystacks II, 1908
Oil on canvas mounted on cardboard
13.6 x 17 in. (34.5 x 43.2 cm)
Monogrammed lower right
Sidney Janis Family Collection (A 656)

Cat. 72 (illus. p. 137)
Lighthouse at Westkapelle, c. 1908
Oil on canvas
28 x 20.5 in. (71 x 52 cm)
Signed lower left
Gemeentemuseum, The Hague, bequest of Salomon B. Slijper, 1971, inv. S 127–1971 (A 682)

Cat. 73 (illus. p. 130)
Dying Sunflower I, 1908
Oil on canvas
24.8 x 12.2 in. (63 x 31 cm)
Signed lower right
Gemeentemuseum, The Hague, bequest of Salomon B. Slijper, 1971, inv. S 123–1971 (A 596)

Cat. 74 (illus. p. 131)
Dying Sunflower II, 1908
Oil on cardboard
26.8 x 13.4 in. (65 x 34 cm)
Signed lower left
Gemeentemuseum, The Hague, bequest of Salomon B. Slijper, 1971, inv. S 124–1971 (A 597)

Cat. 75 (illus. p. 136)
Metamorphosis, 1908
Oil on canvas
33.3 x 21.3 in. (84.5 x 54 cm)
Signed lower left
Gemeentemuseum, The Hague, bequest of Salomon B. Slijper, 1971, inv. S 125–1971 (A 601)

Cat. 76 (illus. p. 140)
Blue Tree, 1908–9
Oil on cardboard
22.4 x 29.5 in. (56.8 x 75 cm)
Monogrammed lower right
Dallas Museum of Art, Foundation of the Arts Collection, gift of the James H. and Lillian Clark Foundation, inv. 1982–26 FA (A 673)

Cat. 77 (illus. p. 141)
Blue Tree, c. 1909
Tempera on cardboard
29.7 x 39.2 in. (75.5 x 99.5 cm)
Signed lower right
Gemeentemuseum, The Hague, gift of Conrad Kikkert, inv. T 99–1934 (A 672)

Cat. 78 (illus. p. 144)
Lighthouse at Westkapelle, 1909
Oil on cardboard
15.4 x 10.2 in. (39 x 29.5 cm)
Signed lower left
Gemeentemuseum, The Hague, bequest of Salomon B. Slijper, 1971, inv. S 137–1971 (A 684)

Cat. 79 (illus. p. 147)
Sea after Sunset, 1909
Oil on cardboard mounted on panel
24.6 x 29.3 in. (62.5 x 74.5 cm)
Signed lower left
Gemeentemuseum, The Hague, gift of Albert van den Briel, 1963, inv. S 47–1963 (A 693)

Cat. 80 (illus. p. 142)
Sea after Sunset, 1909
Oil on cardboard
16.1 x 29.9 in. (41 x 76 cm)
Signed lower left
Gemeentemuseum, The Hague, bequest of Salomon B. Slijper, 1971, inv. S 131–1971 (A 694)

Cat. 81 (illus. p. 145)
Dune I, 1909
Oil on cardboard
11.8 x 15.7 in. (30 x 40 cm)
Signed lower left
Gemeentemuseum, The Hague, bequest of Salomon B. Slijper, 1971, inv. S 133–1971 (A 701)

Cat. 82 (illus. p. 145)
Dune II, 1909
Oil on canvas
14.8 x 18.3 in. (37.5 x 46.5 cm)
Monogrammed lower right
Gemeentemuseum, The Hague, bequest of Salomon B. Slijper, 1971, inv. S 134–1971 (A 704)

Cat. 83 (illus. p. 146)
Dune IV, 1909
Oil on cardboard
13 x 18.1 in. (33 x 46 cm)
Signed lower right
Gemeentemuseum, The Hague, bequest of Salomon B. Slijper, 1971, inv. S 144–1971 (A 707)

Cat. 84 (illus. p. 149)
Lighthouse at Westkapelle, c. 1910
Oil on canvas
53 x 29.5 in. (135 x 75 cm)
Signed lower left
Gemeentemuseum, The Hague, bequest of Salomon B. Slijper, 1971, inv. S 143–1971 (A 687)

Cat. 85 (illus. p. 132)
Avond (Red Tree), 1908–10
Oil on canvas
27.6 x 39 in. (70 x 99 cm)
Monogrammed lower left
Gemeentemuseum, The Hague, inv. T 17–1933 (A 671)

Cat. 86 (illus. p. 133)
Self-Portrait, 1908
Crayon on paper
11.8 x 10.0 (30 x 25.5 cm)
Signed lower left
Gemeentemuseum, The Hague, bequest of Salomon B. Slijper, 1971, inv. T 53–1971 (A 639)
Paris only

Cat. 87 (illus. p. 133)
Self-Portrait, 1908
Crayon on paper
11.8 x 9.6 in (30 x 24.5 cm)
Signed lower left
Gemeentemuseum, The Hague, bequest of Salomon B. Slijper, 1971, inv. T 52–1971 (A 638)
Paris only

Cat. 88 (illus. p. 149)
Zon, Kerk in Zeeland (Sun, Church in Zeeland), c. 1910
Oil on canvas
35 x 24 in. (88.9 x 61 cm)
Monogrammed and dated lower left
Tate Gallery, London, purchased with the assistance of the National Lottery for The Heritage Lottery Fund, The Kreitman Foundation, The National Art Collections Fund, and The Society of Friends of the Tate Gallery, 1997, T 07328 (A 689)

Cat. 89 (illus. p. 150)
Duinen bij Domburg (Dunes at Domburg), c. 1910
Oil on canvas
25.8 x 37.8 in. (65.5 x 96 cm)
Monogrammed lower right
Gemeentemuseum, The Hague, inv. S 83–1957 (A 709)

Cat. 90 (illus. p. 156)
Molen (Mill), 1910
Oil on canvas
59.1 x 33.9 in. (150 x 86 cm)
Monogrammed lower left
Gemeentemuseum, The Hague, bequest of Salomon B. Slijper, 1971, inv. S 147–1971 (A 692)

Cat. 91 (illus. p. 160)
Evolutie (Evolution), 1910
Oil on canvas (triptych)
70.1 x 33.5 in. (178 x 85 cm) (side panels); 72 x 33.5 in. (183 x 87.5 cm) (center panel)
Each panel is monogrammed lower right
Original frames
Gemeentemuseum, The Hague, bequest of Salomon B. Slijper, 1971, inv. S 148–1971 (A 647)

Cat. 92 (illus. p. 157)
Duinlandschap (Dune Landscape), 1911
Oil on canvas
55.5 x 94.1 in. (141 x 239 cm)
Monogrammed lower left
Gemeentemuseum, The Hague, bequest of Salomon B. Slijper, 1971, inv. S 149–1971 (B 1)

Cat. 93 (illus. p. 166)
Still Life with Gingerpot I, 1911
Oil on canvas
26.1 x 29.5 in. (66.5 x 75 cm)
Signed lower right
The Solomon R. Guggenheim Museum, New York, inv. 295.76 (B 2)

Cat. 94 (illus. p. 167)
The Gray Tree, c. 1911–12
Oil on canvas
31.4 x 43 in. (79.7 x 109.1 cm)
Signed lower left
Gemeentemuseum, The Hague, bequest of Salomon B. Slijper, 1971, inv. S 156–1971 (B 4)

Cat. 95 (illus. p. 172)
Landschap met bomen (Landscape with Trees), 1912
Oil on canvas
47.2 x 39 in. (120 x 100 cm)
Signed lower right
Gemeentemuseum, The Hague, bequest of Salomon B. Slijper, 1971, inv. S 151–1971 (B 6)

Cat. 96 (illus. p. 174)
Landscape, 1912
Oil on canvas
24.7 x 30.7 in. (63 x 78 cm)
Signed lower right
Gemeentemuseum, The Hague, bequest of Salomon B. Slijper, 1971, inv. S 150–1971 (B 16)

Cat. 97 (illus. p. 181)
Still life with Gingerpot 2, 1912
Oil on canvas
36 x 47.2 in. (91.5 x 120 cm)
Signed lower right
The Solomon R. Guggenheim Museum, New York, inv. 294–76 (B 18)

Cat. 98 (illus. p. 178)
Bloeiende Appelboom (Flowering Apple Tree), 1912
Oil on canvas
31 x 42.3 in. (78.5 x 107.5 cm)
Not signed
Gemeentemuseum, The Hague, gift of Conrad Kikkert, 1934, inv. S 55–1934 (B 19)

Cat. 99 (illus. p. 177)
Trees, c. 1912
Oil on canvas
37 x 27.2 in. (94 x 69.8 cm)
Not signed
The Carnegie Museum of Art, Pittsburgh, Patrons Art Fund, 1961, inv. 61–1 (B 21)

Cat. 100 (illus. p. 184)
Composition: Trees 2, c. 1912–13
Oil on canvas
38.6 x 25.6 in. (98 x 65 cm)
Signed lower right
Gemeentemuseum, The Hague, bequest Salomon B. Slijper, 1971, inv. S 158–1971 (B 24)

Cat. 101 (illus. p. 187)
Tableau No. 4/Composition No. VIII/Compositie 3, 1913
Oil on canvas
37.5 x 31.5 in. (95 x 80 cm)
Signed lower right
Gemeentemuseum, The Hague, bequest Salomon B. Slijper, 1971, inv. S 159–1971 (B 27)

Cat. 102 (illus. p. 183)
Tree A, 1913
Oil on canvas
39.3 x 26.5 in (100.2 x 67.2 cm)
Signed lower left
Tate Gallery, London, 1977, inv. T o 2211 (B 30)

Cat. 103 (illus. p. 190)
Tableau No. 3, 1913
Oil on canvas
37 x 30.7 in. (94 x 78 cm)
Signed lower right
Stedelijk Museum, Amsterdam, inv. A 6043 (B 33)

Cat. 104 (illus. p. 193)
Tableau No. 1, 1913
Oil on canvas
37.8 x 25. 2 in (96 x 64 cm)
Signed lower right
Kröller-Müller Museum, Otterlo, inv. 531–13 (B 37)

Cat. 105 (illus. p. 200)
Tableau No. 1/Composition No. I/Compositie 7, 1914
Oil on canvas
47.5 x 40.4 in. (120.6 x 101.3 cm)
Signed and dated
Kimbell Art Museum, Fort Worth, Gift of The Burnett Foundation of Fort Worth in memory of Anne Burnett Tandy, 1983, inv. Apg 1983.03 (B 44)

Cat. 106 (illus. p. 201)
Tableau No. 2/Composition No. V, 1914
Oil on canvas
21.6 x 33.6 in. (54.8 x 85.3 cm)
Signed and dated lower left
The Museum of Modern Art, New York, The Sidney and Harriet Janis Collection (B 45)

Cat. 107 (illus. p. 203)
Composition No. IV, Compositie 6, 1914
Oil on canvas
34.6 x 24 in. (88 x 61 cm)
Signed and dated lower left
Gemeentemuseum, The Hague, bequest Salomon B. Slijper, 1971 (B 46)

Cat. 108 (illus. p. 204)
Tableau III, 1914
Oil on canvas
55.1 x 39.8 in. (140 x 101 cm)
Monogrammed and dated lower right
Stedelijk Museum, Amsterdam, inv. A 24589 (B 49)

Cat. 109 (illus. p. 206)
Compositie No. VI/Compositie 9, 1914
Oil on canvas
37.5 x 26.6 in. (95.2 x 67.6 cm)
Signed lower right
Beyeler Collection, Basel, (B 50)

Cat. 110 (illus. p. 208)
Composition in Oval, 1914
Oil on canvas
44.5 x 33.25 in. (113 x 84.5 cm)
Signed lower left
Gemeentemuseum, The Hague, bequest Salomon B. Slijper, 1971, inv. S 160–1971 (B 55)

Comparative illustrations

Map of Holland, c. 1910 (illus. p. 22)
Van Oosthoek Encyclopedia, 1924

Administrative map of Amsterdam and environs, 1896 (illus. p. 48)
Municipal Archives, Amsterdam

Fig. 1 (illus. p. 27)
Mondrian's father, P. C. Mondrian (1839–1921), 1867
Photograph
Gemeentemuseum, The Hague

Fig. 2 (illus. p. 28)
The Mondrian children, c. 1890
Left to right: Carel (1880–1956), Pieter Cornelis (Piet), Johanna Christina (1870–1939), Willem Frederik (1874–1945), and Louis (1877–1943)
Photograph
Gemeentemuseum, The Hague

Fig. 3 (illus. p. 29)
Jacob Olie, *The Stadhouderskade, Amsterdam, with the façade of the Royal Academy of Fine Arts (Rijksacademie)*, July 14, 1897
Photograph
Municipal Archives, Amsterdam

Fig. 4 (illus. p. 32)
Pieter Stortebeker (1828–1898), *Cows beside the Water*
Oil on canvas
Private collection

Fig. 5 (illus. p. 32)
Piet Mondrian, *Copy after Stortebeker*
Oil on canvas
Private collection (A -)

Fig. 6a and b (illus. p. 34)
Gallery Van Wisselingh, located at 194 Kalverstraat, Amsterdam, c. 1893
Photograph
Private collection

Fig. 7 (illus. p. 34)
"Square Gallery" on the first floor of the Stedelijk Museum, Amsterdam
Photograph
Stedelijk Museum, Amsterdam

Fig. 8 (illus. p. 37)
The class of Professor Jan Six, in the library of the Royal Academy, c. 1910
Photograph
Gemeentemuseum, The Hague

Fig. 9 (illus. p. 40)
Jacob Maris, *The Barge*, 1878
Oil on canvas
Gemeentemuseum, The Hague

Fig. 10 (illus. p. 40)
Georg Hendrik Breitner, *Avenue Rokin*, c. 1890
Oil on canvas
Gemeentemuseum, The Hague

Fig. 11 (illus. p. 43)
Willem Maris, *Cows among the Reeds*, c. 1885
Oil on canvas
Gemeentemuseum, The Hague

Fig. 12 (illus. p. 43)
Piet Mondrian, *Irrigation Ditch with Bridge*, c. 1894–95
Oil on canvas
Private collection (A 38)

Fig. 13 (illus. p. 43)
Piet Mondrian, *Irrigation Ditch with Bridge*, c. 1894–95
Watercolor
Gemeentemuseum, The Hague (A 39)

Fig. 14 (illus. p. 49)
Piet Mondrian, *Church at Winterswijk*, c. 1898
Engraving
The Museum of Modern Art, New York (A 60)

Fig. 15 (illus. p. 60)
Jan Voerman, *River landscape with Cows*, c. 1900
Watercolor
Gemeentemuseum, The Hague

Fig. 16 (illus. p. 62)
View of the Stadhouderskade near the Overtoom, before 1910
Photograph
Municipal Archives, Amsterdam

Fig. 17 (illus. p. 63)
Jacob Maris, *The Ferry*
Oil on canvas
Gemeentemuseum, The Hague

Fig. 18 (illus. p. 64)
Piet Mondrian, 1899
Photograph
Gemeentemuseum, The Hague

Fig. 19 (illus. p. 64)
In Simon Maris's studio, c. 1900
Photograph
RKD (Simon Maris Archives), The Hague

Fig. 20 (illus. p. 65)
In Simon Maris's studio, June 8, 1901, after the opening of the Saint Lucas Society exhibition
Photograph
RKD (Simon Maris Archives), The Hague

Fig. 21 (illus. p. 69)
The Gein near Abcoude, with the Oostzijde Mill
Photograph
Municipal Archives, Amsterdam

Fig. 22 (illus. p. 69)
The Kalfje Tearoom on the Gein
Photograph
RKD (Simon Maris Archives), The Hague

Fig. 23 (illus. p. 71)
Simon Maris, *Piet Mondrian painting on his bicycle*, c. 1906–7
Pencil drawing taken from a sketchbook
RKD (Simon Maris Archives), The Hague

Fig. 24 (illus. p. 76)
Trees on the banks of the Gein
Photograph
Municipal Archives, Amsterdam

Fig. 25 (illus. p. 86)
Piet Mondrian and his friends, 1903
Photograph
RKD (Simon Maris Archives), The Hague

Fig. 26 (illus. p. 86)
Piet Mondrian in Spain, 1903
Photograph
RKD (Simon Maris Archives), The Hague

Fig. 27 (illus. p. 92)
Piet Mondrian, *Trees beside the Water*, 1907
Oil on canvas
Gemeentemuseum, The Hague (A 482)

Fig. 28 (illus. p. 93)
Piet Mondrian and Simon Maris on the banks of the Gein, on the grass and under the willows, "among the city people," summer 1904
Photograph
RKD (Simon Maris Archives), The Hague

Fig. 29 (illus. p. 106)
Mondrian in his studio on the Rembrandtplein examining sketches
Photograph
Gemeentemuseum, The Hague

Fig. 30 (illus. p. 106)
Simon Maris, *Mondrian painting on the Gein*, 1906
Pencil drawing taken from a sketchbook
Gemeentemuseum, The Hague

Fig. 31 (illus. p. 110)
Mondrian in his studio on the Rembrandtplein, in front of the still life [A 264] that won him the Willink van Collen Prize in 1906
Photograph
Gemeentemuseum, The Hague

Fig. 32 (illus. p. 115)
Photograph of Mondrian taken by Jacob Vetter, reproduced in Onze moderne meesters (Our Modern Masters), *by the critic F. M. Lurasco*
Work published by Chr. Veldt, 1907
Gemeentemuseum, The Hague

Fig. 33 (illus. p. 116)
Piet Mondrian, *Trees on the Gein: Moonrise*, 1907
Pencil on paper
Gemeentemuseum, The Hague (A 659)

Fig. 34 (illus. p. 128)
Mondrian, hair parted in the middle, wearing a beard and a chain, c. 1908
Photograph
Gemeentemuseum, The Hague

Fig. 35 (illus. p. 131)
R. Denktraan, *Mondrian's studio/apartment, 42 Sarphatipark*, late 1908
Photograph
Gemeentemuseum, The Hague

Fig. 36a, b, and c (illus. p. 135)
Reconstruction of the placement of Avond (Evening), *chosen by Mondrian for the 1909 exhibition.*
Gemeentemuseum, The Hague

Fig. 37 (illus. p. 151)
Piet Mondrian, *Rhododendrons*, 1909–10
Oil on canvas
Present location unknown (A 618)

Fig. 38 (illus. p. 151)
Piet Mondrian, *Rhododendrons*, 1909–10
Charcoal and pastel on paper
Gemeentemuseum, The Hague (A 617)

Fig. 39 (illus. p. 153)
On the terrace of the café Le Dôme, *in Paris*, summer 1907
Photo W. Uhde, *Von Bismarck bis Picasso*, 1938, p. 161
RKD, The Hague

Fig. 40 (illus. p. 162)
Engagement photograph: Greta Heijbroek and Piet Mondrian, in Laren, October 1911
Photograph
Gemeentemuseum, The Hague

Fig. 41a, b, and c (illus. p. 163)
The International Exhibition of Modern Art, October 1911
Photograph
RKD, The Hague

Fig. 42 (illus. p. 164)
The International Exhibition of Modern Art, October 1911
RKD, The Hague

Fig. 43 (illus. p. 165)
Piet Mondrian, *Clocktower in Zeeland*, 1911
Oil on canvas
Gemeentemuseum, The Hague (A 691)

Fig. 44 (illus. p. 170)
Piet Mondrian, *Large Nude*, 1912
Oil on canvas
Gemeentemuseum, The Hague (B 7)

Fig. 45 (illus. p. 174)
Piet Mondrian, *The Sea*, Domburg, August 1912
Oil on canvas
Private collection (B 17)

Fig. 46 (illus. p. 175)
Piet Mondrian, *Two Trees*, Domburg, August 1912
Pencil
Private collection (B 380)

Fig. 47 (illus. p. 176)
Three works by Picasso shown in the second exhibition of the Moderne Kunst Kring (Modern Art Circle) at the Stedelijk Museum, Amsterdam, October 1912
Gemeentemuseum, The Hague

Fig. 48 (illus. p. 180)
Piet Mondrian, *Flowering Trees*, Paris, September 1912
Oil on canvas
Judith Rothschild Foundation, New York (B 20)

Fig. 49 (illus. p. 185)
Piet Mondrian, *Trees*, Domburg, August 1912
Pencil
Private collection (B 394)

Fig. 50 (illus. p. 192)
Writing on the back of a painting: Gemälde No. II /Composition No. XV/Compositie 4, 1913
Oil on canvas
Stedelijk Museum, Amsterdam (B 39)

Fig. 51 (illus. p. 194)
Piet Mondrian, *Façades of Paris buildings*, 1914
Pencil drawing taken from a sketchbook
Private collection (B 410)

Fig. 52 (illus. p. 194)
Piet Mondrian, *Gemälde No. 1/Composition No. XII*, 1913
Oil on canvas
Private collection (B 40)

Fig. 53 (illus. p. 195)
Piet Mondrian, *Study of a Tree 1*, 1912–13
Charcoal on paper
Gemeentemuseum, The Hague (B 10)

Fig. 54 (illus. p. 195)
Piet Mondrian, *Tableau No. 2/Composition No. VII*, 1913
Oil on canvas
The Solomon R. Guggenheim Museum, New York (B 35)

Fig. 55 (illus. p. 196)
Piet Mondrian, *Geinrust Farm and Young Trees*, 1905–7
Gouache sketch
Gemeentemuseum, The Hague (A 447)

Fig. 56 (illus. p. 197)
Piet Mondrian, *Composition No. II*, 1913
Oil on canvas
Kröller Müller Museum, Otterlo (B 42)

Fig. 57a (illus. p. 199)
Composition in Oval with Color Planes 1, with its original frame, 1914
Photograph taken during the exhibition, *Modern Dutch Art*, Brighton, England, Public Art Galleries

Fig. 57b (illus. p. 199)
Page of a letter from Mondrian to the architect J. J. P. Oud, dated March 31, 1921, explaining the placement of the pieces of wood for the frame.
Netherlands Institute, Paris

Fig. 58 (illus. p. 207)
Postcard, *Paris (XIVe arrondissement): Rue du Départ along the Gare de l'Ouest (West Station) on the Right Bank*, c. 1913
Musée Carnavalet, Paris

Fig. 59 (illus. p. 209)
Buildings along the boulevard Edgar-Quinet, seen from the rue du Départ, 1914
Photograph
Gemeentemuseum, The Hague

Fig. 60 (illus. p. 209)
Piet Mondrian, *Parisian façades*, 1914
Pencil. Drawing taken from a sketchbook
Private collection (B 405)

Credits

Publisher
Waanders Publishers, Zwolle
First published in March 2002 by La Réunion des Musées Nationaux

RMN production department directed by
Béatrice Foulon

Editorial coordination
Dagmar Rolf
Assisted by Mathilde Jack

Authors
Hans Janssen
Joop Joosten

Translation of the text
Julie Lawrence Cochran

Text editors
Wendy P. Gottlieb
Anna Lazarus

Graphic Design
Gilles Huot, HDL Design
Assisted by Stephanie Schuller

Typesetter
Frank de Wit

Picture editor
Evelyne David

Production
Jacques Venelli

Text font
Documenta

Illustrations engraved by
GEGM, Gentilly

This work was printed in 2002 on the presses of Imprimerie Kapp & Lahure Jombart, Evreux

Trimming
Kapp & Lahure Jombart, Evreux

Photographic Credits

Amsterdam, Gemeentearchief (Gemeente Archives): cat. 22; fig. 3, 16, 21, 23, 24; map, p. 48.
Amsterdam, Stedelijk Museum: cat. 1; cat. 103, and detail, p. 191; cat. 108 and detail, p. 205; fig. 7 and 50.
Appeldoorn, Gier van Leeuwen Photograph: cat. 24, and detail, p. 72; cat. 33.
Basel, Öffentliche Kunstsammlung: fig. 45.
Borzo Kunsthandel: cat. 64.
Christie's Images Ltd., 2002: cat. 15, and detail, p. 51; cat. 41.
Dallas Museum of Art, Foundation for the Arts Collection, gift of James H. and Lillian Clark Foundation: cat. 76.
Fort Worth, Kimbell Art Museum: cat. 105 (photo by Michael Bodycomb).
Haarlem, Frans Halsmuseum: cat. 39, 48 (photo by Thijs Quispel).
Heino/Wijhe, Hannema de Stuers Foundation: cat. 66 (photo by Tom Haartsen).
The Hague, Gemeentemuseum: cat. 2 to 5, 7, 8 (photo by Strenpers); cat. 9 and detail, p. 44; cat. 10, 11, 13, 14, 16 to 18, 20, 21, 23, 25 to 28, and detail, p. 77; cat. 30 to 32, 34, and detail, p. 87; cat. 34b to 38, 40, 42, 44, 46, 47, 49 to 51, and detail, p. 107; cat. 52, 54 to 56, 58 to 60, 62, 63, 67 to 69, and detail, p. 129; cat. 72 to 75, 77 to 87, 89 to 92, 94, 95, and detail, p. 173; cat. 96, 98, 100, 101, and detail, p. 189; cat. 107, 110; fig. 1, 2, 8, 9 to 12, 13 (photo by Strengers), 15, 17, 18, 23, 27, 29 to 38, 40, 43, 44, 47, 49, 52, 53, 55, 59, 60.
The Hague, Rijksbureau voor Kunsthistorische Documentatie: fig. 19, 20, 22, 25, 26, 28, 39, 41a–c, 42, 46, 57a.
London, Tate Picture Library, Tate Gallery: cat. 88 and 102.
Middelburg, Zeeuws Museum: cat. 70 and detail, p. 139 (photo by Tom Haartsen).
New York, Judith Rothschild Foundation: fig. 48.
New York, The Solomon R. Guggenheim Museum: cat. 93 and 97 (photos by David Heald); fig. 54.
New York, The Museum of Modern Art, 2002: cat. 57 and 106; fig. 14.
Otterlo, Stichting Kröller-Müller Museum: cat. 104; fig. 56.
Paris, Netherlands Institute: fig. 57b.
Paris, Musée Carnavalet: fig. 58 (photo by Briant).
Paris, Musée d'Orsay: cat. 12 (photo by Michèle Bellot), 17 (photo by Gérard Blot), 29, 45, 53 (photos by Michèle Bellot).
Pittsburgh, The Carnegie Museum of Art: cat. 99.
Riehen/Basel, Beyeler Foundation: cat. 109
Sidney Janis Family Collection: cat. 71.
Tom Haartsen Photograph: fig. 4.